The Planetary Turn

I0895760

The Planetary Turn

Relationality and Geoaesthetics in the Twenty-First Century

✦

Edited by Amy J. Elias and Christian Moraru

NORTHWESTERN UNIVERSITY PRESS
EVANSTON, ILLINOIS

Northwestern University Press
www.nupress.northwestern.edu

Copyright © 2015 by Northwestern University Press. Published 2015.
All rights reserved.

Printed in the United States of America

10 9 8 7 6 5 4 3 2 1

Library of Congress Cataloging-in-Publication Data

The planetary turn : relationality and geoaesthetics in the twenty-first century / edited by Amy J. Elias and Christian Moraru.
pages cm
Includes bibliographical references.
ISBN 978-0-8101-3073-9 (cloth : alk. paper) — ISBN 978-0-8101-3075-3 (pbk. : alk. paper) — ISBN 978-0-8101-3074-6 (ebook)
1. Space and time in literature. 2. Space and time in motion pictures. 3. Globalization in literature. 4. Aesthetics. I. Elias, Amy J., 1961– editor of compilation. II. Moraru, Christian, editor of compilation.
PN56.S667P57 2015
809.9338—dc23

2014042757

Except where otherwise noted, this book is licensed under a Creative Commons Attribution-NonCommercial-NoDerivatives 4.0 International License. To view a copy of this license, visit http://creativecommons.org/licenses/by-nc-nd/4.0/.

In all cases attribution should include the following information:
Elias, Amy J., and Christian Moraru. *The Planetary Turn: Relationality and Geoaesthetics in the Twenty-First Century*. Evanston: Northwestern University Press, 2015.

The following material is excluded from the license:
Illustrations and an earlier version of "Gilgamesh's Planetary Turns" by Wai Chee Dimock as outlined in the acknowledgments.

For permissions beyond the scope of this license, visit http://www.nupress.northwestern.edu/.

Knowledge Unlatched

An electronic version of this book is freely available, thanks to the support of libraries working with Knowledge Unlatched. KU is a collaborative initiative designed to make high-quality books open access for the public good. More information about the initiative and links to the open-access version can be found at www.knowledgeunlatched.org.

CONTENTS

PREFACE AND ACKNOWLEDGMENTS

Planetarity: our moment. A way of being and a way of measuring time, space, and culture in the human sciences and on the planet at large. Whether a break with modernity, as some argue, or its extension into the twenty-first century, as others contend, this new moment involves, more than any other geosocial shifts of the modern era, spectacular spatial-cultural reconfigurations on a global scale. Evincing its epoch-making power are, certain critics point out, the overall weakening of the ties between determinate locations and cultural formations such as discourse, identity, and community, and, more specifically, the enfeebling or even severing of the living, connective links between culture and nation-state sovereignty. Other scholars have insisted that planetary modernity is a new cosmopolitanism, a less "bounded" model of cultural origination in which autochthonous "roots" become rerouted first cross-regionally and then globally, inherited filiation yields to voluntary affiliation, and "vertical" derivation gives way to horizontal *dérive* (drifting) and playful self-fashioning. For all their differences, both scenarios share a belief that the contemporary place-culture nexus has been shifting, faster and faster, across cultural practices and disciplines, and that a new form of relationality is emerging worldwide among people and across language groups, national boundaries, and categories of cultural expression.

Confronted with such onto-aesthetic changes, the humanities must revisit, perhaps even jettison, established approaches and formulate new lexicons and descriptive models. A radical upswing in population mobility, global interconnectedness, and, following from them, discourse's "worldly" interdependence demands that theorists of art and culture work out *apposite* accounts of global influences and palimpsests—in Yoko Tawada's poetry, for instance, which, as John Pizer shows in this collection, carries one back to Goethe and Novalis as much as to Japan's history and national language. In the same vein, we need to reformulate national literatures as planetary intertextuality, as Wai Chee Dimock does in her analysis of *Gilgamesh*; we have to rethink the antipodes as rhizomatic connections, as Paul Giles counsels in his essay; we must envision, as Christian Moraru has advocated, a "cosmodern" arts vocabulary that pertains to our planetary time-space stage within and without the United States.

Insofar as they can be traced back to the voyages, "discoveries," and displacements of the early Renaissance, our intellectual challenges, no less than the world realities generating them, are not new; their pervasiveness and intensity are. Whether, once again, the planetary is the Habermasian end point of modernity or it signals that both the modern and its postmodern coda are behind us is not yet clear. In the thick of things at the dawn of the third millennium, we have no unobstructed view of where we stand. What is apparent to many, however, is what the introduction to this book identifies as the "cultural-aesthetic symptomatology" of our juncture. *The Planetary Turn* is devoted to this symptomatology and to the "condition" it appears to attest to. Something is happening. Something is afoot. And this something seems to fit neither the global, neocolonialist models of modernity nor Marxist teleological diagnoses of capitalist globalization; it sits ill with definitions of twentieth-century postmodernism, and it grates against easy celebrations of cultural sovereignty and "difference"; it looks more substantial than an "affectsphere" and significantly less politically articulated than a global revolution. Thus, the questions posed in this book speak to the pressure this condition puts on us to theorize it and recalibrate our critical instruments and aesthetic-critical vocabularies to its newness and oftentimes amorphous, contradictory character. This is what, critically and theoretically speaking, the planetary turn strives for: a decisive reorientation toward the unfolding present and its cultural paradigm.

This book has been made possible by an abundance of intellectual guidance and logistical resources. Therefore, as coeditors, we have a large number of individuals and institutions to thank for their support. We are grateful to our contributors for their goodwill and substantial and patient involvement in this enterprise. We also thank Northwestern University Press for faith in the project and publication of what we believe to be a groundbreaking volume. We are especially indebted to Henry L. Carrigan Jr., senior editor and assistant director at Northwestern, to his staff, and to the two anonymous readers who evaluated our manuscript. We would also like to thank Jered Sprecher for allowing us to use a reproduction of his painting *Quell the Storm* (2010, oil on linen, 48" x 36") on the book cover, as well as the editors of *English Language Notes* for giving us permission to reprint, in modified form, Wai Chee Dimock's article "Recycling the Epic: *Gilgamesh* on Three Continents," first published in *ELN* 51, no. 1 (Spring–Summer 2013): 19–33 (http://english.colorado.edu/eln/).

Christian Moraru expresses his gratitude to the following programs, institutional entities, and people who have supplied much-needed funding, advice, and venues of critical exchange: the German Alexander von Humboldt Foundation, for a 2012 research stipend at Ludwig Maximilian University of Munich; University of North Carolina, Greensboro (UNCG), for a 2012 Summer Excellence Fellowship; also at UNCG, the College of Arts and Sciences, specifically for the assistance extended by the college's dean, Timothy Johnston, over the past few years; UNCG's English Department, its past and present heads, Professor Anne Wallace and Professor Scott Romine, respectively, and its inquisitive and collegial faculty; UNCG's dynamic Atlantic

World Research Network and its director, Professor Christopher Hodgkins, whose support, encouragement, and genuine interest in the thorny issues tackled here have been absolutely invaluable; UNCG's Office of Research and Economic Development and its vice chancellor, Terri L. Shelton; UNCG's International Programs Center, for a 2012 Kohler Research Award and other grants enabling travel and work leading to this book; colleagues and graceful hosts at Ludwig Maximilian University of Munich, University of Konstanz, and University of Freiburg (Germany), University of Limoges (France), University of Maryland, Ohio State University, University of Bucharest, University of Cluj-Napoca, and Transylvania University, Braşov (Romania), and University of Amsterdam and Radboud University, Nijmegen (the Netherlands). Amy J. Elias, superb critic of postmodern and post-postmodern culture, has been a great team player and a most dependable source of what one would call, no doubt, "clarifying moments." John McGowan, John Protevi, and Jeffrey J. Williams have offered great feedback on an earlier draft of a portion of Moraru's individual contribution to *The Planetary Turn*. Jeffrey R. Di Leo's support, friendship, expertise, and hospitality have made a world of difference too. And Henry Sussman's erudition, kindness, and elegant writing continue to be an example one strives to emulate. Gratefully acknowledged is also the support of Marjorie Perloff, David Cowart, Brian McHale, Ursula Heise, Paul Maltby, Emily Apter, Brian Richardson, Jerome Klinkowitz, Monika Fludernik, Jan Alber, Liedeke Plate, Yra van Dijk, Timotheus Vermeulen, Robin van der Akker, Radu Ţurcanu, Basarab Nicolescu, Rodica Mihăilă, Mircea Martin, Ştefan Borbely, Corin Braga, Andrei Bodiu, Caius Dobrescu, Alexandru Muşina, Adrian Lăcătuş, Ion Buzera, and Daniela Rogobete, all of them distinguished scholars and friends who have offered assistance, directly or indirectly.

Amy J. Elias would like to thank and acknowledge the support of the following people and institutional programs: the University of Tennessee's (UT's) Department of English and the Hodges Better English Fund for funding that led to this book's completion, particularly a Hodges Research Grant in summer 2012; Stanton B. Garner Jr., head of the UT English Department during this project, for friendship and championing of this and other faculty research projects; the University of Tennessee Humanities Center, headed by Thomas J. Heffernan, for a fellowship in 2013 that granted time and office space for writing and editing; the College of Arts and Sciences at the University of Tennessee for a 2012 SARIF travel grant enabling work toward this project, and the UT College of Arts and Sciences' dean, Theresa Lee, for unflagging support of humanities initiatives. ASAP: The Association for the Study of the Arts of the Present provided opportunities at its conferences to explore and shape ideas expressed in these pages. Christian Moraru is to be thanked emphatically for sharing his intellectual gifts, prodigious research background, and friendship in this endeavor. Gratefully acknowledged also are Ursula Heise, Amir Eshel, Alan Liu, Richard Grusin, John McGowan,

James Phelan, Jonathan Eburne, Allen R. Dunn, Heather A. Hirschfeld, Thomas Haddox, Judith Welch, Donna Bodenheimer, and the members of the Critical Theory Reading Group at the University of Tennessee for collegial conversations and valuable interchange that helped clarify many ideas fundamental to the individual essay Elias has contributed to this book. Thanks goes to Margaret Dean, Katy Chiles, Urmila Seshagiri, Lisi Schoenbach, and HAH for a roadstead during a rip-tide fellowship year, and to Jonathan Barnes for everything else. James Civis, John Hurt Fisher Research Assistant in English at the University of Tennessee for 2012–13, did an excellent job of editing and formatting initial drafts of the manuscript, and Darren Jackson deserves thanks for translating Bertrand Westphal's essay in *The Planetary Turn*.

Some of the insights set forth in our introduction and essays have been tested out in our classes. We are grateful, therefore, to our undergraduate and graduate students. Christian Moraru would like to recognize, specifically, his UNCG students in post-2010 courses such as English 208: "Topics in Global Literature," English 740: "Studies in Contemporary and Postmodern American Literature," and English 704: "Studies in Contemporary Literary and Cultural Theory." Amy Elias would like to thank University of Tennessee graduate students in English 688: "Planetarity: Postmodernism and After" and undergraduates in English 499 (Senior Seminar): "Virtual Worlds and the Ethics of Character" for helping to explore the worlds of global media and planetary exchange.

Introduction

The Planetary Condition

AMY J. ELIAS AND CHRISTIAN MORARU

As its title suggests, this essay collection attends to the planetary turn in contemporary criticism and theory. Like other critical "turns" before it—postcolonial, postmodern, or global—the shift under scrutiny here concerns artists' and critics' new speculations about our world, one which seems to be outgrowing modernity's reigning sociological, aesthetic, and political-economic systems. Less and less relevant to the twenty-first century, modern paradigms appear increasingly unable to predict, let alone adequately explain, the global operations of technologically enhanced finance capital, cosmopolitanism's struggle to reinvent itself from the ashes of post-empire Europe, and the risk environment brought about by the ever-escalating crises of world ecologies.[1] A reaction to the multiple and steadily widening inconsistency between what the world is becoming and how this change registers in prevalent epistemologies and cultural histories, the critical-theoretical model of *planetarity* attempts a move away from the totalizing paradigm of modern-age globalization—and thus a critique or critical "completion" of globalism—as well as from the irony and hermeneutics of suspicion typical of what came to be known as postmodernism. The postmodern has always been a fraught and unsatisfactory analytical category also because, as Guy Debord, Jean Baudrillard, Fredric Jameson, and David Harvey have maintained, it never severed its compromising ties to late socio-aesthetic modernity, market globalization, and the society of spectacle, simulation, and empty pastiche. Little surprise, then, that, on many fronts today, postmodernism is being relinquished as a dessicated—itself "exhausted"—descriptor of the social macrocosm and world art.[2]

The discourse of planetarity presents itself, in response to the twenty-first-century world and to the decreasing ability of the postmodern theoretical apparatus to account for it, as a new *structure of awareness*, as a methodical receptivity to the *geothematics of planetariness* characteristic of a fast-expanding series of cultural formations. Admittedly transitional, "fuzzy," and frustratingly amorphous at times, these formations nevertheless seem to indicate that there has been a paradigmatic translation of world cultures into a planetary setup in which globalization's homogenizing, one-becoming pulsion is challenged by *relationality*, namely, by an ethicization of the ecumenic process of coming together or "worlding." That is to say, while unfolding within the same historical moment as globalization, planetarity is configured—artistically, philosophically, and intellectually—from a different angle and goes in another direction. It represents a transcultural phenomenon whose economical and political underpinnings cannot be ignored but whose preeminent thrust is ethical.

Synonymous, in a sense, with what Ulrich Beck and Edgar Grande have termed "second modernity," planetarity advances on a plurality of modernization paths, Western and non-Western, "tak[ing] the varieties of modernity and their global interdependencies as a starting point for theoretical reflection and empirical research."[3] In this emerging worldview and critical theory, *the planet as a living organism, as a shared ecology, and as an incrementally integrated system both embracing and rechanneling the currents of modernity is the axial dimension in which writers and artists perceive themselves, their histories, and their aesthetic practices.* Insufficiently systematic so far, planetarity has yet to reach critical mass culturally and stylistically. As such, it has not yet given birth to a well-defined world culture or to a coherent model of relational localisms that might make up this kind of geocultural conglomerate. We submit, however, that the burgeoning critical conversation around planetarity is leading to a better and better marked, more and more consequential set of thematic, discursive, and cultural protocols. Neither entirely new nor everywhere identical in terms of its meaning, material embodiment, and effects, planetary geoculture looks to be a powerful albeit nascent paradigm, leaving its daily imprint on how people imagine themselves and the world in the third millennium.

Our project rests on two principal, intertwined claims. First, planetarity as the location and formal operator of culture must be given pride of place by any rigorous, historically minded effort to come to grips with contemporary representation in general and the arts in particular: *the world rise of the bioconnective is the present-day event horizon.* Thus, planetarity should be distinguished from other, coterminous approaches connoting similarly ecumenic aesthetics and relational scenarios such as "globalization" and "cosmopolitanism." Second, if today's planetary life consists in an incessantly thickening, historically unprecedented web of relations among people, cultures, and locales, to comprehend the planetary must entail grasping the relationality embedded in it. Consequently, relatedness, dialogue, and interactivity are central to major aesthetic initiatives stirring at this stage in world history. Indeed, clusters of problems are coalescing in the twenty-first-century literary and visual arts around social connection, language translation, cultural exchange, trafficking, cross-border mobility, and other forms of "self-other" interplay. If planetarity is the cultural-discursive matrix of innovative art, then the dialogical and the relational may well encapsulate the planetary aesthetic.

Globalization and Planetarity

As a concept, "globalization" might be understood as a world vision, an economic trajectory, a thematic-stylistic repertoire, and a scholarly focus. It designates a highly complex category and array of concerns. Its planetary counterparts, "planetarization" and "planetarity," seem concurrently symbiotic and oppositional concepts insofar as they assume, for many commentators, the equivocal status of global studies offshoots.[4] Globalization, however, may be a fundamentally different animal. Its meaning spans three main semantic zones—internationalization, multinationalism, and transnationalism—each with its specific implications for political, environmental, and ethical global organization.[5] Thus, Nick Bisley interprets globalization as "the set of social consequences which derive from the increasing rate and speed of interactions of knowledge, people, goods and capital between states and societies."[6] His definition falls under the purview of sociology and economics, but the debate about globalization roams across an astoundingly wide panoply of discourses and disciplinary-historical perspectives. Given such a range, even the modern origins of globalization are contested. There are, for instance, those who take a "long view" of the phenomenon as well as those who place its beginnings closer to our time. Certain critics claim that the networks of intercultural contact originated with the seventh- and eighth-century spread of Islam throughout the Middle East, Asia, and Africa; others point to mercantilist Europe and early multinational corporations such as the Dutch East India Company; and still others situate globalization's "golden age" in nineteenth-century colonialism and in the international politics ushered in by industrial-era imperialism. Lopsided, scarcely affecting all people and places with the same force or in the same fashion, its benefits darkly ambiguous and unevenly distributed, globalization, some historians contend, has been in full swing for a while now, if not for ages.

The *longue durée* methodology of a number of authors influenced by the French *Annales* school merges these approaches, stressing that modernity had been globalizing since the late medieval period and only became *manifestly* global after World War II. These critics' broad-compass tack sweeps across whole geographical and geopolitical zones (countries, regions, continents) and historical periods (centuries, epochs). Holding sway inside this camp is Immanuel Wallerstein's "world-systems" theory. In Wallerstein's work, however, the world-system and the global are initially not equivalent; they would become so only in the nineteenth century. Modeled on Fernand Braudel's "Mediterranean world," the "world-system" may have "originated in Europe in the sixteenth century," Wallerstein ventures in *Geopolitics and Geoculture*, but it reached a truly global level hundreds of years later, following several globalizing stages.[7] Likewise, the economic theory of Giovanni Arrighi is centered in systems analysis and posits a 700-year period of development of capital. In this account, the genealogy of capitalism as a succession of "long centuries" privileges certain nations and leads ultimately to the current world hegemony of the United States.[8] Wallerstein and Arrighi both postulate the existence of transhistorical systemic aggregates underlain by capital flows largely indifferent to the actions of human individuals and groups. For both writers and those influenced by their conclusions, political events such as the end of Word War II or of the Cold War do not change the trajectory of the world system but rather serve its developmental purposes.

There are, of course, those who "believe that globalization is a myth, or that, at any rate, it is much exaggerated as a distinctively new phenomenon."[9] Supporting this notion are critics who contest what they see as a Eurocentric bias in many globalization models, namely, an alignment of this historical process with Western modernity and, subsequently, an assumption that the globalizing system functions uniformly and on a world scale.[10] Authors such as Martin Albrow, however, reason that in order for globalization to have any meaning for current economic, social, and cultural systems, we must look for it solely within industrial and post-industrial capitalism.[11] Along the same lines, voices in critical theory, globalization studies, and cognate fields are keen to underline the more recent events leading to a qualitatively new, twenty-first-century globalization. In cultural history and anthropology, for example, many consider the tearing down of the Berlin Wall a watershed in the narrative of globalization. To critics such as Christian Moraru, 1989 is what "mondialization" historian Jean-Pierre Warnier would call *une année charnière*: a "hinge year" opening a historical door onto "thick" or late globalization.[12] That year, we are told, set off the later phase of a momentous shift from a "cubicular" world—Pierre Chaunu's *univers cloisonné*—to one experienced and conceptualized as an incrementally all-pervasive "network."[13] From this standpoint, the Cold War world was a "soft," quintessentially bipolar system, loosely if counterintuitively held together by an antagonist-separatist template whose keystone was the nation-state, with "division" the logic of the Cold War-era geopolitical *dispositif*. Accordingly, territory was parceled out worldwide into walled-in "influence zones" balancing each other and functioning centripetally under the jurisdiction of relatively stable and recognized political centers. Underwritten and kept in place by its mutually "deterring" antinomies of power, "common markets," pacts, and treaties, that world ended, some say, in 1991. The one to come, neoliberal institutions and pundits were eager to assure us, would close economic gaps between rich and poor and heal humanity's historical wounds. Immediately following the fall of the Berlin Wall, it seemed that the new world—or at least the new European-North American world—had a modicum of hope for a post-conflictual state of global affairs. Echoing Woodrow Wilson's 1918 "new world" speech, sweeping, "new world order" pronouncements made by Mikhail Gorbachev and George H. W. Bush fueled that optimism.

But this rhetoric was soon to be punctured by cultural theorists who had grown suspicious of the international political consensus on the putatively universal economic gains of globalization. A case in point, Ken Jowitt wrote of a "new world disorder" and was followed in his apprehensiveness of post–Cold War sanguinity by Zygmunt Bauman, Tzvetan Todorov, Amin Maalouf, Wallerstein, and other chroniclers of "le Nouveau Désordre mondial." Concerned less with the Cold War, Joseph Stiglitz mounted a devastating critique of economic globalization, while Zilla Eisenstein and others laid the disenfranchisement of women and non-white, non-European peoples at the door of globalization's "philosophy," neoliberalism.[14] These critics painted pictures of a hopelessly entropic, world-scale pandemonium triggered by the liquefying of Cold War binaries and by the triumph of neoliberal economics seeping across continents and world financial markets. Their jeremiads outlined how, in a "planetar[ily] diasphor[ic]" age, autopoietic world-systems were bound to bypass human agency and meaningful planning altogether.[15] Before long, such critical exercises in catastrophism were joined by what would amount to a post-1990 flood of more applied and patiently documented analyses of "globalization," "globalism," and the "global age." As a result, contemporary theory underwent a "global turn" comparable to the paradigm-changing "turns" of decades past.[16] Breaks other than the end of the Cold War were offered as equally plausible causes of globalization's acceleration, with the Al-Qaeda attacks on New York's World Trade Center and the Pentagon as main contenders.[17] A Lacanian psychosocial examination of the same historical interval led Phillip E. Wegner, for example, to the conclusion that September 11, 2001, reenacted the earlier crumbling of the Berlin Wall and, more generally, that the Cold War actually ended only with 9/11 and the establishment of a twenty-first-century "New World Order."[18]

Media and technology theorists put forth a rather different perspective. Less interested in periodization, they zeroed in on cultural shifts, claiming that the decisive impetus of globalization was not a political occurrence—such as the demolition of the Berlin Wall or the fall of the Twin Towers—but the advent of wide-reaching communication technologies, including the Internet. Media studies have long examined how film, television, music, and other mediatic forms cross borders and transform cultural landscapes on a vast scale.[19] Epistemic or even ideologically colored political shifts are themselves viewed as indebted to technological advancements and networked media. In works by McKenzie Wark, Paul Virilio, Douglas Kellner, Richard Grusin, and others, the determining factor leading to new types of globalization is the forging of cross-national communication networks through affordable and transportable digital technologies.[20] In the most optimistic accounts, popular protest movements and even political revolution are seen as enabled by media or by newer technological communication networks. Manuel Castells, for example, has written that burgeoning democracy movements throughout the world are deeply indebted to international social networking systems, while Jennifer Earl and Katrina Kimport's work (mimicking studies of transnational advocacy networks in traditionally configured organizations) exemplifies analysis that investigates how World Wide Web affordances enable Web activism that crosses national boundaries and class lines.[21] Similarly, popular authors such as Pico Iyer and Thomas L. Friedman tell "global stories" featuring extensively, if somewhat euphorically, the technologically enhanced milieux of transnational travel and the political "flatness" of a world within the purview of capital.[22]

The globalization accounts supplied by writers like Iyer and Friedman beg a number of questions. For even if statistics on population migration, data dissemination, goods and services transfer, and communications' internationalization were readily available, reliable, and easy to work into a cohesive theory of globalization, conclusions about globalizing trends drawn by political economists would still not necessarily match those by cultural theorists grappling with issues of identity and the cultural productions expressing it. As differentiated benefits accrue to different constituencies across the globe, there is meager consensus today about the advantages and disadvantages of globalization. Nor do all scholars agree on where we are right now in its history. Is globalization accelerating, some ask? Has it peaked? Is it perhaps now mutating into novel forms of local/global organization? If so, then what about the rising, trans-statal "jurisdictional geographies" and their bearings on the leverage, sovereignty, and overall significance of the nation-state?[23] And, again, what is the role of culture, art, and their reception and interpretation in the new geopolitical context? In a recent review, Albrow succinctly formulates the questions that remain unanswered in globalization debates. "In a democratic nation-state," he notes, "we accept the legitimacy of laws and regulations and demand that those responsible for their creation and for their implementation should be publicly accountable. But who are the authorities in global governance? And how can we, now a 'global public,' have any part in the process or exercise any kind of democratic control?"[24] What Albrow underscores is globalization theory's central critical struggle, and, we would add, overall failure to come to terms with issues of political control and technical administration in a developing world monoculture in which fewer and fewer are at home.

Planetary studies responds to these concerns and shortcomings in several ways, two of which are worth highlighting here not only because they carry more weight but also because they intersect with the antipostmodern—and "post-postmodernizing"—reaction delineated earlier. Chiefly eco-cosmological, the first advocates an urgent conceptual shift away from globalization to "worlding"—or more precisely, from *globe* as financial-technocratic system toward *planet* as world-ecology. This reorientation calls for significant changes in perspective, which should eventually lead, we believe, to notably different outcomes in and for the world. Directly and indirectly, such a repositioning was influenced by the growth of environmental movements and ecocritical analysis throughout the twentieth century, especially in the decades when globalization theory was picking up speed.

Galvanized by the 1990s publication of Lawrence Buell's *The Environmental Imagination* and Cheryll Glotfelty and Harold Fromm's *The Ecocriticism Reader* as well as by the 1992 founding of the Association for the Study of Literature and Environment (ASLE), ecocriticism promotes a systematic inquiry into the place of nature in Western thought, oftentimes taking on the sagas and legacies of global modernity and opposing to its abstractions a grounded, phenomenal, earth-anchored ethics and aesthetics.[25]

Largely outside the projects of environmentalism and ecocriticism but ostensibly sympathetic to them was also Basarab Nicolescu's planetarily and cosmically minded "world vision." By the time the French polymath laid out the latter in his 1994 *Théorèmes poétiques* and brought it to bear on the modern schemas of territorially, politically, culturally, and disciplinarily discrete discourse, the world as *cosmological* entity had been part of conversation in the arts and humanities for some time.[26] The notion gained momentum as a critical theme with Yi-Fu Tuan's *Cosmos and Hearth*, Gérard Raulet's *Critical Cosmology*, Félix Guattari's "chaosmotic" and "ethico-aesthetic paradigm" (*Chaosmose*), Anne Phillips's cosmos-based multiculturalism, and other similar, late 1990s and early 2000s increasingly well-configured efforts to swerve from the rhetoric of the globe while drawing, with growing benefit, on the figures of cosmos and cosmology.[27] In hindsight, this looks like an important and necessary discursive stage in the transition from the rhetoric, hermeneutics, and, ultimately, the politics of globalization to planetarity. As a phenomenologically oriented idea, the cosmological appealed to critics, who, before leaving it behind, mined it for fertile, ecological-culturological and ethical tropes, which in turn would pave the way to another key move: from "cosmos" to "planet." Many found this progression justified, for at least two reasons. On the one hand, "cosmos" was too akin to "globe" and "globalization" in that it figured the Earth as a cosmic body, part of a macrosystem organized according to system-specific rules and, more generally, to a rationality some scholars found culturally and epistemologically constraining. On the other hand, the discourse of cosmos and cosmic relationality remained too broad from the vantage point of an anthropologically pertinent scalarity. As Amy J. Elias points out, "the planetary model" and the new "chronotope" it has made available to the arts and their interpretation were "opposed to the dehumanizing context of cosmic space constructed by science and then, as a metaphor for the cybernetic, to scientific rationality."[28]

The planetary field's most significant counter to the global—understood primarily as a financially, economically, and technologically homogenizing force—is its relationality model and return to ethics. Indeed, in our judgment, the best discussions of planetarity gravitate away from global studies' obsessions with economic, political, and technical administration and move closer to the vital problem of the *ethical relation* obtaining in new models of transnationality, internationality, or multinationality. This relational *potenza*—the "strength" of the multitudes of the planet—multiplies the meaning of relatedness and, by the same movement, challenges us to stabilize relational ontosemantics, to articulate what relationality does and stands for in the world.[29] Concomitantly descriptive and prescriptive, analytic and normative ("aspirational"), theories of planetarity unfold a vision not of globalized earth but, as Elias maintains in her *Planetary Turn* essay, of a "world commons," thus helping us conceptualize how cultural productions such as art enable this vision.

This move is particularly indebted to Gayatri Chakravorty Spivak and Masao Miyoshi. The stakes of Spivak's 1999 essay "The Imperative to Re-Imagine the Planet" were profoundly ethical although, in keeping with her poststructuralist and psychoanalytic allegiances, the "imperative" she spoke of was non-totalizing and reaffirmed both a Levinasian ethics and a Derridean courting of the uncanny, of *unheimliche* unhomeliness.[30] In her intervention, Spivak positioned planetarity "to control globalization interruptively, to locate the imperative in the indefinite radical alterity of the other space of [the] planet[,] to deflect the rational imperative of capitalist globalization," and thus "to displace dialogics into this set of contradictions."[31] In line with Emmanuel Levinas's ethics of alterity, she insisted that life on the planet must be "lived as the call of the wholly other." Thus, in Spivak, the planet morphs into a "cosmopolitheia," both an astronomical body and a "defracted view of ethics," as space becomes another name for "alterity."[32] As she wrote a few years later in *Death of a Discipline* (2003),

> I propose the planet to overwrite the globe. Globalization is the imposition of the same system of exchange everywhere. In the gridwork of electronic capital, we achieve that abstract ball covered in latitudes and longitudes, cut by virtual lines. . . . To talk planet-talk by way of an unexamined environmentalism, referring to an undivided "natural" space rather than a differentiated political space, can work in the interest of this globalization in the mode of the abstract as such. . . . The globe is on our computers. No one lives there. . . . The planet is in the species of alterity, belonging to another system. . . . Planet thought opens up to embrace an inexhaustible taxonomy of such names [for a radical alterity and intention toward the other].[33]

The planetary claims of *Death of a Discipline* have provoked replies from various critical quarters. Continuing into the 1990s and the first decades of the third millennium, Spivak's inquiries into issues of translation, comparison and the incommensurable, communication, globalization, subalternity, and regional welfare led her to bring serious charges against globalist imperialism, cosmopolitan arrogance, and the cultural parochialism typically following from both. As a remedy, she proposed solutions as diverse as revaluation of place, familiarization with other languages and thought paradigms, and, more broadly, genuine contact with alterity, even though, in practice, her handling of Levinasian ethics and the semiological indeterminism of poststructuralist extraction at play in her reasoning sometimes risked preventing such dealings and exchanges from working more concretely as an effectively relational, world-transforming dialogics.

Underscoring the same need for renewal on a similarly large scale, Miyoshi's 2001 article "Turn to the Planet: Literature, Diversity, and Totality" grounded its manifestly epochalist-epistemological argument in a planetary paradigm shift. Miyoshi observed that a change of historical proportions had been afoot since the globalizing 1980s; this change, as Neil Turnbull later noted, "heighten[ed] the conceptual importance of the earth" across all material and cultural forms and arenas.[34] Miyoshi too found globalism wanting because, plagued by a structural insufficiency, it appeared exclusionist, touting a universal good but bestowing it only on the privileged few for whom techno-mercantile connectedness operates beneficially. Since "the return to the nation-state," he specifies in his essay, is not a realistic solution, "there is [now] one such core site for organizing such an inclusiveness, though entirely negative at present: the future of the global environment. For the first time in human history, one single commonality involves all those living on the planet: environmental deterioration as a result of the human consumption of natural resources."[35] Acknowledging this "total commonality" as the premise for "map[ping] out our world and [for] engag[ing] in research and scholarship" is a stepping-stone to the all-too-important recognition that

> literature and literary studies now have one basis and goal: to nurture our common bonds to the planet—to replace the imaginaries of exclusionary familialism, communitarianism, nationhood, ethnic culture, regionalism, "globalization," or even humanism, with the ideal of planetarianism. Once we accept this planet-based totality, we might for once agree in humility to devise a way to share with all the rest our only true public space and resources.[36]

In certain respects, Miyoshi's take on planetarity is closer to posthuman environmentalism than to Spivak's cosmopolitan crypto-humanism. Moreover, some of his assertions are not completely clear, fully developed, or entirely persuasive. Together, however, the two critics made a decisive push down a path further blazed by comparatists and theorists such as Emily Apter, Paul Giles, and, in particular, Wai Chee Dimock, whose trans-nationalist, "deep-time" forays and conceptualizations of a new, planet-oriented scalarity and aggregation scheme in literary history have been particularly influential in this burgeoning planetary vocabulary. A quick glance at the amount of scholarship inspired by these three critics' ethical-relational and cross-territorial reconstructions of globalization as planetarity suggests that, historically co-articulated with the global lexicon and concerns as it has been, the planet model may be at this juncture well situated to fulfill, in the humanities at least, earlier dreams of critically "purging" the globe (Apter) or even "overwriting" it (Spivak).[37]

Still somewhat bothersome, of course, is the "terminological quandary" lingering in the interchangeable use of "globalization," "globality," and "globalism," as Marshall Brown has remarked. On the one hand, "globality" has been defined by critics such as Beck as the global's abstract cousin. As such, it "means that we have been living for a long time in a world society, in the sense that the notion of closed spaces has become illusory." "No country or group," the German sociologist concludes, "can shut itself off from others" any longer. Globality also implies "that from now on nothing which happens on our planet is only a local and limited event; all inventions, victories and catastrophes affect the whole world."[38] On the other hand, "by globalism," critics such as Brown "understand an idea, an image, a potential; by globalization[,] a process, a material phenomenon, a destiny."[39]

As far as we are concerned, "globalism" is primarily a *cosa mentale*, a subjective, reflexive-evaluative position designating an attitude or mode of perceiving things "in global perspective." In globalism, we underscore a life perspective and an epistemological stance toward a *global ensemble* wherein the parts communicate and must face up to their interdependence. But, as we have stressed, the global paradigm has not been particularly effective in weighing the cultural, political, and ethical implications of world interconnectivity, and so, to avoid a confusion at once existential, methodological, and terminological, we offer up planetarity as a critical substitute. Retooled around planetary semantics and its ramifications across ethics, phenomenology, and epistemology, world cultures might leave room, in Roland Robertson's assessment, both for "relativism," that is, for a sense that cultures are "bound-up," and for "worldism," or "the claim that it is possible and, indeed, desirable to grasp the world as a whole analytically" while keeping in mind that no "reference t[o] the dynamics of the entire 'world-system'" can afford to lose sight of the complexities, contradictions, and other asystemic features that might leap at us whenever we do not base the analysis too strictly on the "world-systemic, economic realm."[40] It is in this light that, in an essay also chiming in with the positions formulated in *The Planetary Turn*, Min Hyoung Song reaches the conclusion that "there is . . . something sovereign about what gets signified by globalization, a *nomos* that divides, restricts, hierarchizes, and criminalizes. It is a royal epistemology, a striation. Planetarity, then, might be thought of as a different order of connection, an interrelatedness that runs along smooth surfaces, comprises multitudes, and manifests movement."[41] Thus, while flat-out dismissal or wholesale demonization of globalization processes in economy, technology, and culture remains misguided, the planetary perforce builds on the global, critiques it, and, to some degree, "completes" it. But, as Warnier puts it bluntly, if "speaking of the 'globalization of culture' is abusive," the abuse may be even more egregious if planetary culture is still conceived in similarly "globalistic" ways.[42] The "hard" materiality of globalization—a "hard" planet—is or has the tendency of becoming a consistent oneness wedded to selfsameness, a homogenous and "defacing" or disfiguring whole impervious to smaller figures, cultural rhetorics, and voices. Instead, the geoaesthetic planetary ensemble toward which our book's essays variously work designates a "soft" materiality within which relatedness both recognizes and hinges on negotiations of difference and where, as such, being-in-relation may be pressed into service with an eye to fostering ethical relations worldwide.

Cosmopolitanism and Planetarity

A fairly substantial body of critical literature has already gone some distance toward accounting for this ethical relationality on a range of scales. This corpus has coalesced around cosmopolis, the cosmopolite, and cosmopolitanism, a set of time-honored ideas, foci, and geocultural-intellectual models that regained force in the academy and popular press roughly at the same moment as did globalization. As is well known, the ethical-philosophical concept of cosmopolitanism has a long history in the West and elsewhere. The origins of cosmopolitan deliberation can be traced back to the thinkers of ancient Greece and Rome, primarily to the Cynics and the Stoics, who argued for an individual's belonging both to the local-national polity and to humanity's greater commonwealth beyond his or her family, kind, or country, outside which the *kosmopolitēs* must care for and generally be in an ethical relationship with others. Is planetarity, then, simply another word for cosmopolitanism?

To answer, it might be useful to turn briefly to Amanda Anderson's discussion of the dialectical tension between cosmopolitanism and universalism in Western philosophy. Anderson treats cosmopolitanism not as a countermodernity but as a strain of thought within modernity itself. Differentiating between, on the one hand, a Habermasian, public-sphere approach that appeals to a sense of *universal* community, and, on the other, a popularized "cosmopolitan sensibility," she reminds us that cosmopolitanism was revived in the humanities as a reaction to "a strictly negative critique of Enlightenment" and combines a skepticism "of partial or false universals with the pursuit of those emancipatory ideals associated with traditional universalism."[43] Like "strategic essentialism" operating in cultural critique, cosmopolitanism so defined is compatible with some aspects of Marxism and also counters overly restrictive definitions of community sometimes expressed by identity politics. Moreover, it works against the early twenty-first-century reawakening of violent nationalisms and nationalistic identitarian agendas. "In general," Anderson explains, "cosmopolitanism endorses reflective distance from one's cultural affiliations, a broad understanding of other cultures and customs, and a belief in universal humanity."[44] She breaks down cosmopolitan philosophy into two forms. One is "exclusionary" and values only an abstract or cosmic universalism. The other is "inclusionary." In this variant, universalism is shaped by "sympathetic imagination and intercultural exchange." In this sense, we learn, "cosmopolitanism also tends to be exercised by the specifically ethical challenges of perceived cultural relativisms; it aims to articulate not simply intellectual programs but ethical ideals for the cultivation of character and for negotiating the experience of otherness, . . . to foster reciprocal and transformative encounters between strangers variously construed."[45]

Neither moral relativism nor rigidly abstract universalism, this cosmopolitanism parts company with theories of local authenticity and rises at times in history when the world grows in population and, seemingly, in complexity.[46] Such a perspective shores up and qualifies universalism with a much-needed "rhetoric of worldliness" and enlists *translation* as an ideal. Anderson turns to James Clifford's notion of "discrepant cosmopolitanisms," Bruce Robbins's "mobile, reciprocal interconnectedness," Seyla Benhabib's "interactive universalism," and Julia Kristeva's "transnational Humanity" to illustrate the host of positions characterizing this "new cosmopolitanism." She also notes the more radical ideas that begin to swirl around it at this juncture, such as Judith Butler's "reconstructed universality" and Etienne Balibar's real, fictive, and ideal universalities, the last of which is characterized by an "insurrection" against normalcy.[47] Anderson admits, however, that anthropological ethics has not had significant purchase in old or new cosmopolitanisms, which by and large tend to gel instead around more urgent, counter-nationalist, anti-parochial, and non-localist platforms.[48]

Where such philosophical propensities and political programs are concerned, new cosmopolitanism is closest to planetarity as we conceptualize it.[49] Very roughly put, planetarity is to globalization what neo-cosmopolitanism is to universalism. It is true too that, like certain neo-cosmopolitan varieties, some theories of planetarity are less "counter-modernities" than critical rearticulations of modernity's own dialectics, thriving as they do in the contestatory spaces between warring universalism and particularism or between local and global contexts. These interstices are, for example, the sites Ursula K. Heise links to "eco-cosmopolitanism" from an emphatically planetary perspective.[50] Similarly to some versions of neo-cosmopolitanism, a few models of planetarity align themselves openly with a "modified universalism" or new humanisms, affirming the role of shared human experiences and values across cultures. Finally, not unlike cosmopolitan ethics, planetarity puts much stock in encounter with difference, in recognition and toleration of alterity, and in reciprocity and translation as seminal to any peaceful, cross-cultural, and transnational interaction.[51]

The differences between planetarity and twenty-first-century cosmopolitanism, however, should not be discounted. Though ancient and recent cosmopolitanisms take into account behaviors, politics, and lifestyles and thus attend to phenomenological being in the world, cosmopolitanism manifests itself chiefly as a philosophical enterprise whose cardinal thrust is ethical and hermeneutical. It is a kind of knowledge and interpretation of the world, a way one mentally processes environments, assesses them, and endorses attitudes in them. In contrast, the planetary reaches beyond the hermeneutical to the ontological. Planetarity is not, as Susan Stanford Friedman says, just an epistemology, merely an inquisitive *forma mentis*, a mindset eager to take the world in.[52] Planetarity is also *in and of* this world, its modality of being, describing both a phenomenological perception and a new theater of being whose novelty is becoming more conspicuous every day. "You wonder," writes Bharati Mukherjee in her 2004 novel *The Tree Bride*, "if everyone and everything in the world is intimately related. . . . You pluck a thread and it leads to . . . everywhere." And she goes on to ask: "Is there a limit to relatedness?"[53] If there is one, it is that of the cosmos itself, with planetarity both indexing and probing the world as a relational domain. Thus, sympathetic as we certainly remain to cosmopolitanism's spectacular resurgence in critical theory, we define "planet" and "planetary" as a noun and an attribute signifying and qualifying, respectively, *a multicentric and pluralizing, "actually existing" worldly structure of relatedness critically keyed to non-totalist, non-homogenizing, and anti-hegemonic operations typically and polemically subtended by an eco-logic.*

Here, the eco-logical is not a subsidiary appendage, for its logic signals another departure from new cosmopolitan theory. Unlike the latter, which spotlights solely human and largely discursive cultural and intergroup relationships, planetarity opens itself as well to the nonhuman, the organic, and the inorganic in all of their richness. Informed by an ecocritical perspective, it affirms the planet as both a biophysical and a new cultural base for human flourishing. Accordingly, planetarization and its outcome, planetarity, trace a three-layered process whereby (1) the earth *qua* material planet becomes visible to theory and its abstractions as the non-negotiable ecological ground for human and nonhuman life; (2) individuals and societies of the earth as cosmo-polis heed an imperative to "worlding," that is, the creation of an ethical, "diversal," and relational ensemble so as to guarantee the survival of all species; and (3) the phenomenal earth seeps into our conceptual elaborations and ways of seeing the world, thus refounding our interpretative categories, our aesthetics, and our cultural lives.

Axial to the planetarity paradigm are the notion and practice of *stewardship* in the world commons. The regulative principle is either largely absent from or suspect in cosmopolitan debates, where it raises uncomfortable associations with paternalism, colonialism, and monopoly capital. In point of fact, theories of cosmopolitanism are constantly plagued by—much as they struggle to undo and reweave—the historically close and forever taxing relation between, on the one side, cosmopolitan overtures and Orientalist curiosity, and, on the other side, cosmopolitan contact and colonial control.[54] In the ecocritically informed discourse of planetarity, however, "stewardship" may be better positioned to take on politically less fraught connotations. It connotes both an ethics of care for both organic and inorganic planetary resources and a social stance mindful to conserve cultural legacies. At the end of the day, the most controversial aspect of planetary stewardship may not be its paternalistic-colonialist disposition but rather its anthropocentric bent, insofar as it implies that humans hold (and deserve) the privileged role of stewards among animate and inanimate entities that are all together entangled in planetary relation. Stewardship as we conceive it here, however, would be both a recognition of and a counter to the negative effects of the Anthropocene and anthropocentric effects in a global environment.[55]

In asserting a "world commons" as stewardship's theater of operations, planetarity also deviates from cosmopolitanism's well-trodden geographies, itineraries, and spatial fantasies. Cosmopolitan's champions frequently talk about travel and contact, border-crossing, and negotiating difference in unfamiliar territories. In contrast, planetarity's proponents discuss how to make the world a commonly familiar space, a shared resource, and a home for all. Furthermore, the world commons so grasped are not universalist, homogeneous, monocultural, or monological. They imply a complex planetary network including nested but nonhierarchical cultural and material ecosystems—commutual constellations, sites, and forms of life ranging in scale but acknowledging, serving, and honoring a shared, affectively and materially interrelated, inhabited world space.

Planetary relatedness is thus *bioconnective*. Not a monologue but an echo, speaking to us not through a mouthpiece but as through a sonar, cultural discourse and identity come about through the connection of bodies in space and time in the post–Cold War, planetary age. They surface more relationally and dialogically every day, according to the logic of the Greek *dià*: always belatedly, obliquely, by a detour through the world's distant or just "different" places, intervals, and styles. Reading planetarily, then, is necessarily reading comparatively, and this is a main reason we are witnessing, within critical theory, a resurgence of interest in translation as comparative reading and cultural interaction.[56]

Actively *worlding* the world, making it a world of relations, and attending to them: what we are talking about when we talk about the planet in these terms is (1) the planetary configuration or ontological *condition* the planet brings about and (2) an *approach or cluster of approaches* befitting this condition's cultural-aesthetic symptomatology, an apposite understanding of virtual and physical spatiality that constitutes the lived circumstance of interrelatedness. While tribal, feudal, consanguinean, and kindred relationships are usually worked out in face-to-face relations or through established community networks and protocols ordinarily closed to outsiders, woven together into the classical, territorialized, geographically bounded *Gemeinschaft* or "community" type of human association, the relationships typical of planetary contemporaneousness operate across space, launched as they are both from nearby and afar. In that, they are no less concrete or life-enhancing, for they render the planet a cultural geography of distance management, a platform of survival, an aesthetic trope connoting these attributes, and a critical lens through which to evaluate their shape, meaning, and impact. Now that more and more of us are awaking to the fragility of our common world ecosystems as well as to the tenuousness of some of their immediate, national allegiances, a theoretically plausible and critically effective, social and aesthetic model turning on planetary relation is, we think, a matter of urgency.

Planetarity and the Bioconnective Aesthetic

A caveat is in order at this point: the planetary culture notion should be taken as heuristic rather than deterministic. The function we assign it for now is cautiously exploratory; we posit the planetary as an absolutely defining and sole context neither for cultural production nor for its interpretation. As a new episteme, and in contrast to well-known globalization models, the planetary is not, to us at least, a one-world, genetically determinant, uniform, and homogenizing totality. Poised to forge a culture of sharing and participation, harbingers of planetarity have not yet erected a stable and wholly crystallized sustentation for an ecumenically and equitably enjoyed, economic or sociocultural commonwealth. Such an ethical configuration of material planetarity is still to be adequately thought out and built, which is one reason a sufficiently consolidated ecoculture is still on the horizon. Nonetheless, if, "soft" and "loose" as it may be, planetarity furnishes the cultural-discursive matrix of emerging art, then the dialogical and the relational may well encapsulate the operations and values of a planetary imaginary and of its thematic-aesthetic protocols. Moraru has observed that the post-1989 historical intermezzo of "cosmodernism" translates, inside and outside the United States, primarily into an *imaginary*, a way of picturing the world. As the contributors to *The Planetary Turn* notice repeatedly, the planetary imaginary currently making inroads across the arts shows a predilection for certain themes—particularly the arche-thematic "world"—specifically for a sheaf of *metathemes* deployed with characteristically growing frequency around the quasi-omnipresent world subject and its worldly subcategories. And, while a distinctively planetary stylistics is still in the offing, isomorphic to this geothematics seems to be a relational aesthetics visible in artists' keen attention to at-distance interaction, intertextuality, remediation, mash-up, recycling, and quotation. As marginalia to such encodings and interpolations of planetarity, our book asks (1) if a geocultural arena of aesthetic production is taking shape in which the various discourse-engendering functions, narratives, and epistemological tools historically attributed to the operations of the nation-state model are now being put to the test, broken, or refashioned; (2) if the twenty-first century is witnessing the rise of a broader, postnational formation, which is the planet; and (3) if the latter is thus becoming a dominant environment, onto-ethical ground, and conceptual-methodological frame of reference for proliferating socio-aesthetics and critical exercise.

As a material and analytic master framework rather than a fully consolidated system, the planetary is capacious and integrative; it has its ebbs and flows; it transforms and surprises. In keeping with the etymology of the ancient Greek *planaō*, the planetary remains shifty, cannot help turning, literally and linguistically, and so it is neither an ontological nor a hermeneutic given, let alone a completed project. The planetary does not stamp all art objects or all artworks equally, nor does it elucidate them completely. To us, the planet is not only a new cultural landscape throughout which people and their sustaining projections wander, connect, and reproduce, but also a "wondering" domain of twists and turns, perplexities, inquiries, and flashes of insight. Our overall objective is to start mapping this expanse, that is, to begin to read the planetary as a repertoire of aesthetic routines *structurally presupposing and further stimulating relationality.*

This reading prompts at least five categories of query. First, what are planetarity's ethics, politics, and theories of value? Which are the benchmarks, yardsticks, and tools that supply the basis and instruments of planetary criticism? Second, in what ways is this geoaesthetic condition of planetarity new, and how does it rehearse or critically move beyond the forms and tenets of earlier cultural-aesthetic theories or historical movements such as modernism and postmodernism? What new vocabulary do we need to talk about the planetary's distinctive nature? Third, to what extent are geoaesthetic spaces familiar or compatible with the traditional cartographies, analytic grids, narrative recipes, measuring and scalar units, and aggregation entities recognized by "methodological nationalism" and, in particular, by literary history?[57] Fourth, what would a "planetary art" be like? What would mark an unfolding planetary aesthetics, and in what kind of stylistics, if any, are planetarity's relationality and dialogics couched? How might such an aesthetics reframe classical values such as authenticity, originality, and novelty? What do we mean when we claim that the planet animates work X or that author Y operates within a planetary horizon or outlook? Fifth and finally, what is the relation between the universal and the particular, geoculture and local culture, place and planet in artworks stemming from or interpreted through a planetary aesthetic? How does the planetary paradigm's relational-dialogical *poiesis* play out across discourses, styles, and media? How does "world art" promote dialogue among and between people, institutions, traditions, and forms? How are we to receive, decipher, and distribute planetary works?

Planetary Theory and Critical Praxis

In answering these questions, our contributors take steps toward (1) theorizing the planetary condition; (2) devising and testing modalities of reading aesthetic and cultural symptoms of planetarity in a fashion germane to the planetary ethics of relationality; and (3) working out, albeit independently and, for the most part, inductively, a reasonably functional and sufficiently detailed model of the planetary aesthetic and its geocultural *modus operandi*.

With this threefold end in sight, we lead off with John D. Pizer's "Planetary Poetics: World Literature, Goethe, Novalis, and Yoko Tawada's Translational Writing," which addresses the recent planetary turn against the backdrop of eighteenth-century German criticism. Pizer examines the tripartite translation schemes of Goethe and Novalis to stress that Goethe's "world literature" model, so perennially influential in comparative studies, was grounded in a largely Eurocentric literary cosmopolitanism that we might associate nowadays with a similarly oriented globalism. Novalis, on the other hand, envisioned, in Pizer's reading, a proto-*Weltliteratur* in literary fragments that introduced an intermediary, collective, or local level of human contacts that subtly shifted transnational literature from a global cosmopolitanism of cultural interchanges to one similar to contemporary planetary relationality. Today, Japanese-German author Yoko Tawada enacts such planetary consciousness as sensitivity to translation issues in a way that proves, Pizer asserts, more consonant with Novalis's pre-nationalist cosmopolitanism than with Goethe's *Weltliteratur*.

Focusing, in the next chapter, less on the historical genealogy of planetarity and more on its dimensionality, Hester Blum examines the mutual investment of planetary and oceanic studies in the recalibration of the static optics and chronometrics of land. "Terraqueous Planet: The Case for Oceanic Studies" explains how the sea nulls time and space metaphors and abstractions imposed by global capital and nation-sponsored, landed geographies, and, further, how authors like Henry David Thoreau and Herman Melville endorse alternate, materialist, and labor-based understandings of time and space that are so important to our own planetary moment. Both planetary and oceanic studies reveal, Blum concludes, "the artificiality and intellectual limitations of national, political, linguistic, physiological, or temporal boundaries," as well as the risks incurred by a thinking that, wedded too deeply to land-derived tropes and calculations, abstracts earth and sea from human toil, employment, and daily struggle for survival.

In "The Commons . . . and Digital Planetarity," Amy J. Elias aligns the planetary with "the commons" and implicitly offers a rejoinder to the Spivakian poststructuralist ethics of alterity. Elias investigates how the "commons," as a social space organized on the model of neither the nation-state nor the free market, is now brought in line with the idea of the Internet as a new planetary collective. Reviewing key theoretical claims about commons construction within the fields of public economy, digital media, and affect studies, she contends that, because fully functioning common pool resources demand dialogic relationality among users, such theories fail to account for the necessarily ethical foundations of those resources. For, Elias demonstrates, conceptions of human agency, ethics, and law—all suspect in contemporary digital theory for some time—are or should be central to the construction and maintenance of any planetary digital commons.

"The Possibility of Cyber-Placelessness: Digimodernism on a Planetary Platform," Alan Kirby's contribution to *The Planetary Turn*, furthers Elias's inquiry into the digital by nuancing the "digimodernist" coinage he introduced in his 2009 book. As we learn, digimodernism is a descriptor of the present stage, which replaces, Kirby ventures, a now obsolete postmodern paradigm and is characterized by the digitizing of the textual artifact and the technologizing of cultural expressions. Tying into "cyber-placelessness," digimodernism allows Kirby to refute Spivak's claims that planetarity should be set in opposition to computerization. The local, he proposes, can be reinscribed within a globalizing platform by way of a planetary dialectic.

Raoul Eshelman's "Archetypologies of the Human: Planetary Performatism, Cinematic Relationality, and Iñárritu's *Babel*" directly takes on the planetarity views Spivak articulated in *Death of a Discipline*. Not unlike her, Eshelman is skeptical of traditional humanism. His solution, however, is "performatism," the new, anthropologically founded episteme he proposed in his 2008 book. Performatist planetarity, Eshelman argues, casts light on the human as a unified, biosocial construct motivated by the nondiscursive modes of mimesis and intuition. Its dominant technique in artworks is "double framing." This procedure takes a narrative scene or detail and correlates it to the mimetic logic of the whole work so as to manipulate audiences into subscribing to the claims of an artificial, closed construct. Laying out the performative as a textual-interpretive category over and against Spivak's discursive figure, Eshelman illustrates how performatism structures Alejandro Iñárritu's film *Babel* (2006) and, more broadly, how a performatism-guided planetary approach might work.

Also dealing with film, Laurie Edson's "Planetarity, Performativity, Relationality: Claire Denis's *Chocolat* and Cinematic Ethics" too trades on Spivak's planetarity to drive home the point that the relational ethics of planetarity is well poised to replace globalization's treatment of singularities. Her patient examination of Claire Denis's 1988 film *Chocolat* dwells on relationality, performativity, "learning from below," "minor" transnationalism, horizontal networks, and related issues and phenomena instrumental to the planetary.

In "*Gilgamesh*'s Planetary Turns," Wai Chee Dimock seeks to rethink world literature within the paradigm the planetary turn has made available to literary studies. As she observes, revisiting the venerable notion from the standpoint of shared planetary time and space changes our perceptions of world literature from a set of texts in a static canon to mobile cultural material—tropes, motifs, themes, and texts in intercontinental circulation. Focusing on the ways the Gilgamesh epic has been recycled throughout history in different cultural locations, she explicates how literature and ecology are both co-articulated with processes of decomposition and recomposition and how planetary life continuously works archetypal tropes into cultural productions.

Paul Giles warns, however, in "Writing for the Planet: Contemporary Australian Fiction," against what might be described as a "reglobalization" of planetarity, namely, against the notion's lapsing back into a globalist-essentialist trope liable to erase geographical and historical differences among the world's cultures once again. A theoretical-analytic stay against globalizing U.S. market capitalism, the planetary is, in Giles's assessment, also laden with features of the American romantic worldview, and planetary critics would be well advised to keep the term's ambiguities in mind. Against Miyoshi's notion of the planet as unifying totality, planetary consciousness needs to be, Giles further counsels, more tightly bound up with, and supportive of, the pluralizing and "disorienting" perspective of cultural and historical "crosscurrents and crossovers" such as those traced in the nineteenth-century prose of Edgar Allan Poe and Melville as well as in twentieth- and twenty-first-century Australian literature and art criticism of Bernard Smith, J. G. A. Pocock, Tim Winton, Gail Jones, Christos Tsiolkas, and Alexis Wright. These authors are exemplary in that, in Giles's view, they disrupt conventional notions of social scale and human agency and shed light on planetarity as a theater of unequal cultural traffic and barterings.

The Planetary Turn's next chapter, Bertrand Westphal's "The White Globe and the Paradoxical Cartography of Berger & Berger: A Meditation on Deceptive Evidence," specifically tackles the idea of "globe" as totality. In his reflections on Laurent P. Berger and Cyrille Berger's 2001 sculpture *Astre blanc* (*White Star*), Westphal raises questions about the nature of the blank map, uncharted space, and the planet's depopulated areas. In the critic's interpretation, whiteness adduces in Berger & Berger's works "deceptive evidence," a saturation rather than a negation of meaning, which nonetheless evokes images of emptiness, cataclysmic decimation, and "white sands." Applying the geocritical method formulated and tested in *La géocritique: Réel, fiction, espace* (2007) and elsewhere, Westphal understands geographical space as dynamic, mobile, and transgressive. Thus, he helps us discover the complex chromatics of a planet whose multiple colors fade out in the very attempt to colorize it on our geographical and political maps.

"Comparing Contemporary Arts; or, Figuring Planetarity," Terry Smith's chapter, articulates a vision of twenty-first-century world art as characterized by multiple, antinomial temporalities. He argues thus for a current move from modernity through postmodernity, contemporaneity, and planetarity. However, this historical trajectory does not rehearse traditional periodization. Instead, it foregrounds a "splitting" of modernity complete with uneven developments occurring at different rates and times throughout the world. Smith's critical narrative identifies three currents in post-1989 art: remodernist, retro-sensationalist, and spectacularist tendencies flow into the first while aesthetic expression following nationalist/identitarian priorities and Do-It-Yourself art constitute the second and third. In these contexts, planetary figuration comes into play on a number of levels, including world-scales of vision enabled by technology, an aesthetics of disappearance, and the by now ubiquitous imprint of "worlds within the World."

In "Beyond the Flaming Walls of the World: Fantasy, Alterity, and the Postnational Constellation," Robert T. Tally Jr. maintains that through its estrangement techniques, the "discursive modality" of fantasy undercuts the conventions and standards of beauty embedded in national literatures and draws the reader imaginatively into the world and beyond it. Unlike the historical novel, which writers such as Walter Scott saw as serving national interests, fantasy fundamentally attends to planetary otherness and in so doing sets in train an otherworldly literary cartography of the postnational world-system. In his argument, the critic pays special attention to how the 1968 *Time* magazine "Earthrise" photo embodied this otherworldly view of the planet and became the focus of science fiction and fantasy literature as well as the master figure for a utopianism linked to similar meditations on the impossible.

Our book's closing chapter, Moraru's "Decompressing Culture: Three Steps toward a Geomethodology," is something of a hybrid. In the genre's formally and intellectually exploratory spirit, "Decompressing Culture" blends a Deleuzian-Guattarian discourse of worldly territoriality, Levinasian ethics and concerns of space technology, analysis of post-9/11 fiction, and a more provocatively couched axiomatics so as to compose a manifesto of sorts and thus enter a plea on behalf of a certain algorithm of "planetary reading." A systematic description of this interpretive model, he tells us, is as necessary as a strong emphasis on the model's urgency, hence the rhetorical shifts of Moraru's presentation throughout his piece. Moraru enumerates some key planetary themes: the greater elsewhere and the planet itself; remote spaces, customs, and their "others" represented as intrinsic or internal to closer ("our") places, groups, and their habits; a whole gamut of time-space constriction games and the bioconnective imaginings they spawn; and a new sense of togetherness and interdependence the resulting planetary iconology in turn endorses. After laying out the components or steps of his geomethodology, he applies it to works by Joseph O'Neill, Orhan Pamuk, Mircea Cărtărescu, and other novelists, and goes on to conclude by pinpointing the ethical consequences of planetary reading.

Notes

1. See Ulrich Beck, *World Risk Society* (Cambridge, Eng.: Polity; Malden, Mass.: Blackwell, 1999).

2. The literature on post-postmodernism is now threatening to rival in volume the archive of postmodern theory, with scholarship by Mary Holland,

Amy J. Elias, Timotheus Vermeulen, and Robin van den Akker (proponents of "metamodernism"), Alison Gibbons, Caren Irr, Leerom Medovoi, Rachel Adams, Min Hyoung Song, Bharati Mukherjee, and others steadily adding to it. Works addressing the question "What comes after postmodernism?" include Jeffrey T. Nealon's *Post-Postmodernism or, The Cultural Logic of Just-in-Time Capitalism* (Stanford, Calif.: Stanford University Press, 2012); a post-millennial special issue of *symploke* (12, nos. 1–2 [2004)]; a *College English* cluster of essays titled "Twentieth-Century Literature in the New Century: A Symposium" (64, no. 1 [September 2001]: 9–33); and a *Twentieth-Century Literature* special issue edited by Andrew Hoberek, "After Postmodernism: Form and History in Contemporary American Fiction" (53, no. 3 [Fall 2007]). See also Timothy S. Murphy, "To Have Done with Postmodernism: A Plea (or Provocation) for Globalization Studies," in *symploke* 12, nos. 1–2 (2004): 20–34; Robert L. McLaughlin, "Post-Postmodern Discontent: Contemporary Fiction and the Social World," in *symploke* 12, nos. 1–2 (2004): 53–68; Brian McHale, "What Was Postmodernism?" in *Electronic Book Review*, December 20, 2007, http://www.electronicbookreview.com/thread/fictionspresent/tense; Christian Moraru, *Cosmodernism: American Narrative, Late Globalization, and the New Cultural Imaginary* (Ann Arbor: University of Michigan Press, 2011); Neil Brooks and Josh Toth, eds., *The Mourning After: Attending the Wake of Postmodernism* (Amsterdam: Rodopi, 2007); and Terry Smith, *Contemporary Art: World Currents* (Upper Saddle River, N.J.: Prentice Hall, 2011). In "Thirteen Ways of Passing Postmodernism: Introduction to Focus," 3–4, an essay introducing his guest-edited *American Book Review* issue (34, no. 4 [May–June 2013]) on "metamodernism," Moraru shows that the post-postmodern debate has reached the planetary stage. Additional evidence is provided, along these lines, by *Narrative* in the "Postmodernist Fiction: East and West" issue coedited by Wang Ning and Brian McHale (21, no. 3 [2013]).

3. Ulrich Beck and Edgar Grande, "Varieties of Second Modernity: The Cosmopolitan Turn in Social and Political Theory and Research," *British Journal of Sociology* 61, no. 3 (2010): 412.

4. See Christian Moraru, "The Global Turn in Critical Theory," *symploke* 9, no. 1–2 (2001): 80–92. David Held advances the "strong globalization thesis" in the "Afterword" to his anthology *A Globalizing World? Culture, Economics, Politics* (New York: Routledge in association with The Open University, 2000), 171. Christopher J. Kollmeyer takes up Held's weak/strong globalization distinction in "Globalization, Class Compromise, and American Exceptionalism: Political Change in 16 Advanced Capitalist Countries," published in *Critical Sociology* 29, no. 3 (October 2003): 369–91. On "late globalization" and its cultural relevance in world and U.S. context, see, among others, Moraru, *Cosmodernism*, 33–37.

5. Nicholas A. Ashford and Ralph P. Hall, *Technology, Globalization, and Sustainable Development: Transforming the Industrial State* (New Haven, Conn.: Yale University Press, 2011), 4–5. For useful and succinct introductions to globalization, see Jürgen Osterhammel and Niels P. Petersson, *Globalization: A Short History*, trans. Dona Geyer (Princeton, N.J.: Princeton University Press, 2009); Manfred Steger, *Globalization: A Very Short Introduction*, 3rd ed. (Oxford: Oxford University Press, 2013); and Akira Iriye and Jürgen Osterhammel, eds., *Global Interdependence: The World after 1945* (Cambridge, Mass.: Belknap Press of Harvard University Press), 2013.

6. Nick Bisley, in *Rethinking Globalization* (Basingstoke, Eng.: Palgrave Macmillan, 2007), 6, 30, outlines what he sees as the three key engines of globalization: economics, sociology, and politics (23). Bisley lists a number of theoretical models for post–World War II global development including, for economic globalization, those of Samir Amin's *Re-Reading the Postwar Period* (New York: Monthly Review, 1994) and of Alex Callinicos, ed., "Europe on the Edge," a special issue of *International Socialism* 63 (1994). On sociological globalization, Bisley references David Held and Anthony McGrew, eds., *The Global Transformations Reader: An Introduction to the Globalization Debate,* 2nd ed. (New York: Palgrave Macmillan, 2005); and Manuel Castells's *The Information Age* trilogy: *The Rise of the Network Society, Vol. 1: The Information Age: Economy, Society, and Culture* (Oxford, Eng.: Blackwell, 1996); *The Power of Identity, Vol. 2, The Information Age: Economy, Society, and Culture*, 2nd ed. (Hoboken, N.J.: Wiley-Blackwell, 2009); and *End of Millennium, Vol. 3, The Information Age: Economy, Society, and Culture* (Hoboken, N.J.: Wiley-Blackwell, 1998). Discussing political globalization, he cites, among others, Ankie Hoogvelt, *Globalization and the Postcolonial World: The New Political Economy of Development*, 2nd ed. (Baltimore: Johns Hopkins University Press, 2001); and Randall D. Germain, *Globalization and Its Critics: Perspectives from Political Economy* (Basingstoke, Eng.: Palgrave Macmillan, 2000). Germain's more recent book on world administration and finance, *Global Politics and Financial Governance* (Basingstoke, Eng.: Palgrave Macmillan, 2010), also deserves mention.

7. Immanuel Wallerstein, *Geopolitics and Geoculture: Essays on the Changing World-System* (Cambridge, Eng.: Cambridge University Press; Paris: Maison des Sciences de l'Homme, 1991), 140. Wallerstein's autopoietic globalization is articulated in his books *The Modern World-System,* volumes I–IV, all reissued in 2011 by the University of California Press; see too Immanuel Wallerstein's *Utopistics, or Historical Choices of the Twenty-First Century* (New York: New, 1998).

8. See Giovanni Arrighi, *The Long Twentieth Century: Money, Power, and the Origins of Our Times* (New York: Verso, 2010), originally published in 1994.

9. Allan Cochrane and Kathy Pain, "Chapter 1: A Globalizing Society?" in *A Globalizing World? Culture, Economics, Politics*, ed. David Held (New York: Routledge in association with The Open University, 2000), 23.

10. In the context of media studies, for instance, this perspective informs Don Slater's *New Media, Development and Globalization: Making Connections in the Global South* (Cambridge, Eng.: Polity, 2013).

11. See, for example, Martin Albrow, *The Global Age: State and Society Beyond Modernity* (Stanford, Calif.: Stanford University Press, 1997).

12. Jean-Pierre Warnier, *La mondialisation de la culture*, 3rd ed. (Paris: La Découverte, 2004), 32. Also see Moraru, introduction to *Cosmodernism*, 15–75.

13. On Pierre Chaunu's *univers cloisonné*, most relevant is the author's book *Histoire, science sociale: La durée, l'espace et l'homme à l'époque moderne* (Paris: Société d'édition d'enseignement supérieur, 1974).

14. Ken Jowitt, *New World Disorder: The Leninist Extinction* (Berkeley: University of California Press, 1992). Zygmunt Bauman refers to Jowitt's book in *Globalization: The Human Consequences* (New York: Columbia University Press, 1998), 59. For Tzvetan Todorov, see *Le nouveau désordre mondial: Réflexions d'un Européen* (Paris: Robert Laffont, 2003). On the "chaos" of the

contemporary world, the reader might consult Amin Maalouf's recent book *Le dérèglement du monde* (Paris: Grasset & Fasquelle, 2009); and Immanuel Wallerstein's article "New Revolts Against the System," *New Left Review*, 2nd series, 18 (November–December 2002): 37. Joseph Stiglitz develops his critique most famously in *Globalization and Its Discontents* (New York: W. W. Norton, 2003). Zillah Eisenstein's views have been set out in *Against Empire: Feminisms, Racism, and the West* (New York: Zed Books, 2004).

15. Allan Cochrane and Kathy Pain refer to Paul Q. Hirst and Grahame Thompson's 1996 book *Globalization in Question: The International Economy and the Possibility of Governance,* 2nd ed. (1999). "Planetary dysphoria," Emily Apter explains in the closing chapters of her latest book, is a "geo-psychoanalytic" concept that captures the essence of our planet's "dark ecology" or "state of the world at its most depressed and *unruhig* [restless], awaiting the triumphant revenge of acid, oil, and dust." See Apter's *Against World Literature: On the Politics of Untranslatability* (London: Verso, 2013), 338, 341.

16. We refer the reader to the essays in Frank J. Lechner and John Boli, *The Globalization Reader* (Malden, Mass.: Blackwell, 2000); and in Fredric Jameson and Masao Miyoshi, eds., *The Cultures of Globalization* (Durham, N.C.: Duke University Press, 1998). Some critics point to a "postglobal age." See, in this regard, Ulrike Bergermann, Isabell Otto, and Gabriele Schabacher, eds., *Das Planetarische: Kultur-Technik-Medien in postglobalen Zeitalter* (Munich: Wilhelm Fink, 2010).

17. See Slavoj Žižek, *Welcome to the Desert of the Real: Five Essays on September 11 and Related Dates* (New York: Verso, 2002), and his *First as Tragedy, Then as Farce* (New York: Verso, 2009); Douglas Kellner, "Globalization, Terrorism, and Democracy: 9/11 and Its Aftermath," http://pages.gseis.ucla.edu/faculty/kellner/essays/-globalizationterroraftermath.pdf; as well as Kellner's *From 9/11 to Terror War: Dangers of the Bush Legacy* (Lanham, Md.: Rowman and Littlefield, 2003).

18. See Phillip E. Wegner, *Life between Two Deaths, 1989–2001: U.S. Culture in the Long Nineties* (Durham, N.C.: Duke University Press, 2009), especially the introduction.

19. See, for example, Terhi Rantanen, *The Media and Globalization* (London: Sage Publications, 2004); William Uricchio, *We Europeans? Media, Representations, Identities* (Bristol, Eng.: Intellect, 2009); Tanner Mirrlees, *Global Entertainment Media: Between Cultural Imperialism and Cultural Globalization* (New York: Routledge, 2013).

20. McKenzie Wark, *Virtual Geography: Living with Global Media Events* (Bloomington: Indiana University Press, 1994) and *Telesthesia: Communication, Culture, and Class* (Cambridge, Eng.: Polity, 2012); Paul Virilio, *The Information Bomb* (New York: Verso, 2006); Douglas Kellner, *Media Spectacle and Insurrection, 2011: From the Arab Uprisings to Occupy Everywhere* (London: Bloomsbury Academic, 2011); Richard Grusin, *Premediation: Affect and Mediality after 9/11* (London: Palgrave Macmillan, 2010). Sources discussing the relation of media and technology to globalization are myriad and range through political positions and disciplinary contexts. A few examples might include David Tabachnick and Toivo Koivukoski, *Globalization, Technology, and Philosophy* (Albany: SUNY Press, 2004); Kevin Robins and Frank Webster, *Times of the Technoculture: From the Information Society to the Virtual Life* (London:

Routledge, 1999); and Kaushalesh Lal, *Information and Communication Technologies in the Context of Globalization: Evidence from Developing Countries* (New York: Palgrave Macmillan, 2008).

21. Manuel Castells, *Networks of Outrage and Hope: Social Movements in the Internet Age* (Cambridge, Eng.: Polity, 2012); Jennifer Earl and Katrina Kimport, *Digitally Enabled Social Change: Activism in the Internet Age* (Cambridge, Mass.: MIT Press, 2011).

22. See, for instance, Pico Iyer's *The Global Soul: Jet Lag, Shopping Malls, and the Search for Home* (New York: Random House, 2000) and Thomas L. Friedman's books *The Lexus and the Olive Tree: Understanding Globalization* (New York: Picador, 2012) and *The World Is Flat 3.0: A Brief History of the Twenty-First Century* (New York: Farrar, Strauss and Giroux, 2006).

23. Saskia Sassen takes on "the development of new jurisdictional geographies" in "Neither Global nor National: Novel Assemblages of Territory, Authority, and Rights," published in *Ethics and Global Politics* 1, no. 1–2 (2008): 61–79.

24. Martin Albrow, "Who Rules the Global Rule Makers?" in *La Vie des idées* (November 3, 2011). The text is also available in English at the mirror site "Books and Ideas," http://www.booksandideas.net/Who-Rules-the-Global-Rule-Makers.html.

25. Lawrence Buell, *The Environmental Imagination: Thoreau, Nature Writing, and the Formation of American Culture* (Cambridge, Mass.: Belknap Press of Harvard University Press, 1996); Cheryll Glotfelty and Harold Fromm, eds., *The Ecocriticism Reader: Landmarks in Literary Ecology* (Athens: University of Georgia Press, 1996).

26. Basarab Nicolescu, *Théorèmes poétiques* (Paris: Rocher, 1994).

27. Yi-Fu Tuan, *Cosmos and Hearth: A Cosmopolite's Viewpoint* (Minneapolis: University of Minnesota Press, 1996), 187–88; Gérard Raulet, *Critical Cosmology: On Nations and Globalization—A Philosophical Essay* (Lanham, Md.: Lexington Books, 2005), especially 65–80; Félix Guattari, *Chaosmose* (Paris: Galilée, 1992); Anne Phillips, *Multiculturalism without Culture* (Princeton, N.J.: Princeton University Press, 2007), 42–72.

28. Amy J. Elias, "The Dialogical Avant-Garde: Relational Aesthetics and Time Ecologies in *Only Revolutions* and *TOC*," *Contemporary Literature* 53, no. 4 (Winter 2012): 749–50.

29. For the concept of *potenza*, see Antonio Negri, *Art and Multitude: Nine Letters on Art, Followed by Metamorphoses: Art and Immaterial Labor*, trans. Ed Emery (London, Eng.: Polity, 2011), 30. Maurizia Boscagli translates Negri's *potenza* as "strength" in *Insurgencies: Constituent Power and the Modern State*, trans. Maurizia Boscagli, with a New Foreword by Michael Hardt (Minneapolis: University of Minnesota Press, 2009). Boscagli's note on p. 337 defines potenza as "strength . . . resid[ing] in the desire of the multitude."

30. Gayatri Chakravorty Spivak, "Imperative to Re-Imagine the Planet," originally published in *Imperatives to Re-Imagine the Planet/Imperative zur Neuerfindung des Planeten*, ed. Willi Goetschel (Vienna: Passagen, 1999). Reprinted in *An Aesthetic Education in the Era of Globalization* (Cambridge, Mass.: Harvard University Press, 2011), 335–50.

31. Spivak, "Imperative to Re-Imagine the Planet," 348.

32. Ibid., 349.

33. See Gayatri Chakravorty Spivak, *Death of a Discipline* (New York: Columbia University Press, 2005), 72–73. For earlier formulations of this idea, see her *A Critique of Postcolonial Reason: Toward a History of the Vanishing Present* (Cambridge, Mass.: Harvard University Press, 1999) and "Imperative to Re-Imagine the Planet."

34. Neil Turnbull, "The Ontological Consequences of Copernicus: Global Being in the Planetary World," *Theory, Culture & Society* 23, no. 1 (2006): 133.

35. Masao Miyoshi, "Turn to the Planet: Literature, Diversity, and Totality," *Comparative Literature* 53, no. 4 (Fall 2001): 295.

36. Ibid., 296.

37. Some of these titles include Moraru's *Cosmodernism*; Ursula K. Heise's by now classic *Sense of Place and Sense of Planet: The Environmental Imagination of the Global* (Oxford: Oxford University Press, 2008); Wai Chee Dimock's articles "Literature for the Planet," *PMLA* 116, no. 1 (January 2001): 173–88, and "Scales of Aggregation: Prenational, Subnational, Transnational," *American Literary History* 18, no. 2 (Summer 2006): 219–28 as well as her trailblazing book, *Through Other Continents: American Literature across Deep Time* (Princeton, N.J.: Princeton University Press, 2008); Amy J. Elias, "Interactive Cosmopolitanism and Collaborative Technologies: New Foundations for Global Literary History," *New Literary History* 39, no. 3 (Summer 2008): 705–25; Joni Adamson, "American Literature and Film from a Planetary Perspective: Teaching Space, Time, and Scale," *Transformations* 21, no. 1 (Spring–Summer 2010): 23–41; Frances Ferguson, "Planetary Literary History: The Place of the Text," *New Literary History* 39, no. 3 (Summer 2008): 657–84; Susan Stanford Friedman, "Planetarity: Musing Modernist Studies," *Modernism/Modernity* 17, no. 3 (September 2010): 471–99; Caren Irr, "Toward the World Novel: Genre Shifts in Twentieth-First-Century Expatriate Fiction," *American Literary History* 23, no. 3 (Fall 2011): 660–79; Leerom Medovoi, "'Terminal Crisis?' From the Worlding of American Literature to World-System Literature," *American Literary History* 23, no. 3 (Fall 2011): 643–59; Mark Poster, "Global Media and Culture," *New Literary History* 39, no. 3 (Summer 2008): 685–703; Mary Louise Pratt, "Planetary Longings: Sitting in the Light of the Great Solar TV," in *World Writing: Poetics, Ethics, Globalization*, ed. Mary Gallagher, 207–23 (Toronto: University of Toronto Press, 2008); and Min Hyoung Song, "Becoming Planetary," *American Literary History* 23, no. 3 (Fall 2011): 555–73.

38. Ulrich Beck, *What Is Globalization?* trans. Patrick Camiller (Cambridge, Eng.: Polity, 2000), 9–10. Otherwise treading carefully, Beck is getting here on a slippery slope toward a notion of the world as fully integrated "totality."

39. Marshall Brown, "Globalism or Globalization?" *Modern Language Quarterly* 68, no. 2 (June 2007): 143. Brown's definitions can be inconsistent (see, e.g., 137).

40. Roland Robertson, "Social Theory, Cultural Relativity, and the Problem of Globality," in *Culture, Globalization, and the World-System: Contemporary Conditions for the Representation of Identity,* ed. Anthony D. King (Minneapolis: University of Minnesota Press, 2000), 73.

41. Min Hyoung Song, "Becoming Planetary," 568. Song draws from Carl Schmitt's controversial *The Nomos of the Earth*, Paul Gilroy's *Postcolonial Melancholia*, and Hardt and Negri's three-volume opus on global-era multitudes.

42. Warnier, *La mondialisation de la culture*, 107.

43. Amanda Anderson, "Cosmopolitanism, Universalism, and the Divided Legacies of Modernity," in *Cosmopolitics: Thinking and Feeling Beyond the Nation*, ed. Pheng Cheah and Bruce Robbins, 265–89, especially 278 and 265 (Minneapolis: University of Minnesota Press, 1998).

44. Ibid., 267.

45. Ibid., 268, 269. Quoting from Bruce Robbins's *Secular Vocations: Intellectuals, Professionalism, Culture* (New York: Verso, 1993), 181, Anderson notes that cosmopolitanism "enables an embrace of worldliness in two senses: '1) planetary expansiveness of subject-matter, on the one hand, and 2) unembarrassed acceptance of professional self-interest, on the other.' "

46. Anderson, "Cosmopolitanism," 267, 274, 276.

47. See Robbins, *Secular Vocations*, 197; James Clifford, "Traveling Cultures," in *Cultural Studies: Now and in the Future*, ed. Larry Grossberg, Cary Nelson, and Paula A. Treichler, (New York: Routledge, 1992), 108; Seyla Benhabib, *Situating the Self: Gender, Community, and Postmodernism in Contemporary Ethics* (New York: Routledge, 1992), 153; Judith Butler, "For a Careful Reading," in *Feminist Contentions: A Philosophical Exchange*, ed. Linda Nicholson (New York: Routledge, 1995), 130–31; Etienne Balibar, "Ambiguous Universality," *differences* 7, no. 1 (1995): 48–74; and Julia Kristeva, *Nations without Nationalism* (New York: Columbia University Press, 1993)—all discussed and quoted in Anderson. Our summary here follows her language. For an updated formulation of "agonistic universalism" by Butler, see *Contingency, Hegemony, Universality: Contemporary Dialogues on the Left* (New York: Verso, 2000) and *Dispossession: The Performative in the Political* (New York: Polity, 2013). Also see Benhabib's *Another Cosmopolitanism* (New York: Oxford University Press, 2008) for a more recent discussion of the pragmatic ethics of interactive cosmopolitanism.

48. Anderson cites David Hollinger's *Postethnic America*; Martha Nussbaum's "Patriotism and Cosmopolitanism"; and Arjun Appadurai's postnationalist stance from "Patriotism and Its Futures" (*Public Culture* 5 [1993]: 411–29). Hollinger's distinction between pluralism and cosmopolitanism is particularly important to our discussion. Pluralism endows certain groups with specific privilege and protects culture, while cosmopolitanism has been typically more oriented to the individual and disputes claims to cultural integrity (*Postethnic America: Beyond Multiculturalism* [New York: Basic Books, 1995], 85–86, quoted in Anderson, 278).

49. Shared topics and areas of theoretical concern inform such studies as the transatlantic cosmopolitanism reconstituted by Susan Manning and Andrew Taylor's *Transatlantic Literary Studies* (2007), Paul Gilroy's *The Black Atlantic* (1993), Kwame Anthony Appiah's *Cosmopolitanism: Ethics in a World of Strangers* (2006); the contributions to *Hemispheric American Studies*, edited by Caroline Field Levander and Robert S. Levine (2008); Yunte Huang's books, chiefly *Transpacific Displacement* (2002); Paul Jay's *Global Matters: The Transnational Turn in Literary Studies* (2010); Paul Giles's *Antipodean America: Australasia and the Constitution of U.S. Literature* (New York: Oxford University Press, 2013); and the Spring 2003 *Modern Fiction Studies* special-topic issue on the "trans-American imaginary," guest-edited by Paula M. L. Moya and Ramón Saldivar. To be sure, the list could go on.

50. Heise, *Sense of Place and Sense of Planet*, 50 and following. Heise further develops her eco-cosmopolitan argument in *Nach der Natur: Das Artensterben und die Moderne Kultur* (Berlin: Suhrkamp, 2010).

51. For an interesting contrast between a focus on rights in the context of globalization, on the one hand, and ethics within the framework of planetary cosmopolitanism, on the other, consult the audio dialogue between Judith Butler and Spivak, "A Dialogue on Global States, 6 May 2006," *Postmodern Culture* 17, no. 1 (2006).

52. Susan Stanford Friedman writes in her 2010 article "Planetarity: Musing Modernist Studies" (*Modernism/Modernity* 17, no. 3 [September 2010]): "As I use the term, . . . planetarity . . . is an epistemology, not an ontology" (494).

53. Bharati Mukherjee, *The Tree Bride* (New York: Hyperion, 2004), 231.

54. "Heterogenizing" interplays with the global are outlined in Roland Robertson's concept of "glocalization," while in "creolizations" the global is further customized, blending into native mixtures more aggressively, and even goes "slumming."

55. For a posthuman critique of the human-nonhuman hierarchy embedded in classical ecocriticism, see Heise, *Nach der Natur*, especially 115–49. Much has been made recently in ecocriticism of the "Anthropocene era," Paul Crutzen's 2002 term for the geologic-chronological age in which humans radically affect and alter the planet's ecology; see Jan Zalasiewicz et al., "Are We Now Living in the Anthropocene?" *GSA Today* (February 2008): 4–8.

56. See, for example, Spivak's *Death of a Discipline* (2005); Emily Apter's *The Translation Zone* (2006) and "Untranslatables: A World System," *New Literary History* 39, no. 3 (Summer 2008): 581–98; Wai Chee Dimock, "Planetary Time and Global Translation: 'Context' in Literary Studies," *Common Knowledge* 9, no. 3 (Fall 2003): 488–507.

57. Paul Gilroy, "Planetarity and Cosmopolitics," *British Journal of Sociology* 61, no. 3 (September 2010): 620. For "methodological nationalism" and the cosmopolitan reaction to it, see Ulrich Beck, "Toward a New Critical Theory with a Cosmopolitan Intent," *Constellations* 10, no. 4 (2003): 453. On postnational/post-territorialist aggregation and its role in new literary history, see Wai Chee Dimock's pioneering articles and books, especially *Through Other Continents*.

The Planetary Turn

Planetary Poetics

World Literature, Goethe, Novalis, and Yoko Tawada's Translational Writing

JOHN D. PIZER

Because of its cosmopolitan and global orientation, as well as its focus on transnational interchange, Johann Wolfgang Goethe's *Weltliteratur* (world literature) paradigm has been engaged in a variety of works in which scholars are in the process of developing an emerging planetarity paradigm. While Goethe saw *Weltliteratur* as a still-evolving phenomenon in his time, it has acquired a somewhat overdetermined character due to the disparate way critics have defined and appropriated it since 1836, when the term became widespread through the publication of the *Gespräche mit Goethe* (*Conversations with Goethe*), collected and edited by his former amanuensis Johann Peter Eckermann, where it was first enunciated in print. Goethe initially employed it in 1827, at a time when the fervent nationalism in Germany attendant to the successful conclusion of the Napoleonic Wars had been effectively suppressed through the edicts of the Congress of Vienna, executed with Machiavellian skill under the leadership and guidance of Austrian statesman Klemens Metternich. The almost coercively imposed cosmopolitanism that inspired Goethe's coinage was already crumbling by 1836, leading literary historians subsequently to associate *Weltliteratur* with canonicity, the global marketing of literature, and closed circulation. The ongoing planetary turn, on the other hand, has more the resonance of a provisional, open-ended dialogue. While it must be stressed that precisely such free, unclosed, interactive exchange among the practitioners of culture across national boundaries informs all of Goethe's elucidations of his paradigm, elucidations marked by a fragmentary and uncohesive character, many critics today, including those who are preoccupied with the planetarity phenomenon, have lost sight of this circumstance and associate *Weltliteratur* with a hoary traditionalism. Therefore, the juxtaposition of "world literature" and planetarity as quite disparate, if not antithetical, paradigms is unsurprising. Such a juxtaposition is evident, for instance, in Emily Apter's essay "Untranslatables: A World System," published in a 2008 special-topic issue of *New Literary History* devoted to "Literary History in the Global Age": " 'World Literature,' " Apter writes in "Untranslatables," "is the blue-chip moniker, benefiting from its pedigreed association with Goethean *Weltliteratur*. World Literature evokes the great comparatist tradition of encyclopedic mastery and scholarly ecumenicalism. It is a kind of big tent model of literary comparatism that, in promoting an ethic of liberal inclusiveness or the formal structures of cultural similitude, often has the collateral effect of blunting political critique." After summarizing other transnational literary models such as Pascale Casanova's notion of a "world republic of letters" and certain recent Kantian cosmopolitan/cosmopolitical formulations, the critic remarks that "'planetarity' would purge 'global' of its capitalist sublime, greening its economy, and rendering it accountable to disempowered subjects."[1] In contrasting world literature's putative tendency toward neutralizing effective political discourse with planetarity's positive ecological and socially inclusive trends, Apter does not imply that Goethe himself is to blame for creating an "association" with *Weltliteratur* that seems possessed of reactionary, or at least conservative, political and literary tendencies. However, given the circumstance that it may be difficult if not impossible to strip "world literature" of such linkages, a distinct but related conceptual constellation might be more fruitful in helping steer the course of the planetary turn.

The early German romantic author Friedrich Leopold Hardenberg, whose nom de plume was "Novalis," never used the term "Weltliteratur" in his writing. However, in his 1979 article "Novalis und die Idee der Weltliteratur" ("Novalis and the Idea of World Literature"), Thomas Bleicher shows that in many ways Novalis's writing anticipates Goethe's notion. Only 28 when he died in 1801, Novalis did not experience the coerced Metternichian cosmopolitanism that led Goethe to postulate the concept of an evolving *Weltliteratur*. Romantic cosmopolitanism in Novalis's day was grounded, at the political level, in the transnational hopes generated in the late eighteenth century by the Enlightenment and the French Revolution. Whereas Goethe's musings on world literature have a scattered, unsystematic character simply because he only sought on random occasions to define and elucidate his paradigm, the radically unclosed, fragmentary structure of Novalis's proto-*Weltliteratur* musings is consistent with his unmethodical methodology, partaking of a deliberate strategy evident in most writings associated with early German romanticism. Both Goethe and Novalis focused on the commerce-driven nature of an increasingly European-wide literary exchange.[2] However, typically for an early German romantic, Novalis's ideas on such transnational literature were more open-ended, utopian, and approximative than is the case with Goethean *Weltliteratur*. While Goethe's paradigm is grounded in the dialectic of the universal and the particular, planetarity in this digital age of solitary (albeit not necessarily isolated) men and women hunched in front of their computers but interconnected through the Internet is more informed by the dialectic of the individual and the collective. As the title to Barbara Senckel's important 1983 study of Novalis's "anthropology" indicates, his thought shuttles between the poles of *Individualität und Totalität*—individuality and totality (though in some cases he does consider the local and the particular, as we will see)—and this circumstance may allow us to bring this early romantic into a more fruitful contiguity with the unfolding planetary turn than would the effort to elucidate a productive intersection between planetarity and Goethean *Weltliteratur*. Nevertheless, my drawing upon some theorists who are beginning to work toward the development of a planetary consciousness while excluding others is governed by my wish to highlight potentially useful zones of filiation between contemporary planetarity, on the one hand, and the cosmopolitan world literature ideas expressed by both Goethe and Novalis, on the other. Not recognizing this filiation, in my view, would risk the failure of twenty-first-century literary criticism to ground historically its attempt to bring about the planetary turn.

The following chapter has four intersecting areas of focus. The first will explore what Goethe intended by the term *Weltliteratur*, especially in the historical context of its genesis, and what role this paradigm, along with the broader concept of world literature, has been playing in the recent emergence of the "planet" as a cross-culturally oriented framework for comparatism. I will then look at Novalis's proto-*Weltliteratur* literary fragments and examine how they are relevant to the nascent planetarity paradigm. Indeed, though they precede Goethe's thoughts on *Weltliteratur* chronologically, they are in some ways more valuable to a truly planetary turn because they are less rooted in a specifically western European framework. Goethe, at times, consciously associates *Weltliteratur* with European literature, and he primarily elucidates his term as a means to create greater balance and cosmopolitan insight among literary circles of the western European nations. Novalis's proto-world literary fragments, on the other hand, adopt a relational model that seeks an ideal romantic transcendence of cultural production grounded in discrete nation-states. In this regard, his enunciations take a more authentically transnational turn than do those of Goethe.

My examination of comments by Goethe and Novalis on the general principle of *Weltliteratur* will be followed by a brief comparison of their tripartite translation schemes, a key element in their respective ideas on world literature and of significance for the planetarity notion. Finally, I will explore a recent work by the Japanese-German author Yoko Tawada as exemplary of planetary consciousness, a consciousness, in her case, grounded in a reflective sensitivity to issues connected to translation in the broadest sense of that term. Tawada's poetics are located in what Apter, in the title of her 2006 book, terms "the translation zone." Tawada's stories and poetry are hyperconscious of the avenues through which transnational cultural exchange is mediated in and through language. As I will show, she consistently evokes a planetary hybridity rooted in a practice of border-crossing relationality more resonant with Novalis's pre-nationalist cosmopolitanism than with Goethean *Weltliteratur*. Goethe's paradigm was largely generated by a prophetically accurate fear that the xenophobia triggered by the Napoleonic Wars fought after Novalis's death might soon reemerge. Tawada's writing is generally devoid of such fear. Given her uniquely acute attunement to how language mediates transnational encounters, Tawada is included in this essay not only because of her exemplary planetary poetic praxis, but also because her writing illustrates the major role translation plays, according to Goethe and Novalis, in planetary interlingualism.

Goethe's *Weltliteratur* in a Planetary Context

The publication of Fritz Strich's *Goethe und die Weltliteratur* (*Goethe and World Literature*) in 1946 was significant for two reasons. First of all, its appendix brought together the passages scattered throughout Goethe's diaries, letters, and conversations in which Goethe, starting in 1827 and ending in 1831 (the year before his death), employed the term "Weltliteratur." This gathering of all Goethe's enunciations (albeit sometimes in abridged form) on *Weltliteratur* into one brief (397–400) contiguous compilation has enabled scholars to access these remarks without the effort of combing through editions of his collected works. Secondly, Strich's own interpretation of *Weltliteratur* as an expansive cosmopolitan paradigm allowing one to regard the most noteworthy works of Europe, the Far East, and America as a broad literary network collocated through Goethe's visionary gaze inaugurated the postwar tendency to link *Weltliteratur* to various forms of globalist discourse, a trend most strikingly manifest once the "age of globalization" began after the collapse of the Soviet Union and the concomitant end to the Cold War. To be sure, Karl Marx and Friedrich Engels had forecast, in their 1848 *Communist Manifesto*, the birth of a "Weltliteratur" from all the various national literatures, going beyond Goethe in predicting their dissolution by bringing them into allusive contiguity with national industries, which they saw as disappearing through bourgeois world capitalism and—so they hoped and were calling for in the revolutionary year 1848—the unification of the proletariat on a global scale.[3] However, such internationalism collapsed with the failure of the 1848 Revolution, ushering in the intense nationalism of the Western world, which lasted until the end of World War II. Thus, until the appearance of Strich's book—and indeed in Strich's own prewar engagement with Goethe's paradigm—the cosmopolitan resonance of *Weltliteratur* was largely ignored by critics, who tended to focus on canonicity, transnational commerce, and reception as indicative of an author's relative world literary status.[4] The National Socialist "scholar" Kurt Hildebrandt went so far as to claim that, for Goethe, *Weltliteratur* was the product of Aryan populations who experienced the Renaissance, and that Goethe's perception was racially oriented.[5]

Apter's previously cited association of *Weltliteratur* with "blue-chip," "pedigreed," and thus canonic works is not simply justified by such developments in the reception of Goethe's paradigm, a phenomenon also evident in Strich's monograph and which continues today, but in Goethe's own treatment of the subject. In language that anticipates almost verbatim the claim of Marx and Engels in the *Communist Manifesto*, Goethe asserted that national literature signified little at the time and that the epoch of *Weltliteratur* was at hand.[6] However, he also equated world literature with European literature, primarily because the infrastructure and communication advances enabling border-crossing literary discourse at that moment were restricted to western Europe.[7] In addition, he prophesized what would become the literature market-driving dictates of popular tastes, a trend one would strive in vain to resist but which he believed to be only a temporary current (*Strömung*). He therefore urged the serious-minded to create their own modest "church," presumably as a means to preserve the viability of elevated literature. He issued this recommendation in the course of his famous pronouncement that the world, in the current age, was nothing more than an expanded fatherland.[8]

The interconnection between cosmopolitanism, on the one hand, and qualitatively superior literature/discourse/intellectuals, on the other, is also evident in a number of the fragments from Strich's appendix. Strich himself strongly contributed to the association between *Weltliteratur* and canonicity in *Goethe und die Weltliteratur*. He argues that much work that has crossed national borders and was widely read and translated does not deserve the *Weltliteratur* appellation because such texts might be mere popular diversions (*Unterhaltungsliteratur*), sensationalism, or fads, and so are likely to disappear from the global literary catalogue as quickly as they rose to the top of international bestseller lists. With respect to Goethe's contemporaries, Strich cites the example of August von Kotzebue, who, during the Age of Goethe, had the greatest international commercial success of all German-language authors but lacked the capacity to achieve enduring renown. According to Strich, the German term *Weltliteratur* signifies not only supranational (*übernationale*) but also supratemporal (*überzeitliche*) validity.[9] However, establishing the linkage between *Weltliteratur* and canonicity was not Strich's primary purport in his book; much previous scholarship had cemented this bond, which has endured—as the passage from Apter indicates—to this day. Rather, in the wake of the extreme, murderous xenophobia that gripped the Axis powers, especially Germany, during the Second World War, Strich, a Swiss-German scholar, wanted to hold up Goethe as an exemplar of genuine cosmopolitanism to the German-speaking nations. He also hoped to recuperate Germany's deservedly damaged reputation with respect to transnational, globalist outreach, a reputation the German-speaking regions just as deservedly enjoyed during Goethe's lifetime. The subsequent imbrications scholars (including Apter, with her allusion to *Weltliteratur*'s "ecumenicalism")[10] have highlighted in their work between cosmopolitanism and *Weltliteratur* show Strich was quite successful in this regard.[11]

There is no question but that Goethean *Weltliteratur* is marked by a certain degree of elitism. Goethe stresses in one instance that it is cross-border, translinguistic collaboration among the most advanced intellectuals and scientists that is enhanced through world literary dialogue. In many cases, leading thinkers from one nation are in a better position to judge the merits of writers in another than critics who share the nationality of the authors under discussion. As an example, he argues that Thomas Carlyle's biography of Friedrich Schiller exhibits greater perspicacity than might be found in the perspective of Schiller's fellow Germans, and finds the opposite is true with respect to Shakespeare criticism.[12] He also contended—and this is frequently overlooked by critics who believe Goethe first perceived world literary interchange as occurring at a wide-ranging international level—that the different lands had already been taking note of each other's literary products for some time, and that *Weltliteratur* signified productive social interchange among a rather select group—"die lebendigen und strebenden Literatoren" ("the lively striving men of letters")—as he told a group of scientists in 1828.[13] Given planetarity's stress on outreach to "disempowered subjects," Goethe's underscoring of an elite few who participate in the world literary dialogue would seem to indicate that his *Weltliteratur* paradigm, in this respect, is less than ideal in helping guide the planetary turn. However, Goethe was not always consistent in this regard. In his last note on the concept, he remarks that the consequence of *Weltliteratur* for the diverse nations would be the ability to more quickly benefit reciprocally from each other's advantages.[14] Goethe's concept is so deeply rooted in respect for alterity that Homi Bhabha was able to use it as a heuristic instrument in turning to the work and lives of the planet's most dispossessed citizens. Alluding to *Weltliteratur*'s germination through the dislocations caused by the Napoleonic Wars, Bhabha comments "that transnational histories of migrants, the colonized, or political refugees—these border and frontier conditions—may be the terrains of world literature."[15] Rüdiger Görner, who stresses the open-ended nature of *Weltliteratur* as Goethe envisioned it, goes so far as to claim that "Goethe was indeed the first European writer who had recognized, in the aftermath of the French Revolution, that the sufferings of emigration would dominate civilization henceforth."[16] This is what makes Goethe a natural ally, despite his elitism, of those who, like Bhabha, see *Weltliteratur* as productive in elucidating and promoting the thought of the marginalized and disenfranchised.

Goethe's oscillation between an emphasis on national literatures as enriched through cosmopolitan intercourse and the global (or at least European-wide) networks enabling this border-crossing dialogue has inspired Claudio Guillén's assertion that Goethean *Weltliteratur* commences at the national level, "thus making possible a dialogue between the local and the universal, between the one and the many."[17] In her introduction to *Sense of Place and Sense of Planet* (2008), a work which anticipates and helps inaugurate the planetary turn, Ursula K. Heise challenges the very notion of the local; a work such as Douglas Adams's *The Hitchhiker's Guide to the Galaxy* creates an interplanetary tableau in which Earth itself, the entire globe, is articulated as a quite discrete particular space *tout court*, so that Adams's book "redefines the meaning of the word 'local.'"[18] Through discussions of globalization, contemporary advocates of cosmopolitanism begin to move away from national and even locally based modes of identity, in Heise's view, thus hinting at the possibility of a truly planetary consciousness.[19] Already in his seminal essay "Turn to the Planet: Literature, Diversity, and Totality" (2001), Masao Miyoshi points to "the spread of desocialized individualism," a process that has come about through globalization, and bluntly speaks of the growing inefficacy of the local and national domains as sites of positive contestation in the public, cultural sphere.[20] He goes so far as to argue that there is no going back to the nation-state model and proclaims that "literature and literary studies now have one basis and goal: to nurture our common bonds to the planet—to replace the imaginaries of exclusionist familialism, communitarianism, nationhood, ethnic culture, regionalism, 'globalization,' or even humanism, with the ideal of planetarianism."[21] Whether such a radically planetary approach on the part of literary scholars is desirable or even viable may be subject to debate, but it does suggest that Goethean *Weltliteratur*, with its oscillation between the local and a grounding in discrete national literatures, on the one hand, and the transnational/universal, on the other, may not be useful as a heuristic tool in the service of "planetarianism," even when it is adapted to Bhabha's version of an anti-exclusionist approach to the cultures of marginalized groups.

The next major work to suggest a planetary approach to literary studies, and which has had a major influence on comparatism, is Gayatri Chakravorty Spivak's 2003 volume *Death of a Discipline*. The discipline Spivak finds to be in the process of demise is Comparative Literature. She suggests that its impending doom is caused by a homogenizing globalization, which imposes a uniform "system of exchange" across the planet.[22] She objects to the very term "globe," a place, she claims, no one actually inhabits. The place we inhabit is the planet, albeit on loan, and planetary—as opposed to global—thought is Other-directed, grounded in alterity, and capable of reenchanting the terrestrial sphere—uniform and drab when conceptualized as "globe"—through its ability to reinvest it with the "unheimlich," the sense of ineffable mystery that can make everyday life interesting. Antithetical to such planetary uncanniness, to Spivak's mind, is world literature, which she associates with English-language hegemony on a global scale. She fears the universal spread of world literature anthologies, which, she predicts, will lead to such scenarios as the reading by Taiwanese students of Chinese-language classics like *The Dream of the Red Chamber* in English-language translation made available in extremely abridged form in textbooks or compendia published in the United States.[23] Spivak worries about the specter of "U.S.-style world literature becoming the staple of Comparative Literature in the global South" because it would undermine the possibility that Comparative Literature on a planetary scale could be enriched by cultural and linguistic diversity.[24] In her view, comparatism under the sign of planetarity is viable only when the discipline's practitioners, including those in America, are conversant with the languages of the Southern hemisphere and possess a more than superficial acquaintance with that region's cultures; she proposes that an attention to the latter's nuances would be enhanced through an Area Studies-style immersion into their particularities. Thus, a world literature approach as defined by Spivak—monolingual, univocal, and culturally hegemonic—is completely opposite to Comparative Literature as a field of study undertaken with a planetary consciousness. Indeed, in her opinion, world literature is strongly contributing to the slow "death" of Comparative Literature as a discipline.

In my 2006 book *The Idea of World Literature*, I have submitted that "World Literature" as an introductory-level humanities course—a pedagogical domain primarily to be found, contrary to Spivak, in colleges and universities across the United States—must be conceptually disentangled from the Goethean *Weltliteratur* paradigm. *Death of a Discipline* is not exactly guilty of conflating "World Literature" with *Weltliteratur*, but Spivak does treat Goethe's concept rather negatively in criticizing Franco Moretti's widely cited 2000 essay "Conjectures on World Literature." Partly inspired by Immanuel Wallerstein's world-systems theory, Moretti argues for a "distant" reading that examines broad transnational trends in literature rather than engaging in a New Critical–style "close reading" attentive to often minute textual details and informed by philological rigor. Given Spivak's desire that comparatism should inculcate an appreciation of the "Otherness" of texts, especially those of marginalized cultures in little-studied languages—a telos of planetarity quite distinct from that of Miyoshi—her dissatisfaction with Moretti's approach is unsurprising, even though part of Moretti's intention in practicing distant reading is to bring "cultures that belong to the periphery of the literary system" into critical consciousness through broad examinations of literary genres and styles.[25] Moretti opens his essay by complaining that literary studies have not lived up to the promise held by Goethe's approach and proposes that "we return to that old ambition of *Weltliteratur*: after all, the literature around us is now unmistakably a planetary system."[26] He realizes that this return cannot involve studying all literatures from all times, but rather must attempt to show how these literatures are "interrelated," constituting "one world literary system."[27] In her critique of Moretti, Spivak recognizes as positive his attention to the periphery but maintains that "there is something disingenuous about using Goethe, Marx, and Weber as justification for choosing world systems theory to establish a law of evolution in literature," because such an approach relies on the work of others from the periphery itself to fill in the necessary details. Though she does not use the term, Spivak virtually suggests that adherents to Moretti's model would have to engage in a kind of scholarly outsourcing.[28] Indeed, Moretti more or less admits this; he realizes that simply more reading of texts written in a plethora of languages is not possible, so a reliance on the work of those who focus on something other than western European narratives (Moretti's specialization) must be part of the equation.[29]

In her 2006 essay "Scales of Aggregation—Prenational, Subnational, Transnational," Wai Chee Dimock suggests a form of planetarity that incorporates *Weltliteratur* in a manner that taps into the local/universal dialectic of Goethe's paradigm. In so doing, she avoids both the homogenization Spivak associates with world literature and the perhaps literally all-too-farsighted scale proposed by Moretti in his world literary system conjectures, even though Dimock refers neither to Goethe nor to his concept in her essay. Bhabha, however, persuasively locates, via Mikhail Bakhtin, in the subnational and prenational elements of Goethe's work, in its local and particular dimensions, the possibility of a transcendent historical synchronicity. Indeed, for Bhabha, Bakhtin's reading of Goethe evokes the uncanny, that liminal sense of mystery Spivak would resurrect in her planetary approach to Comparative Literature.[30] Whereas the subnational and prenational tendencies in Goethe's oeuvre, which inspire transnational topographies in the thought of Bakhtin and Bhabha, were enabled by the circumstance that Goethe never lived in a genuine, politically integrated German nation (which did not undergo its first unification until 1871, almost forty years after Goethe's death), Dimock grounds her triadic terms in the principle of an "unbundling and rebundling" of the humanities proposed by a variety of scholars, a paradigm shift that would occur with respect to both discipline and national tradition, that is to say, would presuppose, for example, the elimination of the exclusive (and exclusionary research) of American literature in departments of English and American Studies. Pre-, sub-, and transnational literary studies would examine marginalized cultures and endangered languages not affiliated with the nation-state, creating a "species-wide platform" linking the disciplines of anthropology, history, and literary studies in a manner suggestive of planetary comparatism, enriched, as proposed by Spivak, through an Area Studies–type of immersion into cultural and linguistic localities and particularities.[31]

In arguing for a transnational methodology mindful of localized details, Dimock's approach is germane to the universal/particular dialectic inherent in Goethean *Weltliteratur* and at the same time anticipates a recent effort by Reinhard Meyer-Kalkus, who wants to take "world literature beyond Goethe," as the title of his 2010 essay indicates. The maneuver is prompted by the recognition that contemporary writers are no longer bound by discrete ethnic/linguistic/national affiliations, as is evident in the large number of authors who were originally Iranians, Turks, or Arabs but now reside in Germany and write in German. Meyer-Kalkus also argues for the need to closely examine the prenational "preliminary stages" of the planet's literatures.[32] Thus, like Dimock, albeit in his case consciously drawing on Goethe's paradigm, he endorses a study of literature informed by pre-, sub-, and transnational constellations and concludes that transnationalism is a relatively recent phenomenon the tendencies of which scholars can only perceive when they "put their ear to this rail network of the new cultural mobility."[33] His intervention presents a model of how, when oriented by planetary consciousness, literary studies may rely on Goethe's *Weltliteratur* paradigm but move beyond it.

It is worth recalling that Goethe developed his thoughts on *Weltliteratur* at a time of almost literally coercive cosmopolitanism. He had been horrified at the extreme xenophobia that flared up when the tide turned against the French in the last years of the Napoleonic Wars. He was enough of a visionary to sense that extreme nationalism might overwhelm Europe in the near future, as it did beginning in 1848 and lasting until 1945. In the conversation with Eckermann on January 31, 1827, in which Goethe made his most often-cited pronouncement concerning the advent of *Weltliteratur*, he speaks of a "pedantic darkness" that will befall the Germans if they do not cast their gaze beyond the narrow circle of their own environs, a darkness he sensed in the last stages of the Napoleonic Wars. There is a note of urgency when he claims that all must do their part to accelerate (*beschleunigen*) the epoch of *Weltliteratur*.[34] Subsequent to the collapse of the Soviet Union, the world also entered into an era of cosmopolitanism, coercive not through a network of agents such as those who served Metternich but through economic necessity; English became the world language of multinational capitalism on a universal scale, and national governments lost the ability effectively to regulate commercial activity. Cosmopolitanism continues to be thought of, at least among most intellectuals, rather favorably, as long as it is attuned to, and celebrates, cultural differences.[35] The negative term used to describe the cultural/economic coercion and homogenization of our time, the dark side of contemporary cosmopolitanism, is "globalization." This is evident, for example, in *Death of a Discipline*, when Spivak refers to globalization as "the imposition of the same system of exchange everywhere." She differentiates between the "globe" as uninhabited cyberspace and the "planet" as the locus of diversity and difference.[36] This kind of contrast explains the move, exemplified by the essays in this volume, toward planetary thinking and away from globalism/globalization, toward a heterogeneous rather than uniform cosmopolitanism.[37]

Novalis's Proto-Planetary Idealism

These considerations precede a consideration of Novalis's proto-*Weltliteratur* musings in order to highlight the radically different historical context in which he evolved them. Nationalism had not yet swept through Germany, and the French Revolution had not yet aroused deep antipathy toward France. Early German romantic cosmopolitanism was marked neither by a sense of coercion nor by a sense of urgency, as it was in the later stages of Goethe's life, when he made his observations on *Weltliteratur*. This lack of duress in Novalis's proto-*Weltliteratur* formulations imbues them with a certain idealism, indeed utopianism, and this aspect renders them productive in the envisioning of a liberatory planetarity. Novalis's proto-*Weltliteratur* fragments also lack the elitist dimension characteristic of certain elucidations by Goethe of his paradigm. In their preface to *Multitude: War and Democracy in the Age of Empire*, Michael Hardt and Antonio Negri define the multitude as "an open and expansive network in which all differences can be expressed freely and equally, a network that provides the means of encounter so that we can work and live in common." Unlike the "people" or the "masses," the "multitude" is a diverse, differentiated collection of individuals.[38] While Novalis addressed his remarks to the educated, he seems to favor literary networks among writers, which, he thinks, would counteract the pablum marketed to the multitude of readers around the world (whom mass literature marketers themselves have tended to regard as a homogeneous collection of potential buyers). As noted previously, Goethe, by contrast, proposed the formation of a modest "church" that would stoically but quiescently constitute a countertrend to literary mass marketing. Where Goethean *Weltliteratur*, as Apter suggests, is the model for a globally based but somewhat rarified Comparative Literature, Novalis's proposals speak to a more planetary stance. For, if planetarity is to encompass some form of "world art," a truly cosmopolitan organization seeking to promote a planetary aesthetics through a creative commercial approach directed toward diverse networks of readers in resistance to the current worldwide marketing of literature geared to the lowest common denominator of manipulated mass cravings for mindless entertainment might be a desideratum, even though such a strategy might also be regarded by some as elitist.

The rather speculative, visionary character of Novalis's thought is evident in his aphorisms on cosmopolitanism; he claims a truly complete human must live simultaneously in a variety of locations and in other humans, with a broad circle and multiple events constantly present to mind. In this way, presence of spirit (*Gegenwart des Geistes*) will turn the individual into a genuine cosmopolitan (*Weltbürger*) and make one thoughtfully active.[39] A genius has the ability to act on the basis of both imagined and real objects and to engage with these objects. Without the capacity to act as a suprasensual being (*ein übersinnliches Wesen*) capable of being outside oneself and conscious while rising beyond the realm of the senses, one could not be a cosmopolitan, indeed, one could only be an animal.[40] The European stands above the German, the German stands above the Saxon, and the Saxon above the citizen of the (Saxon) city of Leipzig. Above the European (and apparently above all) stands the cosmopolitan. This seems a relatively practical, politically rooted evaluative scale, but Novalis goes on to remark in this fragment that all the more limited, confined entities—the national, temporal, local, and individual—can be universalized. The individual coloring of the universal is its "romanticizing" element: "Thus every national, and even the personal, God, is a romanticized universe."[41] Such dialectical interplay between the cosmopolitan and universal, on the one hand, and the local/national/individual, on the other, promotes a self/Other dialogue unbound by political and economic constraints. Grounded in his studies of early romantic philosopher Johann Gottlieb Fichte's idealism, Novalis's fragments concerning the relationship between the ego and the external world posit that personal consciousness itself creatively shapes what lies outside it; the human spiritual sanctum and the phenomenal universe external to it are so profoundly interconnected that, as the previous quote suggests, the national God and the personal God constitute a romanticized—that is to say, wholly integral—universe. Such early romantic thought is unencumbered by worries on how to cope with extreme national/political divisiveness. This virtually unmitigated relationality between the self and all that is external to it, such unimpeded interactivity on the part of the true cosmopolitan, may be attractive in formulating utopian ideals for a planetary paradigm, ideals resistant to the repressive elements of globalization. The danger, of course, is the potential for solipsistic egoism on the part of interlocutors who might see in Novalis's Fichtean cosmopolitanism more the opportunity for a literal self-sufficiency than the ability to employ a romantically invested imaginary in seeking genuine dialogue and an understanding of what lies outside the personal sphere. It should also be added that Novalis had some reservations concerning the sweeping character of Fichtean consciousness and self-knowledge and recognized that what is found through reflection already appears to exist.[42]

Central, in Novalis, to a cosmopolitan engagement with the world through the romantic imagination is poetry, and his projection of a "poeticizing of the world" is the fulcrum of his proto-*Weltliteratur* reflections.[43] To this end, Novalis called for "the establishment of a literary-republican order, which is of a thoroughly mercantile-political character, an authentic cosmopolitan lodge."[44] Cosmopolitan societies and lodges constituted an essential aspect of intellectual life in eighteenth- and early nineteenth-century Germany, as reflected in the popularity at that time of orders such as the Illuminati and the Freemasons. Goethe was deeply involved with such orders, albeit not always on a friendly footing when he felt they threatened the established political system.[45] In commenting on this and other passages in which Novalis proposes to establish an "intellectual knightly order,"[46] Bleicher speculates that the writer may have imagined that such an organization would use the knightly orders and Freemason lodges of the Middle Ages as a model; like most other early German romantics, Novalis was fascinated by this period, and one of his most widely read works, *Die Christenheit oder Europa* (*Christendom or Europe*, 1799), expresses a yearning for the kind of politically and religiously harmonious Europe that Novalis—a Protestant—believed was in existence prior to the Reformation. Bleicher compares Novalis's pronouncements concerning a literary/republican/intellectual order to the kind of *Weltliteratur-Bund* (world literature federation) constituted by today's global PEN Club.[47] However, while PEN tends to work toward goals such as writers' freedom from governmental oppression, and, concomitantly, resistance to all forms of censorship, Novalis's emphasis on the mercantile character of the proposed fellowship points in the direction of promoting the sale and marketing of poetic literature on a worldwide scale. After all, Novalis proclaims elsewhere that the spirit of commerce (*Handelsgeist*) is the great spirit awakening countries, cities, and works of art; it is the spirit of culture and of the perfection (*Vervollkommnung*) of the human race. He distinguishes between the historical spirit of commerce, slavishly adherent to the needs of the moment, and the creative (*schaffenden*) spirit of commerce.[48]

A central domain of *Weltliteratur* for Goethe, Novalis, and those who seek to interpret and develop this paradigm today is constituted by the theory and practice of translation. Indeed, in his well-received book *What Is World Literature?* (2003), which contains an illuminating overview of the genesis of Goethe's *Weltliteratur*, David Damrosch argues that works can be categorized as belonging to the select genre named in his title only when they circulate widely throughout the planet—and are critically enhanced—by means of translation.[49] Certainly, even if one agrees with Spivak and many others that reading in translation is detrimental to authentic comparatism, the planetary turn cannot do without it. The tripartite translation schemes proposed by both Goethe and Novalis can be helpful here. At the first level of Goethe's model, the translator creates a prose version of the text, which faithfully transmits the content presented in the source language. The second-level rendering reflects the stylistic tendencies of the translator as grounded in his or her own language. At the third level, the translator foregoes precisely such tendencies, giving up an adherence to the grammatical and stylistic conventions of the target language and surrendering them to the rhythms and nuances of the source language. This method will lead to an initial sense of estrangement on the part of the reader but ultimately enhances the suppleness and structural range of the target language.[50]

Such an approach is reminiscent of one of the qualities Novalis associates with romantic poetry, namely, the art of making the object (*Gegenstand*) of the literary work both alien (*fremd*) and familiar, as well as attractive.[51] However, his classificatory scheme is somewhat distinct from that of Goethe. As Novalis claims, a translation is either grammatical, infused with the power to alter (*verändernd*), or mythic. Grammatical translations, not unlike those at Goethe's first, prosaic level, require scholarly knowledge (*Gelehrsamkeit*) but are conventional and demand only discursive ability on the part of the translator. Like Goethe's second-level translation, those renditions with the potential for changing the character of the source-language text are most frequently carried out by authors themselves: they must be undertaken by what Novalis calls the (source-language) poet, who allows the poem to speak according to the idea (*Idee*) of both individuals, the original author and his or her translator. However, Novalis's third category, the mythic translation, is quite unique. He contends that renderings of this kind do not completely convey the content of the actual work of art but only its ideal. As such, no fully realized model of this type of translation yet exists; only luminous traces (*helle Spuren*) of such efforts are available. Not just books, but everything can be translated in these three modes.[52] In its hint at language's lack of self-sufficiency, Novalis points forward to a similar notion in Walter Benjamin's celebrated 1921 essay "Die Aufgabe des Übersetzers" ("The Task of the Translator"), with its notion of an originary, prelapsarian language only glimpsed in trace form through the palimpsest of the source language and the target languages into which it is translated. Novalis's scheme also suggests a utopian relationality potentially valuable for planetary thought, but Goethe's third-level translation concept, Other-directed and grounded in a realizable alterity, may constitute a more practical path toward a productive twenty-first-century geoaesthetics.

Neither Goethe nor Novalis eschews a national, indeed vaguely nationalist dimension with respect to the relationship between translation and world literature. Goethe believed that Germans would play a central role as interpreters (*Dolmetscher*) in the world literary marketplace. Indeed, whoever speaks German will find himself or herself in the market where all nations offer their wares, but it is also the case that every translator is a mediator in the literary intellectual trade.[53] In a study of early German romanticism, Andreas Huyssen argues that the early German romantics saw Germans as master translators on a global scale. Therefore, the German nation is destined to lead Europe into a golden age. In discussing Novalis's myth-centered translation postulate, Huyssen notes that at this level, the individuality of neither the original author nor of the translator is relevant. Mythic translation cannot be practically realized; rather, its articulation points in an eschatological manner toward a future in which all humanity will be poetic and is also a corollary to Novalis's declaration that all poetry is translation. The mythic translator translates reality into myth, and mythic translation is a cipher for the aimed-for romanticizing of the world, through which harmony will reign, and peace, love, religion, and poetry will predominate.[54] Novalis's mythic translation is a constitutive element of what Huyssen refers to as an early Romantic "literary spiritual utopia of a German *Weltliteratur*."[55] However, in proposing a relational practice on a universal scale and not restricted to just rendering words and syntax from one national tongue into another, Novalis's all-encompassing notion adds a unique dimension to planetary thinking.

Tawada's Planetary Poetics

In her recent essay "Planetarity: Musing Modernist Studies" (2010), Susan Stanford Friedman explains that "planetarity as I use the term is an epistemology, not an ontology. On a human scale, the 'worldness' the term invokes—to echo Glissant—means a polylogue of languages, cultures, viewpoints, and standpoints on modernism/modernity. It requires attention to modes of local and translocal meaning-making and translation, to processes and practices of perception and expression on a global scale."[56] In her description of what she intends the term "planetarity" to signify, Friedman unintentionally summarizes the poetics of the contemporary German-Japanese language author Yoko Tawada. Unlike most other German-language writers for whom German is not the mother tongue, Tawada is a true authorial polyglot; she writes as much in her native Japanese as in German. The most consistent focus of her oeuvre is precisely the "local and translocal meaning-making and translation" highlighted by Friedman; Tawada constantly reflects on how meaning and modes of expression as well as signification vary according to their local and translocal contexts. She is "polylogue" in the sense that her attention is not solely focused on the interface between the languages, cultures, and topographies of Japan and Germany; her second language is Russian, and she has traveled and taught in the United States. The attention she pays in her writing to "processes and practices of perception and expression" has a truly "global" reach. She concentrates more on how perception and knowledge alter from one language and topography to another rather than attempting to articulate an ideal overarching realm of being transcending linguistic diversity, an ontology pursued by Novalis, Benjamin, and, albeit not in his translation theory, by Goethe. This concluding section will examine Tawada's planetary poetics as exemplified by her 2007 collection of poetry and prose entitled *Sprachpolizei und Spielpolyglotte* (*Speech Police and Polyglot Play*).

Tawada is one among a large and increasing number of contemporary German writers who are foreign-born inhabitants of that country, non-native speakers, and not ethnically German. Other, more commercially successful writers who immigrated to Germany and first learned the language there include the Russian-born Wladimir Kaminer, Turkish-born Emine Sevgi Özdamar, and Syrian-born Rafik Schami. While they and many other immigrant German writers frequently thematize issues such as transnational understanding (or a lack thereof), cultural border-crossing, and interlingualism, none are as attuned as Tawada to the way language mediates relationality between and among diverse populations. This linguistic relationality is at the core of a planetary turn that would—or should—not simply assume that the global English spoken by the globe's elites will be planetarity's exclusive mode of communication.

In his study *A Transnational Poetics*—which, although it focuses on English-language literature across the globe, is sensitive to interlingual issues—Jahan Ramazani characterizes Melvin Tolson's book of poems *Harlem Gallery* as informed by "polyglot hybridity and pan-cultural allusiveness."[57] More than other German authors of the present, Tawada's work exhibits these traits because of her hyperawareness of the linguistic, and often translational, dimension of inter-national human (mis)understanding. This makes her work especially exemplary for a planetary poetics that draws upon world literary thinking. There is a perpetual liminality shaping Tawada's works. They are almost always situated at the intersections between and among cultures considered by most people to be discrete with respect to language and thought. Working against this assumption, Tawada demonstrates the inherent interrelationality of such cultures, indeed their often-overlooked imbrication in the current age. In this way—and again, rather uniquely among German-language authors—she carries on the world literary dialogue envisioned by Goethe and Novalis, on a planetary scale but without any trace of the former's elitism and of the latter's romantic eschatology.

In the opening poem of *Sprachpolizei und Spielpolyglotte*, "Slavia in Berlin," the entire planet is constellated through paronomasia, catachresis, and other forms of wordplay. The first line, "Ich nahm Abu Simbel von meinen Kamerun und ging/Los Angeles" ("I took Abu Simbel from my Cameroon and went/Los Angeles"), connects three distinct geographic entities through the short-circuiting misapplication of place names substituted for any other potential nouns that might create lucid syntax and signification.[58] Marjorie Perloff describes the poem as a tableau "in which ordinary German street conversation is viewed from the angle of the foreign visitor, who processes simple directions and bits of information according to the place-names they contain," where such terms as "Ägypten" (Egypt) and "Finnland" suggest, through homonymic relationality, German terms such as "gibt es" (there is, there are) and "finden" (to find).[59] However, the sheer jumble of such proper place names brought into a striking and unexpected contiguity through wordplay also forces the reader to consider how meaning is constituted in and through signifiers for various localities. In their untraditional phonemic and syntactic imbrications, they make one reflect on how translocal signification is created when the words standing in for multiple geographic sites across the globe literally collide. In this case, "worldness" comes into consciousness through the concatenation of random cities, countries, and so on. The poem concludes with the line "Du gehst in den Taunus zurück,/und ich fahre zu dem Bahnhof Nirgendzoo" ("You travel back to the Taunus/and I travel to the train station Nowherezoo"), whereby the narrative "I," Slavia, indicates that her auditor returns to the comfort of a real existing site, the Taunus region of the state of Hesse, perhaps the auditor's home, while Slavia travels to the train station "Nowherezoo," a pun on "nirgendwo."[60] This "nowhere" is also everywhere, as it is (also) a zoo with animals from throughout the globe. Thus, it is a cipher for the disoriented border-crossing traveler in a poem that evokes all corners of the planet in a jumble of paranomasic place-name signifiers; at the end of the poem as at its beginning, Slavia is—and is traveling—everywhere and nowhere, even when she seems to be in—and traveling from—Berlin.

In an interview conducted around the time *Sprachpolizei und Spielpolyglotte* was published, Tawada noted that the German verb for "translate," *übersetzen*, also signifies the steering of a boat from one shore to the other. Perloff cites this passage in conjunction with another in which Tawada speaks of how, when an author whose native language is a "minor" tongue starts writing in a "major" language, the target language itself becomes transformed, and even the way the "magical" is sensually perceived may manifest itself in "the *target* language."[61] We have observed that, for Goethe, the stylistics, semantics, and even the sensual dimension of the target language can be enhanced at the third level of translation. In *Das Märchen* (*Fairy-Tale*, 1795), where a boatman shuttles passengers—and "translates" Goethe's text—back and forth between prosaic and poetic/eschatological realms, Goethe also exploits the dual potential of *übersetzen*, which evokes the meaning noted by Tawada when the stress in pronunciation falls on the first syllable rather than the second. As Huyssen notes in describing Novalis's early romantic world literature utopia, poeticizing the world is to be equated with the creation of the fairy-tale world; the world is "translated"—carried over—to the fairy-tale. Playing on the dual signification of "übersetzen," Huyssen comments that, for Novalis, because poetry is translation (*Übersetzung*), it also brings about the conveyance (*Über-setzung*) of the human race into a golden age and thereby redeems it.[62] Tawada does not engage in such fairy-tale eschatology; her planetary poetics locate and elucidate magic solely in the domains of words and syntax, but, as with Goethe and Novalis, this magic is instantiated when *Übersetzung* takes place in the most inclusive sense of both acts signified by this term. In the longest text of the *Sprachpolizei und Spielpolyglotte* collection, "U.S. + S.R. Eine Sauna in Fernosteuropa" ("U.S. + S.R. A Sauna in Far East Europe"), the narrator opens with the tableau of a boat traveling the short distance from a Japanese point of embarkation to the Russian territory of Sakhalin, an island wrested from Japan by the Soviet Union at the close of the Second World War. Tawada's evocation of the ship as resonant with interlingual, intercultural dialogue almost magically makes the vessel itself, and not just the maritime territory it traverses, into a borderland where Russia and Japan, Russian and Japanese, are intertwined. Thus, the boat becomes a metonym for translocal space, indeed, for the intertextual, interlingual blendedness of the planet itself. It carries out the act of "Übersetzung" in both senses of the word, ferrying passengers from one nation (Japan) to another (Russia), but also translating back and forth between Russian and Japanese culture through the medium of a third language, German. In this way, the narrative becomes a sort of Benjaminian palimpsest, revealing cross-cultural truths through the collocation of all three national entities and tongues, along with allusions to English and Korean. The linguistic character of the journey is established at the outset, when after declaring that there is always something solemn and ceremonious (*Feierliches*) about disembarking from a ship and thus establishing the solemn significance of the act of *Übersetzung*, she notes that she is balancing on the "tongue" that the ship has extended out to the mainland.[63] As in English, the German term for "tongue"—*Zunge*—is a synonym for language. The narrator's description of her balancing, rather precariously, on a "tongue" at the outset of this story-essay foregrounds the self-consciously multilingual milieu, labile with respect to univocal meaning, she will soon establish not only on the boat but in her wanderings on Sakhalin itself.

Tawada frequently interrupts the present-time narrative to reminisce about Sakhalin's earlier history and linguistic ambience. The narrator remarks that the southern half of the island, under Japanese rule from the end of the Russo-Japanese War until the end of World War II, bore the name "Karafuto." *Kara* means "emptiness" and *futo* is the Japanese term for "sudden." Thus, in the narrator's private etymology, "Karafuto" signifies "a sudden emptiness." She realizes that this etymology cannot be accurate, but, at the outset of the next segment, finds herself standing "on the empty place or square" (*Platz*) in Karafuto.[64] There is a rather sudden shift here from the narrator's pondering the significance and etymology of *Karafuto* to the mise-en-scène of her actually standing on its empty square. As is the case throughout this story-essay, there is no discursive transition between narrative segments; they are only indicated through double-spacing. Similar to Novalis's proto-*Weltliteratur*-oriented postulations, translation occurs on two levels here: *Übersetzung* takes place in both nuances of the term. Verbally, Tawada renders *Karafuto*, through an admittedly creative etymological act, into the German for "a sudden emptiness"—*eine plötzliche Leere*. The reader is thereupon *instantly*—without any narrative transition—transported to the *empty* square in Karafuto, where the narrator abruptly stands. Again, this double move lacks any sense of Novalis's eschatological metaphysics. Instead, to once more cite Friedman's definition of planetarity, Tawada puts into play an etymologically grounded epistemology by paying "attention to modes of local and translocal meaning-making." "Sudden emptiness" constitutes Tawada's self-consciously creative, translocal act of meaning-making, while her constant focus on the labile modes of signification on Sakhalin—alternating between Russian and Japanese and transmitted in German—inspires the reader to reflect on "processes and practices of perception and expression on a global scale."[65] The etymologically faithful but awkward rendering of "Karafuto" not only constitutes an example of what Perloff refers to as "the stubborn literalism of Tawada's logic," but also allows the author, through subtle paronomasia, to "translate"—*<u>über</u>-setzen*—her readers from a linguistically to a topographically oriented narrative segment with the barest hint of a bridge, a bridge as *Zunge*, as tongue, a "mother" (Japanese) and German tongue with a Russian ambience.[66]

Christian Moraru has recently argued that translation, in order to have validity in the current age, must become more reflective and self-referential. Translation is as much about the translator and the text he or she creates in the target language as it is about the work and author of the source language.

Citing contemporary theorists of translation such as Lawrence Venuti (whose thinking was strongly influenced by Goethe's third-level translation axiom), Moraru asserts that if "relational semantics and the contingent critique it capacitates" are self-reflective enough, its practitioners "look 'laterally,' around the translator's world and into him- or herself."[67] Tawada's planetary poetics render transparent the process of self-reflection and self-referentiality Moraru finds to be desiderata for translation and translation theory in the present age. Her work thus becomes exemplary for the double act/double significance of *übersetzen* as suggested by Goethe and Novalis in their respective world literary and proto-world literary models. Tawada both self-consciously foregrounds the act of translating words and sentences from one tongue to another and transports the reader from one shore to more distant shores, from the globe of the creating but solitary ego to the planet relationally inhabited, as Spivak indicates, by the self and the Other.

Notes

1. Emily Apter, "Untranslatables: A World System," *New Literary History* 39, no. 3 (Summer 2008): 582.

2. See Thomas Bleicher, "Novalis und die Idee der Weltliteratur," *Arcadia* 14, no. 3 (1979): 254–70.

3. Karl Marx and Friedrich Engels, *Werke* (Berlin: Dietz, 1959), 4:466.

4. See, for example, Ernst Elster, "Weltlitteratur und Litteraturvergleichung," *Archiv für das Studium der neueren Sprachen und Literaturen* 107 (1901): 38–39; and Fritz Strich, "Weltliteratur und vergleichende Literaturgeschichte," in *Philosophie der Literaturwissenschaft*, ed. Emil Ermatinger (Berlin: Junker und Dünnhaupt, 1930), 422–41. This latter essay focuses not only on the necessity of selectivity and superiority in critically establishing what works belong to *Weltliteratur*, but also on the genetically specific popular (*völkisch*) quality of the various national literatures. At this time, Strich argued that an author could not be regarded as worthy of world literary status if his work did *not* reflect the characteristics of his nation and people. For example, by virtue of the cosmopolitanism exhibited by the German author Heinrich Mann, a putatively "French" quality, this author does not deserve to be characterized as belonging to the pantheon of *Weltliteratur* (429–30).

5. Kurt Hildebrandt, *Goethe: Seine Weltweisheit im Gesamtwerk*, 2nd ed. (Leipzig: Philipp Reclam, 1942), 471.

6. Fritz Strich, *Goethe und die Weltliteratur* (Bern: Francke, 1946), 397.

7. Johann Wolfgang Goethe, *Gedenkausgabe der Werke, Briefe und Gespräche*, ed. Ernst Beutler (Zurich: Artemis, 1948–54), 14:907.

8. Ibid., 14:914–15.

9. Strich, *Goethe und die Weltliteratur*, 14.

10. In a similar vein, Apter has alluded to *Weltliteratur*'s "commitment to expansive cultural secularism" in *The Translation Zone: A New Comparative Literature* (Princeton, N.J.: Princeton University Press, 2006), 41.

11. I discuss how contemporary scholarship has addressed the interrelationship between these concepts in "Cosmopolitanism and *Weltliteratur*," *Goethe Yearbook* 13 (2005): 165–79.

12. Strich, *Goethe und die Weltliteratur*, 398.

13. Ibid., 399.

14. Ibid., 400.

15. Homi K. Bhabha, *The Location of Culture* (London: Routledge, 1994), 12.

16. Rüdiger Görner, "Goethe's Cosmopolitanism," in *Cosmopolitans in the Modern World: Studies on a Theme in German and Austrian Literary Culture*, ed. Suzanne Kirkbright (Munich: Iudicium, 2000), 37. In making this claim, Görner cites Goethe's epic poem *Hermann und Dorothea* (1797), which creates a poetic encounter between refugees from the French Revolution and a prosperous, more easterly settlement as yet untouched by the revolution's violence (36–37). The encounter culminates in the betrothal of the female refugee Dorothea with Hermann, a local young man who is strongly rooted in the familial and community domains where the narrative takes place. Goethe's poem makes it clear that Dorothea will easily accommodate herself to her new world and positively contribute to it.

17. Claudio Guillén, *The Challenge of Comparative Literature*, trans. Cola Franzen (Cambridge, Mass.: Harvard University Press, 1993), 40.

18. Ursula K. Heise, *Sense of Place and Sense of Planet: The Environmental Imagination of the Global* (Oxford: Oxford University Press, 2008), 3.

19. Ibid., 6.

20. Masao Miyoshi, "Turn to the Planet: Literature, Diversity, and Totality," *Comparative Literature* 53, no. 4 (Autumn 2001): 289.

21. Ibid., 295.

22. Gayatri Chakravorty Spivak, *Death of a Discipline* (New York: Columbia University Press, 2003), 72.

23. Ibid., xii.

24. Ibid., 39.

25. Franco Moretti, "Conjectures on World Literature," in *Debating World Literature*, ed. Christopher Prendergast (London: Verso, 2004), 152.

26. Ibid., 148.

27. Ibid., 149.

28. Spivak, *Death of a Discipline*, 107–8 n1.

29. Moretti, "Conjectures on World Literature," 149.

30. Bhabha, *The Location of Culture*, 143.

31. Wai Chee Dimock, "Scales of Aggregation: Prenational, Subnational, Transnational," *American Literary History* 18, no. 2 (2006): 225.

32. Reinhard Meyer-Kalkus, "World Literature beyond Goethe," trans. Kevin McAleer, in *Cultural Mobility: A Manifesto*, ed. Stephen Greenblatt (Cambridge, Eng.: Cambridge University Press, 2010), 114.

33. Ibid., 121.

34. Goethe, *Gedenkausgabe der Werke*, 24:229.

35. See, for example, the essay collections Vinay Dharwadker, ed., *Cosmopolitan Geographies: New Locations in Literature and Culture* (New York: Routledge, 2001); and Pheng Cheah and Bruce Robbins, eds., *Cosmopolitics: Thinking and Feeling beyond the Nation* (Minneapolis: University of Minnesota Press, 1998).

36. Spivak, *Death of a Discipline*, 72.

37. The term "globe" certainly did not have negative connotations for Goethe. Indeed, Goethe's *Weltliteratur* concept was largely inspired by his reading of the French journal *Le Globe*. See Heinz Hamm, *Goethe und die französische Zeitschrift "Le Globe": Eine Lektüre im Zeichen der Weltliteratur* (Weimar: Böhlau, 1998).

38. Michael Hardt and Antonio Negri, *Multitude: War and Democracy in the Age of Empire* (New York: Penguin, 2004), xiii–xiv.

39. Novalis, *Schriften*, ed. Paul Kluckhohn and Richard Samuel, 2nd ed. (Stuttgart: Kohlhammer, 1960–75), 3:560.

40. Ibid., 2:420.

41. Ibid., 2:616.

42. Ibid., 2:112. In her book *Delayed Endings* (Athens: University of Georgia Press, 1987), Alice A. Kuzniar notes that, for Novalis, the ego is actually "a negative entity, ever impure and ever striving," a postulate that comes to the fore in his *Fichte Studies* (81). He thus almost literally cuts the ego down to size and forces it, as an "ever striving" entity, to reach out to the Other. This makes Novalis's view of the personal ego compatible with the valuation of alterity one associates with the planetary turn. On Fichtean consciousness and self-knowledge, also see Clare Kennedy, *Paradox, Aphorism and Desire in Novalis and Derrida* (London: Maney, 2008), 21–24.

43. Novalis, *Schriften*, 3:677.

44. Ibid., 4:268–69.

45. W. Daniel Wilson's study *Unterirdische Gänge: Goethe, Freimaurerei und Politik* (Göttingen, Ger.: Wallstein, 1999) is especially instructive in this regard.

46. Novalis, *Schriften*, 3:464.

47. Bleicher, "Novalis, " 265.

48. Novalis, *Schriften*, 3:464.

49. See David Damrosch, "Introduction: Goethe Coins a Phrase," in *What Is World Literature?* (Princeton, N.J.: Princeton University Press, 2003), 1–36.

50. Goethe, *Gedenkausgabe der Werke*, 3:555–56

51. Novalis, *Schriften*, 3:685.

52. Ibid., 2:439–40.

53. Goethe, *Gedenkausgabe der Werke*, 14:932–33.

54. See Andreas Huyssen, *Die frühromantische Konzeption von Übersetzung und Aneignung: Studien zur frühromantischen Utopie einer deutschen Weltliteratur* (Zurich: Atlantis, 1969), 131–38.

55. Ibid., 173.

56. Susan Stanford Friedman, "Planetarity: Musing Modernist Studies," *Modernism/Modernity* 17, no. 3 (September 2010): 494.

57. Jahan Ramazani, *A Transnational Poetics* (Chicago: University of Chicago Press, 2009), x.

58. Yoko Tawada, *Sprachpolizei und Spielpolyglotte* (Tübingen: Konkursbuch Verlag Claudia Gehrke, 2007), 7.

59. Marjorie Perloff, *Unoriginal Genius: Poetry by Other Means in the New Century* (Chicago: University of Chicago Press, 2010), 137.

60. Tawada, *Sprachpolizei und Spielpolyglotte*, 10.

61. Perloff, *Unoriginal Genius*, 137 (emphasis in original).

62. Huyssen, *Die frühromantische Konzeption von Übersetzung und Aneignung*, 133 (italics in original).

63. Tawada, *Sprachpolizei und Spielpolyglotte*, 124.

64. Ibid., 149.

65. Friedman, "Planetarity," 494.

66. Perloff, *Unoriginal Genius*, 143.

67. Christian Moraru, *Cosmodernism: American Narrative, Late Globalization, and the New Cultural Imaginary* (Ann Arbor: University of Michigan Press, 2011), 169, 170.

Terraqueous Planet

The Case for Oceanic Studies

HESTER BLUM

To measure distance at sea is to measure time on an interstellar scale. We demarcate the globe by temporally defined lines of longitude and latitude whose origins come from seafaring. The ocean is in permanent opposition to landmarks, inscriptions, and other localizing mechanisms presuming stasis; the imaginary lines that subdivide the globe were conceived as a way to abstract and solidify oceanic location in the face of the unstable surface of planetary terraqueous space. Fixing degrees and minutes and seconds—the ordinal terms of global location—has relied historically on the ability to measure a position relative to the sun and other stars. Before global positioning systems, this could only be done by means of accurate sea clocks, sextants, and charts that allowed mariners to plot their relative position among the poles of Greenwich, the stars, and the bobbing horizon. Thus, by definition, to know one's place at sea was to know one's place on the planet—even more, in the universe. And yet, in literary and philosophical history the nautical environment, despite covering more than 70 percent of the earth's surface, has been seen as a non-specific place, one outside of time, beyond time, or hostile to time. A "sea which will permit no records," in Herman Melville's phrase,[1] could register as a medium both of generation and annihilation.

The presumed abstraction of time and space at sea, though, is a land-based perspective that emerges from an understanding of the planet as subdivided into political rather than ecoglobalist categories. How might our understanding of planetary time and space be reoriented—cast adrift—when considered from the vantage point of the earth's oceanic spaces? This essay meditates upon the planetary turn from the perspective of the coincident and complementary field of oceanic studies. Both positions share the fundamental presumption that the nation-state is an insufficient unit of comparative analysis. As Gayatri Chakravorty Spivak proposes, thinking about the planet allows for an understanding of ecological, cultural, and political relations as functioning independently of the state- or capital-based exchanges familiarly identified as globalism.[2] In Wai Chee Dimock's formulation, a planetary sense of deep time serves a similar purpose in dislocating our approach from nation-based temporalities.[3]

Along the same lines, oceanic studies seeks to reorient our critical perspective, finding capacious possibilities for new relational forms—dispersion, erosion, flotation, confluence, solvency—adapted from the constitutively unbounded examples provided by the ocean. And recent geophysical changes to the seas caused by global climate change demand critical attention as well, as part of a history of knowledge circulation plotted along sea routes. As Kären Wigan writes of what has also been called New Thalassology, "No longer outside time, the sea is being given a history, even as the history of the world is being retold from the perspective of the sea."[4] Rather than viewing planetary exchange as something that takes place transnationally, between geographically abstracted states, oceanic studies unmoors our critical perspective from the boundaries of the nation. Planetary and oceanic shifts are invested, in part, in recognizing the artificiality and intellectual limitations of national, political, linguistic, physiological, or temporal boundaries in studying forms of literary and cultural influence and circulation.[5] A fundamental premise of oceanic studies is that such recognized patterns of nation- and capital-based relationality dissolve in the space and time of the sea.

In what follows, I consider the relationship between theories of oceanic studies and planetarity in terms of their mutual investment in recalibrating—even annihilating—the gauges of time and space. The science of latitude and longitude provides one critical vocabulary for understanding how space and time are weighed in a planetary balance. I also invoke several scenes of oceanic and planetary accounting in the works of Henry David Thoreau and Herman Melville, the U.S. writers who have arguably been the most identified with ecoglobalist and oceanic perspectives. Thoreau, for instance, surveys a body of water that had been imagined bottomless and finds that theories of the infinite in fact have greater explanatory power once the measurement of infinity has been countermanded. Melville, too, provides a model for thinking through comparative notions of planetary location in theorizing time as either horological (clock-based, locally relevant) or chronometrical (idealized, spiritual—that is, Greenwich Mean Time). Thus, I draw on these two American writers for their insistence on the necessity of materialist, labor-based practices when postulating philosophical understandings of time and space. This point, I contend, is urgent in our current planetary moment: metaphorizing earth and sea, abstracting them from the effects of human actors, has severe consequences both environmentally and politically. Oceanic studies is predicated on a belief in the sea's imaginative and material resources. Both kinds are under constant threat, a contingency that helps account for the field's present emergence at our moment of climate change.

"The Whims of Tides and Mariners"

We must think of the sea and the ships that butt about it as emphatically embodied: even more so than in Michel Foucault's now-familiar closing proposal in his essay "Of Other Spaces," where he writes that the ship has been not only "the great instrument of economic development . . . but has been simultaneously the greatest reserve of the imagination."[6] Granted, when considering reserves of the imagination, we must be mindful, too, of the gas and mineral sources that make the liquid and frozen seas the target of mining, extraction, and other ecological threats, especially in a period of global climate change propelled by human actions. These threats, for example, are producing new varieties of imperialist territorial claiming: in 2007 Russia—seeking to secure raw materials at the North Pole, an oceanic region with no land or stable ice—claimed not the sea or "pole" but the tectonic plate beneath the seafloor.[7] More recently, at the opposite pole, Russia also drilled into the sub-glacial Lake Vostok (over 13,000 feet under the Antarctic ice cap), the liquid contents of which are estimated to have been under ice and thus untouched for 25 million years. And Russia is, of course, not the only nation making new claims to oceanic spaces. The United States, Canada, China, Denmark, Britain, and Norway are among the other circumpolar nations seeking new access to resources in or beneath the water. In addition, global warming produces new access to planetary sea routes. The fabled Northwest Passage through the seas of the Canadian Arctic archipelago, which provides a northern sea route from the Atlantic to the Pacific Oceans, had been unsuccessfully—often fatally—sought for half a millennium. However, by 2009 the Arctic pack ice had been reduced to the point of open-water navigation through the Canadian and Russian Arctic. The ship of Foucault's imagination thus produces economic development at the potential cost of the very reserves it traverses.

However, there is another aspect of the sea's materiality that is overlooked in formulations such as Foucault's and environmentalists' discourse: the figure of the sailor, the laboring body that brings human presence to the ocean in the first place. The sailor is crucial to oceanic studies not just as the agent of maritime commerce, transit, and mythology, but also for his literal outlandishness: the sailor typifies the historic dissolution of the protections afforded by national affiliations in the space and time of the sea.[8] As the first intra-planetary travelers, sailors were imagined free from many of the constraints of social and political life. Yet they faced hostile environmental conditions as well as repressive hierarchical structures aboard ship, neither of which could be mediated by the protections of statehood or citizenship. The two regularities in the lives of seamen were the disciplinary practices of maritime navigation and time management: the taking of celestial readings, the keeping of the log, the maintenance of watches or shifts as clocked by the hour. The labor of mariners, in other words, was the metronome of humanized oceanic time.

And yet in the modern Western cultural imagination, seamen's mobility accounts in part for their roughness, their dissolution, and their potential for agitation. In his preface to *On the Shores of Politics*, Jacques Rancière recognizes the centrality of these aspects of sailors and identifies as well the reasons for their imaginative obliquity to the history of states:

> The sea smells bad. This is not because of the mud, however. The sea smells of sailors, it smells of democracy. . . . Before taking us down into the famous cave, Socrates tells us a lot about triremes, incorrigible sailors and helpless pilots. Entering the cave we bid farewell to this fatal and seductive seascape. The cave is the sea transposed beneath the earth, bereft of its sparkling glamour: enclosure instead of open sea, men in chains instead of rows of oarsmen, the dullness of shadows on the wall instead of light reflected on waves. The procedure whereby the prisoner is released and offered conversion is preceded by another, by that first metaphoric act which consists in burying the sea, drying it up, stripping it of its reflections and changing their very nature. In response to these assaults we know, however, that the sea will take its revenge. For the paradox of the undertaking is that hauling politics onto the solid ground of knowledge and courage entails a return to the isles of refoundation; it means crossing the sea once more and surrendering the shepherds' resurrected city to the whims of tides and mariners.[9]

The oceanic counterpoint to Plato's famous cave analogy might change how we perceive both shadow and substance in the world, Rancière offers. Drying out the sea as a philosophical figure strands those odorous, boisterous aspects of the political world represented in his figure by seamen. And in invoking the "revenge" that the sea might seize in its response to being rendered peripheral by political and philosophical orders, Rancière underscores both the sea's inhumanity and its embodiment. (We will see this suggested in Melville's work as well.) The political world in Rancière's formulation cannot be accurately assessed from the vantage point of the stability and desiccation of the "solid ground of knowledge." Instead, we might take the bobbing, surging, unfixed shadows on the cave wall as an encouragement to understand political and planetary questions as similarly composed of a matter whose substance owes more to the ductility of the watery world than has been heretofore measured. Democracy requires an accord with the "fatal and seductive" aspects of the imaginative and material oceans.

The sea of Rancière's imagination is no longer figured as the world outside of hearth and self, or even at the margins of the planet understood in terms of political geography. His figure asks us not to assess the ocean from a position on land but to locate ourselves among the "whims of tides and mariners" in order to shape a new and different vision of the world. A land-based perspective takes its stability from what we might see as a kinesiological notion of proprioception: we understand our position in the world in relation to stimuli generated from within the perceiving body itself.[10] In other words, in the kinesiological model a person's balance is derived not only from some intrinsic stability, or from contact with the floor, but from his or her visual, tactile, and other sensory awareness of and contact with the relative permanence of his or her surroundings. (This is why, for example, it is more difficult to balance with one's eyes closed.) The fluid environment disallows such comparative forms of understanding. In this sense, the "enclosure" of the cave in Rancière's Platonic figure comes as a stabilizing force that stands in contrast to the riotous a-referentiality of the sea. Absent the "sea legs" necessary to anchor one's vantage point and corporal positioning, an oceanic perspective takes disequilibrium as its state of being. As I maintain elsewhere in my work, critical positions premised on a planet organized by relations between states and capital circulation could profit from an embrace of disequilibrium and learn from the sea's ways of gauging interchanges that are both cosmic and measurable in some new form.

"Not Continent but Insular"

Consider, as an instance of the longitudinal logic of oceanic studies, the familiar figure of the eco-materialist Thoreau at Walden Pond. The pond was both repository and wellspring for his imaginative project, his determination "to explore the private sea, the Atlantic and Pacific Ocean of one's being alone."[11] Throughout his writings, Thoreau is insistently mindful of the coincidence of the practical and poetic dimensions of natural spaces. In *Walden*, for instance, he writes of the pond, "when you look into it you see that earth is not continent but insular. This is as important as that it keeps butter cool" (391–92). Recognizing land as an "insular" plot, its existence contingent on water's recession (both locally and on a planetary scale), makes Thoreau's voyage of self-discovery reliant on an oceanic reorientation of geographic terms. That is, the act of setting the land in a relation to water rather than to an orienting pole allows him, instead, to create an imaginative "sea." Experiential knowledge of the pond, Thoreau proposes, produces imaginative capital; he is interested in the epistemological payload of the insularity of land as well as in the experiential knowledge of the pond.

The pond's ability to serve theoretically as Thoreau's ocean in miniature is not necessarily more important, however, than its mundane powers of butter-cooling. When Thoreau ventures out to survey the bottom of Walden Pond, which locals had long thought to be literally and figuratively unfathomable, he sensibly takes up "compass and chain and sounding line," finding it "remarkable how long men will believe in the bottomlessness of a pond without taking the trouble to sound it" (549). He records over one hundred readings, noting the variance in the pond's length and breadth, its coves and bars. The results of his labor are printed in *Walden* as a map—the only illustration or diagram in the book—with all the various depth measurements provided and labels to mark the pond's dimensions. Thoreau's scientific documentation of Walden's foundation is not entirely clinical, nor is it intended to anesthetize any more ethereal contemplation of the pond's imaginative depths. In fact, Thoreau finds that "not an inch" of the pond's rather unusual depth "can be spared by the imagination." He wonders, "What if all ponds were shallow? Would it not react on the minds of men? I am thankful that this pond was made deep and pure for a symbol. While men believe in the infinite some ponds will be thought to be bottomless" (551). An imagination capable of considering the infinite might find its reflection in deep waters. Yet Thoreau has taken the trouble to quantify the pond's dimensions, to expose the myth of its infinitude. Although factual accounting here could limit his range of interpretation, Thoreau argues that geophysical knowledge grants him broader ground for contemplation. A belief in bottomlessness or the infinite is a passive belief, borrowed from conventional thinking rather than one sounded independently; it is a belief without referent or logical scale. What Thoreau has done, instead, is to seize the physical fact of the pond's depth out of the realm of the unknowable, to mark it with his own intellectual and mechanical labor. The ability to fix a location, to establish a point of reference, frees the subject to contextualize, and then reproduce, any other readings from the perspective of the point thus fixed. In setting the pond in material relation to the world instead of retaining its symbolic value for abstraction, Thoreau thus rescues unknowability as a philosophical problem rather than an empirical one.

The notion of the earth as "insular" rather than "continent[al]" exemplifies the perspectival shift proposed by the planetary turn and oceanic studies alike. Just as the Copernican revolution outmoded a Ptolemaic model of the heavens by revealing the small, subject Earth to be peripheral to the Sun, an oceanic revolution—if of different proportion—repositions continental land as circumscribed, minimized, and mere island amid the waters that dominate the globe. From the earliest days of nautical travel, those venturing upon the deep faced an indefinitely proliferating unknown, one that reduced the once Ptolemaic earth to a receding spot of dark on the horizon. Columbus famously dealt with the existential horror that oceanic distance threatened in his men by keeping two logbooks for his 1492 voyages to the Americas. One book recorded the actual distance traveled, according to the navigational tools of the time. But as that distance became attenuated beyond what the expedition had expected, Columbus doctored a second, public logbook meant to be read by the crew, a log that radically shortchanged their daily advance and thus assuaged the men's fear that they would sail off the edge of the earth. Columbus judged nautical distance in balance with the psychic distance in space and time that could be reasonably understood by his frightened crew members adrift at sea: the tools of measurement at sea were therefore relational. Even though Columbus's move, unlike Thoreau's, falsified aqueous information in order to deny the materiality of relation, both posit the unknown as something other than immediate or empirical.

But against which control might Columbus's men have observed the truth? At every moment, every coordinate, the maritime world of the ship lists, heaves, rolls, plunges, and rocks. Should an impulse to stability even obtain at sea? In the oceanic world, such celestial reflections resist metaphorics in favor of a metaphysics that more closely resembles a better (albeit more abstract) physics. The Galilean utterance "and yet it moves" is a state of being in the space of the sea, particularly in its evocation of the measurement of the relative position of planetary bodies to one another. In Father Mapple's sermon at the beginning of *Moby-Dick*, Melville illustrates this very equivocality in the figure of Jonah, who has run to sea rather than submit to God's command to preach to the residents of Nineveh. The presumption behind his flight is, in part, that God's reach would hold no purchase at sea. In Melville's telling via Father Mapple (the seamen's chaplain), the divine light from which Jonah seeks obscurity is no blinding flash. Instead, it illuminates the oceanic contours of contingent systems of valuation. Here is Jonah in his cabin, looking at an actual lamp:

> Screwed at its axis against the side, a swinging lamp slightly oscillates in Jonah's room; and the ship, heeling over towards the wharf with the weight of the last bales received, the lamp, flame and all, though in slight motion, still maintains a permanent obliquity with reference to the room; though, in truth, infallibly straight itself, it but made obvious the false, lying levels among which it hung. The lamp alarms and frightens Jonah; as lying in his berth his tormented eyes roll round the place, and this thus far successful fugitive finds no refuge for his restless glance. But that contradiction in the lamp more and more appals [*sic*] him. The floor, the ceiling, and the side, are all awry. "Oh! so my conscience hangs in me!" he groans, "straight upward, so it burns; but the chambers of my soul are all in crookedness!"[12]

Jonah's dilemma is something like this: aligning himself with the light of his conscience or God's commands will put him in "permanent obliquity" with the structure of the material world around him. Neither Jonah's eye nor the lamp can find repose; their spatial dislocation from truth becomes an unceasing movement for which every moment renders obsolete the movement that had preceded it. Melville makes material the process by which oceanic spaces force "awry" the referents with which one normally organizes a sense of the world.

Throughout *Moby-Dick* Melville stages similarly equivocal scenes of planetary orienteering. One of the more memorable passages in the novel takes on an added dimension when considered in terms of the oceanic forms of location. I refer here to the scene in "The Quarter-Deck" in which Ahab lays out for the crew his true motivation for the voyage: not a general whale hunt, but his monomaniacal pursuit of the white whale that had devoured his leg. The only significant opposition that Ahab encounters comes from the first mate, Starbuck, whose worldview is shaped by his Christian belief; Starbuck finds blasphemous the idea of taking "vengeance on a dumb brute." Ahab's famous response reveals his own indifference to answering the questions that undergird causality. His desire is to obliterate causality without understanding it: "All visible objects, man, are but as pasteboard masks. But in each event—in the living act, the undoubted deed—there, some unknown but still reasoning thing puts forth the mouldings of its features from behind the unreasoning mask. . . . That inscrutable thing is chiefly what I hate; and be the white whale agent, or be the white whale principal, I will wreak that hate upon him" (163–64). Captain Ahab accepts that there is an unfathomable force that governs action in the world; yet the "unknown but still reasoning thing" that determines causality as embodied by the whale is for him only something to hate and destroy rather than to seek to understand in relation to Judeo-Christian ideology, or to zoology, or to eco-biology. Irrelevant to him, in other words, is the question of whether Moby Dick's seeming malice toward Ahab originated with the whale, or with some broader, unseen force on whose behalf the whale acted. In accepting that the oceanic world provides no answers, only "inscrutable" agency against which to rail, Ahab provides a fatalistic (and ultimately fatal) counterpoint to Columbus and Jonah, who push against oceanic uncertainty by falling back on structures of thought borrowed from the relative stability of terrestrial philosophies.

Chronometric and Horological Conceits

Neither Columbus's nor Jonah's experiences were exceptional; oceanic measurement is ever provisional. At its most speculative, we find the blind form of navigation known as "dead reckoning" (or "ded. [deduced] reckoning"), an unreliable method employed only when celestial referents are hidden and other navigational tools incapacitated, whether by weather or circumstance. Using dead reckoning, a sailor guesses a ship's position based on probable drift in the time elapsed, as well as on any prior knowledge of the currents or conditions. Even more rigorous modalities of navigation are based on forms of conditional triangulation. Latitude, or one's angle from the equator on a north-south axis, is determined by plotting the sun's altitude either at noon or by the star Polaris by means of a tool such as an astrolabe or a sextant (pre-satellite-based global positioning systems in the age of sail). These readings are in turn compared with the celestial charts and navigational manuals produced by other, earlier voyagers. But this is an imperfect science. The swell of the waves, the haziness of the horizon, or atmospheric changes all make accurate readings an ideal rather than a reality. Determining longitude or one's distance on an east-west axis from the prime meridian that runs through Greenwich, England, is a more difficult proposition, requiring a measurement not just of space but also of time. (Even the Greenwich prime meridian is only a provisional convenience, for historically it faced challenges from a rival meridian in Paris.) Measuring both space and time is necessary given that the earth rotates fifteen degrees every hour, and calculations relative to the prime meridian must account for the temporal turn. Much like Columbus's two logbooks, navigators needed to keep two clocks: one set to a local time in which the sun at a 90-degree angle signified noon and one set to an unchanging Greenwich mean time. Before the invention of a more accurate sea clock by John Harrison in 1761, which kept time well over a much longer duration without adjustment, longitude was exceptionally difficult to calculate accurately by any specialists other than expert astronomers—to be sure, not by the average ship's navigator.

The prime meridian is invoked by Pascale Casanova as a way to locate literature in time and space. "Just as the *fictive* line known as the prime meridian, arbitrarily chosen for the determination of longitude, contributes to the *real* organization of the world and makes possible the measure of distances and the location of positions on the surface of the earth," she writes in *The World Republic of Letters*, "so what might be called the Greenwich meridian of literature makes it possible to estimate the relative aesthetic distance from the center of the world of letters of all those who belong to it."[13] For Casanova, this time extends latitudinally—measuring north and south, forward and backward in time. In Melville's novel *Pierre; or the Ambiguities*, however, spatiotemporal location has a longitudinal logic. The novel's title character had spent his youth imagining himself as the linear climax of his family's genealogical promise, but after a series of rash and incestuous actions force a rupture and disintegration of that familial line, he embraces a new temporal theory. An ephemeral, incomplete pamphlet Pierre encounters upon renouncing the family estate pronounces that all wisdom is "provisional." The pamphlet's own contingency is reinforced by beginning and abruptly terminating in the word "if" (as well as in its subtitle, "Being not so much the Portal, as part of the temporary Scaffold to the Portal of this new Philosophy").[14]

Pierre finds in the pamphlet a philosophy that both draws from and defines an oceanic, planetary perspective. It begins by stipulating that the human soul is irreconcilably distant and out of tune with divine truth, and gives names to those two poles by incorporating time-keeping nomenclature. By this theory, humans keep expedient "horological" or terrestrial time (say, Eastern Standard Time), while God keeps idealized "chronometrical" or celestial time (Greenwich mean time), one akin in its accuracy, we are told, to the chronometers crafted by John Harrison. In the following extended figure of a ship attempting to navigate while in China—taking readings with respect to the Greenwich time then 120 degrees or eight hours away—Melville asks the question of how one might live in one time knowing that the other exists:

> But though the chronometer carried from Greenwich to China, should truly exhibit in China what the time may be at Greenwich at any moment; yet, though thereby it must necessarily contradict China time, it does by no means thence follow, that with respect to China, the China watches are at all out of the way. . . . Besides, of what use to the Chinaman would a Greenwich chronometer, keeping Greenwich time, be? Were he thereby to regulate his daily actions, he would be guilty of all manner of absurdities:—going to bed at noon, say, when his neighbors would be sitting down to dinner. . . . Nor does the God at the heavenly Greenwich expect common men to keep Greenwich wisdom in this remote Chinese world of ours; because such a thing were unprofitable for them here, and, indeed, a falsification of Himself, inasmuch as in that case, China time would be identical with Greenwich time, which would make Greenwich time wrong. (212)

This is not just a post-lapsarian observation or the realization that one's local or mundane existence can only be recognized as such in the knowledge of a universal or ideal time. In Melville's conception both the terrestrial and the celestial remain live, synchronic, and in relation, together constituting an oceanic third space in which the horologue and the chronometer triangulate an ever-askew subject position. And in the provisional truths established in the spatiotemporal logic of the pamphlet, we see not only the freighted time of Dimock's planetary conception, but also Spivak's alternative to globalism. That is, if the terms of globalism flatten all planetary distance—if such a notion makes Greenwich mean time or the logic of capital the universal standard—then an oceanic sense of planetarity allows for a protean understanding of space and time alike, one that rests uneasily on Rancière's "whims of tides and mariners." We can see in this as well Gilles Deleuze's identification of the characteristic "deterritorialization" of American literature, for which "everything is departure, becoming, passage, leap, daemon, relationship with the outside."[15]

China time versus Greenwich time, insular earth versus continent earth: both oceanic and planetary studies add a geometric and conceptual dimension to our standard practices of referentiality. By this I mean that if relations are normally plotted linearly, in a point-to-point trajectory, then the example of oceanic spatiotemporal accounting registers in a third if not fourth dimension, necessitating a celestial or interstellar connection in order to describe one's place in the world. An oceanic standard helps, too, to give new meaning to the figure of the "turn" in thinking of planetarity, as well as in the many turns of recent decades (the transnational, the linguistic, the temporal, the spatial, and the hemispheric, among many others). The fact that these reorientations are predicated on the use of the word "turn" suggests an orienteering impulse, one that presumes routes whose transits have a continuity, a linearity, a cartography. To "turn" is to have had a path, a line of demarcation.

While the terminus of that turn might be unknown or imagined, it has an established trajectory, a traceable origin. And yet what a turn produces is a triangulation: the point from which one begins and the point at which one ends might be more closely located on the triangular axis. Nonetheless, the longer, perpendicular route is necessitated, even mandated, by imagining such intellectual routes as "turns." One of the fundamental premises of the emerging field of oceanic studies is that such patterns of relationality dissolve in the space and time of the sea.

Notes

1. Herman Melville, *Moby-Dick; or, The Whale*, vol. 6 of *The Writings of Herman Melville*, ed. Harrison Hayford, Hershel Parker, and G. Thomas Tanselle (Evanston, Ill.: Northwestern University Press; Chicago: Newberry Library, 1988), 60.

2. See Gayatri Chakravorty Spivak, "Planetarity," in *Death of a Discipline* (New York: Columbia University Press, 2003), 71–102.

3. See Wai Chee Dimock, *Through Other Continents: American Literature across Deep Time* (Princeton, N.J.: Princeton University Press, 2006).

4. Kären Wigan, introduction to "AHR Forum: Oceans of History," *American Historical Review* 111, no. 3 (June 2006): 717. See also the "Theories and Methodologies" cluster on oceanic studies in *PMLA* 125, no. 3 (May 2010): 657–736.

5. In these terms we might locate oceanic studies at the critical intersection of a Spivakian notion of space and a Dimockian sense of time.

6. Michel Foucault, "Of Other Spaces," trans. Jay Miskowiec, *Diacritics* 16, no. 1 (Spring 1986): 27.

7. I discuss Russia's North Pole "land" grab in my article "John Cleves Symmes and the Planetary Reach of Polar Exploration," *American Literature* 84, no. 2 (June 2012): 243–71.

8. I make this argument in more detail in my article "The Prospect of Oceanic Studies," *PMLA* 125, no. 3 (May 2010): 670–77.

9. Jacques Rancière, *On the Shores of Politics*, trans. Liz Heron (London: Verso, 1995), 2.

10. This extends into a corporeal (and labor-aware) dimension of Dimock's spatiotemporal concept. Pascale Casanova also writes that "literary space creates a present on the basis of which all positions can be measured, a point in relation to which all other points can be located" (*The World Republic of Letters*, trans. M. B. DeBevoise [Cambridge, Mass.: Harvard University Press, 2004], 88).

11. Henry David Thoreau, *Walden; or, Life in the Woods*, in *A Week, Walden, The Maine Woods, Cape Cod*, ed. Robert F. Sayre (New York: Library of America, 1985), 578. All references hereafter are to this edition and are noted parenthetically.

12. Melville, *Moby-Dick*, 44–45. All references hereafter are to this edition and are noted parenthetically.

13. Casanova, *The World Republic of Letters*, 88 (emphasis in original).

14. Herman Melville, *Pierre; or, The Ambiguities*, vol. 7 of *The Writings of Herman Melville*, ed. Harrison Hayford, Hershel Parker, and G. Thomas Tanselle (Evanston, Ill.: Northwestern University Press; Chicago: Newberry Library, 1971), 210–11. All references hereafter are to this edition and are noted parenthetically.

15. Gilles Deleuze and Claire Parnet, *Dialogues II*, trans. Hugh Tomlinson and Barbara Habberjam, rev. ed. (New York: Columbia University Press, 2002), 36.

The Commons . . . and Digital Planetarity

AMY J. ELIAS

> The only sense in which we are Communists is that we care for the commons: the commons of nature, the commons of what is privatized by intellectual property, the commons of biogenetics. For this, and only for this, we should fight. Communism failed absolutely, but the problems of the commons are here.
>
> —Slavoj Žižek

> We must be able to explain success as well as failure of efforts to achieve collective action. . . . Mobs, gangs, and cartels are forms of collective action as well as neighborhood associations, charities, and voting.
>
> —Elinor Ostrom

Everyone knows what a "commons" is: it's a public, community location open to all, controlled singly by no one, and somehow linked to public beliefs and communication. Synonyms for the word "common"—such as "ordinary," "everyday," "widely known," "usual," "jointly shared," "standard," "low born"—have a range of connotations, but all imply a leveling, a state of equality where no one has a special or notable designation, status, or rank. "Common law" is law developed through customs and usages rather than through statutes; at a university, "the Commons" is often a communal dining hall or a public green. We like people with whom we have something "in common," people with whom we share an abstract commons such as a personality or lifestyle.

Experts define a commons as a shared resource in which all stakeholders have an equal interest: "Nothing belongs to anyone, yet everything belongs to everyone."[1] Yet "the commons" is in the category of tricksy things that disappear when you try to touch them, like fog, floating soap bubbles, or financial markets. Calling something a commons gives it a pseudo-utopian halo, an implication of equality and sharing aligned with *fraternité* in the best sense, but we tend to forget that a modern commons is often an enclosed space dependent on an exclusionary border that designates an inside and an outside, brother and Other. We also tend to forget how commons are created in modern societies: a commons is produced either from within itself, a *mise en abyme* situation in which one requires a commons to define a commons (in such cases of exemplary democracy, few commons actually see the light of day), or from a paradox, in which developing a commons depends on the military power, beneficence, or sheer will of autocrats, bureaucrats, entrepreneurs, or wealthy patrons in the private or power sectors. (How many public parks in the United States originated from private gifts from wealthy patrons or from acts of imminent domain by government?) Many places that most people believe to be commons, such as public parks, or university quads, or waterways, are often revealed to be private or legislated spaces when someone becomes angry or litigious about how others are using the space. Certainly, that's one of the things that the various Occupy movements of 2011 illustrated; occupiers who camped out in Zuccotti Park, seemingly a commons area, found themselves the target of hostility from passersby as well as from the actual owner of the park, Brookfield Office Properties. The point is that not only are archaic commons, such as an agrarian society's grazing area, necessarily defined differently in modern, urbanized contexts, but also that in order to function efficiently and fairly, a commons might need to be mediated by authority and law.

Today, a reconsideration of the commons is, implicitly or explicitly, everywhere redefining the concept on a planetary scale. At a moment of world population explosion and depletion of natural resources, the rhetoric of the planetary commons is central to environmental studies; within the context of global finance capitalism, notions of the financial commons preoccupy sociology and economics; as world nations experience increased travel and labor mobility and weakening of nation-state boundaries as a result of globalization, the commons comes to the fore in cultural theories of cosmopolitanism and in world democracy movements. But we need a better sense of the sociological and anthropological work tackling the problem of the commons—or, more accurately, common pool resources—if our conversation about this often under-theorized topic is to avoid the dangerous political poles of communitarian fantasy or political authoritarianism. In our new twenty-first-century zeal to create a *global* commons, we should remember that there is a material history to commons creation, development, and management to which attention must be paid.

A rethinking of the commons began with research about simple commons (or common pool resources [CPRs]), moved to consideration of complex CPRs, and expanded exponentially with the rise of the global environmental movement and its early adoption of commons discourse.[2] Deliberations about the commons today almost always take as their starting point a 1968 paper in the journal *Science* by biologist Garrett Hardin, who presented a theory of the commons that argued for its inevitable tragic outcome. He claimed that, in any commons, people will be motivated to increase their own profit by optimizing their use of the common resource; however, if everyone does this, the resource itself will be rapidly depleted, since its longevity and health are predicated not on everyone's maximum individual profit based on maximum individual yield, but on maximum profit based on maximum *resource* yield, ideally distributed equitably among resource users. Hardin's famous example is that of the herdsmen's common grazing area:

> Picture a pasture open to all. It is to be expected that each herdsman will try to keep as many cattle as possible on the commons. Such an arrangement may work reasonably satisfactorily for centuries because tribal wars, poaching, and disease keep the numbers of both man and beast well below the carrying capacity of the land. . . .
>
> As a rational being, each herdsman seeks to maximize his gain. . . . The rational herdsman concludes that the only sensible course for him to pursue is to add another animal to his herd. And another; and another. . . . But this is the conclusion reached by each and every rational herdsman sharing a commons. Therein is the tragedy. Each man is locked into a system that compels him to increase his herd without limit—in a world that is limited. Ruin is the destination toward which all men rush, each pursuing his own best interest in a society that believes in the freedom of the commons. Freedom in a commons brings ruin to all.[3]

Hardin maintained that relying on morality to regulate the commons will not circumvent this tragedy, for morality is "system-sensitive," depending often on context, and is thus impossible to determine unilaterally.[4] For instance, he maintains that in places of low population density and huge bison herds, a hunter's killing a bison just for the tongue meat would be less ethically fraught than the same act would be if the dependent population were large and only a thousand bison remained on the earth. He asseverates that to ask individuals to restrain themselves for the general good by means of conscience will also lead only to tragic outcomes, for those who break the rules and operate selfishly will be more successful over the long run and eventually dominate the system.

Hardin's social Darwinism is much maligned in leftist circles, but often overlooked is the fact that he also called for an "exorcism" of Adam Smith's "invisible hand" theory from economic affairs, rejecting the assumption "that decisions reached individually will, in fact, be the best decisions for an entire society."[5] Because people have no motivation to act ethically in relation to the commons and have every incentive to shirk, free-ride, cheat, or respond opportunistically *regardless of the economic system that is in place*, Hardin concluded that the only way to avoid the tragedy of selfish overuse was to regulate the commons either through privatization (that is, markets) or through governmental oversight. "The social arrangements that produce responsibility," he wrote, "are arrangements that create coercion, of some sort. . . . The only kind of coercion I recommend is mutual coercion [such as taxes], mutually agreed upon by the majority of the people affected."[6]

My question is this: what impact has such thinking had on today's discussion of the planetary commons, particularly in the context of digital culture and media studies, where talk of the commons has always been part of the indigenous language? Perhaps the rhetoric of "open source" and "digital commons" did not originate when the first computational machines were created, but certainly it is characteristic of cyber research after the birth of the Internet Protocol Suite in 1982, the introduction of hypertext, and the creation of the World Wide Web (WWW). The Internet may have been born of the military-industrial complex, but it was from the start considered by developers to be a commons space, and commons thinking fundamentally drove innovation in it. In the second decade of the twenty-first century, however, as telecommunications goes global, technologies such as smartphones become ubiquitous, and platforms such as social networking systems encroach on the open grazing lands of cyberspace, privatization is wildly disputed among developers and users. As more and more of our material and informational reality gets transferred to the oversight of machines and stored in the cloud, who owns these machines and these clouds (and how ownership impinges on the nature of the WWW as a global informational commons) will become increasingly central to, among other things, fundamental definitions of individual and group autonomy, collective oversight of resources, property rights, profit distribution and labor production, and privacy rights.

This is not a new insight. In fact, the wars over online privatization have been waged for so long that weariness, cynicism, and naive utopian accommodation are now easily identified rhetorical norms in digital culture studies. Movies have been made about this. Thus, rather than rehearse yet again the stories of Napster and other start-ups that ran into a wall of privatization, in this article I'd like to go back to basic definitions and address the complexities of the commons—what it is, how it operates, and what controversies surround its management. Specifically, I will consider three ways that the figure of the commons is now being reimagined, after decades of contestation, to answer Hardin's original theory and also how these reconceptions are impacting discussion regarding the planetary media environments of the Internet and World Wide Web.

The word "digital" is of course a plenum, designating everything from social networking sites to Krzysztof Wodiczko's public video projections; to talk about "digital planetarity," then, risks further complicating and perhaps confusing the discussion with multiply overlapping digital domains, scales, platforms, and aesthetics. I therefore set my sights primarily on theory and have deliberately picked three radically different domains in which the commons is apprehended—public economy, discussions about digital culture and open source, and affect theory—in order to illustrate how a range of approaches can be used to address the problem of the planetary digital commons. At the site of commons inquiry in digital media studies, distinctions between "planetarity" and "globalization" become clear: it is precisely the issue of the commons—as a social space that is organized neither on the nation-state model nor on the neoliberal global model—that is most aligned with the idea of the Internet as a new planetary collective. The last section of this chapter evaluates the effectiveness of these three avenues of theory for addressing central issues related to the planetary digital commons. Since the second of the three example discourses—namely, the debate about open source and property rights—should be familiar to most readers involved in technology studies, I will focus primarily on the other two, though all address two questions I see as key to any discussion of digital planetarity: What does it mean to understand life online as living in the planetary commons? And what direction might be posited for commons life in this virtual, planetary space?

Elinor Ostrom, Public Economy, and The Commons

A significant counter to Hardin's "tragedy of the commons" scenario emerged in public economics through the work of Elinor Ostrom, who in 2009 was awarded the Nobel Prize for Economics "for her analysis of economic governance, especially the commons."[7] Ostrom made two unique contributions to theories of the commons. First, she turned to game theory to try to map and understand interactions between appropriators of, and outcomes within, common pool resources (CPRs).[8] Second, she tested projected CPR outcomes against those of actual field settings and case studies, assessing the predictive capacities of game theory and also the results of lab experiments in relation to documented human use of CPRs across the globe.

Ostrom is clear that simple and complex common pool resources require different oversight to operate efficiently and fairly. Complex CPRs may call, for instance, for the inclusion of experts to provide research background and information to CPR appropriators/managers as well as to supervise the implementation of sanctions stipulated by them. "Providers," she says, are "those who arrange for the provision of a CPR," and a "producer" is any person "who actually constructs, repairs, or takes actions that ensure the long-term sustenance of the resource system itself." In some cases, providers and producers are the same people, but in other cases they are not: Ostrom gives the example of a national government providing the financing and design of an irrigation system and then arranging with local farmers to produce and maintain it, at which point the farmers themselves become the providers as well as the producers. A group of many people or more than one firm can be the producer of a CPR, but "the resource units . . . *are not subject to joint use or appropriation*." For example, a number of fishermen may control a common fishing ground as providers and/or producers, but "fish harvested by one boat are not there for someone else."[9] Thus, "CPR appropriators who organize themselves to govern and manage a CPR are faced with some problems that are similar to those of appropriating private goods and other problems that are similar to those of providing public goods."[10]

Ostrom also clearly asserts that interdependence is the state in which appropriators of a *material* resource (recognized as such) find themselves, and the motivation for acting interdependently in good faith is the maximization of profit, however defined. She specifically rejects a view frequently seen in much popular and academic discussion, where "interdependence" within a commons is presented as a moral good and ethical goal or outcome.[11] In other words, the commons in much of Ostrom's work is not the happy if somewhat vaguely defined space of an ethical cosmopolitanism, nor is it a contestatory sphere of planetary intercultural communication.[12] Practically speaking, in Ostrom's view, acting interdependently means coordinating action strategies to obtain higher joint benefits or reduce joint harm. A commons is the shared bedrock of survival, where success or failure is defined in terms of a functioning economy of goods.

Ostrom's research seems shaped by a pragmatic approach to human nature. She implicitly rebuts conceptions of the commons based on the evolutionary basis of human altruism,[13] but she also ignores or is not aware of a poststructuralist radical interrogation of individual self-determination and agency that might inhibit the pursuit of a commons. Much more down to earth, she understands a commons as a benefit to material life but humans as beings subjected to constant temptation to act opportunistically in relation to resources. Her research avoids utopian promises that a commons will revamp human subjectivity and concludes instead that CPRs and their situational contexts themselves do not produce ethical outcomes. She posits that people basically need to be ethical *going in* to the CPR situation or be given incentives to act ethically once the CPR is operating. "The capacity to design their own rules," Ostrom argues, "will not enhance the outcomes achieved by the nontrusting and narrowly selfish individuals of the world, but will enhance the outcomes of those who are prepared to extend reciprocity to others and interact with others with similar inclinations."[14] Based on lab experiments measuring cooperation in different simulated CPR circumstances, Ostrom contends that there are at least three kinds of settings that seem unlikely to be improved by self-organization: those where people "have no expectation of mutual trust and no means of building it"; those in which "mistrust is already rampant, and communication and continued interactions do not reduce the level of distrust"; and settings in which many people "are willing to extend reciprocity to others but lack authority to create their own self-governing institutions."[15] In order for a CPR to function optimally, appropriators themselves must have the opportunity to lay down rules, monitoring systems, and penalties.

In fact, the central problem facing any self-organized group seeking to operate a CPR is "the commitment problem," or adhering to the principles of the CPR without an external enforcer. Unlike Hardin, Ostrom thinks that though this problem will inevitably arise, a resulting "tragic" outcome is not inevitable. In the face of great temptation to break rules for personal gain, producers/appropriators "have to motivate themselves (or their agents) to monitor activities and be willing to impose sanctions to keep conformance high."[16] Research has shown, she also reports, that "users of a resource system will continue to harvest resource units, without trying to self-organize, unless they perceive that the benefits they would receive from a change in their rules will be greater than the costs involved."[17]

Highly relevant to *The Planetary Turn*'s axial focus on relationality is a CPR's communicational dynamic. Notably, Ostrom's team found that *face-to-face communication played a significant role in the successful functioning of CPRs in laboratory situations.* After running a series of game models with test subjects, her group concluded that "the inability [of subjects] to communicate [with one another] limited the durability of their agreements." However, "in a decision environment where subjects were given repeated opportunities to communicate [face-to-face and without having to pay for the opportunity], subjects offered and extracted promises of cooperation and chastised one another when conformance was not complete, thereby increasing their joint yield significantly above that obtained prior to communication." In their experiments, they also found that the highest yield of a CPR was gained, and the defection rate from agreements was lowest, when subjects/appropriators had "the right to choose a sanctioning mechanism [for rules-breakers] and a single opportunity to communicate" face-to-face.[18]

This flies in the face of Hardin's tragedy scenario, but, as Ostrom notes, also of assumptions by theorists of noncooperative games, such as John Nash, who see "words alone . . . as frail constraints when individuals make private, repetitive decisions between short-term, profit-maximizing strategies and strategies negotiated by a verbal agreement."[19] These theorists maintain that what keeps people honest are enforceable contracts (the Hobbesian-based model of interaction), not whether they were able to communicate with one another. Olstrom's own research indicates otherwise:

> In many of these [CPR dilemmas], but not all, individuals overcome the temptations present to overuse the CPR. They do this by communicating their desires to reach acceptable sharing agreements. They build trust in these agreements by extending reciprocity through the use of personal heuristics like measured reactions. In difficult settings, they use measured reactions to bolster their agreements as well as imposing sanctions on those who violate agreements. Individuals who extend reciprocity to others and who learn to craft their own effective rules can accomplish more than individuals who do not,

> especially when they can identify others following the same heuristics. Such individuals achieve more than predicted by noncooperative game theory as currently understood.[20]

It seems that communication between producers of a CPR is not only central to its most efficient operation but also may sometimes offset the "tragedy of the commons."

This may be good news for planetarity, specifically for any discussion of the "planetary commons," for this is one area in which digital technologies can contribute unprecedented benefactions. If face-to-face communication plays a significant role in the construction and operation of successful common-pool resources, the "digimodernist" global world of the twenty-first century can facilitate such interactions cheaply, at a pace and on a scale that has never been seen before in human history.[21] Real-time, direct written language-based online chat (such as instant messaging), social networking systems (such as Facebook), and proprietary voice-over-IP services combined with software applications (such as Skype) offer now-familiar and easily accessed means to overcome distance on a global level, and more advanced technologies are being created daily. Many of these communications platforms allow people to meet "virtually face-to-face" in real time. If their potential for expediting and simplifying communications is not hampered by politicians or corporations, these new communications systems offer previously unparalleled opportunities for CPR providers and appropriators to create new commons on a planetary scale. At the same time, of course, privatization and politics are working to limit access to this type of ownership and control, which is increasingly available only to those who can afford it, to those whose governments allow it, to those whose communication and digital literacy is sufficiently advanced to use it, to those who speak the *lingua franca* of the digital system, and to those who are logged into systems that have security sophisticated enough to control misuse and surveillance. These are not trivial limitations.

Equally important, while Ostrom does not completely reject Hardin's pessimistic hypothesis and, as noted above, she fundamentally agrees with Hardin that people will be tempted to use the commons selfishly, her research offers tested criteria that can lead to appropriators' equitable use of CPRs with optimum output. Whereas Hardin saw tragedy as inevitable and thereby advocated governmental or privatized oversight as the *only* means to regulate a commons and avoid its misuse, Ostrom and her team submit that the commons tragedy is one possible outcome among many and suggest lab-tested strategies for CPR use that might avoid Hardin's prognoses under certain circumstances.[22] The good news is that as research on CPRs has evolved, there has been a convergence of studies concerning collective action and common pool resources that presents these as "social-ecological systems" (SES). These are complex CPR systems (such as the world's oceans) that need to be studied so that CPR investigators learn how to describe and empirically and reliably predict their operation. As Amy R. Poteete, Marco A. Janssen, and Ostrom note, *scale* is important when considering a full SES. Such systems are characterized by a nested hierarchical structure in which subsystems function as semi-autonomous units that interact across scales or system levels and are often challenged by changes in leadership and resources.[23] This seems an obvious point, but it poses particular difficulties when trying to organize and predict the behaviors of the system as well as of the appropriators of complex CPRs such as the stratosphere—or the World Wide Web. Thus, contrary to popular notions that often picture the commons as a vast, open, mutually supportive collective, these studies indicate that CPRs operate in all kinds of ways, can be nested within one another on all kinds of scales, and can be overseen by all kinds of appropriators. As a result, a CPR must be considerably researched up front, before it is implemented, if it is to yield maximum profit (as defined by its maximum carrying capacity) for all appropriators. Otherwise, producers can expect a long period of trial and error, potentially devastating to the CPR, before the CPR usage problems are resolved.

It would seem that logistical and administrative planning—the mundane bureaucratic stuff of organization building rather than the sexy utopian call to collective action—is key to the viability and sustainability of a common pool resource. Centering on the components of CPRs and the logistics of their operation, Ostrom clearly thinks that common pool resources are good things and that it is imperative for researchers and policymakers to address the issue of the global commons.[24] Yet her projects and those studies building upon them tend neither to posit ideal CPR environments that might be instituted by public policy advocates nor to formulate regulations and laws setting restrictions on CPR creation. What Ostrom attempts to reveal are the nuts and bolts of CPRs: what they need in order to thrive and which questions are still left to be investigated in relation to their genesis and operation in the real world.[25] This work is perhaps most important to the large and exponentially growing conversation about behaviors in cyberspace—particularly behaviors in contexts directly or indirectly related to digital arts such as MMORPWs (massively multiplayer online role-playing worlds) and SNSs (social networking systems, such as Facebook).

To illustrate, a very old example comes to mind, one referencing the oldest functioning Multi-User Domain Object-Oriented (MUD or MOO) and familiar to anyone working in digital culture studies. In 1993, freelance journalist Julian Dibble made digital culture history when he published a *Village Voice* article titled "A Rape in Cyberspace: How an Evil Clown, a Haitian Trickster Spirit, Two Wizards, and a Cast of Dozens Turned a Database into a Society."[26] Dibble documented "the Bungle Affair" in LambdaMOO, an early text-based, real-time Internet multiplayer game or MUD (Multi-User Dungeon).[27] This incident involved a gamer who appeared inworld as Mr. Bungle, an evil clown. At around 10:00 pm PST on a Monday in March 1993, when the virtual world was populated with many users, the gamer logged in and Mr. Bungle went to the "living room" and began running a "voodoo doll" script which allowed him to control other characters' actions. Targeting specific characters, he caused them to engage in sex acts and perverse self-mutilations that they could not stop, and "his distant laughter echoed evilly in the living room with every successive outrage" until someone named Zippy used a different script (a gun that enveloped targets in an impermeable cage of protection) to stop his rampage.

One might write off the incident as a very early example of online "trolling" (malicious behavior), now a staple of almost any online community (one thinks of the horrible below-the-line comments on YouTube or the treatment of newbies in MMORPGs). To us today, the LambdaMOO incident is hardly shocking, and people who don't think much about the Internet often write it off as a just another stupid online prank. For LambdaMOO after all wasn't "real-life": it was "just a middlingly complex database, maintained for experimental purposes inside a Xerox Corporation research computer in Palo Alto and open to public access via the Internet."[28] In fact, the incident probably would not have garnered the international attention it did if it were not for Dibble's provocative analysis of what happened next.

Dibble made clear that the Bungle Affair was so distressing, first, because it ended up having real-world effects: the avatars that had been violated in the virtual world were controlled by real people logging in from different geographical locations, and those people felt *themselves* traumatized by Mr. Bungle's "rape" of their avatars. The incident brought to light questions concerning the relationship between real-world and online personae—and online ethics incumbent on those personae—that we are still hashing through today in discussions about the psychological implications of intermeshed human-avatar identities, from online relationships to gameworld role-playing. Second, the Bungle Affair raised queries about how real-world acts translate into online contexts: as Dibble notes, while everyone using LamdaMOO that day saw a "rape" happen, violated users chastised Mr. Bungle for his lack of "civility"—not the ethical terminology we would normally apply to rape. Actions, particularly violent ones, somehow had double meanings, or new meanings, in the inworld context; there was an ontological as well as an ethical problem to be overcome when a line of code became an act of real-world, personal violation.

Third, and most important to the discussion of cyberspace CPRs, the long-term questions generated by the Bungle Affair concerned the nature of commons governance in online communities. One LambdaMOO user named evangeline, "who identified herself as a survivor of both [this] virtual rape . . . and real-life sexual assault, floated a cautious proposal for a MOO-wide powwow on the subject of virtual sex offenses and what mechanisms if any might be put in place to deal with their future occurrence."[29] Following her post, another user named legba called for Mr. Bungle's "toading" (the deletion of his account from the MOO—essentially a "death sentence") for "raping Starsinger." While many in the collective agreed to this, it could not be done without unilateral action from a "wizard," one of the master programmers of the MOO. In the case of LambdaMOO, this was Pavel Curtis, a Xerox researcher and the MOO's principal architect, who had early on issued a declaration that wizards would not be involved in day-to-day, mundane operations of the virtual world. LambdaMOO was in a quandary:

> Since getting the wizards to toad Mr. Bungle . . . required a convincing case that the cry for his head came from the community at large, then the community itself would have to be defined; and if the community was to be convincingly defined, then some form of social organization, no matter how rudimentary, would have to be settled on. And thus, as if against its will, the question of what to do about Mr. Bungle began to shape itself into a sort of referendum on the political future of the MOO.[30]

The online community met to discuss options: various participants expressed their opinions about the action and what its consequences should be, and this played through a number of political positions from libertarianism to anarchism to dictatorial fiat. In the end, the band of MOO users reached a stalemate, and it was only through the unauthorized act of a wizard—JoeFeedback, who acted alone and toaded Mr. Bungle—that the matter was immediately resolved. The long-term outcome of the Bungle Affair for LambdaMOO was the institution of a "new regime" that included a petition-and-ballots system that would allow citizens to define and impose sanctions and a procedure for adjudicating conflicts, "an ad hoc arbitration system in which mutually agreed-upon judges have at their disposition the full range of wizardly punishments."[31]

Ostrom's CPR research becomes visible here. In particular—and contradicting much utopian rhetoric upholding the idea that online cooperation is natural or automatic—the Bungle Affair supports Ostrom's claims that cooperative ethics and civility must be either part of the appropriator's disposition going *in* to the CPR situation (in Mr. Bungle's case, it was not) or must be cultivated by specific procedures of CPR operation that appeal to the self-interest of appropriators. In contrast to the hymns of praise we hear so often for "flow" or horizontal structure and self-organization that eschew unilateral rules and hierarchy, the LambdaMoo appropriators learned that in a completely open commons there are no checks and balances on behavior, and that this can bring such a sodality to a grinding, even traumatizing, halt.[32]

But the LambdaMoo incident posed additional questions that apply today to any digital commons. What constitutes an online community and what are the rules governing such a commons space? Who should decide those rules: the commons provider, producer, or appropriator? If there is always an "admin" behind the scenes who has control of the code—always a "man (or corporation) behind the curtain" who has the ability to act unilaterally to toad players, manipulate the platform, or pull the plug on an entire virtual environment—can cyberworlds ever truly be "commons"? Or are they just commons more complex than we had imagined, in fact perfectly illustrating Ostrom's contention that some CPR situations call for administrative oversight by commons providers or even require the inclusion of experts to oversee sanctions created by appropriators. (If they do need administrative monitoring, then we should be discussing how appropriators of cyber-CPRs might negotiate and legally formalize sanctions rules with providers. This of course leads us, as we shall see below, to the property rights problem diagnosed by open source advocates.) And significantly, in view of the present discussion, Dibble's article raises the question of human ethics in digital space. If, as Ostrom claims, even minimal face-to-face communication plays a decisive role in the successful functioning of CPRs, what will replace this human interaction in the digital environment, particularly if we haven't yet come near to sorting out the relation between online personae and real-life human identity in digital worlds? As we try to engender and maintain commons across cultures on a planetary scale, will new, Skype-like platforms that "actually" offer us the chance to see one another's faces be perceived by us as the same ethical situation as face-to-face meetings, or will this be a third, avatar space between fiction and reality for which we need to revise our negotiating and commons-building skills?

The Digital Commons, the Anticommons, and Open Source

New media studies analyzing the nature of "cyberspace as commons" have been another rejoinder to Hardin's theory, which is cited frequently in debates about "open source ethics." In fact, open source is the most easily recognized commons desideratum in digital culture contexts. In the work of writers such as James Boyle, David Bollier, Lawrence Lessig, Clay Shirky, Diana Saco, Carolyn Guertin, Manuel Castells, and many others, the conversation about the network society has fundamentally defined scholarship concerning the Internet, World Wide Web, and online cultures.[33] One could argue that this inquiry was in fact birthed with the Internet itself. But certainly with the development of Richard Stallman's GNU Unix operating system, with its "CopyLeft" rules of appropriation, and the FOSS (Free/Libre and Open Source) software movement, combined with newer ideas about "net neutrality" and the development of peer-to-peer file-sharing software, the idea of the global Internet as a public commons took permanent hold.[34] Yet as early as 1998, it was clear that bellicosity regarding the Internet Commons was focused primarily on property distribution rights and copyright laws. Douglas Noonan, for example, proposed that the Internet is a commons because it "meets both criteria of (1) nonexcludability and (2) rivalrous consumption."[35] The second criterion has been examined extensively, and the first is not used primarily to assess commons resources but rather to gauge to what extent things meet the definition of public or collective goods.[36] The overlap between theories of the commons and of public goods continues in deliberations about the digital commons because such inquiries often involve arguments about copyright and management of open-source software.[37]

Those of us in language studies might note the key role played by metaphor in these debates. The Internet is in fact understood in terms of property rights when the dominant trope organizing discussions is that of "cyberspace as place" or planetary space. Dan Hunter has pointed out how frequently the "cyberspace as place" metaphor is used in legal scholarship, thereby fostering a regulatory environment. This metaphor, he contends, is "leading us inexorably towards an undesirable policy outcome: the staking out of private claims in cyberspace and concomitant reductions in the public 'ownership' of the space"—one version of "the tragedy of the anticommons."[38] "Anticommons" is a term Hunter appropriates from James Boyle, a major player in the open source movement who writes prolifically about the need to keep the Internet an open commons space.[39] Boyle writes that "we are [now] in the middle of a second enclosure movement," an "enclosure of the intangible commons of the mind" that mimics in many ways the English enclosure of arable lands in the nineteenth century.[40] He makes the case that, historically, intellectual property law worked to protect the intellectual commons, but that key changes in intellectual property rights are now radically extending those rights' traditional boundaries—such as the troubling move by the European Database Directive to attempt to copyright compilations of *facts*.[41] However, Boyle cites two important differences between the nineteenth-century enclosure of the arable commons and the movement attempting to regulate intellectual property today: (1) the "commons of the mind" (unlike the arable commons) may be "non-rival," that is, one person's use does not preclude or undermine use by another, and (2) this use is also "non-excludable," meaning that the good can be used and duplicated again and again by many people without its diminishment. The second of these sounds like a good thing in relation to the arable commons, but in the context of the digital commons, it could actually undermine incentive to create the resource in the first place, for creators of products would not be able to regulate copying of, block usage of, or charge for their creations.

There are also ways to wreck an online commons that are unique to its digital character. With the development of the WWW, for instance, the strategy of overloading websites became an intentional, premeditated method for hacking and disrupting websites and public access to them. Critics such as Noonan point out that sophisticated users often can easily overload different links in the network chain, "reducing the value of other transmissions congested at that point" and thereby "pos[ing] collective-action dilemmas" related to bandwidth and its use.[42] In the same vein, Gian Maria Greco and Luciano Floridi stress that overloaded bandwidth ("*bandwidth exploitation*") and spam ("*information pollution*") should be considered online forms of Hardin's "exploitation" and "pollution of the commons."[43]

Boyle's thesis, however, is that "a global network actually *transforms* our assumptions about creativity and innovation so as to reshape the debate about the need for incentives." He specifically references the collaborative work at the heart of the free software and open source movements: here, one does not simply donate work to a public domain, but rather the domain itself is "a continual accretion in which all gain the benefits of the program on pain of agreeing to give their additions and innovations back to the communal project."[44] This definition makes the similarities between open source and commons clear. His notion of distributed production—whereby smaller groups work on chunks of a problem and then coordinate results—implicitly accords with Ostrom's assertion that complex CPRs will need to be broken into smaller coordinated units. Boyle also is not adverse to intellectual property regulation but tends to see the Internet as a vast experiment in new kinds of commons production that may or may not be compatible with some forms of intellectual privatization: "our concerns about the excesses of intellectual property were simply the ones that Jefferson, Madison, and Macaulay gave us so long ago."[45] But important to Boyle's argument as well as to others' in his camp is the idea that it doesn't matter *why or with what attitudes* people engage in this commons behavior (for instance, the love of others, participation in a gift economy, or potlatch), just that often they *will* work within distributed production without proprietary/exclusion laws and that if governance processes are needed, these too can be assembled through distributed methods.

Yet I would venture to ask in what ways our perspectives on, say, Wikipedia would change if we saw it less as a flashpoint for discussions of copyright and intellectual property rights and more as an example of participatory, digital art on a global scale that avoided the "cyberspace as place" metaphor. Joseph Michael Reagle has made a strong case, for example, that "Wikipedia is both a community and an encyclopedia" and "a good faith collaborative culture."[46] His presentation of Wikipedia dovetails perfectly with Ostrom's definition of well-functioning commons communities, for he see it not as the completely open, egalitarian, and free space of public contribution often praised or bemoaned in popular discussions but rather as a highly defined and policed community effort. Reagle examines the three core community policies outlined on Wikipedia's metapages ("Neutral Point of View," "No Original Research," and "Verifiability") as commons principles formulated by providers and supported by appropriators that keep the wiki from locking into self-interested points of view, and he analyzes the multiple vehicles for user interaction (the page editing, the talk/discussion page associated with each article, Wikizine bulletin, Wikiprojects,

Wikipedia-related blogs, aggregators, and podcasts) as if they were dialogical, face-to-face encounters between appropriators.[47] He strongly implies that appropriators' attitudes matter, but that they need to be reinforced by rules and oversight.

As pointed out above, retracing all the ins and outs of the discussion about open source and the "anticommons" would be to rehearse an exchange foundational to the entire field of digital culture studies. It is important to note, however, that Ostrom's work rarely is mentioned in this exchange, which concentrates not on how to make a commons or on its actual operational logistics but on intellectual property rights and laws built upon the "cyberspace as place" metaphor. Thus we see how two approaches to the digital commons can talk past one another—or, put more positively, address very different aspects of commons creation. On the one hand, the feuds about open source call attention to right of access to CPR platforms (software), and this skews the conversation toward the "cyberspace as place" metaphor. Since open access to the digital commons is the primary concern, theories extolling open source tend to center on property and access rights: rather than examining closely the ethics of appropriators or providing clear definitions of the territory that is threatened, this conversation converges on new, privatizing "enclosure movements" and warns against the construction of an "anticommons" that both locks out new CPR producers and administrators and radically limits the actions of all appropriators. On the other hand, Ostrom's work in the field of public economics tends not to focus on the threat of privatization or regulatory oversight (though she does acknowledge and, clearly, disapprove of this) and instead delineates the concrete operations of common pool resources themselves. Her work may in fact prove to be central to the effectiveness of arguments in the other camp: it is difficult to preserve the freedoms of an ill-defined commons.

Certainly, however, Ostrom's work speaks to many assertions that a global digital commons will emerge organically from the inorganic space of online life. Rejecting a strict Hobbesian view of sociality,[48] but also rejecting an easy communality, Ostrom emphasizes that trust, reciprocity, and ethical relationality all maintain a role in the successful operation of a CPR while also insisting that the CPR does not always create these ethical attributes (a claim implicit in some open source positions, such as Boyle's) but rather that it depends on them. Relationality is the condition of the commons, but relation can be mere adjacency, coterminous occupation, contiguity, or even hostile cohabitation that collectively builds and sustains nothing. A healthy and operationally successful CPR grows from appropriators' *ethical* relationality—reciprocity and trust—and while a CPR can be constructed so that it fosters and grows mutual trust, it also hinges on the ethical maturity and trust of administrators and appropriators *entering* the CPR situation. Nonetheless, Ostrom's theory, centered as it is on the logistics of CPR operation, does not help determine where and how this ethical maturity may be developed.

Affect Theory and the Planetary Commons

So there is still a piece missing in theories of the digital planetary commons. What is not put in place in hypotheses about the commons in biology, public economics, or digital culture studies appears, in effect, to be the generating operational principle, which is neither legal nor logistical but ethical and based upon rational communication. A critical investigation known as "affect studies" attempts to remedy this oversight and find this missing ethical piece, and yet it too seems, at this point, shy of this goal. But before fleshing out that claim, I'd like to examine affect studies as a third entry point to current constructions of the planetary digital commons.

Affect studies range across a number of disciplines, topics, and scales, and here I'd like to look at only a few examples that speak to the relation between affect and commons creation. For instance, Michael Hardt and Antonio Negri have addressed the problem of the mislaid keystone in the commons edifice by bringing together affect studies and theories of the commons in a Deleuzian-inflected model of global collectivity. In *Commonwealth*, Hardt and Negri (H&N) champion the term "love" as a concept for inducing a new sociality, of bringing about a new notion of the social predicated upon, or birthing, a new subjectivity in a Foucaultian sense.[49] Hardt asserts that currently we lack "a political concept of love" that would unite political interest and our affective lives, would operate on multiple scales and in the encounter with difference, and would help us to transform our world but also give us a lasting foundation upon which to build a new one.[50] This may or may not be true, and, indeed, one can think of examples, from Socrates's hemlock to Christ's Passion to modern anti-apartheid movements, where love seemed to have serious political dimensions and was theorized, accordingly, as a transformative social power.[51] Nonetheless, H&N argue that "love is a process of the production of the common and the production of subjectivity," and, moreover, that "love—in the production of affective networks, schemes of cooperation, and social subjectivities—is an economic power."[52]

With Spinoza and Bergson in the background, H&N maintain that love is joy and the recognition of an external cause, God, which they immediately secularize to "love of nature as a whole." To this they add a twist of Deleuze and Guattari, to the effect that this joy/love is corrupted in two ways. First, it is made into "identitarian love, or love of the same" in which love becomes love for "those most like you." This love includes family love, race love, patriotism: "Family, race, and nation, then, which are corrupt forms of the common, are unsurprisingly the bases of corrupt forms of love." Combating these is the mandate to love the Other: "The mandate to love thy neighbor, then, the embodiment of each and every commandment for the monotheistic 'religions,' requires us to love the other or, really, to love alterity."[53] Anyone familiar with the biblical story of the Good Samaritan will not be surprised; however, the great monotheistic religions do not assert that love is love of alterity *per se*. This is H&N's Deleuzian move, which also requires a radical secularization of love that simultaneously imbues the affect itself with transformational, even sublime, power. Second, for H&N, corrupt forms of love stem from a "process of unification or of becoming the same," namely, from what Deleuze and Guattari in *A Thousand Plateaus* call a despotic formation. Such forms include the unity of the state but also the unity bestowed by identity politics. What H&N essentially want is love as a line of flight, an immanence in movement without *telos*, or an assemblage (that is, a multitude) but not a unity (that is, a nation).[54]

This is the basis of their hypothesis that a commons derived from emotion, from love, is not the same as a unity. Instead, they posit, this commons is made up of "multiple singularities"—that is, it is more like a Leibnitzian universe or a Deleuzian plane of consistency. The powers of love are, first, its creation of the common as social relation (in Marxist terms, these would be its powers of association and rebellion); second, its force "to combat evil," defined as a corruption of the common; and third, the ability to form "the multitude," the name for a new collective released from the shackles of identity and *telos* associated with Marxist definitions of the proletariat.[55]

And how do we learn love? Where do we learn the reciprocity and trust necessary to the function of the commons? The authors conjecture that "the deployment of love has to be learned and new habits have to be formed through the collective organization of our desires, a process of sentimental and political education. Habits and practices consolidated in new social institutions will constitute our now transformed human nature."[56] (This is the move that radically departs from the doctrines of major monotheisms: the transformation of human nature itself.) Since, however, H&N disregard religion, nation-state, and ethnicity-based communities, they don't answer the questions of how human nature can be transmuted and what might be the nature of the new social institutions that alter it. Clearly these institutions hold considerable power and seem to iterate the claim often made in digital culture studies that a commons *produces* the community and ethos that sustains it. And so it appears that H&N's utopian version of the planetary common is the reworking, through Deleuzian metaphysics, of an old Marxist dream: the rise of a global underclass undivided by race, class, ethnicity, or beliefs, which will bond together in brotherly love born out of opposition to material oppression and will be collectively organized by new social institutions that will both guide action in the new material common and help to transform human subjectivity.[57]

For Hardt, love, as affect, has this sublime power, but it also operates as a metaphor for something like "collective spirit." It is both an operand in the creation of the common and a figure for an eternally open and nonteleological political collectivity: the multitude, another name for the common itself as a new form of being. It may thus be important that H&N continually refer to "the common" rather than "the commons." The former connotes a larger, more abstract territory than the latter, a reorganization of Being rather than a reorganization merely of space or material resources.[58] Where love *comes from*—from what ethics or ontologies it is born and why it is created instead of something else, such as competition—is not clear. H&N sidestep the very problem they set out to solve, which is how love can serve as the catalyst and foundation for a new global collectivity. Love here is alpha and omega: the affect (love) links to a Deleuzian line of flight (in H&N, "exodus") and transforms the global workforce into a multitude and commonwealth, but love also is the *result* of global collective organization that brings about a new ontology. The difference from older Marxisms as well as from the concrete, worldly ethics of monotheism—and, to me, an unsatisfying swerve into metaphysical vagueness—is the turn from politics to ontology in the interest of pure utopianism. Real, lived human communities such as the family or the group with shared ethnic history are suspect and discarded while the common is defined as eternal, the opening of a space of nonteleological possibility inhabited by the multitude, which evinces a new subjectivity born from love and exodus.

Hardt has defended these ideas in his dialogues with Lauren Berlant, who herself explores the notion of affect as bedrock for the foundation of a commons. Like Hardt, Berlant sees affect as an opening, providing new access to the social: as a psychosocial concept, it replaces older terms that connote stasis and normativity or that have lingering associations with Hegelian, teleological idealism or with "great man theory" of the "Zeitgeist" type.[59] Berlant's approach to affect blends the notion of "a spirit of an age" (as a kind of general feeling about the present) with modern psychology and theories of globalization: individually felt affects can be shared generally, as an intuition about the times, and may thus lead to transformations in perception and even to new social formations. Berlant is interested in how the singular becomes the general, how the local becomes the global—that is, how affect experienced viscerally by one person indicates a shift in the culture at large—but unlike H&N, she does not say that affect necessarily gathers the planetary multitude or that love is the key to any affective collectivity. Like Ostrom, who is cautious about the dangers of understanding common-pool resource communities as inherently positive and collegial, Berlant seems wary of Hardt's "love" as a recuperated institutional fantasy and psychic investment.[60] While to some extent she shares H&N's Deleuzianism, Berlant allows only that "affective atmospheres are *shared,*" that "affect, the body's active presence to the intensities of the present, embeds the subject in a historical field, and that its scholarly pursuit can communicate the conditions of a historical moment's production as a visceral moment."[61]

In *Cruel Optimism*, Berlant is interested in historicizing the present as a point in time when affect is itself a new kind of subjectivity, an intuitionism that is fundamental to the cognitive mapping abilities of an "affective class" that is the global "precariat." This new subjectivity is born of shock—the shock of the triumph of finance capital that makes apparent that the old promises of upward mobility, the welfare state, and the fantasy of "the good life" no longer hold for most people. These people experience a crisis reaction that jolts *habitus*, the collective affects that are the culmination of institutional fantasy: "a rhythm of life, a habit, all of the things that are affectively inculcated in one's orientation towards the world are institutions."[62] Unmoored from stable social foundations and denied a progressive or even a custodial future, the precariat loses faith in, and sees for the first time, the ideological, fantasy narrative that structures its lifeworld; affects associated with that lifeworld are inadequate to the new precarious reality in which it finds itself. The affective class, living in a time of constant threat and crisis, feels that something is off-kilter, and it uses its intuitions to map a new epistemological and political landscape. The disaffected cross traditional class lines, and they respond to the crisis-event of the present in radically different ways but through the same means: intuitively and viscerally, through affective reactions to social changes and intuitions of alternatives to the status quo. Berlant writes that "a shift between knowing and uncertain intuitionisms enables us to think about being in history as a densely corporeal, experientially felt thing whose demands on survival skills map not the whole world in one moment but a way to think about the history of sensualized epistemologies in the atmosphere of a particular moment now (aesthetically) suspended in time."[63]

Berlant reasons that this is a postwar phenomenon related to the collapse of the welfare state, no longer upheld by what used to be strong political narratives. She claims that this moment in the twenty-first century constitutes a historical *situation*, "a state of animated and animating suspension that forces itself on consciousness, that produces a sense of the emergence of something in the present that may become an event." Consequently, we experience the present as a kind of duration, an "impasse" or a "glitch" that "is lived as adjustment, remediation, or adaptation." Brilliantly, she writes that this is "a space of time lived without a narrative genre. . . . An impasse is a holding station that doesn't hold securely but opens out into anxiety."[64] Berlant thus brings together affect, contemporary sociality, politics, psychology, and art: each refracts affective intuitions about a present that voices its truth slantwise, in not-yet-formed articulations.

Berlant's notion of the present as duration or "impasse" that is lived as adjustment, remediation, or adaptation is completely compatible with the notion of the planetary commons as metaphysics of flow, queering of time, or digital stream.[65] Like H&N, she sees the new commons as a provisional, a-teleological space of lived possibilities, inhabited by those disaffected with, or reeling from, the aftershocks of global capital. While H&N stress the rhyzomatic nature of this commons, Berlant underscores its psychosomatic foundations. The commons is a kind of "nervous system," an affective atmosphere that is shared.[66] Thus if there is a collectivity forming from the precariat's affective perception of the present, it is the "affectsphere," the social commons located not in the future but in the "becoming-event" of the present, the becoming-historical of the affective, "prehended" event.[67] The commons that is germinated—this provisional, affective, atmospheric commons that we might call, using an older language, "common sense"—is not based on "love" but does put people into relation (with others, with the world) and features other affects central to relationality, including those "involving proximity, . . . friendship, . . . aversions."[68] Unlike Hardt, Berlant leaves open the ethical valence of this affective commons that is also the historical present, though she strongly implies that it is a positive collectivizing movement.

But how is affect theory addressing media studies and its particular focus on a planetary digital commons? Situated within the province of digital culture studies, Richard Grusin's work might provide one answer. Like Berlant, Grusin understands "the real" to be thoroughly mediated. His focus, however, is not on somatic or even on ideological intervention, though his argument builds upon both of these ideas. His primary concern is with what he terms "the affective life of media": "Our contemporary media forms and practices also collapse into a single heterogeneous action a number of specific human and nonhuman, cognitive and affective, interactions, which create affective feedback loops in conjunction with our everyday media forms and practices."[69] For Grusin, these feedback loops—this affective life of telecommunications—are distinctly *not* derived from an ethics of love, nor do they reflect a kind of intuited Real that allows cognitive mapping in the historical present. In fact, they specifically foreclose the latter. The real world has become the world of digital communications: in the twenty-first century, specifically after the 9/11 attacks on the World Trade Center, we live in a state of culture that is "hypermediated" into "diverse and interconnected media formats of social networking" and where televised and Internet newscasting invent a cultural logic that Grusin terms "premediation."[70] "Premediation" is a specific effect of news coverage and journalistic reporting in all technological platforms. It is a kind of temporal distortion or flattening of time in which the news and social networking services constantly try to articulate, in the present, all possible immediate or near-future disaster scenarios in order to anticipate them. They do so in order both to assuage citizens' fear of being surprised by terrifying natural, economic, or social acts and (in collusion with political power) to keep the citizenry in a state of anxiety that precludes real political action. Thus, rather than distracting viewers, the media construct "an affect of anticipation." Affect here fashions a collective in Berlant's sense, but this affect does not spontaneously make its presence felt in response to conflicts defining a social milieu. The collective affect is, instead, fully controlled and created by communications venues, which thereby become "agents of juridicality" as well as "governmentality": there is a "social networking among the executive branch, the military, and the media."[71] In some ways, this is a newer, global, informational version of the twentieth-century "military-industrial complex." Public broadcasts as well as other information formats together produce "premediation," or the affects of anticipation. Anything that happens seems, to the public, to be inevitable, and the possibility of an unmediated future is staved off.

Building upon Niklas Luhmann's theory of autopoietic systems, Grusin argues that "there is . . . an ontological aspect of premediation in which [media guarantee that] the future is always remediated at the very moment that it emerges into the present." Rather than an event, the "future present" will be a present that is the product of, and completely defined within the parameters of, information systems and communications technology, "the continuation of a recursive system of irritation and stabilization."[72] The media don't exist to patrol government or even to report events to the citizenry: they exist solely to reproduce themselves, and to produce a false continuity between past, present, and future that may in fact collude with the aims of power.[73] As Grusin writes,

> More like designing a video game than predicting the future, premediation is not concerned with getting the future right, as much as with trying to map out a multiplicity of possible futures. Premediation would in some sense transform the world into a video or computer game, which only permits certain moves . . . [and] only some of those possibilities are encouraged by the protocols and reward systems built into the game.
>
> . . . In fact it is precisely the proliferation of competing and often contradictory future scenarios that enables premediation to prevent the experience of a traumatic future by generating and maintaining a low level of anxiety as a kind of affective prophylactic.[74]

The difference between premediation and video games, however, is that in a game there are a limited number of possible moves allowed by the system. Premediation works not with the possible but with the virtual: it remediates (or puts into technological formats) *in the present* the virtual potentialities of *future* actions to generate possibilities for such occurrences. All of these possibilities are "real" in the sense that they all have an effect in the present regardless of which ones turn out to be true. Grusin notes that "to think of premediation as virtual [à la Deleuze], and therefore as real, is to refuse this metaphysical distinction [between true and false] and to insist instead on the efficacy, or force, of the multiplicity of premediations in and of themselves—no matter how the future might actually turn out." Premediation's main effect is to change "the relationship of proximity, closeness, or intimacy to embodiment" into a kind of "distributed affect."[75]

Grusin's vision of the affective commons is the most pessimistic of those I've noted here. Unlike H&N, Grusin sees little emancipatory potential in such a commons, for it would be produced within an autopoietic media system whose gaze is turned only upon itself in its many forms and networks of distribution. From the perspective of his account, which is compatible with popular world-systems theories, the members of Berlant's precariat seem to be cogs in a machine, manipulated by the system according to its own needs for self-reproduction and self-extension.[76] If there is a "real" outside of this system, it is increasingly difficult for people to access; in the proliferation of social media that constitutes our modernity in the twenty-first century, there may indeed be, as Berlant claims, an "affectscape," but for Grusin, this is not based in human psychology and intuition. It is instead constructed through an overload of information geared to produce a low-level intensity. Grusin maintains that the media manufacture content that becomes "common sense" and short-circuits the precariat's relation to the real; the media commons is a homeopathic machine that stays or inhibits political action by constantly producing the affect of paralyzing anxiety in the citizenry.

In its various forms, affect theory thus positions the planetary commons as a somatic or cognitive miasma, circulating through media and culture and determining human perception and social action. It may be defined positively ("love") or negatively ("premediation"), but in all of its formulations, affect implies the irrelevance of human rational agency. The planetary commons in this theoretical sphere is shared intuitive *perception* rather than shared communal *project*. Such a definition easily supports the bleakest pictures of the coming media technocracy and biopolitical control. But even at its most optimistic, such a planetary commons offers the possibility only of affective cognitive mapping and somatic intuition of political oppression, duplicities, and hypocrisies. People may think, "Something has gone wrong: I feel it to be so, and I will join with others who feel it to be so." But how to build upon this feeling in a way that leads to an egalitarian, productive planetary commons constructed at various scales is a question that remains largely unanswered. While affect theories give provocative reasons why collectivization might occur, it is left to other conceptual models to account for the actual rise and maintenance of the commons, as well as for the ethical values needed to maintain its productivity and fair use.

Worlding the Technological Commons

In his concert performance *Stripped, Live*, the British comic Eddie Izzard quipped that after downloading, the new version of iTunes "starts asking you questions, like, 'Will you sign a new agreement with iTunes?' I've signed many agreements with iTunes. I don't know what they want from me anymore. Surely they know that I agree with them."[77] Whether we agree with iTunes, as a global conglomerate redefining the digital commons, is part of the fun here.

It would seem that today, in fact, a reconsideration of the commons is, implicitly or explicitly, everywhere. As the planet is seen more and more as a closed system, and as technology advances into territories once reserved for science fiction,[78] the planet as commons becomes increasingly tied to notions of the common media grid. Different perspectives situated within biology, property rights law, digital culture studies, political economy, and affect theory speak of the wedding of the planetary commons to the technological sublime, the machinic territory of the posthuman. The shadows of Deleuze and Guattari loom over this theoretical scene, which implies that Pierre Macheray was prescient in 1979 when he predicted a shift from Hegel to Spinoza in contemporary thought: in articulations of the commons, across discourses and disciplinary borders, we see the language of flow, becoming, posthumanism, alterity, and affective and somatic relationality often privileged over that of rational planning, ethics based in *habitus*, dialogic relationality, and institution-building.[79]

In the context of digital culture and global media studies, the commons is treated differently than it is in environmental studies, comparative arts, ethics, or even political economy. The textual and remediated territory of the Internet seems to elude a humanism interpreted as embodied performative mimesis.[80] Cyberspace also poses unique problems to a planetarity defined, in Spivak's terms, as recognition of materiality, placedness, and difference.[81] While I hesitate to agree with Mark Poster that "global culture can only be global media culture," certainly it is true that "the human/information machine link introduces new configurations of the binaries of space and time, body and mind, subject and object, producer and consumer, indeed all the constituents that form cultures."[82] In response, cyber-theorists and open source advocates often appear to adopt radically different perspectives on the commons and on the possibilities for human agency in it. Some advocate a Habermasian conception of communicative agency and public sphere, in which human initiative and self-determination (based in fundamental needs of survival and communication within social systems) are frequently understood to be ingredients central to the construction of creatively imagined, collaborative digital commons.[83] And yet critics from these same fields have also issued some of the most frightening predictions about global surveillance and mind control in this online environment.

Oftentimes, researchers and advocates in the open-source technology camp who campaign with zeal for a planetary digital commons seem undisturbed by the idea that "flow" may come at the price of the human, perhaps even at the price of the organic. Autopoiesis is, after all, a machinic idea, and systems theories proliferating in digital culture studies routinely drift in the direction of Singularity religiosities.[84] In the most ecstatic as well as the bleakest pictures of the emerging technological planet (such as the global-collective-as-Matrix image), the most human of concepts—that of a commons, a collectively managed territory promoting survival but also a shared space of negotiated *values*—may be precisely what is occluded, wresting control from people and placing it in the domain of machines and networks, undermining notions of human agency, and overriding humans' ability to rationally plan and negotiate their realities by streaming affect through our cognitive processing centers and/or short-circuiting, through new legal and illegal surveillance, our determination of public space.

It may be difficult to be jubilant about digital planetarity as it is currently being configured if it just mirrors older notions of globalization—that is, if the digital commons we create is just a new platform for creating us in its own image and according to the dehumanizing logics of the market, or if the digital commons is merely a way to funnel free labor to multinational corporations. In 2013 I visited the website for "hack/reduce," a Boston-based nonprofit organization supported by the state of Massachusetts and MIT that advertises its membership as "a meritocracy based around community and innovation." I was perplexed to see that this "hacker" organization touting open-source rhetoric and collaborative organization was funded by, among other entities, Microsoft, IBM, Dell, Google, and Bain Capital Ventures.[85]

Of course, it is precisely in the territory of the digital that the most vehement protests and subversive action are taking place against privatization and market appropriation of the planetary commons—from the Hackers on Planet Earth (HOPE) annual conferences featuring speakers such as The Yes Men and Steve Rambam to global online actions by Anonymous and Wikileaks. On the side of these protests and informed by research such as Ostrom's, we are not simply championing theoretical naïveté when we assert that "a broader theory of human behavior views humans as adaptive creatures who . . . learn norms, heuristics, and full analytical strategies from one another, from feedback from the world, and from their own capacity to engage in self-reflection and imagine a differently structured world. They are capable of designing new tools—including institutions—that can change the structure of the worlds they face for good or evil purposes."[86] Such a claim does not necessarily impose anthropomorphic machinery upon the planet and its life forms. Rather, it is recognition that humans are clever little animals who occupy the top of their planetary food chain, and often it is good for everyone's and everything's survival when these social mammals learn to collaborate.

Certainly, the planet will be impacted by technology, as is most apparent in such initiatives as "Hack the Planet," a geoengineering project to technologically control the planet's weather. In his book of the same title, Eli Kintisch quotes Stewart Brand, author of the original *Whole Earth Catalog*, as noting, in 2009, "Whether it's called managing the Commons, natural infrastructure maintenance, tending the wild, niche construction, ecosystem engineering, mega gardening, or intentional Gaia, humanity is now stuck with the planet's stewardship role."[87] If *stewardship* of the planet is to be the goal of the new planetary commons—and I think it is the only option linked to human survival—then perhaps we should pay more attention to Ostrom's model, which seems to me to offer the most reasonable discussion of operational commons and a particularly useful set of cautions when planning a digital commons that will inevitably operate on a planetary scale. But, as I've tried to show, her model needs to be supplemented by some kind of discourse—philosophical, religious, affective—that posits a way to fashion its ethical keystone. This is the starting place for the good-faith values that will organize and maintain the planetary commons. These are not necessarily "traditional values" (though they are not necessarily radically new values either) and they will not come naturally to the human animal. They must be constructed in the spirit of the commons itself—relationally, collaboratively.

Oddly, therefore, looking at the planet as digital commons may require us to develop a new form of humanism rather than an anti-humanism (Rosi Braidotti's work is particularly useful in this regard).[88] Surprisingly, in the end, planetary cyberspace in fact may not be incompatible with Spivak's demand for a re-cognition of humanity through planetary dialogue. For some time now, I have been researching, and thus steeped in, the ethics and politics of dialogue and have come to understand that there is often an excluded middle in both constructivist and essentialist theories of human agency—namely, the territory of negotiation between the phases of construction and adoption, and, located between identity and exchange, the negotiated selfhood that provides the very territory of dialogics. In other words, if we do not assume an autopoietic system (even one based in affect) acting similarly at all levels of the planetary system and training persons to act in accordance with its own objectives, and if we can, without theoretical embarrassment, posit that effective human action requires rational planning, the missing ethical linchpin in current theories of the commons must be forged through dialogic exchange between persons in a public sphere. What Mr. Bungle made clear, and what new research about online civility illustrates, is that in lived human contexts, relationality does not necessarily equal dialogue. Ethics and the politics of ethics matter. The birth of the digital planetary commons need not be divorced from conceptions of human agency, ethics, law, and optimism, if these are what it takes to build a commons that is not a hive or a sweatshop.[89]

I have written elsewhere about the linkages between planetarity and dialogism; in the discourse of the planetary, we see a concept opposed to "the global" and a return to the idea that survival depends on dialogic relation, on persons able to negotiate with their surroundings—with other persons, with cultural and natural environments.[90] In Ostrom's theory of common pool resources, we see how important dialogue is to maintaining integrity and good faith in commons interactions, even if these need to be undergirded by law that is itself of our own making. We need to think much more about how dialogue and negotiation—the face-to-face relation—are not just possible but *imperative* to any functioning commons, even to one encompassing the planet, in cyberspace.

Notes

The first epigraph is from Slavoj Žižek (speech, Occupy Wall Street after a march near Washington Square Park in New York City, Oct. 9, 2011). A video of the speech was online at http://www.youtube.com/watch?v=Xjcm2djpimQ&feature=player_embedded.

The second epigraph is from Elinor Ostrom, "Analyzing Collective Action," supplement, *Agricultural Economics* 41, no. S1 (November 2010): 156.

1. Tibor R. Machan, "Introduction: The Commons," in *The Commons: Its Tragedies and Other Follies*, ed. Tibor R. Machan (Stanford, Calif.: Hoover Institution, 2001), xxi.

2. For an example of how concerns of the environmental movement merge with commons research, see Susan J. Buck, *The Global Commons: An Introduction* (Washington, D.C.: Island, 1998).

3. Garrett Hardin, "The Tragedy of the Commons," *Science* 162, no. 3859 (December 13, 1968): 1244.

4. Ibid., 1245.

5. Ibid., 1244.

6. Ibid., 1247. Analysts of Hardin's essay align him with various politics; recently, Rob Nixon has shown how his "antipastoral logic" often resonates with neoliberalism's "hostility to shared goods, a hostility inseparable from the neoliberal drive for resource appropiation and for dismantling regulatory oversight, whether by international, nation-state, or local bodies." However, as Nixon does note, this is precisely opposite to Hardin's objective, which was a call for more (possibly governmental) oversight of commons areas; his primary concern was population control, and, alarmingly, he called for a repeal of the UN Universal Declaration of Human Rights, asserting that the size of families should be regulated by the state. See Nixon, "Neoliberalism, Genre, and 'The Tragedy of the Commons,'" *PMLA* 127, no. 3 (May 2012): 597.

7. The Royal Swedish Academy of Sciences, "The Prize in Economic Sciences 2009," press release, October 12, 2009, http://www.nobelprize.org/nobel_prizes/economics/laureates/2009/press.pdf.

8. "The term 'common-pool resource' refers to a natural or man-made resource system that is sufficiently large as to make it costly (but not impossible) to exclude potential beneficiaries from obtaining benefits from its use." Examples include ocean fisheries and groundwater resources. CPRs come in two strata: the *resource system* associated with *stock* ("groundwater basins, grazing areas, . . . parking garages," etc.) and *resource units* (RU) produced by the system associated with *flow* ("the acre-feet or cubic meters of water withdrawn from a groundwater basin or an irrigation canal, the tons of fodder consumed by animals from a grazing area, . . . the [number of] parking spaces filled," etc.). Each stratum is dependent on the other. With renewable resources, one factors in a replenishment rate: "as long as the average rate of withdrawal [i.e., "appropriation"] does not exceed the average rate of replenishment, a renewable resource is sustained over time. CPR access can be limited to a single individual or firm or to multiple individuals or teams of individuals who use the resource system at the same time." Appropriators may themselves "consume the resource units," may "immediately transfer ownership of resource units to others," or may "use

resource units as inputs into production processes." For instance, fishermen can use an RU in the process of making something else (such as irrigating a field) or sell it directly, thereby transferring ownership (such as selling fish at market). See Elinor Ostrom, *Governing the Commons: The Evolution of Institutions for Collective Action* (Cambridge, Eng.: Cambridge University Press, 1990), 30–31.

9. Ibid., 31.

10. Ibid., 33.

11. For one example of the many Declarations of Interdependence, see Interdependence Movement, "Declaration of Interdependence," http://www.interdependencemovement.org/declaration_form.php. A comfy and undertheorized sense of the commons as moral ground and ethical position permeates Jay Walljasper's *All That We Share: How to Save the Economy, the Environment, the Internet, Democracy, Our Communities, and Everything Else That Belongs to All of Us* (New York: New, 2010), which is linked to the "On the Commons" commons movement strategy center website at http://www.onthecommons.org/all-that-we-share.

12. I would put Appiah's theory of cosmopolitanism in the first camp; see Kwame Anthony Appiah, *Cosmopolitanism: Ethics in a World of Strangers* (New York: W. W. Norton, 2006). Spivak's view would be a part of the second; it is more muscular, recognizing the role that economic disparity and cultural difference will play in any intercultural contact, but her Derridean assumptions lead her to valorize difference as such and can construct only an abstract planetary commons made and unmade in a perpetual cycle of unmasking, undoing, and rearticulation. See Gayatri Chakravorty Spivak, *Death of a Discipline* (New York: Columbia University Press, 2003).

13. "Yet by now," Nixon notes, "most sociobiologists accommodate a broader vision of species self-perpetuation, one that acknowledges how altruism—forms of apparent selflessness—may be genetically beneficial, enhancing the prospects of collective survival. Hardin's genetic-generic method fails to acknowledge the evolutionary role that the paradox of selfish selflessness may play." See Nixon, "Neoliberalism," 594.

14. Elinor Ostrom, Roy Gardner, and James Walker, *Rules, Games, and Common-Pool Resources* (Ann Arbor: University of Michigan Press, 1994), 329.

15. Ibid., 328.

16. Ostrom, *Governing the Commons*, 44.

17. Amy R. Poteete, Marco A. Janssen, and Elinor Ostrom, *Working Together: Collective Action, the Commons, and Multiple Methods in Practice* (Princeton, N.J.: Princeton University Press, 2010), 236–38. The authors here cite previous research by Ostrom as well as by Robert L. Axtell, including "The Emergence and Evolution of Institutions of Self-Governance on the Commons" (working paper, Department of Computational Social Science, George Mason University, Fairfax, Va., 2013).

18. Ostrom, Gardner, and Walker, *Rules, Games, and Common-Pool Resources*, 171, 193.

19. Ibid., 145.

20. Ibid., 327–28.

21. "Digimodernism" is Alan Kirby's term for the new digital era. See his essay in this volume, as well as Kirby, *Digimodernism: How New Technologies*

Dismantle the Postmodern and Reconfigure Our Culture (New York: Continuum, 2009).

22. I am closely paraphrasing Hess and Ostrom here. See Charlotte Hess and Elinor Ostrom, "Introduction: An Overview of the Knowledge Commons," in *Understanding Knowledge as a Commons*, ed. Charlotte Hess and Elinor Ostrom (Cambridge, Mass.: MIT Press, 2007), 7.

23. See Poteete, Janssen, and Ostrom, *Working Together*, 243–45.

24. "Since our future is dependent on our joint use of the global commons [defined as ecological environments], we either must face up to the issues discussed in this volume [concerning use of land, water, and atmosphere] or find ourselves destroyed by our own indifference to the major set of problems facing us as we near the twenty-first century" (Elinor Ostrom, foreword to *The Global Commons*, by Buck, xiv).

25. Ostrom herself notes that her studies have implications specifically for public policy. See Ostrom, Gardner, and Walker, *Rules, Games, and Common Pool Resources*, 193–94.

26. Julian Dibble, "A Rape in Cyberspace: How an Evil Clown, a Haitian Trickster Spirit, Two Wizards, and a Cast of Dozens Turned a Database into a Society," *Village Voice* (December 23, 1993), http://www.villagevoice.com/2005-10-18/specials/a-rape-in-cyberspace/full/.

27. At the time of this writing, LambdaMoo was still operating; see its gateway at http://www.cc.gatech.edu/classes/cs8113e_99_winter/lambda.html.

28. Dibble, "A Rape in Cyberspace."

29. Ibid.

30. Ibid.

31. Ibid.

32. In contrast, see Clay Shirky's hyperbolic utopianism concerning digital commons, open source, and horizontal organization in *Cognitive Surplus: How Technology Makes Consumers into Collaborators* (New York: Penguin, 2010) or Steven Johnson's pean to interconnectivity in *Future Perfect: The Case for Progress in a Networked Age* (New York: Riverhead, 2012).

33. See, for example, James Boyle, *The Public Domain: Enclosing the Commons of the Mind* (New Haven, Conn.: Yale University Press, 2008); David Bollier, *Viral Spiral: How the Commoners Built a Digital Republic of Their Own* (New York: New, 2008); Lawrence Lessig, *The Future of Ideas: The Fate of the Commons in a Connected World* (New York: Random House, 2001); Clay Shirky, *Cognitive Surplus*; Diana Saco, *Cybering Democracy: Public Space and the Internet* (Minneapolis: University of Minnesota Press, 2002); Carolyn Guertin, *Digital Prohibition: Piracy and Authorship in New Media Art* (London: Continuum, 2011); and Manuel Castells, *The Rise of the Network Society*, Vol. 1, *The Information Age: Economy, Society, and Culture* (Oxford: Blackwell, 1996).

34. For a discussion of GNU and FOSS in relation to commons research, see Sam Williams, *Free as in Freedom: Richard Stallman's Crusade for Free Software* (Sebastopol, Calif.: O'Reilly, 2002); Eric S. Raymond, *The Cathedral & the Bazaar: Musings on Linux and Open Source by an Accidental Revolutionary* (Sebastopol, Calif.: O'Reilly, 1999); and Charles M. Schweik, "Free/Open-Source Software as a Framework for Establishing Commons in Science," in *Understanding Knowledge as a Commons: From Theory to Practice*, ed. Charlotte Hess and

Elinor Ostrom (Cambridge, Mass.: MIT Press, 2007), 277–310. Net neutrality is the principle that states that Internet providers, governments, or corporations cannot prevent consumer access to networks that are part of the Internet, which access also includes manipulating down-access speeds to competitors; see Marlene H. Dortch, "Federal Communications Commission," FCC 05–151, September 25, 2005, http://hraunfoss.fcc.gov/edocs_public/attachmatch/FCC-05–151A1.pdf. For a key statement about the challenges to intellectual property law posed by Internet and digital culture, see the National Research Council's report *The Digital Dilemma: Intellectual Property in the Information Age* (Washington, D.C.: National Academy, 2000).

35. Douglas S. Noonan, "Internet Decentralization, Feedback, and Self-Organization," in *Managing the Commons*, ed. John A. Baden and Douglas S. Noonan, 2nd ed. (Bloomington: Indiana University Press, 1998), 189.

36. In economics, a public good is defined as a good available to all ("nonexcludable") and one in which one person's use does not subtract from another's use ("nonrivalrous"). For the classic statement on public goods, see Paul A. Samuelson, "The Pure Theory of Public Expenditure," *Review of Economics and Statistics* 36, no. 4 (1954): 387–89. A public good is therefore distinguished from common pool resources, where subtractability or rivalry plays a major role in the viability of the resource (one person's use has the potential to subtract from another's use). Charlotte Hess and Elinor Ostrom provide a useful short discussion of the difference between public goods, private goods, and CPRs in "Introduction: An Overview of the Knowledge Commons," especially on pages 7–10.

37. See, for example, Steven Weber's discussion of open source and/as the commons, in *The Success of Open Source* (Cambridge, Mass.: Harvard University Press, 2004), particularly his summary on pages 243–48. Justyna Hofmokl contends that Internet goods do not fall into the common pool category at all; see "The Internet Commons: Towards an Eclectic Theoretical Framework," *International Journal of the Commons* 4, no. 1 (2010): 226–50. Noonan posits a criterion of "rivalrous consumption" important to studies claiming that digital spaces contradict Hardin's original "tragedy of the commons" scenario—not, as Ostrom maintains, because users can find ways to negotiate resource use but because the goods that electronic sites make available are (1) nonmaterial and (2) cannot be depleted (downloading a pdf from a website does not reduce the number of pdfs available later to others); see "Internet Decentralization, Feedback, and Self-Organization." However, Karthik Jayaraman argues that it is not participation in commons based peer production (CBPP) but *lack* of participation in it that has more impact on a CBPP project's success ("Tragedy of the Commons in the Production of Digital Artifacts," *International Journal of Innovation, Management and Technology* 3, no. 5 [2012]: 626).

38. Dan Hunter, "Cyberspace as Place and the Tragedy of the Digital Anticommons," *California Law Review* 91, no. 2 (2003): 499, 444.

39. Boyle gets the term from Michael A. Heller and Rebecca S. Eisenberg, "Can Patents Deter Innovation? The Anticommons in Biomedical Research," *Science* 280, no. 5364 (1998): 698–701.

40. James Boyle, "The Second Enclosure Movement and the Construction of the Public Domain," *Law and Contemporary Problems* 66, no. 33 (Winter/Spring 2003): 37.

41. Dan Hunter notes that "the anticommons effect occurs when multiple parties [though not everyone using a resource] can prevent others from using a given resource so that no one has an effective right of use." He correlates the digital anticommons to the situation in Japan following the 1995 Kobe earthquake, in which rebuilding was stymied because of "a 'world class' tangle of property" rights claims in the area that led to an "anticommons" situation ("Cyberspace as Place," 502, 510, 513). Hanoch Dagan and Michael A. Heller define a liberal commons in "The Liberal Commons," *Yale Law Journal* 110, no. 4 (2001): 553. Michael A. Heller's theory is outlined fully in *The Gridlock Economy: How Too Much Ownership Wrecks Markets, Stops Innovation, and Costs Lives* (New York: Basic Books, 2008).

42. Noonan, "Internet Decentralization, Feedback, and Self-Organization," 189. Noonan also responds to George Gilder's warning in "Feasting on the Giant Peach" (*Forbes ASAP*, August 26, 1996) about the tragedy of the Internet commons in relation to the problem of spam (which would be akin to pollution of the CPR) and points out that in order to maintain order online, we probably will see the creation of "privatized, proprietary, secure intranets, enmeshed in a broader public Internet framework" (192).

43. Gian Maria Greco and Luciano Floridi, "The Tragedy of the Digital Commons," *Ethics and Information Technology* 6 (2004): 76 (emphasis in original), 78, 74.

44. Boyle, "Second Enclosure Movement," 44 (emphasis in original), 45.

45. Ibid., 49.

46. Joseph Michael Reagle Jr., *Good Faith Collaboration: The Culture of Wikipedia* (Cambridge, Mass.: MIT Press, 2010), 1.

47. Reagle, *Good Faith Collaboration*, 12, 53ff.

48. There is no space here to analyze how Hobbes's own theory has been oversimplified in recent discussions to make it seem the über-neoliberal theory of state-managed, pro-capital force—something a bit astray from Hobbes's notion of the Leviathan as commonwealth, created when every man makes an agreement with every other man to give the right to govern.

49. See Michael Hardt and Antonio Negri, *Commonwealth* (Cambridge, Mass.: Belknap Press of Harvard University Press, 2009).

50. Michael Hardt, "For Love or Money," *Cultural Anthropology* 26, no. 4 (2011): 676.

51. Hardt and Negri's appropriation and secularization of much of Christian theological thought is consistent with neo-Marxism's recent moves in that direction. See, for instance Alain Badiou's celebration of universalism and the immanent event in *St. Paul: The Foundation of Universalism*, trans. Ray Brassier (Stanford, Calif.: Stanford University Press, 2003); or Slavoj Žižek, *The Fragile Absolute: or, Why Is the Christian Legacy Worth Fighting For?* (New York: Verso, 2009).

52. Hardt and Negri, *Commonwealth*, 180.

53. Ibid., 181, 182.

54. For Deleuze and Guattari, the rhizome also produces the unconscious; exceeds unity; replaces transcendence with immanance; rejects dualism; is neither One (a totality) nor multiple in the sense of aggregative, but rather is dimensional motion; is not subject to social authority. It has no "general" or hierarchical

structure and is linked to micropolitics, and it is a machinic assemblage of desire. For a presentation of these rhizomatic traits, see Gilles Deleuze and Félix Guattari, *A Thousand Plateaus: Capitalism and Schizophrenia*, trans. Brian Massumi (Minneapolis: University of Minnesota Press, 1987).

55. Hardt and Negri, *Commonwealth*, 195.

56. Ibid., 195–96. One hears echoes here of Boyle's claim that the digital commons will itself alter user subjectivity. There is some neuroscience supporting this claim: see, for example, work on neuroplasticity and emerging work on the relation between playing video games and altered brain patterns.

57. Joss Hands's excellent analysis in *@ Is for Activism* of H&N's "commons multitude" identifies many of the same questions I raise here and below. Hands accounts for and locates H&N's heralded "new social institutions" in the arena of dematerialized and somewhat autonomous labor that is situated in the bodies of laborers themselves (thinking and feeling work in a new information economy) brought about by the growth of cognitive and affective work related to media expansion (170).

58. In her excellent discussion of Negri's notion of "the common" in relation to the "inoperative community" of Jean-Luc Nancy, Helen Morgan Parmett notes that "the common" was formulated through the Italian "Autonomia" movement and emerged in the 1970s as a way to theorize the collective as living labor. Parmett distinguishes the relevant theorists on the basis of "their differing ontological theories of being as alterity (Nancy) and being as immanent totality (Negri)." See Helen Morgan Parmett, "Community/Common: Jean-Luc Nancy and Antonio Negri on Collective Potentialities," *Communication, Culture & Critique* 5 (June 2012): 174, 175.

59. During a joint interview that also included Hardt, Berlant notes that "Unlike Michael, who is trying to think love as a better concept for suturing or inducing the social, I'm trying to think about what the affects of belonging are without attaching them to one or another emotional vernacular [such as love]. . . . We're thinking of the affective phenomenology of these conditions, not how to do it." See Heather Davis and Paige Sarlin, "'On the Risk of a New Relationality': An Interview with Lauren Berlant and Michael Hardt," *Reviews in Cultural Theory* (2008): 9.

60. On this topic, see Lauren Berlant, "A Properly Political Concept of Love: Three Approaches in Ten Pages," *Cultural Anthropology* 26, no. 4 (2011): 683–91.

61. Lauren Berlant, "Intuitionists: History and the Affective Event," *American Literary History* 20, no. 4 (2008): 845–46 (emphasis in original). For a different treatment but support of this claim to shared affect, see Teresa Brennan, *The Transmission of Affect* (Ithaca, N.Y.: Cornell University Press, 2004); and Nigel Thrift, *Non-Representational Theory: Space, Politics, Affect* (London: Routledge, 2007). Thrift's work is particularly important to Berlant's theories of the affective present.

62. Quoted in Davis and Sarlin, "'On the Risk,'" 12.

63. Lauren Berlant, *Cruel Optimism* (Durham, N.C.: Duke University Press, 2011), 64.

64. Ibid., 5, 199.

65. Berlant acknowledges her debt to queer theory's rethinking of time and reciprocity within a new phenomenology and particularly her use of Michael D. Snediker's *Queer Optimism: Lyric Personhood and Other Felicitous Persuasions*

(Minneapolis: University of Minnesota Press, 2008) and Sara Ahmed's *Queer Phenomenology: Orientations, Objects, Others* (Durham, N.C.: Duke University Press, 2006).

66. Berlant takes this term from Michael Taussig, *The Nervous System* (New York: Routledge, 1992).

67. Again, the echoes of Deleuze and Guattari, Bergson, and Foucault are clear here, as becoming and prehended event are elevated over being and analysis. As Berlant writes, "Life in the impasse turns from threat to aim. To enter experience without eventilizing it will mean knowing something is afoot without forcing prediction into being, as though it would be possible to place one's affect on a kind of confident cruise control. The literary figures grow something like that: a historically capacious, neointuitive sense of becoming-present" (*Cruel Optimism*, 70–71).

68. Berlant, "A Properly Political Concept of Love," 687.

69. Richard Grusin, *Premediation: Affect and Mediality after 9/11* (London: Palgrave Macmillan, 2010), 103–4.

70. Ibid., 3. Grusin notes that he adopts the concept of "logic" from "late 1980s American cultural studies . . . It is meant to hold on to the Foucauldian sense that there are rhetorical and conceptual continuities across different discursive and biopolitical formations" (5). He prefers affect theory to trauma theory, which he believes is more "reli[ant] upon various psychoanalytical methodologies" (7).

71. Ibid., 154, 42, 43.

72. Ibid., 48, 55. Grusin is basing his analysis on that of Niklas Luhmann from *The Reality of the Mass Media*, trans. Kathleen Cross (Stanford, Calif.: Stanford University Press, 2000).

73. Grusin, 55.

74. Ibid., 46.

75. Ibid., 61, 91, 94.

76. In addition to the overwhelming impact of Luhmann's systems theories, Immanuel Wallerstein's work on mini-systems, world empires, and world economies has grown in influence. See Immanuel Wallerstein, *The Essential Wallerstein* (New York: New, 2000); and David Palumbo-Liu, Bruce W. Robbins, and Nirvana Tanoukhi, eds., *Immanuel Wallerstein and the Problem of the World: System, Scale, Culture* (Durham, N.C.: Duke University Press, 2011).

77. Eddie Izzard, *Stripped, Live*, directed by Sarah Townsend (UK: Universal, November 23, 2009), DVD.

78. See Steven Shaviro's *Connected, or What It Means to Live in the Network Society* (Minneapolis: University of Minnesota Press, 2003), in which he examines network society as it has been prefigured by science fiction.

79. See Pierre Macherey, *Hegel or Spinoza*, trans. Susan M. Ruddick (Minneapolis: University of Minnesota Press, 2011).

80. See Raoul Eshelman, *Performatism, or the End of Postmodernism* (Aurora, Colo.: Davies Group, 2008).

81. See Spivak, *Death of a Discipline*.

82. Mark Poster, "Global Media Culture," *New Literary History* 39, no. 3 (2008): 698, 689.

83. It is important to note that Habermas himself moved to a more open frame for the commons as he considered the problem of the contemporary nation-state—

namely, the post–Cold War consolidation of the European Union and what it might mean for new political configurations. On the ground, and in the twenty-first century, the public sphere is undergoing transformations Habermas cannot yet articulate but that seem tied to environmental thinking. See Jürgen Habermas, *The Postnational Constellation: Political Essays*, trans. and ed. Max Pensky (Cambridge, Mass.: MIT Press, 2001).

84. For a position both outlining and resisting such Singularity thinking, see Jaron Lanier, *You Are Not a Gadget: A Manifesto* (New York: Alfred A. Knopf, 2010); for a critique of social media networks, see Geert Lovink, *Networks without a Cause: A Critique of Social Media* (Cambridge, Eng.: Polity, 2011).

85. See the "membership" and "about" pages at http://www.hackreduce.org/.

86. Ostrom, "Analyzing Collective Action," 160.

87. Quoted in Eli Kintisch, *Hack the Planet: Science's Best Hope—or Worst Nightmare—for Averting Climate Catastrophe* (Hoboken, N.J.: Wiley, 2010), 234.

88. See Braidotti, *The Posthuman* (Cambridge, Eng.: Polity, 2013).

89. Hands writes, "To conceive the multitude and its production of the common as something other than a swarming aggregation of atoms, and as a political entity, requires the application of a theory of mediated rational communication" (*@ Is for Activism,* 172).

90. See Amy J. Elias, "The Dialogical Avant-Garde: Relational Aesthetics and Time Ecologies in *Only Revolutions* and *TOC*," *Contemporary Literature* 53, no. 4 (2012): 738–78.

The Possibility of Cyber-Placelessness

Digimodernism on a Planetary Platform

ALAN KIRBY

There are always problems attendant upon historicizing the present. First, descriptive terminology seemingly accurate at one historical moment is quickly outdated and replaced by newer, ostensibly more accurate characterizations of the time period, which in turn are often shown to be programmatic, exclusionary, partisan, or self-interested. Historical accounting is also a complex cumulative process: *post-factum* historicizations need to account not only for current and recently past events but also for the characterizations of events proposed when the events themselves were unfolding. And yet, if formed on the basis of the best and most complete information available, period descriptors can generate new perspectives on the past as well as stimulate new perspectives on, and spur innovation in, the present.

Both in my essay "The Death of Postmodernism and Beyond" and in my book *Digimodernism*, I utilized such a new descriptive term that attempted to historicize the present: "digimodernism."[1] In these texts I argued, first, that the overriding fact of our cultural time, and one with which all analyses of the contemporary must begin, is the digitization of the text. This digitizing trend, leading into multiple domains of reading and writing activity, is by now several decades old; it emerged in the mid-to-late 1980s with the creation and development of the Internet and accelerated as technologies associated with portable telephony have reached critical mass. Since then, text has been taking digital form everywhere and in ways all too familiar to us. Thus, nowadays the typewriter turns into the word processor; the private letter gives way to the e-mail and the scribbled note to the text message; the atlas is superseded by Google Maps and the road map by in-car satellite navigation; the personal diary becomes the online blog; the book or multivolume encyclopedia is displaced by Wikipedia; celluloid photographs and films are digitized, while genre movies morph into computer games; recording media such as the videotape and the vinyl record are superseded by digital formats, a process facilitated by online file-sharing platforms that sync with portable media devices such as the iPod; broadcast media abandon analog for digital transmission; and the death of print is said to be presaged with the unveiling of digital "e-book readers." The list could easily go on. This immense systemic shift or cluster of transformations, which doubtless date back to, or were first identified during, the immediate postwar period, have an intense speed and relentless momentum, perhaps making it too easy to overstate their long-term historical significance. To describe this cluster of shifts as "digimodernism" and the primary event or set of events of our cultural time may seem controversial since the word replaces the older and more accepted concept of "postmodernism" as period descriptor. On the one hand, adopting the new term appears to necessitate an overhaul or even jettisoning of assumptions about the period covered by the postmodern paradigm, which, as an account or explanation of the present, has held sway in some circles since the early 1970s. On the other hand, this identification of the cultural primacy of digitization may also seem self-evident, although its precise formulation may be more elusive.

My second argument has been that because these reorientations form a systemic pattern with certain paradigmatic traits affecting artistic form, content, production, reception, economics, and value, they should be seen *en bloc* as a new cultural dominant in the terms that Fredric Jameson adapted from Raymond Williams. Thus, the dominant in question requires its own descriptive label, "digimodernism," and should be read as displacing a postmodernism whose exhaustion, retreat, or neutralized diffusion into the sociocultural milieu has become evident.

This does not simply mean that, as one critic wrote recently, the postmodern has given way to the Internet.[2] What I call "digimodernism" both encompasses the artistic-creative and connects and intermeshes it with the discursive-critical, consequently incorporating and remediating the postmodern. It includes Facebook and Twitter as well as popular movies such as *300* (Snyder, 2007) and *Avatar* (Cameron, 2009) and auteur films such as *The Boss of It All* (von Trier, 2006), *Ten* (Kiarostami, 2002), and *Life in a Day* (Macdonald, 2011). Digimodernism foregrounds certain highly sophisticated contemporary narrative video games such as *Metal Gear Solid 4* (2008), but it equally speaks to a shift to semi-narrativized, "low" genres in television like "reality TV" or docusoap formats, and popular, highly narrativized, and long-running series such as *The Office* (BBC, 2001–03), *Peep Show* (Channel 4, 2003–present), and *Lost* (ABC, 2004–10). If digimodernist podcasting revitalizes radio, long assumed to be in terminal decline, digimodernist textuality also redefines such forms as the short story or the novel—as, for example, with Jennifer Egan's "Black Box" (2012) or *A Visit from the Goon Squad* (2010), the latter of which contains a PowerPoint presentation as part of its narrative, or with Chris Ware's *Building Stories* (2012), an unbound graphic novel in a box that materializes hypertext format. As an expansive set of aesthetic tendencies characterized predominantly by their location within digitally based performance, digimodernism extends to artistic undertakings such as Antony Gormley's *One & Other*, in which 2,400 individuals successively performed for one hour each over 100 days on the fourth plinth in Trafalgar Square in London in summer 2009. Gormley's project, streamed online to a global audience that commented on the performances on Twitter, was attacked by pseudonymous contributors to the London *Guardian*'s cultural blog who were seemingly unaware that the textual principles applied by Gormley inhered equally in the format of the message board and online forum used by these critics: evanescence, "ongoingness" or openness, haphazardness and improvisationality, and multiple and variegated authorship.[3] These in fact are among the principal features of the digimodernist text. Moreover, both the artistic event itself and the critical response it elicited in this case opened out toward a planetary cultural practice or discourse, a trend that is the focus of this essay.

Digimodernism and Its Peers

As a theory about the emergence of a new cultural dominant beyond postmodernism, "digimodernism" is a political reading of contemporary culture and art. Not intended to be programmatic, it does not dogmatically claim that the postmodern suddenly went extinct, though, like other recent interrogations of the postmodern paradigm, it maintains that a certain conceptual ground-clearing is now necessary. It has accorded with assertions elsewhere about the supersession of postmodernism, such as Andrew Hoberek's 2007 claim that "declarations of postmodernism's demise have become a critical commonplace."[4] Digimodernism, which begins with a revolution in the materiality of the text, differs in its intellectual emphasis from those "–isms" that concentrate primarily on the content of texts whose material form remains wholly or largely traditional and familiar. A digimodernist analysis highlights, for instance, the displacement of theater as cinema's "other" by the video game, which increasingly supplies the archeological, mythological, or ludic aesthetic of genre movie-making; likewise, such an approach foregrounds the effects of the filmic intromission of the computerized between the directorial/teleological and the found/external of traditional cinema. But this interpretation also emphasizes how the postmodern is sedimented in digimodernist platforms such as Wikipedia. For digimodernism, as the form of the word suggests, the relationship of the socio-technological with the textual-cultural is neither causal nor contextual; it is symbiotic. Moreover, digimodernism's techno-textual aesthetics cannot be read as inevitably more rewarding or successful than are print or analog aesthetics, though a sense of approbation of the digital aesthetic is apparent in many historicizations of the cultural present.

The period of the rise of planetary digimodernism is therefore that of the retreat of First World postmodernism, and—due in no small part to the ambiguous nature of the latter—the relationships between the two are multiform and complex. An abundance of meanings has been invested since the 1970s in the term "postmodernism" to the degree that today it seems plausible to consider it under the aegis of Wittgenstein's notion of "family resemblances," that is, as a term whose many usages do not share any one common feature but are instead held together by "similarities, relationships, and a whole series of them at that."[5] The various meanings of the word "postmodernism" have always appeared to form "a complicated network of similarities overlapping and criss-crossing: sometimes overall similarities, sometimes similarities of detail" with no *Merkmal or* unifying element.[6] Said to signify that which was fundamentally plural and multiform, "postmodernism" as a concept embodies multiple and even contradictory instantiations in the aesthetic and cultural spheres. If we can distinguish many varieties of postmodernism from one another, we might also agree that different versions or manifestations of postmodernism might not share the same end date or even the same moment of superannuation, form of extinction, or rate of retreat or passing. Postmodernism thus might be said to experience many (and many kinds of) deaths, some of which cannot be described appropriately in terms of a biological image. The end of postmodernism, prefigured in the term's own proliferation of meaning to the point of near-evanescence, will be multitiered and will take place at different times in different contexts. This would explain why the notion of the "end" of postmodernism can seem straightforward to some and untimely to others, tediously old hat ("a critical commonplace") or nonsensically premature.

While there is no space here to explore or even to enumerate the many ways that postmodernism has withered as a cultural dominant since the turn of the twenty-first century, we can easily point to visible examples of its waning in the arts: the comfortable assimilation and therefore historical saturation of postmodernism in such conservative cultural spheres as the children's cartoon (Pixar, DreamWorks), the middlebrow novel (Jasper Fforde, etc.), and the Oscar-winning movie (*Shakespeare in Love* [Madden, 1998]); the loss of any sense of threat, subversion, or novelty from the work of a postmodern street artist like Banksy; and the relative decline of art forms associated with 1980s postmodernism such as music video, pop music-based subculture, and spectacular television. Such postmodern remnants contrast, for example, with newer participatory digital arts like vcasting or participatory cultural platforms such as Pinterest. Postmodernism may now seem facile and generically repetitive or nostalgic, even bordering at times upon *ennui*. However, hybrid postmodern-digimodernist texts are easily identified—movies such as *The Cabin in the Woods* (Goddard, 2012) or the Harry Potter series (2001–11), by which postmodern tropes are retooled through an encounter with digimodernism. If the term "postmodernism" seems in literary criticism and academic studies to have gone out of fashion or to have been reduced to a historical category akin to romanticism, the importance of this process should not be overstated. On a theoretical level, the historical passing of postmodernism may occur according to a conceptual absorption, dispersal, or recontextualization. In response to the counter-argument that the characteristics of digimodernism are encompassed by the rubric of postmodernism, it can be asserted that, at the very least, the digitization of the text is a vast and significant cluster of processes, so much so that its cultural consequences merit study and definition in their own right. Such study would provide the basis for a minimalist digimodernism.

As a theory attempting to name what follows from and develops out of postmodernism, digimodernism counts among its peers Raoul Eshelman's performatism, Nicolas Bourriaud's altermodern, Christian Moraru's cosmodernism, Gilles Lipovetsky's hypermodernity, and Robert Samuels's automodernity.[7] It distinguishes itself from these other characterizations through its foregrounding of the technological basis of contemporary cultural expressions. Digimodernism today is not defined as a fully developed aesthetic norm or arts movement, though it is associated with certain aesthetic patterns; it is primarily a theory of cultural practice. In this sense, it can compete with other current characterizations of the present or may complement them, as it does with Timotheus Vermeulen and Robin van den Akker's notion of "metamodernism." For instance, performatist and digimodernist readings of *Lost* or Yann Martel's *Life of Pi* (2001) might be combined to rewarding effect.

On the other hand, digimodernism needs to be set apart from theories of digital media to which it bears a superficial resemblance. For one thing, digimodernism traces the radical disruption of the very notion of "media," for it describes a moment at which much traditional media (such as print newspapers, books, analog recording, and film) are systemically demonetized.[8] More importantly, the manifestations of digimodernism belong as much to "old" media like cinema and radio as to "new" digital media and permit for the older forms a historicizing account of transformations and continuities. An example of such transformation might be the contrast between the postmodern tropes of the original, mechanical-analog *Star Wars* film trilogy (Lucas, Kershner, and Marquand, 1977–83) and the digitized and digimodernist traits of the later prequel trilogy (Lucas, 1999–2005). A digimodernist analysis of *Avatar* would focus on the film's earnest recuperation, via the technologies of digital motion capture or 3D cinema, of the devices of children's literature or mythology; in this example, digimodernism can be seen to approach the "digital revolution" from the perspective of cultural criticism, interrogating, for instance, how an entirely new technological basis of cultural production and dissemination is translated into textual forms and meanings.

Cyber-Placelessness

Digimodernism is thus understood as a newly dominant cultural paradigm based on the transformations and configurations associated with digitization, and its theorization might chime with a twenty-first-century planetary turn via the apparent placelessness opened up by the Internet and the technologies of portable telephony. At least since William Gibson's novel *Neuromancer* (1984), published almost thirty years ago and now central to both the science fiction and postmodern canons, computerization has been thought to give rise to an autonomous field called "cyberspace" that abolishes or transcends the location-specific or the geographically particular. In *Neuromancer,* cyberspace is evoked as a "consensual hallucination experienced daily by billions of legitimate operators, in every nation"; it is the protagonist's "distanceless home, his country, [a] transparent 3D chessboard extending to infinity," and a "nonspace."[9] Cyberspace might be understood to recuperate the materially sited within the computerized, and to anticipate the formation of contingent online communities and exchanges composed of and engaged in by individuals based anywhere in the "real world."

That the Internet permits a supranational, global, or radically delocalized space requires some immediate caveats, however. First, as a digitized location, cyberspace is not the same as the "nonplaces" in the "real world" theorized by Marc Augé, Melvin Webber, or Henri Lefebvre. Moreover, the Internet is not a universally accessible or occupied space: a study published in September 2012 by Tim Berners-Lee's World Wide Web Foundation suggests that only one in three of the world's population use it, the number falling below one in six in Africa.[10] While these proportions are presumably rising, even countries that represent highest use and access to cyberspace show, when compared to one another, marked disparities or variations in terms of both the amount of time people spend online and the scale or nature of their involvement in international, planetary discursive exchanges, and these strongly uneven usage statistics are doubtless connected to differences of users' gender, age, or social background.

Nevertheless, that the Internet and World Wide Web appear to permit a global or delocalized circulation of discourse remains a commonplace in digital humanities studies. The socio-historical starting point of this digitized possibility is an easily recognizable one: sitting with his or her laptop or iPhone in a departure lounge in Slovakia, a hypothetical academic can buy books to be delivered to his or her home in England or onto his or her portable e-book reader, consult scholarly journals published in Australia or Minnesota, read reviews written in Mexico or South Africa, submit a paper proposal to a university in Peru, e-mail an editor in India, argue on message boards with readers based in Greece or South Korea, and so on. Postmodernism set the stage for this. In the same year as *Neuromancer*, as well as Jameson's "Postmodernism, or, the Cultural Logic of Late Capitalism," David Lodge published *Small World*, a satirical portrait of late twentieth-century academia globalized through an international conference circuit itself enabled by the expansion of affordable air travel and improvements in communications. Lodge's internationalized academics also saw their nation-based critical perspectives transformed by 1960s theorists, some of whom, such as Roland Barthes and Hans Robert Jauss, appear lightly disguised in Lodge's novel. The work of some of these authors appeared to transcend the narrowness of traditional academic disciplines and boundaries, and, here already, the delocalization of discourse, specifically academic discourse, was inextricable from contemporary tendencies in cultural theory. My hypothetical twenty-first-century academic is stationary, not in transit; he or she moves through a digitized, not a stratospheric, plane of worldwide discursive exchanges. Yet with his or her PowerPoint lectures, seminar blogs, and Skype supervisions, this academic performs at this one sitting web-based activities that represent only a fraction of the distance-annihilating, textual digitization of his or her working life, which itself assumes the internationalism of perspective that Lodge's academics experienced.

Today, it might seem as if the Internet, the World Wide Web, and portable telephony permit a worldwide diffusion of literary or cultural discourse that triumphs over a previous straitened sitedness, breaking open geographical privilege, destabilizing hierarchies based on location, and promising a utopian equality and freedom within the digital sphere. The Internet and the World Wide Web do provide a structural platform that moves us toward the planetary in the form of cyberspatiality, a digitized placelessness or delocalization. However, it looks to me as though this unremitting and inescapable movement toward cyberspatiality is constantly being constrained by or negotiated in terms of an awkward reintegration of a "real world" sitedness. The local or geographically particular reemerges persistently, and it would appear at this presumably early stage in the history of cyberspace, unavoidably, to skew and compromise the digital drive toward delocalization. Berners-Lee defined the Internet in 2012 as "a global conversation," but he also cautioned against the undermining and distortion of its discursive scope by socioeconomically determined inequalities of access and governmental restrictions such as the notorious "great firewall of China." His advocacy of a "web for all" takes for granted, apparently, the political, social, economic, and personal benefits of an ever wider and more closely knit cyberspatiality.[11]

Gayatri Chakravorty Spivak's account of planetarity, on the other hand, sets the concept over and against both economic globalization and computerization. Defining globalization as the financialization of the world by which the latter becomes exploitable and controlled in order to yield capitalist profits, she states emphatically that "the globe is on our computers. No one lives there. It allows us to think that we can aim to control it. The planet is in the species of alterity, belonging to another system; and yet we inhabit it, on loan."[12] Thus, planetarity involves "a more sensitive and attuned way of understanding the materiality of the world and our collective place and responsibility as humans within it."[13] Spivak asserts that we are called to be not global agents but planetary subjects. This is in the spirit of other critics' calls for a planetary ethos—Ursula Heise, for example, calls not for globalism but for an "eco-cosmopolitanism."[14] If planetarity is indeed not "on our computers" and also lies, as Christian Moraru argues, beyond the postmodern, then the status of digimodernism might seem problematic as a theory of what follows the postmodern, for it is focused on the cultural consequences of clusters of flows across computers.

One example might clarify the tension between the local and the planetary that characterizes digimodernism. Digimodernist cinema can exist because of delocalizing, globalizing digital technologies; yet it chooses repeatedly topics concerning, and ideologically moves toward, a planetary environmentalist ethos as the other, planetary side of delocalization. In *Avatar*, for instance, digital motion capture as a production process becomes identical with the narrative's reach toward cross-cultural empathy and works to ground its environmentalist politics. Systemically, digitization appears primarily, though not monolithically, to achieve a triumph over or alienation from the geographically local, whether localism is embodied in a village, city, nation, or social grouping based on race, religion, lifestyle, or class. Favoring the mythopoeic, often infantilized, "other" of video games, American popular digimodernist cinema slides quickly over the details of the proximately territorial toward what may appear at different times a space vastly expanded and unique to itself or a space voided of content. In parallel to this turn in digimodernist cinema, a digimodernist Internet—via, for example, Web 2.0 formats, which were embryonic at the turn of the twenty-first century, when Spivak was writing—foregrounds the body of and the scope for worldwide discursive exchanges that break out again from the geographically proximate. In both cases, digimodernism appears as the *possibility* of a planetary cultural practice, its potential prompt, mediator, and platform: its impulse toward either a "global" or "planetary" scale is relentless but ambiguous both structurally and ideologically.

Such a practice occurs, of course, specifically within a digitized platform. Just as *Avatar*'s Occidental bias is obliterated at the level of theme but reinserted at another narrative or structural level, so the geographically proximate is not annihilated by digitization but is instead re-placed. Therefore, a spiral obtains: through digitization, the local is overcome or recedes; the planetary scale emerges "in the species of alterity," that is, as other to us, a space we cannot enter, a "nonspace." Yet "we inhabit it" as a "distanceless home." In consequence of this, we reintroduce our locality within it, reconfigured. At last, this reintegrated locality is supplanted or recedes anew, and so the spiral keeps turning. It is possible thus to regard cyberspace (figured, for instance, in the textual "place" of Peter Jackson's 2001–2003 *Lord of the Rings* film trilogy) simultaneously as a universe closed in on itself, as a larger locality overwhelmingly determined by hegemonic (cultural, economic, political, social) power flows from the "real world," as a nowhere, and as an emblem of a Spivakian planetarity belonging to us collectively and placing responsibility on all. Whether in the guise of a vaster Occident, as a seemingly universal state, as an eco-cosmopolitan home, or as an autonomous field, the specter of digimodernist textual place(lessness) glimpsed at different points within a spiral is unceasingly awakened by the technology that permits it. Two case studies will seek to unpack this process.

Digimodernism and the Bookstore

Founded in 1995, Amazon.com is almost the same age as the World Wide Web itself and perhaps its most enduring commercial success story. Amazon emblemizes the influence and effects of Web HTTP protocol, browsers, and hyperlinking on the distribution of literary texts and other art forms. The obvious point to make would be that Amazon enacts the dematerialization and hence the delocalization of the bookshop. An individual interested in purchasing a novel in the 1980s would have probably needed to identify a specific store with a unique address found on a particular street, travel to it, and, once inside, locate the volume desired, transfer it to a cash desk, pay for it, and then take it home. The personal acquisition of books or their distribution from publisher to consumer therefore took place in terms of spatial otherness and specificity. Amazon delocalizes these processes into cyber-commerce: a twenty-first-century person Googles a website, types in the name of a desired book, traces it, and purchases it via a series of mouse clicks, data inputs, and changes of screen; the book is delivered to his or her residence a certain time later. Displacement in the physical world with its geographical specificity dissolves into the digital acts of scrolling up and down screens and manipulating the functionality of a website. Moreover, with this digitization of the text and transaction process, which also delocalizes the consumer, comes an equivalent and identical shift on the part of the distributor: bricks-and-mortar bookstores have a limited capacity of titles given inherent restrictions in retail floor space, but Amazon's locations primarily in commercial districts permit it to hold a far wider range and to sell at lower prices.[15] Delocalization through digitization affects both purchaser and seller, and the consequence is a generalized placelessness: books can be ordered anywhere an individual possesses an Internet connection; the metropolis's historic advantage in giving consumers literary access is weakened as the city/country cultural divide is largely dissolved; titles published abroad are now easily obtained; books are held apparently nowhere and seem to emerge through one's letterbox as if by magic.

However, this seemingly hocus-pocus transferral of the object can be oversimplified or overstated, and not only because even in the 1980s there were ways of purchasing books remotely. Like a "real" bookstore such as Blackwell's, Amazon has a head office located in a particular city (Seattle); it abides by the business regulations of a certain locality; it too has an organizational hierarchy and a full-time staff; and it also owns warehouses found on specific geographical sites. As a bookseller, it is, then, indistinguishable from Blackwell's in everything except its eschewal of site-specific retail, that is, its elimination of the shop as a customer interface point. And, to a degree, it achieves this by a sleight of hand by which part of that interface, namely, the material translation of the book to the customer's home, passes from the aegis of the bookseller to that of the local postal service; it is outsourced but not digitized, and so it remains geographically determined. Accordingly, delocalization is partial and above all experiential for the consumer: the book purchase is lived as location-free because an "actually existing" store has constructed it as such and, perhaps as importantly, sold it as such.

If, for its customers, Amazon's delocalized presence is in practice limited and less than novel, its *planetizing* impulse strikes one as stronger on the supply side, where it looks like it gives access to the whole world's sum of commoditized texts in both bound and electronic forms. This appearance is marketed through the corporate logo, where an arrow pointing from the first to the fourth letter of Amazon is meant to suggest alphabetical and therefore expressive completeness. Amazon can therefore stand as both synecdoche of and precursor to the Internet as repository of the globe's textual output in digital form. At a historical point where the Internet's discursive scope still seems to be exponentially expanding, the sense that "the world" is present in one or another format online would appear *experientially* persuasive. It is true that by exploiting delocalization solely to achieve a more effective means of commodity exchange, Amazon leans toward globalization rather than planetarity; however, its activities suggest that Spivak's distinction between the global and the planetary should be seen as aspects of, or emphases within, one impulse rather than as adversaries in a zero-sum game.

Postmodernism has likely foreshadowed this element too. In a novel often used by critics to define the characteristics of postmodern metafiction, Italo Calvino's *If on a Winter's Night a Traveler* (1980), we see the bookstore positioned as synecdoche for local-global tension. The novel self-reflexively describes how a reader of it acquires the volume in a bookshop, and this extended passage highlights many of the recognized traits of postmodern globalization: the flattening of cultural hierarchies and the dissolution of cultural boundaries; the commercialization of art or the repositioning of the artist and text in terms of a system of commodity relations; the precession of intertextuality; and a contemporary textual overload culminating in the text's superseding the "real world" it might once have reflected:

> You went to the bookshop and bought the volume. Good for you.
>
> In the shop window you have promptly identified the cover with the title you were looking for. Following this visual trail, you have forced your way through the shop past the thick barricade of Books You Haven't Read, which were frowning at you from the tables and shelves, trying to cow you. But you know you must never allow

> yourself to be awed, that among them there extend for acres and acres the Books You Needn't Read, the Books Made For Purposes Other Than Reading . . . With a rapid maneuver you bypass them and move into the phalanxes of the Books You Mean To Read But There Are Others You Must Read First, . . . the Books You've Been Planning To Read For Ages, . . . the Books Read Long Ago Which It's Now Time To Reread and the Books You've Always Pretended To Have Read And Now It's Time To Sit Down And Really Read Them.[16]

In contrast to this kind of postmodern Library of Babel, digimodernism represents a shift of perspective from material overabundance of texts and phenomenological, experiential overload to dematerialization and isolation of texts contained in the digital literary purchase. On Amazon, the individual title is sought by name or author or keyword; browsing across a range of juxtaposed volumes in search of a serendipitous discovery seems precluded, though this too can be overstated. If in a city bookstore a dedicated customer with time reserves might inspect and come to master, over several days, its entire current stock according to the categorizations and display principles imposed on it, Amazon's vast holdings render this unfeasible. Yet Amazon compensates for this loss through digitization, which permits the customer to search those holdings more haphazardly, typing any keyword into a search engine designed to yield a range of possibilities both individualized and open-ended. Browsing an overwhelming quantity of materialized, site-specific, retail-classified titles becomes in Amazon's domain the idiosyncratic exploration of an immense mass of dematerialized, delocalized, consumer-classified titles. Calvino's comedic fantasy of personalized book display principles is achieved through digitization, though without industrial satire or readerly guilt. In short, browsing reemerges, reconfigured, in digital form.

Moreover, while functionally producing an experiential-digital apparent placelessness, Amazon's web pages for individual titles are poised to attempt textually the semi-rematerialization of its stock. The potential customer is informed about the book's number of pages, its language and dimensions, as though to compensate him or her for being unable to touch the physical thing prior to delivery; the site permits the consultation of the book's front and back covers, its contents or random pages within it in order to mimic the way a potential buyer might scrutinize or dip inside a possible purchase in an old-fashioned bookshop. As well as returning to the customer the physical qualities of the book and the results of its physical inspection, Amazon reproduces much of a book's industrial paratext, such as its endorsements and blurb, reinforcing the sense of a published, materialized object. Equally, the listing of other titles bought by customers who "purchased this item" restores the experience within the bookstore evoked by Calvino, whereby acquired volumes are necessarily juxtaposed and intermeshed with others. Whereas a visit to an urban Barnes & Noble involves tracing a single item from the total stock, Amazon appears to present a commercial context unique to each title and enhanced by its "sales ranking" system and its derivatives. In addition, the web pages provide for each paperback or hardcover a set of "customer reviews" or their possibility; again, they seem to restore to the lonely individual at his or her laptop or iPad the sense that he or she would immediately get in a store of his or her choosing, buying, and responding to books within a real, if unstable, community of readers.

These are, however, ambiguous outcomes of Amazon's platform and marketing strategies. Each of the features of Amazon's web pages can equally be regarded as a digitization, a dematerialization: the book's shape is not felt in how it rests in one's hands as one stands before a commercial bookshelf but spreads across a computer screen; other book lovers do not mill around one but are present only as the words they have previously typed on their keyboards. On the whole, Amazon's digitization and distribution of books would seem coterminous with dematerialization and delocalization and to unfold toward a textual-commercial globalization. Yet, simultaneously, Amazon is hamstrung by the necessity to negotiate with the physically, materially, and geographically specific: the company's approach to cyber-placelessness requires it to digitally recuperate and reconfigure that intractable specificity and can thereby function as a mediator of a planetary cultural practice *malgré lui*.

Digimodernism and the Reader(s)

Quantitatively, the default setting of metaliterary discourse on the Internet is represented by "bookchat," a term coined by Gore Vidal to describe an informal discussion of literature driven by readers outside the professional world of academia. As Vidal suggests in his essay "The Bookchat of Henry James," the term "bookchat" is not necessarily derogatory.[17] Instead, it refers to the articulation of a quest for readerly pleasure that can sometimes be rigorous but is nevertheless amateur, weakly theorized or non-theorized, and focused above all on recent publications and living authors. Thus, while it is often highly uneven in terms of quality, bookchat looks like one of the inescapable social consequences of a widespread interest in literature, with parallels in popular discussions of politics and sports figures. Today, it operates on three levels of diffusion: the age-old localized and interpersonal oral conversation; the more recent regional or national article or debate in generalist print media such as newspapers and magazines or in broadcast media such as television and radio programs; and the contemporary digitization of this discourse. The online dissemination of journalism is currently allied to the message board, blog, or web forum and permits a slippage from the first and second to the third of these levels. That it triumphs over local or national restrictedness to achieve a worldwide reach is easy to assume but also too simplistic. I have previously discussed the dialogic quality of one example—an online article and its comments thread, the London *Sunday Telegraph*'s "110 Best Books: The Perfect Library"—and will here go back briefly to this article's discursive geography.[18]

Illustrating the category of bookchat, "110 Best Books," for which no author was credited, belongs to a more recent subgenre often denigrated collectively as "lists" or the tendentious journalistic itemization and ranking of allegedly important texts. However, not all such lists are equal. In the absence of a developed consensus such as exists for, say, opera or pre-1914 art, the film critic polls carried out and reported every ten years by *Sight & Sound* magazine represent the medium's closest approach to a publicly established and recognized canon of its works. Likewise, the results of the intermittent writer polls in rock music magazines such as the *New Musical Express* and *Rolling Stone* seek, without the institutional weight of an academic department or institution, to shape into a canon what might otherwise be a near-chaos of artistic value. Here, the media take on the task of constructing a collection of texts of enduring worth in a social context that academia often is either unwilling or unable to address. Such "lists" therefore reflect shifts that have occurred since the 1970s and 1980s in the academy and are broadly related to postmodernism's negation of universal taste values as well as to its insistence upon pluralism and emancipatory destabilization of all universal axiological hierarchies.

Published in 2008, "110 Best Books: The Perfect Library" contradictorily but unself-consciously evinces both cultural-theoretical layers. The vestige of Enlightenment universalism implicit in its title is reflected in its choice of texts from an age of canonical solidity (the *Iliad* and the *Odyssey*, *Paradise Lost*, etc.), while it valorizes hitherto marginalized forms such as romance novels, children's literature, and science fiction in a manner that could be seen as broadly postmodern. As bookchat, it gives disproportionate weight to recently published texts, while it seeks to sustain the conceit of a "library" by including works of history, life writing, and philosophy. Spatially or geographically, it reflects the linguistic, national, social, and political particularity of its publishing house as refracted through its staff writers and their perceptions of the newspaper's print edition readership. Consequently, it favors texts originally written in English, by British or especially southern English authors, that instantiate a politically or socially conservative worldview. This skewing is visible across the eleven categories, which feature such narrowly focused and/or appreciated texts as Anthony Trollope's *The Barchester Chronicles* (1855–57); Jean Plaidy's *The Plantagenet Saga* (1976–82); Arthur Ransome's *Swallows and Amazons* (1930); Delia Smith's *How to Cook* (1998–99); Peter Mayle's account of middle-class English expatriation, *A Year in Provence* (1989); Lynne Truss's plea for grammatical rigor, *Eats, Shoots and Leaves* (2003); and the *Diaries* (1993, 2000, and 2002) of Alan Clark, a right-wing English politician. Though in the long run the list may have little if any inherent importance, its biases are interesting and may derive from a commercial imperative to confirm, and at most only tentatively extend, the tastes of the publication's audience. This closed cultural economy may be qualitatively just as evident in the *Sight & Sound* or rock music polls, or, indeed, in the *Los Angeles Times*'s list of "61 Essential Postmodern Reads," which featured predominantly American novels.[19]

Uploaded to the newspaper's website, digitized and opened to a potentially worldwide readership, "110 Best Books" received 679 below-the-line comments before the thread was closed two years later. The overwhelming majority of comments identify, with varying degrees of hostility, even ferocity, what the comment posters consider untenable omissions from the list or biases in its selection. A systemic or structural tension is apparent between the global scope of the discursive forum and the local specificities both of the *Sunday Telegraph*'s staff writers and many of its website "below the line comment" participants, since a large proportion of the latter, in seeking to address the perceived shortcomings of the former, finally only reproduce their biases within their own national, linguistic, or social particularity. A number of comments by presumably Italian posters decry the absence of Alessandro Manzoni's *The Betrothed* (1827, 1842), while an even greater number of seemingly American posters lament the exclusion of Ayn Rand. Romanian, Persian, and South American writers are proposed by contributors with names indicative of these areas; the Bible and the Quran are put forward in devout terms; successive posters call for multiple authors who all happen to be from the same country. Both above the line and in the comments thread, a universality hypothetically permitted by the digital online platform is repeatedly returned to a geopolitical or cultural narrowness in a spiral of critique and disavowal. The provision of a conceivably worldwide forum for discussion appears to permit only the often aggressive juxtaposition of local perspectives, which seek to displace each other competitively rather than to interconnect in an enriching manner. In the tradition of bookchat, general principles of selection or value are not seriously addressed, while the posters rarely acknowledge each other but instead react to the original list such that the thread devolves mostly into a succession of disconnected interjections in a discursive void.

The thread also throws into relief one of the more obvious local distortions of the worldwide impetus of the Internet, which, accordingly, overcomes geographical distances only to foreground linguistic groupings, such that contributors in Seattle, Belfast, or Adelaide can argue and interact discursively while individuals separated by ten miles and a language barrier cannot. Spatial difference is attenuated as a discursive limitation and overwritten by patterns of language usage; the Internet's geography is mapped less by regions, states, or continents than by formations of linguistic competence nevertheless anchored in those geopolitical units. To the distributions of native speakers are added patterns of diaspora, expatriation, and second-language acquisition, all three strongly and evidently marked by histories of imperialism and more recent economic and political inequalities or power relations. In this instance, an article apparently conceived not on a national but on a regional scale, through the perceptions and preferences of writers and readers from the southern English home counties, is turned by the Internet not into an international or planetary conversation but into a kind of Anglo-Globe-ish colloquy, grouping together a contingent and self-selecting subsection of individuals worldwide who happen, for whatever reason and on varying levels of ability or cultural access, to speak English. Similar discursive forums in other languages will reflect similar historically shaped *lingua franca* that necessarily cross borders but fall well short of planetary discourse. Patterns of linguistic competence may overlap and sidestep, without erasing, their economic or political determinants; the latter are identified in the "110 Best Books" readers' comments in expressions of resentment at a perceived English "prejudice" and "egocentricity."

The "110 Best Books" thread also raises the question whether such aggressive localism is inevitable in such a format, or whether, as the Internet's connective impulse continues to be felt, such localism may eventually weaken or be mitigated by planetary perspectives. There would seem to be some grounds for the latter: if affordable international travel of the sort enjoyed by Lodge's academics enhanced certain cultural exchanges, then cross-border online debate may over time lead to both original publications and to comment threads that are less narrow and more open. Three factors, however, would need to be taken into account.

The first is the anonymity or pseudonymity of the posters in these debates, particularly its capacity to strip their contributions of particularizing and contextualizing meaning. It is difficult to isolate and overcome the national or social specificity or bias of contributors who do not present themselves in such spatial terms—one can only guess that those posters calling for Rand or Manzoni are Americans or Italians evincing their distinctive national tendencies, since in fact they are not geographically constituted or self-identified on the thread. In this sort of forum, the planetary risks being swamped by departicularization.

Second, a successful planetary cultural or meta-literary discourse, either online or in the "real world," may need an expansion of foreign language acquisition, liable to disrupt, and moving beyond, the acceptance of English as the only language of economic globalization. By such acquisitions I do not, however, mean those by which the economically or politically marginalized appropriate or submit to the discourse of the hegemonic center. In the "110 Best Books" thread, global power flows are culturally evident, challenged, mimicked, and unresolved, even unresolvable, and this particular cyberspace locality dissolves into incoherently expanded locality or localities where communication fails and resentment festers. While no transcendental perspective is available, the discursive limitations and inadequacies of Anglo-Globe-ish debate are painfully conspicuous and linguistically underpinned.

Thirdly, the emergence of a truly worldwide discussion of literature would presumably require a sharing of terms of reference with regard to aesthetic value. Some kind of agreement or common framework of literary interest or achievement is, in all likelihood, necessary to debates if they are to have an influence in a significantly widespread online community. This is a far-reaching suggestion, and the trace of Enlightenment universalism evoked and then traduced so brazenly by "110 Best Books" becomes very apposite: if eighteenth-century notions of a "public sphere" constructing shared values have been undermined by twentieth-century critiques frequently identified and historicized as postmodern, then a truly planetary online dialogue among readers would seem to presuppose some sort of (perhaps digimodernist) return to, or movement toward, an aesthetic and philosophical commons. But how this might happen and whether its outcome would be for good or ill are another matter.

Conclusion

Digimodernism would seem to carry the gene or DNA of a symbolic signifying totality, by which it is refocused from a cultural dominant onto an immensely vast and problematically placeless textual singularity. A figure, or prefiguration, of this totality emerges with Amazon and the Internet as a whole, and also with the e-book reader: famously capacious and aggregating serial volumes, the device primarily resembles a multilocational, portable, and personal library rather than the individual book with which it is conventionally contrasted. In 2011, for the first time, the judges of Britain's Man Booker prize received the more than 100 novels submitted by e-book reader rather than through the post, in a historical shift unlikely to be reversed. As the *Sunday Telegraph* article and comments thread suggests, the question is whether this textual concentration tending toward singularity can find a unitary community of readers and writers liberated from sited particularity, and, if so, on what terms.

I have argued that a digimodernist tendency to delocalization or placelessness is simultaneously relentless, bound up in processes of dematerialization and departicularization, and negotiated awkwardly with an intractable "real world" and its power flows such as those shaped by economic globalization. As for what kind of mapping of semi-delocalized, public, and digital texts might emerge, it is partially but not wholly true to say that this is up for grabs. Berners-Lee's online "global conversation" awaits its content. In practice, neoliberal globalization tirelessly seeks to flood every discursive void. If, as I have submitted, digitization is the dominant cultural fact of our time, it cannot be seen in reductively negative or simplistically celebratory terms. Instead, we may need to consider that Spivak's planetary dream, which presupposes an attitude of sympathy, responsibility, and tact toward our shared home, the earth, and its variegated inhabitants, can be fulfilled through a digitization whose impulses, however, tend powerfully both to planetarity *and* its travesty. This is more than encouraging but less than optimistic.

Notes

1. See Alan Kirby, "The Death of Postmodernism and Beyond," *Philosophy Now* 58 (November/December 2006): 34–37; and Alan Kirby, *Digimodernism: How New Technologies Dismantle the Postmodern and Reconfigure Our Culture* (New York: Continuum, 2009).

2. See Hari Kunzru, "Postmodernism: From the Cutting Edge to the Museum," review of "Postmodernism" exhibition at the Victoria and Albert Museum, London, *The Guardian*, September 15, 2011, http://www.guardian.co.uk/artanddesign/2011/sep/15/postmodernism-cutting-edge-to-museum.

3. See online comments to Charlotte Higgins, "The Birth of Twitter Art," *The Guardian*, July 8, 2009, http://www.guardian.co.uk/commentisfree/2009/jul/08/fourth-plinthy-antony-gormley.

4. Andrew Hoberek, "Introduction: After Postmodernism," *Twentieth-Century Literature* 53, no. 3 (2007): 233.

5. Ludwig Wittgenstein, *Philosophical Investigations*, trans. G. E. M. Anscombe (Oxford: Blackwell, 1958), 32, 31.

6. Ibid., 32.

7. See Raoul Eshelman, *Performatism, or the End of Postmodernism* (Aurora, Colo.: Davies Group, 2008); Nicolas Bourriaud, *The Radicant*, trans. James Gussen and Lili Porten (New York: Lukas and Sternberg, 2009); Christian Moraru, *Cosmodernism: American Narrative, Late Globalization, and the New Cultural Imaginary* (Ann Arbor: University of Michigan Press, 2010); Gilles Lipovetsky, *Hypermodern Times*, trans. Andrew Brown (Cambridge, Eng.: Polity, 2005); and Robert Samuels, *New Media, Cultural Studies, and Critical Theory after Postmodernism: Automodernity from Žižek to Laclau* (New York: Palgrave Macmillan, 2009).

8. This paragraph was rewritten in January 2013 as, in France, Virgin Megastore, and, in Britain, Jessop's, HMV, and Blockbuster went into administration. Rendered uncompetitive by digitized textual production and distribution, each can be seen as a victim of digimodernist economics, though reductivism should be avoided when the hand of neoliberalism is also so apparent.

9. William Gibson, *Neuromancer* (Ace Books, 1984; New York: Ace Trade Paperback, 2000), 51, 52, 62. Page references are to the 2000 edition.

10. "Sweden Tops Tim Berners-Lee's Web Index," *BBC News Technology*, September 5, 2012, http://www.bbc.co.uk/news/technology-19478298.

11. Ibid.

12. Gayatri Chakravorty Spivak, *Death of a Discipline* (New York: Columbia University Press, 2003), 72.

13. See, among other similar comments, Katie Smith's short essay on Spivak, http://www.globalautonomy.ca/global1/glossary_pop.jsp?id=PR.0024.

14. See Ursula K. Heise, *Sense of Place and Sense of Planet: The Environmental Imagination of the Global* (Oxford: Oxford University Press, 2008), 205–10.

15. See Chris Anderson, *The Long Tail: Why the Future of Business Is Selling Less of More* (New York: Hyperion, 2006).

16. Italo Calvino, *If on a Winter's Night a Traveler*, trans. William Weaver (1980; repr., New York: Everyman's Library, 1993), 4–6.

17. Gore Vidal, "The Bookchat of Henry James," in *Armageddon? Essays 1983–1987* (London: André Deutsch, 1987), 157–67.

18. See Kirby, *Digimodernism*, 106–11. The article cited is "110 Best Books: The Perfect Library," *Sunday Telegraph*, April 6, 2008, http://www.telegraph.co.uk/culture/books/3672376/110-best-books-The-perfect-library.html.

19. "61 Essential Postmodern Reads: An Annotated List," *Los Angeles Times*, July 16, 2009, http://latimesblogs.latimes.com/jacketcopy/2009/07/the-mostly-complete-annotated-and-essential-postmodern-reading-list.html.

Archetypologies of the Human

Planetary Performatism, Cinematic Relationality, and Iñárritu's *Babel*

RAOUL ESHELMAN

When Gayatri Chakravorty Spivak coined the term "planetarity" in her 2003 essay *Death of a Discipline*, she described her project as an "experience of the impossible."[1] The planet—as opposed to the homogeneous "globe" of globalization—is in her understanding a catachrestic figure into which the most varied experiences of alterity are inscribed. Crucial to this figure is a specific understanding of the human as being "intended toward the other" and the stress on ethical (collective) responsibility for others and education.[2] Spivak, who is skeptical of both technocratic and environmental perspectives that would allow unified approaches to the planet, wants to pursue readings that "dis-figure" "transcendental figurations" like "mother, nation, god, nature," which for her represent an "inexhaustible taxonomy" of possibilities for critical interrogation.[3] In Spivak's planetarity, the human is no longer written off as an illusory effect of discourse but is reinstated as a privileged, originary figure that is "set" towards otherness. In this way, planetarity tacitly shifts the source of the deconstructive project from the textual to the human. The human, in turn, is conceived from the start as a split figure irreducible to any sort of unified experience, including a planetary one (hence the "impossibility" of her project). Planetarity itself, however, is not thinkable without the ethical urgency implied by the reappearance of the human as the basic unit of reckoning in a globalized world.

Spivak's half-anthropological, half-deconstructive approach to the planetary is a good indicator of the fundamental changes that were taking place in the humanities as well as in the arts around the turn of the century. Both academics and creative artists were reacting to the exhaustion of postmodern strategies that had no positive place for the human, which was always *there*, of course, but merely as a fall guy for an endlessly receding, ironic critique of its transcendental pretensions. However, Spivak's—and, of course, not only Spivak's—turn toward ethical anthropology opened up room for a whole slew of positive instantiations of the human that were previously not thinkable in a world where textuality was the main focus of attention and radical irony the principal mindset. Spivak, for example, restricts the human to a specifically ethical and intellectual mode. However, if we take her reasoning to its logical conclusion, many of the "transcendental figurations" reduced by deconstruction to mere effects of discourse must also be rethought as specifically human, universal dispositions. The most powerful of these are the dispositions toward love (the erotic), toward beauty (the aesthetic), and toward belief (the religious). The anthropological turn in critical thinking and the arts is thus more than just a belated correction of a small blind spot in the postmodern episteme. Rather, in its broadest implications, it shifts our entire mode of thinking from one of critical irony to one of anthropological affirmation. This kind of affirmation is perhaps no less "impossible" in global terms than Spivak's deconstructive project. However, it is infused by an entirely different logic than that which guides the still influential post-structuralist theories and still prevailing postmodern strategies. In short, it marks the beginning of a saliently different episteme whose contours are becoming ever sharper with the passage of time.

This is also the starting point of my own approach to planetary relations. Like Spivak, I am skeptical of both technocratic and ecological approaches suggesting that either technical innovations (electronic media) or a common theme (the environment) will transgress all linguistic and ideological boundaries and somehow bring us closer on a planetary scale. And, also like Spivak, I do not look to traditional humanism as a source of inspiration or value. It is not enough to simply postulate the return of love, beauty, and belief in a human guise. Rather, our goal must be to work out, as precisely as possible, the way the human is now being constructed in the arts on a global scale, and to examine how those constructs interact with our perceptions of political and social reality. In the last dozen years or so, based on analyses of numerous media, genres, and individual works, I have developed a theory called performatism, which sets forth the minimal requirements of this new, anthropologically founded episteme.[4] Because I have treated performatism at length elsewhere, I will not outline it in detail here. However, because the theory can be expressed in terms of two minimal propositions, it can be introduced quickly to those unfamiliar with it.

In the emerging episteme of performatism, to begin with, the human appears as a unified bio-social construct (it is neither entirely natural nor is it entirely an effect of discourse). Obviously, the details of the human or humans as construct or constructs vary from case to case. However, they all share one common trait: they have a primarily mimetic and intuitive, rather than a discursive and intellectual, motivation. "Mimesis" is used here in the way that it is understood by René Girard and Eric Gans: it assumes that foundational or primary forms of human interaction occur through imitation of others. Such imitation has both a violent and a reconciliatory potential and is prior to all discourse (you do not need language to imitate the actions of an other, who in mimetic terms is always a potential rival).[5]

One can make this clearer by contrasting the mimetic approach to Spivak's notion of the human. In her view, which follows the so-called ethical turn commencing in the late 1980s, the human subject is "intended toward the other," and this relation is mediated by a discourse that occludes access to that other as much as it enables it. Hence the emphasis on grappling with an alterity that paradoxically "contains us as much as it flings us away" and on "educat[ing] ourselves into this peculiar mindset."[6] Hence also the insistence in practical terms on reading, on "inviting the kind of language training that would disclose the irreducible hybridity of all languages," and on having graduate students learn the subaltern "languages of the Southern Hemisphere."[7] Spivak's "impossible" planetary project, in short, works by unceasingly interrogating the refractory interface with the other that is discourse. The immediate result is a "pluralization [that] may allow the imagining of a necessary yet impossible planetarity."[8] In the performatist episteme, by contrast, the human is conditioned not by the belatedness and particularity of discourse, but by the originary experience of mimesis and intuition *prior to discourse*. In their constructs of the human, performatist narratives tend to privilege characters who have trouble using discourse (hence the prevalence of taciturn, simple-minded, and autistic characters) or to forefront visual, intuitive forms of communication at the expense of discourse by allowing discursively deficient characters to prevail within the work as a whole. One case in point is Mark Haddon's novel *The Curious Incident of the Dog in the Night-Time* (2003), in which the hero, who suffers from a mild form of autism, lacks the ability to use language in anything but a literal way and yet triumphs in the end.[9] Another common strategy is to construct works in such a way that a discursive critique or deconstruction is easily achieved but leads to nothing in the way of understanding the text. Thus, in works like Ian McEwan's *Atonement* (2001) or Yann Martell's *Life of Pi* (2001), we realize at the end that a narrating character has been lying to us—but we do not care, because the aesthetic power of the preceding stories has forced us into a position of wanting to believe rather than of wanting to be skeptical.[10] While it seems "impossible" from a poststructuralist or postmodern perspective to forego or marginalize discourse, this is precisely what performatism does—and also what makes it irreducible to postmodernism. As I will show further on, this occlusion of discourse opens the way for a planetary approach that does not become bogged down in the particularities of local discourse every step of the way.

In critical practice, this necessitates a shift from poststructuralist theories emphasizing discourse to theories aimed at mimesis and the intuition. Girard's scapegoat theory, Gans's generative anthropology, Jean-Luc Marion's post-metaphysical phenomenology, and Peter Sloterdijk's spherology, to name the most notable, all address these issues directly and in depth (it goes almost without saying that all are marginal or play no role at all in present-day academic discussions in the arts).[11] Both in artistic practice and in theory, the human is no longer restricted to a merely ethical mode, but now includes originary aesthetic, erotic, and religious attributes derived specifically from the mimetic and intuitive interaction between humans.

This non-discursive interaction, in turn, achieves results that poststructuralism rejects as "metaphysical" or simply chimerical. Most notably, these include the experience of successful, unifying identification with an other (occurring when someone's mimetic gesture is successfully picked up and used by someone else), the experiencing of presence (triggered by the transparent immediacy and efficacy of the successful mimetic transfer between two humans), and the experiencing of totality (caused by imposing formal closure on a field of experience). The unthinkable, transcendent "others" of postmodern practice and poststructuralist theory—unity, presence, and totality—are made real in art through the performative occlusion of discourse.[12] Discourse, language, and translatability remain practical problems, but ones that can be bridged, albeit imperfectly, through mimesis. The mimetic transfer of value between humans—and not the endlessly obscure discourse of those humans—becomes the principal focus of attention.[13] At the same time, though, mimesis contains a raw potential for violence that continually undercuts the contractual solutions to human strife produced by Enlightenment and Reason. For this reason mimetic theories like performatism or Gans's generative anthropology assume that violence is an originary, insoluble aspect of human existence—and, concurrently, that transcending that violence is an imperative of human existence, albeit one that cannot be fulfilled entirely. This peculiar focus on the ever-present potential for violence, on the one hand, and the impossible need to transcend it, on the other, distinguishes performatism from critical poststructuralist theories (which are dedicated to dismantling the illusion of transcendence and avoid addressing "foundational" problems like violence directly) and humanist ones (which assume that violence can be resolved through contractual means or by resorting to reason).

The second distinguishing feature of performatism—its dominant technique—is what I call double framing. Double framing operates by taking some particular element in a work—usually an odd or unbelievable scene, situation, or detail, sometimes also an odd bio-social disposition—and confirming its mimetic or intuitive logic on the level of the work as a whole. The reader or viewer is in effect faced with a self-confirming construct that forces him or her to accept formally a scenic or visual given that is *prima facie* unbelievable or dubious in terms of prevailing discursive logic.[14] A good narrative example is the movie *American Beauty* (1999), which in purely discursive terms seems to be nothing more than an ironic, scathing satire of "ugly" American suburban life. The film narrative, however, concludes by linking a single odd scene (the twirling plastic bag Ricky Fitts calls animated, beautiful, and benevolent) with Lester Burnham's posthumous speech, which not only repeats Ricky's words verbatim but also suggests we can only appreciate the beauty of the world after we, too, have died. Lester's and Ricky's "unbelievable" intuitions do not completely occlude the discursive critique of American middle-class life contained in the film, but they provide a strong—and in fact logically irrefutable—counterpoint to that critique by offering a metaphysically optimistic perspective that practically forces us to *believe* (at least within the formal confines of the work). The film makes us experience transcendence as performance, which is to say through specifically aesthetic or artificial means whose universal—one might also say planetary—validity has yet to be fulfilled. Granted, it is possible to "ignore" this experience, but only at the expense of ignoring the form of the work itself.

The double frame imposes upon us a tautological, mimetically or intuitively defined free space that separates itself willfully from the boundless field of discourse, in the same way the human in its mimetic or intuitive mode is separate from discourse. This free space implicitly—and sometimes also explicitly—instantiates both the aesthetic and the transcendent as core elements of the human. By raising formally separated, idiosyncratic instances of mimetic and intuitive experience to a higher, more complex formal level, which always necessarily includes some form of discourse, performatist works force viewers or readers to believe in an artificial, closed construct (as opposed to having them "dis-figure" an endless skein of discursive figurations). Viewers and readers can always resist the logic of these closed aesthetic constructs in intellectual terms. However, intuitively they have little choice but to identify with what is being projected onto them. In short, the act of receiving the aesthetic construct is experienced formally as an act of transcendence—the viewer or reader is remade through the form of the work (*per formam*). Similarly, the palpably artificial, often highly manipulative way in which this transferral is conducted points to the existence of a higher authorial power rather than to the endless regress of discourse into which the postmodern author is usually said to disappear. The authorial position in performatism marks the point of undecidability between the human as a self-constructing force and as a construct received from a higher, as yet unknown (theist) source. The degree to which authoriality and the apprehension of transcendence are projected and experienced varies from work to work, but both are fundamental to the new episteme.[15] All in all, the strategy of double framing occludes the endless proliferation, pluralization, and dissemination peculiar to discourse by forcibly imposing artificial, closed categories onto its seemingly endless, open field. Whereas in Spivak's "classical" planetarity the focus is on the discursive figure, in *performatist planetarity* it is on the *category* or *frame*, which imposes a certain problematic aesthetic and political order on the global field of human relations while at the same time reopening the horizon of transcendence for the human via the frame.

Just how widespread is the performatist paradigm in narrative? My own, necessarily selective interpretations in *Performatism, or the End of Postmodernism* (2008) suggest that it started in the mid-1990s and became ubiquitous as of the mid-2000s. However, it is perhaps most convincing if the reader simply takes the criteria outlined above and applies them herself to the narrative works she has read or viewed in the last five years or so. Do these works stress discursive competence or occlude it? Do these works highlight freewheeling boundary transgression or impose frames and categories on characters? Do these works imply we are caught in an endless regress of irony or do they provide specific narrative resolutions transcending that irony? Are the actions of characters in these works dependent on outside discourse or do they exhibit simple forms of agency that are uniquely their own? If your answers consistently land on the latter part of the binary options listed, you will begin to intuit yourself that we are dealing with an *epistemic shift* toward a new epoch and not with random permutations in an endless regress of post-historical filiations.

Archetypologies: A Planetary Perspective on the Episode Film

Performatist planetarity is, as already noted, no less "impossible" than Spivak's anthropologically revised brand of deconstruction in the sense that its "God's-eye view" can never be realized entirely or thought separately from the particulars that it encompasses. It does, however, open up entirely different possibilities for approaching planetary relations in the arts. These possibilities are in no way ideal or utopian—they are inevitably accompanied by a kind of *quid pro quo* with discursive logic that will always make their full realization "impossible"—but they occur in a mode of affirmation that is foreign to the anthropologically supplemented poststructuralism propounded by Spivak and many others. As noted above, this mode of affirmation allows the experiencing of unity, presence, and totality in a way that is quite literally unthinkable in postmodernism and poststructuralism. In the following remarks I would like to develop a planetary perspective for performatism using Alejandro Iñárritu's movie *Babel* (2006) as a point of departure.

As an "impossible" gesture, performatist planetarity suggests the possibility of an affirmatively conceived global relationality among humans that is unthinkable in its entirety. It is therefore all the more interesting to address a case in which this "impossible" point of view is brought into play nonetheless. This case is the movie *Babel*. The work belongs to a cycle of recent films that radically garble or interrupt narrative sequences while in the end linking together what at first seem to be entirely disconnected episodes or strands of plot.[16] Rather than radically diffusing our sense of linear time by allowing "sheets" of time to overlap fluidly (as described by Deleuze in regard to, say, Andrei Tarkovsky's *The Mirror* [1975] or Alain Resnais's *Last Year in Marienbad* [1961][17]), these movies all *reorder* time in such a way that linearity, although radically interrupted and scrambled, can be reconstructed after the fact. The emphasis lies on presenting time in discrete, temporarily disconnected chunks that are experienced all the more intensely because they at first appear to have no connection to a greater *telos* or to the other narrative segments to which they are juxtaposed. The formal discreteness of the time chunks and the intensity which they convey lead, one way or the other, to a specifically aesthetic experience of temporal and spatial immediacy. This temporal reordering and aesthetic immediacy is experienced by the viewer as specifically authorial and artificial, in the sense that it has neither a psychological (dreamlike or hallucinatory) nor a semiotic motivation (it is not the result of linear film narrative being broken up because images interact uncontrollably with other images by way of audiovisual associations).[18] Quite simply, it can only be explained as the willed effect of a higher force—an author—and it confronts us with the question as to why such an author is imposing this radical new order upon us. This kind of movie plays out to a lesser or greater degree the ambivalence between authoriality and theism noted above. Is the work "merely" the whim of a strong-willed author or is the strongly conceived work the symptom of a still higher force that we cannot yet entirely comprehend? The fact that these movies can all be logically reordered in the end in spite of all initial confusion implies that there is. Moreover, the aesthetically charged individual chunks or scenes of the movie tend to be set off in a way that indicates that there is a unity of experience on a lower level, which is necessarily congruent with unity of experience on a higher narrative or structural level (the double frame noted above). The degree to which this necessity is felt depends a great deal on the particulars of the given movie, but it is a defining feature that sets these more recent episode films apart from comparable works from the 1960s or 1970s.

Babel takes these basic strategies and raises them to a global level. The film sets in motion three internally linear plot lines (in Morocco, the Mexican-American borderlands, and Japan) that are continually juxtaposed with one another on the narrative level but which eventually prove to be out of sync on the story level (there is no way of determining their temporal and causal relations until near the end of the film; the Japanese story line, for example, runs four or five days after the Moroccan story line has ended, and the Mexican-American story line takes place immediately after the end of the Moroccan one). The specific selection and positioning of the time chunks can be explained only by reference to an *author*—a specifically human point of origin—and not to the signs or discourse that in poststructuralist thinking always already conditions that point of origin before it even begins. The film asserts itself as a specifically human construct whether we like it or not, and it takes our ability to understand the authorship of the human to its outermost limits.[19]

The movie not only scrambles time, but also juxtaposes four extremely different cultures. There is a comfortable and leisurely American "suburbanscape"; the dirt-poor, austere peasant life of Morocco; an upper-middle-class Japanese milieu marked by high tech, neon, and the impersonal coolness of

Tokyo's urban ambience; and, finally, the vibrant disorder of Iñárritu's native Mexico. Although dissimilar in almost every conceivable way, each of these cultural venues has its own peculiar aesthetic and achieves its own kind of dignity through that aesthetic. Iñárritu and his cameraman Rodrigo Prieto use the natural grandeur of the Moroccan mountains and their intimate acquaintance with Mexican local color to full effect, but they are no less generous in their cinematic presentation of Tokyo's skyline, street life, and interiors, avoiding as they do both the clichéd Japan of *Lost in Translation* (2003) and the easily achieved critique of urban haste in *Koyaanisqatsi* (1982). (This applies no less to the short American suburban segment, which is marked by the inner warmth and child-friendly clutter of the home.) Through slow, panoramic pans, nature (the Moroccan mountains) is presented as equivalent to culture (the Tokyo skyline) and the other way around, with the Mexican scenes containing a carnivalesque jumble of both. On the other end of the scale, all three venues are implicitly connected by detailed close-ups of quotidian objects (most notably water, wells, fountains, animals etc.) that speak to a planetary commonality between cultures at the most elemental level.

This aesthetic framing and affirmation of local particularities is accompanied by a categorically, rather than discursively, guided construction of the human. This asserts itself through what I would like to call *archetypologies*. These are authorially framed, aesthetically sublimated chunks of reality that are particular and local and yet also seem to have a primordial, archetypal core. *Babel* and other performatist works present us with templates for perceiving reality that are circumscribed, bounded, and particular but that at the same time remain anchored in what appears to be timeless scenes or situations open to the intuition rather than to discourse. Archetypologies are hence more than mere empirical typologies and less than universal archetypes: they are categories with an originary "feel" but lacking an a priori justification, as is the case, I might add, with C. G. Jung's archetypes, which are always already "there" in the collective unconscious waiting to unfold through individuation, or with Northrop Frye's archetypal criticism, which would reduce all literary forms to a set of fixed, quasi-organic categories. Summing up, one could say that archetypologies are free-floating, aesthetically generated frames or categories rooted in direct modes of human interaction underpinned primarily by the intuition and mimesis; they are symptomatic of a broader epistemic mindset that has become impatient with approaching human reality through the endless critique of discourse. Archetypologies make possible a planetary approach to culture by generating overarching categories that allow us to compare different cultures in their mimetic and intuitive operations beneath the threshold of discourse.

We can observe the way these archetypologies work at first hand in *Babel*. At first, the differences between the various characters seem to outweigh any similarities, in particular because they bear the typical imprints of their own cultures. Culture, in turn, appears as a unity of nature and socially normed artifice that frames the characters in very different ways. This can be seen most directly in the way that sexual drives are presented. The literally most visible instance is that of the exhibitionism practiced by Chieko and Yussef's sister Zohra. In social terms the circumstances are completely different: the emotionally traumatized Chieko exposes herself to strangers in anonymous urban settings, whereas Zohra exposes herself to Yussef in a semi-incestuous way that is no doubt motivated by the goatherd family's extreme isolation (in accordance with utterly different social norms Chieko goes unpunished even when she exposes herself to a policeman, whereas Yussef and Zohra are beaten by their father). The causal logic of the film strongly suggests, however, that we must regard (natural) sexuality and culturally mediated agency as a kind of bio-social unity. For example, the film makes a direct connection between Yussef's sexual drive and his desire to use the hunting rifle (he is masturbating when his brother calls him to go shoot). There is also a less explicit suggestion that the Japanese father's status as a hunter/loner contributed to his wife's suicide (she killed herself with a gun and was found by Chieko, leading to the latter's trauma). Sexual desire is channeled into certain social actions that take place within the framework of local norms and moral categories, and that in turn may have natural repercussions (wounding, death) that once again merge into social acts. Through an irresistible, authorial, totalizing gesture the film renders these very different bio-social acts equivalent without suggesting any sort of intrinsic superiority of one over the other; they are offered to us as visual pieces of evidence rather than as discursive conundrums. At the same time, on a root level and in spite of all local differences, *Babel* suggests that all cultures function in a similar, mimetic way—in the presence of face-to-face encounters. Language—as hinted at by the "Babel" of the movie's title—gets in the way of this mimetic interaction all the time, but this interference is, in spite of the symbolically loaded title, not the movie's central interest.

This can be seen in the specific ways in which language is thematized within the film itself. While linguistic problems impede communication in a number of instances, most notably when the American husband in Morocco aggressively tries to get medical help for his wounded wife, language itself does not seem to be an unbridgeable gap (the husband is helped by a loyal and very patient local guide and translator). The Mexican nanny Emilia calms her young charges at bedtime by speaking Spanish with them (which they appear to understand). It is also probably no accident that the film makes a point of treating language as a bio-social, rather than as a simply encultured phenomenon: the Japanese teenager Chieko is a deaf-mute who communicates through lip-reading, sign language, and writing. Forcing others to communicate with her face-to-face, her disability underscores the reduction of language to an originary state of visual contact and presence. The film seems to be saying that understanding, rather than being a linguistic or even cultural problem, is based on the willingness to respond mimetically to an other's distress, that is, to react sympathetically to his or her immediate emotional state or situation. I might also point out that the role played by the media in all this is contingent. Various mediatic forms from long-distance phones and cell phones with video functions to television make instant communication with faraway partners possible, but the essentials of communication always take place face-to-face or locally (as when Detective Mamiya reads Chieko's note shortly after their meeting). In *Babel*, the privileged medium of planetarity is definitely film, which is able to combine the local and particular with an overarching narrative perspective that overrides language. Film makes its case to us by appealing to the intuition (from *intuere*, "to look at"), which is prior to language; it argues by presenting us chunks of visual evidence rather than devolving into an endless skein of discursive figures.

If "Babel" in the biblical sense does not explain the movie very well, what, then, is the causal logic behind its plot? Many critics have remarked about the "butterfly effect" that supposedly motivates the film's plot (i.e., the notion that a small local change in an unstable non-linear system—the flap of a butterfly's wing—can result in large differences on a higher level—a hurricane). On the story level this is perhaps true (the Japanese father's gun indeed sets off the Moroccan and Mexican catastrophes), but not on the narrative one. There can be no ethical responsibility on the part of the Japanese father for Yussef's action, which results, as noted above, from a mixture of sexually motivated bravado and mimetic rivalry with his brother.[20] The planetary point being made here is quite the opposite from the banal "we-are-all-responsible-for-one-another" type of thing that some critics see in the movie's message. Rather, the film seems to be saying that ethical responsibility is first and foremost a local and, indeed, individual matter that is mediated by bio-socially defined culture. The film as a whole raises those local, particular matters to a higher plane—planetarity—in an aesthetically affirmative way but does not suggest any discursively guided resolution. The film makes the impossible possible by forcing us to apprehend very different ethical decisions and outcomes in terms of an aesthetic totality that always remains below the threshold of a semantic generalization. The totalizing gesture of the film—its double frame—forces us to turn inward towards the film's (human) particulars once again if we wish to understand it. However, it also forces us to consider what the demonstrably artificial and manipulative frame might be excluding.

The question thus necessarily arises as to whether the combined gesture of aesthetic totalization and a focus on individual ethical decisions leads to an "uncritical" attitude towards global and/or local power structures. This can be tested more closely by examining how public power and private ethical behavior interact in the plot. Here as elsewhere in the film, there does not seem to be any unity in the various outcomes. The different story lines are resolved through highly divergent combinations of political interventions and private gestures: the shooting of Ahmed, the capture of Yussef and his father by the Moroccan police, and Yussef's confession; the arrest and deportation of Amelia by the American Border Patrol and her reunification with her son; the rescue of Susan by the American authorities and Richard's leave-taking from his Moroccan guide; and the fatherly consolation of Chieko by the Japanese detective.

The film's argumentation here uses two overlapping, bio-socially defined archetypologies. The first is political and encompasses the relations between power, patriarchy, and individual dignity. In the Moroccan story, police power and patriarchal violence appear as mutually confirming practices: the Moroccan police officer slaps around the villagers in much the same way that the father slaps around his children, and the police officer threatens to "cut off [Yussef's] balls" if he is lying. Bio-social and political behaviors merge here into a punitive, degrading unity. Yussef, however, acts ethically in the sense that he takes the full burden of guilt upon himself (we later see this confirmed in a television image). In the second, Mexican-American case, state authority asserts itself in an impersonal and bureaucratic, though perhaps no less emasculating guise; it is the extended, intrusive actions of the studiously polite American border guard that eventually causes Emilia's nephew Santiago to bolt with the car (the dubious decision to abandon her and the children in the desert is all his own). Finally, in the Japanese story line, police authority dissolves into caring patriarchal behavior (that of the detective consoling Chieko in lieu of the absent father). On the highest plane, we have international diplomatic tensions between America and Morocco, which resists American claims, inspired by its global viewpoint rather than by knowledge of local conditions, that the tourist has been a victim of terrorism (it is an "arche" position lacking knowledge of typological, local particulars). The movie's archetypology is rooted in an analysis of immediate, face-to-face social relations with variable ethical choices and open-ended outcomes. It presents us with a (necessarily incomplete) typology of political and patriarchal power relations and—I think quite deliberately—does not attempt a sweeping ideological critique of those relations, which would involve returning to a discursive mode.

Instead, it argues by presenting us with a second archetypology that might be called "relations of caring" and that exists coextensively with the archetypology of patriarchal power relations. The Japanese detective Mamiya, Yussef's father, Emilia, the Moroccan translator, the American husband Richard, and even the American Border Patrol searching for the lost children all exhibit different kinds of caring behavior that intersect in unpredictable ways with patterns supplied by the film's archetypology of patriarchal power. The mere exertion of power does not exclude ethical, caring behavior (Detective Mamiya, the Border Patrol), and, conversely, a victimary or powerless status does not guarantee proper ethical action (as when Santiago abandons his aunt and the children in the desert, or when Yussef takes a potshot at the bus). By breaking up the story lines into discrete, juxtaposed chunks, the film reveals the specific interaction of the ethical and the political in an artificial, specifically aesthetic mode. On the one hand, we achieve a planetary, Godlike view of these relations, and on the other, we feel as if we are direct participants in them; our position as viewers is simultaneously universal and particular, authorial and figural.[21]

The reason for this is due not just to a personal whim of the moviemakers but is also structural, a result of the epistemic shift from the metaphysical pessimism of postmodernism to the metaphysical optimism of performatism. Spivak's postmodern ethics, which are representative of much of poststructuralist critical thinking, are rooted in resistance to an all-encompassing system of domination and exploitation that she calls "capitalist imperialism."[22] Capitalism as a means of production, though, has no real economic rival—if we take Spivak at her word, socialism "at its best" is parasitic upon capitalism but is not an autonomous means of production in its own right.[23] Hence also Spivak's emphasis on the alterity of pre-capitalist societies as a source of resistance[24] as well as upon the obscurity of local languages that cannot be assimilated to "hegemonic" languages like English. As Alain Badiou has pointed out in his essay on ethics and evil, the radical pathos of this and similar stances subordinates the political to the ethical. These positions assume the existence of a self-evident "radical Evil" from which the definition of Good is derived; consensus on this radical Evil is achieved through "opinion," which is to say discourse.[25] Good, rather than being a quantity that can be defined in terms of positive truth processes, is reduced to a set of human rights to the "non-Evil" (the right not to be mistreated, exploited, marginalized, etc.). Spivak's position, in sum, depends on the ethically motivated, "impossible" participation in the experience of being subaltern (of being other) and of protecting that subalternity from hegemonic exploitation. It is this experience or defense of otherness, rather than a positive political program or alternative economic mode of production, that confounds the hegemony of "imperialist capitalism."[26]

How critical or politically relevant, then, is a movie like *Babel*, which avoids victimary logic and discursively founded ethics? In answering, a great deal depends on recognizing in it the quality or capability that I have called aesthetic. This aesthetic is not supplementary ornamentation—pretty images or snazzy editing meant to distract us from critical interrogation of the existing order—but is what gives the archetypologies their political bite. The archetypologies may be thought of in this sense as artistic practices that, to borrow a phrase of Jacques Rancière's, enact a "distribution of the sensible" that "disturbs the clear partition of identities, activities, and spaces."[27] The archetypologies impose new forms of artistically mediated order upon us that are analogous to the political destabilization of existing order, and they do this by appealing to the intuition rather than to discursive reason. It is noteworthy in this regard that *Babel's* presumably "contrived" aesthetic quite accurately anticipated numerous aspects of the Arab Spring. In Tunisia, for example, the rebellion was set off by the degradation of a single individual, Mohammed Bouazizi, an educated young man who was prevented by the police from earning money as a street vendor; his fiery, sacrificial suicide led to mass protests that eventually toppled the regime and then quickly spread to other countries, aided by both the mass media and social networking. The main driving force behind the uprisings was less programmatically guided discourse than mimesis—imitation of others' actions—and one of its main features seems to have been an attempt to assert individual dignity in the face of authoritarian repression (the uprising in Tunisia was originally dubbed "The Dignity Revolution"). Obviously, the way the Arab uprisings were conducted and the reasons they arose are much more complex and less coherent than anything that can be conveyed in a film.[28] However, *Babel*'s archetypological approach managed to foreground a number of their crucial features before the fact: the importance of individual dignity and ethical responsibility, the high tech-aided mimesis by which the rebellions spread, and even the bio-social issue of women's right to show their own bodies within Islamic societies.[29] Thus, the film's supposedly "contrived" narrative form demonstrates the urgent need to grasp planetary developments both in terms of their temporal simultaneity and of their categorical overlap—the Arab uprisings not only took place more or less simultaneously but were also soon projected back onto Western experience (the "Occupy" movements in the West sometimes used the slogan "We are Tahrir Square"). Although *Babel* has been criticized, perhaps justifiably, as a compromise between auteur and Hollywood norms,[30] it is precisely this sort of formal compromise on which the performatist planetary perspective hinges: being able to intuit distant cultures will always remain an artificial, and necessarily incomplete, venture.

The Planetary: A Performatist Approach

I have chosen *Babel* as a point of departure not because it marks a new sub-genre or cycle of planetary narrative—the movie has not found any immediate imitators, and it is not likely to do so—but because it undertakes a radical "redistribution of the visible" that can help us rethink the way we approach narrative art after the end of postmodernism and critically address current global problems (and problems of globalization). Using *Babel's* radical aesthetic vision as a jumping-off point, I would like to provide a brief, three-point outline of how this vision can be used to help articulate a performatist approach to the planetary.

1. *Politics of performatist planetarism.* Performatist planetarism is an aesthetic and political project in the sense that this is used by Rancière, which is to say as the "sensible delimitation of what is common to the community."[31] It would undertake the study of how archetypologies are used to order the world in narrative works of art (and, by extension, how they assert themselves

in sociopolitical reality). Performatist planetarism would reconstruct the contours of local particulars but would simultaneously examine them in terms of *overarching categorical assumptions about human social interaction*. This project is "impossible" to achieve in the sense that "arche" (what is originary and general) and "typology" (what is empirical and particular) will never fall together entirely. Both perspectives are however necessary if we are not to fall into making abstract, a priori generalizations about human cultural behavior, on the one hand, or to fetishize its unrepresentable differences, on the other.

2. *Anthropology of performatist planetarism*. Performatist planetarism has a specific anthropological justification. It does not regard the human as a mere effect of language or discourse and stands in contradistinction to rhizomatic and deconstructive paradigms that use the term "human" to supplement discursive or relational figures. Instead, performatist planetarism tries to explain the human in terms of *bio-social unities as they arise under different cultural conditions*. These bio-social categories may be thought of (among other things) in terms of sexuality and human (dis)ability as well as in terms of caring vs. mimetically motivated violence, which arguably both have a partially biological basis. Planetary performatism studies the way the bio-social is projected onto the aesthetico-political (and vice versa). The goal is not to establish a rigorous system of binary categories resulting from their overlaps (that would be structuralism warmed over), but to engage in a kind of intuitionism that would reconstruct newly arising, aesthetically mediated archetypologies of the human in a global context. I also do not envision this intuitionism as a merely hermeneutic operation. As noted earlier, there already exist well-founded theories from thinkers like Gans, Marion, Sloterdijk, and Girard, which seek to describe the intuition or the mimetic aspects of human existence in categorical terms, and it would be imperative to draw on such theories when constructing archetypologies on a planetary level.

3. *Agency in performatist planetarism*. Performatist planetarism is interested in agency and event rather than in the endless, incremental play of discourse and with the resulting emphasis on failure, misprision, misrepresentation, contingency, and dysfunctionality. The point is not that agency and event are always positive and must always succeed, but that they act as catalysts for the archetypologies outlined above. Archetypologies in fact may be thought of as coalescing immediately around events or unexpected redistributions of order; they suggest (but do not guarantee) the possibility of change rather than the endless differentiation of that which has always already been, and they assume that bio-socially defined human agency—rather than discursively defined subjectivity—is the driving force behind such events. Agency, in turn, is linked closely with authorship, with the ability to produce closure and structure in the field of the real. The degree to which both humans and fictional characters can successfully "author" their reality is an important focal point of performatist planetary analysis.

The programmatic points outlined above can help us move beyond the endless reapplication of the poststructuralist critique of discourse, away from a totalizing critique of capitalism, and toward a more differentiated approach describing how human interaction takes place within a global capitalism that imposes constraints—but also opens up certain free spaces—for local cultures and the individuals acting within them.

Notes

1. Gayatri Chakravorty Spivak, *Death of a Discipline* (New York: Columbia University Press, 2003), 102.

2. Ibid., 73.

3. Ibid., 72–73.

4. See my *Performatism, or the End of Postmodernism* (Aurora, Colo.: Davies Group, 2008).

5. For an in-depth discussion, see the descriptions of mimesis and mimetic crisis in Eric Gans, *Signs of Paradox: Irony, Resentment, and Other Mimetic Structures* (Stanford, Calif.: Stanford University Press, 1997), 13–29.

6. Spivak, *Death of a Discipline*, 73.

7. Ibid., 9–10.

8. Ibid., 92.

9. For more on this, see my article "Transcendence and the Aesthetics of Disability: The Case of *The Curious Incident of the Dog in the Night-Time*," *Anthropoetics* 15, no. 1 (Fall 2009), http://www.anthropoetics.ucla.edu/ap1501/1501eshelman.htm.

10. For more on these and similar strategies, see "Performatism, or the End of Postmodernism," in my *Performatism*, 1–36.

11. See, most notably, René Girard, *Things Hidden since the Foundation of the World*, trans. Stephen Bann and Michael Metteer (Stanford, Calif.: Stanford University Press, 1987); Eric Gans, *Signs of Paradox*; Jean-Luc Marion, *Being Given: Toward a Phenomenology of Givenness*, trans. Jeffrey Kosky (Stanford, Calif.: Stanford University Press, 2002); and Peter Sloterdijk, *Bubbles: Spheres, Volume I: Microspherology*, trans. Wieland Hoban (Los Angeles: Semiotext(e), 2011).

12. Performative utterances, which transcend the literal side of discourse, are obviously intrinsic to discourse itself (Derrida's *Politics of Friendship*, to which Spivak repeatedly returns, plays continually on this theme). In deconstruction, though, the "performative contradiction" is simply another binary opposition that ultimately can only be worked through in terms of a critique of discourse. In performatism, the position is reversed: we are confronted with situations in which discourse is deliberately occluded, suppressed, or reduced to sheer banality, so that we are forced to focus on the performative, non-discursive side of communication.

13. Spivak's emphasis on cultivating the "idiomaticity of nonhegemonic languages" (*Death of a Discipline*, 10) comes strangely close to the romantic view equating language with ethnic essence (the difference being that in Spivak's case an endless hybridization is possible—see ibid., 12). It is also characteristic of this quasi-romantic position that language itself can be "hegemonic" at all.

14. For more on this, see "Performatism, or the End of Postmodernism," in my *Performatism*, 1–36.

15. It is important to emphasize, in case the point is not sufficiently clear, that transcendence and authoriality are experienced performatively and not thematically: performatism is not a religious revival. The deconstructive approach also acknowledges religion, but once more in terms of an undecidable discursive strategy marking the outlines of an unreachable future (see Derrida's use of "the messianic" in *Politics of Friendship* or *Specters of Marx*, or Spivak's frequent references to "teleopoesis").

16. Similar movies include Quentin Tarantino's *Pulp Fiction* (1994), Robert Altman's *Short Cuts* (1993), J. P. Anderson's *Magnolia* (1999), Petr Zelenka's *Buttoners* (1997), Christopher Nolan's *Memento* (2000), Erik Poppe's *Hawaii, Oslo* (2004), and Michel Gondry's *Eternal Sunshine of the Spotless Mind* (2004). For a critical overview of the theme, see David Denby, "The New Disorder: Adventures in Film Narrative," *The New Yorker*, March 5, 2007, 80–85.

17. See "Peaks of Present and Sheets of Past: Fourth Commentary on Bergson" in Gilles Deleuze, *Cinema 2: The Time-Image*, trans. Hugh Tomlinson and Robert Galeta (Minneapolis: University of Minnesota Press, 1989), 98–125.

18. I am referring here to Gilles Deleuze's basic opposition between motion-images and time-images. In my view, it is not possible to describe this type of movie using this opposition, which has no way of accounting for the extreme temporal disjunction driven by narrative manipulation rather than by images. For more on this, see my *Performatism*, 89–99.

19. David Denby, whose view is representative of those critics who dislike the movie's "puzzle-box" narrative structure, objects to the "pretentious fatalism and structural willfulness" he thinks marks *Babel* and similar films and dismisses it as a "highbrow globalist tearjerker" ("New Disorder," 84).

20. Denby argues that "in 'Babel,' the privileged carelessness of the First World characters, giving their guns away and leaving their kids behind, plants the seeds of what goes wrong" ("New Disorder," 84). This one-sidedly "global" reading ignores the local side of the film, which explicitly emphasizes individual ethical responsibility.

21. For opposing views from a poststructuralist perspective, see Todd McGowan, "The Contingency of Connection: The Path to Politicization in *Babel*," *Discourse* 30, no. 3 (2008): 401–18; and Sebastian Thies, "Crystal Frontiers: Ethnicity, Filmic Space, and Diasporic Optic in *Traffic*, *Crash*, and *Babel*," in *E Pluribus Unum?: National and Transnational Identities in the Americas / Identidades nacionales y transnacionales en las Américas*, ed. Sebastian Thies and Josef Raab (Münster: LIT Verlag; Tempe: Bilingual, 2008), 205–28. McGowan's (Lacanian) and Thies's (culturalist) readings of *Babel* stress the impossibility of communication and the possibility of forging lasting or real social bonds. Thies writes that "human understanding is shown to fail in a world shaped by post-modern mobility and the mediascapes of the information age, yet divided by postcolonial cleavages between post-Fordist and Third World societies" (220), and McGowan maintains that "nothing underwrites the social bond but a contingent moment" (413). Thies notes critically that "seemingly insurmountable ethnic conflicts" in the film "are resolved by means of a surrogate narrative resolution" (225), whereas McGowan (who avoids addressing the film's use of narrative

closure) maintains that the point of the film "lies in accepting the disturbance that the encounter with excess brings" (414) and in demonstrating "that the real Other is an absence" (415). The film's peculiar authorial aesthetic with its intent toward closure and order is either seen as an irritating supplement or simply ignored, and the failure of communication and social bonding in a globalized world is a foregone conclusion.

22. Spivak, *Death of a Discipline*, 54.

23. "Socialism at its best would persistently and repeatedly wrench capital away from capitalism." Ibid., 100.

24. "The planetarity of which I have been speaking in these pages is perhaps best imagined from the precapitalist cultures of the planet." Ibid., 101.

25. See Alain Badiou, *Ethics: An Essay on the Understanding of Evil*, trans. Peter Hallward (London: Verso, 2001), 8–10.

26. Spivak, *Death of a Discipline,* 51.

27. Jacques Rancière, *The Politics of Aesthetics: The Distribution of the Sensible*, trans. Gabriel Rockhill (London: Continuum, 2004), 13.

28. Other reasons usually mentioned include unemployment, underemployment, rising prices, corruption, and authoritarian rule. Economic protest seems to have been directed more against crony capitalism than capitalism per se, and nowhere was socialism touted as a viable alternative. For more on this see Suzanne Maloney, "The Economic Dimension: The Price of Freedom," in *The Arab Awakening: America and the Transformation of the Middle East*, ed. Kenneth Pollack et al. (Washington, D.C.: Brookings Institution, 2011), 66–75.

29. The topic of exhibitionism treated in the movie became a political issue in Egypt when a female blogger, Aliaa Magda Elmahdy, exposed herself on a website as a protest against Islamic fundamentalism.

30. This has been done most compellingly by Marina Hassapopoulou in "*Babel*: Pushing and Reaffirming Mainstream Cinema's Boundaries," *Jump Cut: A Review of Contemporary Media*, no. 50 (Spring 2008), http://www.ejumpcut.org/archive/jc50.2008/Babel/index.html. Hassapopoulou, who thinks the movie is postmodern, concludes that "*Babel* is perhaps the best we can expect in terms of mainstream experimentation—at least for now. *Babel* could be as close to getting viewers to actively (not just retrospectively) think about the film's form and content as mainstream postmodernism can get. . . . In making viewers question the causality of events, temporal continuity and narrative space, *Babel* demonstrates how contrived continuity actually is in film. Nonetheless, in the case of *Babel*, the film's narrative compromises defeat the possibility of an unfettered artistic creation and suggest that the film's ultimate aim is to be—as *Babel*'s tagline says—'understood.' "

31. Rancière, *The Politics of Aesthetics*, 18.

Planetarity, Performativity, Relationality

Claire Denis's *Chocolat* and Cinematic Ethics

LAURIE EDSON

In a remarkably self-conscious way, much of the literature and art of our postcolonial age bears witness to the realities of transnationalism and diaspora. In a post-1989 world distinctively marked by increased movements of people, culture, materials, and capital, as well as by shifting national borders and evolving geostrategic alliances, theorists, like artists, continue searching for new ways to think about the contemporary realities taking shape on our planet. Thus, inherited notions of identity and nation have been increasingly probed, refined, problematized, and called into question; models that implicitly rely on oppositional thinking ("us/them") appear to have lost ground to more nuanced discussions seeking to underscore the complex relationality that characterizes human life. In the pages that follow, I examine some of the important work in relationality and planetary thinking in order to propose Claire Denis's film *Chocolat* (1988) as an exemplary artistic intervention that takes up these issues and permits insight into some of the most pressing ethical issues of our time. In "performing" the houseboy's identity in ways undercutting imperial silencing and assimilation of colonial subjects, in dramatizing the development of a child's precognitive emotional reality as she enters into relation with those around her while learning about colonial power relations, and in calling attention to the fissures in its own status of authoritative representation as it opens up a space for the emergence of voices and perspectives of silenced "others," *Chocolat* lays, I argue, the groundwork for a planetary ethics.

With a view toward conceptualizing a more just and ethical world, numerous theorists have moved away from thinking along "global" lines and have preferred, of late, to speak in terms of the planet—the place or space of exchanges and sharing that we all inhabit, in the words of Gayatri Spivak, "on loan." "Planet-thought," she explains, requires that "we imagine ourselves as planetary subjects rather than global agents."[1] "Planetarity" leans in a different philosophical direction from that of "globalization," which seems to privilege an all-embracing unit bent on erasing singularities. Kwame Anthony Appiah is one of many who have drawn attention, in this context, to the ethical imperative of attending to the particular and the local. In *Cosmopolitanism: Ethics in a World of Strangers*, he stresses an ethics of relationality and reminds us that "the problem of cross-cultural communication can seem immensely difficult in theory, . . . [yet] when the stranger is no longer imaginary, but real and present, sharing a human social life, . . . you can make sense of each other in the end."[2] Keen on particularity and deeply aware of the ways in which categories of knowledge themselves shape analyses and understanding, Appiah is among those concerned about avoiding the kind of totalizing discourses of globalization that would imply dominance and whose full articulation activates exclusionary mechanisms. If he locates the ethical intervention he calls for, on the one hand, in empirical reality ("when the stranger is no longer imaginary, but real and present, sharing a human social life, . . . you can make sense of each other in the end") and, on the other hand, in existing disciplines, Spivak extends this approach into the domain of a new, planet-oriented Comparative Literature. In her important chapter on "Planetarity" from *Death of a Discipline*, she suggests that a planetary Comparative Literature might move beyond ethnic studies with its grounding in "the authority of experience" and instead seek to defamiliarize the home, to render it uncanny. Planetarity would also involve "learning to learn from below"; it would "persistently and repeatedly undermine and undo the definitive tendency of the dominant to appropriate the emergent."[3]

The Relational, the Performative, and the Planetary Subject

The "learning to learn from below" idea has been gaining momentum. Part and parcel of this development is, for instance, Françoise Lionnet and Shu-mei Shih's argument for "minor transnationalism."[4] While postcolonial studies have tended to focus on *vertical* relations between colonizer and colonized, a dynamic that has historically worked to reinforce oppositional thinking of the above-mentioned "us/them" kind, the newer transnational model draws attention to the *lateral* networks existing among marginalized, subaltern, and minority people of different places. Theoretically, with its focus on the always-already hybrid nature of culture, minor transnationalism carries on the work of Edouard Glissant's *Poétique de la relation* and builds on ideas about the ethical importance of cultural diversity such as those brought forward by Amin Maalouf in *Les identités meurtrières*.[5] Paul Gilroy, too, studies horizontal networks among groups of people in *The Black Atlantic*, drawing on Glissant as well as Deleuze and Guattari's conception of the rhizome in *Thousand Plateaus*; in his introduction, he describes, in fact, his study as "the rhizomorphic, fractal structure of the transcultural, international formation I call the black Atlantic." Gilroy's book is meant as a response to the work of scholars whose views, he felt, are still informed by unexamined concepts of political-cultural nationalism and ethnic particularism. As he sees it,

"Marked by its European origins, modern black political culture has always been more interested in the relationship of identity to roots and rootedness than in seeing identity as a process of movement and mediation."[6] To shift focus away from theories that relied on the integrity or "purity" of modern nation-states and toward the movements and exchanges between various locales, Gilroy proposes as his starting point the image of ships traveling through the spaces between Europe, Africa, the Caribbean, and the Americas. As he puts it, the image of sailing ships foregrounds not only the Middle Passage but also the reality of cultural, artistic, and political diffusion and influence. All that influence, in turn, contributes to the presence of an inherent multiplicity *within* identity that profoundly marks who we are and, in the words of Maalouf, serves an important ethical function. "When one observes in oneself, in one's origins and in the course one's life has taken, a number of different confluences and contributions, of different mixtures and influences," writes Maalouf, "then one enters into a different relationship both with other people and with one's own 'tribe.' It's no longer just a question of 'them' and 'us': two armies in battle order preparing for the next confrontation."[7]

As theorists keep probing our accepted formulations of identity, nation, and related notions, writers, composers, and filmmakers too have been problematizing these concepts in innovative ways, often taking great care not to blindly manufacture "truths" about people and communities along the lines of gender, class, race, or sexuality. Because verbal, visual, and aural representations powerfully shape ideas about culture, artists play an important ethical role in providing that which, in building on the work of Gilroy, Mary Louise Pratt calls "a counterdiscourse to the centrism of metropolitan accounts."[8] By querying the dominant perspective of the metropolitan and exposing how such a construction depends on silencing the presence and perspective of the non-dominant already living within the metropolitan borders, theorists such as Pratt, Gilroy, and Homi K. Bhabha show how "the cultural temporality of the nation inscribes a much more transitional social reality."[9] Instead of a historicist narrative of the nation, Bhabha, for example, favors strategies that avoid any attempt to assert authority, such as attention to the performative. In "DissemiNation: Time, Narrative, and the Margins of the Modern Nation," he sets forth his ideas about the nation as "an obscure and ubiquitous form of living the *locality* of culture. This locality is more *around* temporality than *about* historicity . . . more hybrid in the articulation of cultural differences and identifications—gender, race or class—than can be represented in any hierarchical or binary structuring of social antagonism." Questioning whether "the *emergence* of a national perspective—of an elite or subaltern nature—within a culture of social contestation . . . can ever articulate its 'representative' authority in that fullness of narrative time," Bhabha locates a doubling, a conceptual ambivalence, where people are both "the historical 'objects' of a nationalist pedagogy" and "the 'subjects' of a process of signification." The "pedagogy" is already sedimented, historically crystallized; the latter is ongoing, fluid, performative. For Bhabha, it is through the intervention of the performative that the nation "becomes a liminal form of social representation, a space that is *internally* marked by cultural difference and the heterogeneous histories of contending peoples, antagonistic authorities, and tense cultural locations."[10] Spivak, too, notes the importance of the performative as a key element in the analysis of identity and culture; as one attends to what she calls "the performative of the other, in order not to transcode but to draw a response," the hope is for heightened communication and understanding across diverse cultures, which may culminate, if managed ethically, in a heterogeneous transnationalism or cosmopolitanism that remains alive, vibrant, and characteristically geared toward forming new relations or transforming those already in place.[11]

The planetary space of such transnational or cosmopolitan exchanges is much different from the one implied by hegemonic globalization in that, unlike the global, the planetary does not seek to reduce or assimilate the particular. It is along these lines that Emily Apter has pointed to planetarity's philosophical difference from globalization. "Wai Chee Dimock, Gayatri Spivak, and Edward Said," Apter specifies, "have taken planetary criticism in other directions, focusing . . . on using planetarity to impede globalization's monolithic spread: its financialization of the globe and proselytism of orthodoxies of likeness and selfsame."[12] In valuing heterogenous particularities, Apter, Dimock, and others extend the work of Spivak and Gilroy and remind us that "planetarity" derives its allure, in part, from its emerging, not-yet-fixed status. The term, Dimock says, "stands as a horizon impossible to define, and hospitable in that impossibility. . . . It is a habitat still waiting for its inhabitants, waiting for a humanity that has yet to be born, yet to be wrested from a seemingly boundless racism."[13]

In trying to come to grips with planetarity's evolving condition, it is perhaps useful to return to ideas formulated by Michel Foucault, especially in such key texts as "Theatrum Philosophicum" and "Nietzsche, Genealogy, History." Foucault is one of many theorists to have questioned what he calls the humanist desire to totalize or explain the present by dissolving singular events into ideal continuities.[14] As he points out, any ideology bent, at the outset, on discovering influences, origins, teleologies, models, groundings, or any other type of continuity remains bound to a metaphysics of presence and will be unable to recognize difference, discontinuity, or disparity. Whenever a continuity is thus postulated, a frame can be and usually is established that inevitably valorizes certain variables at the expense of other information. Thinking explicitly outside this model, Foucault, in "Theatrum Philosophicum," proposes the *event*. "The *event*," as Foucault writes, "is always an effect produced entirely by bodies colliding, mingling, or separating." Neither a state of things nor a concept, the event is "devoid of any grounding in an original, outside of all forms of imitation, and freed from the constraints of similitude," in particular from those imposed by the "model" (that which one follows, imitates, or otherwise reproduces).[15] Foucault's essay is a concisely formulated critique of the model as well as the philosophy of representation. Along with Deleuze, he offers up a different kind of philosophical thought, one that would embrace divergence instead of remaining caught in the rigid system of oppositional or bipolar thinking inherited from Plato's thought and its grounding in the original, the prototype, and the paradigm of resemblance. For our purposes here, it is noteworthy that this bipolar thinking continues to underwrite a postcolonial Eurocentrism and impedes an ethical planetarity from coming into being. Foucault sets out to replace the philosophy of representation with one of phantasms, where the latter arise between "surfaces" and acquire meaning there, "freed from the dilemmas of truth and falsehood and of being and non-being." Instead of picturing the phantasm as something already shaped, we should conceive of it, he submits, "without the aid of models."[16] The philosopher argues, in this vein, the necessity of freeing thought from the model, that is, from the concept (for which he substitutes the event), no less than from representation, oppositional thinking, and categories. Foucault's event, then, seems to resonate with Bhabha's performative.

Chocolat: An Other Performance

Of late, there has been a spate of movies that investigate hybrid identity, transnationality, and the relational aesthetics and ethics implicit in planetarity. They raise important questions: How might artists represent the planetary subject's participation in vertical, "pedagogically" nationalist, mimetic, and "stabilizing" structures, as well as in lateral, fluid, trans-categorical and transnational processes, an ambivalence captured by Bhabha's "doubling" and germane concepts reviewed in this chapter's opening section? What techniques and strategies might a moviemaker employ to allow the *performative* to emerge within representation so as to illuminate the problems swirling around the subject's ambivalent status?

While cinema has traditionally provided a fertile ground for exploring the *performative* and its function in undermining ossified categories of analysis, the planetary era's filmmakers have shown great interest in this issue. A case in point is Claire Denis, who has treated this problem in the context of France's imperial past. In her award-winning film *Chocolat*, she questions French colonial history, specifically the role of the dominant perspective in that history's public representation.[17] One of a number of movies revisiting France's colonial past (*Outremer* [1990] and *Indochine* [1992] are two other examples), *Chocolat* provides a significant counter-discourse to that dominant representation as well as a sophisticated analysis of the way subjects are socially constructed, all the while staging the inability of mainstream discourse to account for the inconsistencies in its own narrative.[18] As the film unfolds, it becomes clear that its centering perspective is a white French woman named France who returns to Cameroon, where she spent her years as a child growing up under French colonialism, with the black houseboy Protée her only friend. Yet *Chocolat* is by no means a nostalgic return to some ideal past, nor is it the story of a woman in search of her roots. Instead, *Chocolat* proves to be an artistic intervention that allows the double silent minority perspectives of a child and a houseboy to seep onto center stage so as to reveal the inadequacies of colonization's hegemonic representation.

In imagining minority standpoints and enabling them to emerge in her film, Denis tackles some of the issues Spivak deals with in "Can the Subaltern Speak?" published, incidentally, the same year as *Chocolat*. As Spivak writes, "It is impossible for contemporary French intellectuals to imagine the kind of Power and Desire that would inhabit the unnamed subject of the Other of Europe. It is not only that everything they read, critical or uncritical, is caught within the debate of the production of that Other. . . . It is also that, in the constitution of that Other of Europe, great care was taken to obliterate the textual ingredients with which such a subject could cathect, could occupy (invest?) its itinerary."[19] As we shall see, Denis succeeds in creating a film that, in imagining what Spivak calls the Other of Europe, does so by simultaneously critiquing dominant representational strategies. In this, she joins an ethical project that Spivak finds already in Foucault. "Foucault," Spivak observes, "is correct in suggesting that 'to make visible the unseen can also mean a change of level, addressing oneself to a layer of material which had hitherto had no pertinence for history and which had not been recognized as having any moral, aesthetic, or historical value.'"[20]

The story of *Chocolat* takes place in two distinct time periods: the present moment of France's return to Cameroon, where she accepts a ride into town with a black man and his son, and the past time of her African childhood under colonization. While riding in the back seat of the car and gazing out the window, her daydreams enable a flashback to the earlier years, and so the film transitions to the space of her memories, where she appears to us as a child. *Chocolat* thus stages another kind of doubling, in which France occupies a subject as well as an object position in relation to her mature self; at the same time, she is a subject in relation to her younger self, and, in that, very much a subject-in-process. In this way, *Chocolat* works against cinematic conventions that create the illusion of a unified, coherent "I" who occupies a coherent national space in a coherent historical interval. The "I" the movie illuminates is already hybrid, a planetary subject, and the character's name suggests that Denis is drawing attention to the country's hybrid identity as well, questioning an outmoded concept of identity that no longer applies to either the individual or the nation.

In presenting France as an isolated, young, naive child growing up in colonial Cameroon, Denis opens up a space for exploring how subjects are socially constructed. The child does not yet know about racism; she has not yet grasped the power relations between colonizers and colonized; and she has not yet ossified her own experiences into concepts she can understand. As she tries to make sense of what surrounds her, she lacks representations that might help her interpret her experiences. Her parents are strangely absent for her; her best friend is the houseboy Protée. As an isolated child in need of emotional connection, France relies solely on Protée, and yet we gather that she does not understand much about him. Nevertheless, they form a strong bond. He protects her even though she remains very much a stranger to him. They communicate more with gestures and silent understanding than with words, all of which poses problems of interpretation for the audience. There are, in effect, no easy answers here; Denis has deliberately created a film in which spectators become aware of the extent to which their own interpretive responses are already conditioned by conventions and categories of knowledge.

Instead of relying, as we usually do, on our cognitive apparatus to interpret the relationship between France and Protée, we can turn instead to the focus on emotion that the film develops at length. Dimock is one of the scholars who have recently singled out emotion as a critically underrated topic. "*Cognition*," she remarks, "is no longer the sole player, the sole determinant of consciousness, and the unfailing ally for language. *Emotion* has entered the field [the study of consciousness] as a new, undertheorized, and potentially more interesting research topic, with as yet unpredictable implications." She points to the challenge of neuroscientists such as Antonio Damasio who have argued for a precognitive, neurophysical ground for emotion. "We first register objects in a 'nonlanguage form,' " Dimock explains, "for our core consciousness rests on a mental substrate at once precognitive and prelinguistic: a '*nonverbal*, *imagined* narrative' that serves as the neurophysiological ground for our powerful emotions."[21] Keeping in mind Dimock's words about the undertheorized importance of emotion, especially in the context of relationality, performativity, and planetarity, and in light of Denis's desire to open up possibilities for the emergence of non-dominant perspectives regarding colonialism, it is useful to notice how Denis shifts attention to the thickening of the emotional relationship between France and Protée as they grow accustomed to each other. Two episodes seem especially important in terms of the powerful emotional bond that links France to Protée and grounds her trust in him.

The first takes place during the night when France is so frightened by the howling of a hyena that she comes into her mother's bedroom for protection, only to discover that she is also fearful and cannot protect her. The mother calls Protée into the room, hands him a gun, and gives him a chair to sit in all night in case the hyena attacks, but Protée does not obey. As we see in the next scene, Protée leaves the bedroom to go out into the night with the little girl on his shoulders, shouting loudly at the hyena, matching his power and force with that of the hyena. We gather that this experience affects France in deep ways, as a powerful difference has just been created in her unconscious between her mother's perceived weakness and Protée's agency, bravery, and power. This scene serves to cement the growing emotional tie France feels with Protée as it distances the child from her mother.

The second pivotal episode unfolds the following day, when, on a visit to the neighboring Norwegians, France notices the bloodied corpses of the animals the hyena has killed during the night. A close-up shot of France's traumatized and uncomprehending face as she looks to Protée for help announces the emotional importance of this scene. The camera shows Protée pondering the incident as he surveys the carnage, then taking a bloodied chicken's leg and gently setting it down next to France's hand. The girl tentatively touches the leg, after which Protée draws some marks on France's arm with blood. To the little girl, this act is full of meaning, for as they prepare to leave, we see that she is carefully holding her arm away from her body as though protecting the inscription. Neither France nor the spectator understands exactly what has taken place here, but we do sense that the connection France feels with Protée has been strengthened considerably, since he is the one who succeeded in bringing closure to her fear by "containing" it within the act of the blood inscription. For the young girl living in Cameroon, separated from others her age, living in emotional solitude, and encountering incomprehensible experiences of fear and death, Protée becomes her single pillar of support.

Whereas the story of French colonialism in Cameroon has historically reflected the colonizers' standpoint, Denis provides a powerful counter-discourse as she tells the story from a perspective that is generally obscured: that of the white female child who happens to be in Cameroon simply because her father is a French administrator. From her angle, we catch sight of the layering down of affective reality as she enters into relation with the people, objects, and landscape around her. From the same perspective, we also get glimpses into the African people's lives, which remain hidden to her parents and the other white colonials. She enters the world of the black workers and participates in their games, transgressing the rigid divide between colonizer and colonized.[22] The film thus opens up a space that reveals how authoritative colonial discourse necessarily blocks out the natives' reality.

As the film unreels its story about French Cameroon, the houseboy's voice is ostensibly silenced. Throughout, Protée is represented as a calm and quiet presence simply serving his colonial family, always polite, performing his functions effortlessly and patiently. Like a piece of furniture, he is simply "there," as if he had no life or thoughts of his own.[23] He is meant to appear as an object of perception not only for the members of the colonial family, but for the spectator of the film as well. Nevertheless, in certain key scenes the director allows his agency and subjectivity to break through, as we shall see below. *Chocolat* thus stages the dehumanization and erasure of the colonized under colonial rule while simultaneously pointing to the existence of a subject-in-process underneath that treatment, a presence who nevertheless remains invisible to the colonizer's eye. In this sense, too, Denis's film is *performative* and provides the kind of doubling Bhabha deems instrumental to a critique of colonial power.

Although seemingly peripheral to the film's narrative, a few scenes in *Chocolat* take up the strategic function of reminding the viewer that Protée has a life of his own, outside his household role. At such moments, the movie hints that it withholds a great deal of information about Protée and that, by implication, colonial authority does not extend as absolutely as the spectator may be tempted to imagine. One brief nighttime episode, for instance, presents Protée talking with a woman. During the conversation, he is comfortably relaxed, smiles, and otherwise behaves in ways we have never seen before; this scene contrasts sharply with that in which he is rigidly dressed in a tuxedo, silently standing at attention and awaiting orders. Another revealing moment that jolts the spectator into realizing that Protée exists as a subject in his own right, endowed with an agency the colonial context either ignores or stifles, comes up during his interaction with the black schoolteacher who helps him write a letter to his parents. From this brief encounter we learn that Protée has a family, that he sends his parents money, and that his sister is getting married. This segment, too, serves to show the spectator that Protée exists outside the narrative frame of the film, more exactly outside the position colonialism has assigned him. Here as well, Denis advances and performs Bhabha's argument about the colonizer's "other" always exceeding the discourse purporting to contain his or her otherness within "totalizing" and "authoritative" representations.

As if to puncture the illusion of seamless authority over its subjects, the movie allows Protée's affective life to come through now and then despite the rigid colonial dictates that he fulfill his duties obediently and generally comply submissively and mechanically, as a non-person of sorts, devoid of inner life. Protée is indeed expected to act but not feel, obey but not question. Despite his decorum, self-control, and success in mastering a neutral façade in front of his masters, his frustration comes to the surface as he kicks the empty buckets of water he has just poured so that Aimée, France's mother, can have her shower. His mounting tension erupts through the façade a second time, when he believes that he has been seen naked by France and Aimée while taking his own shower. These two scenes let us know how difficult it is for Protée to preserve the neutral status quo affectively speaking. As spectators of the film, we thus have access, briefly, to a side of Protée's inner life that no colonial whites see. Through its technique of doubling—Protée is simultaneously silent object of perception and subject endowed with agency and emotion—*Chocolat* opposes that which its cinematic presentation portrays, namely, dominant discourse's efforts to construct Protée as a human automaton devoid of inner complexity and processes.

To be sure, this construction remains consistent across the movie. Even when newcomers threaten to disrupt the status quo, Protée's demeanor does not change. With the arrival of Luc Ségalen, who threatens norms of proper behavior by inserting himself into the female space of Aimée (he spends time reading to her in the garden), Protée steps into the scene in an attempt to disrupt the transgression. In the scene where Aimée reaches out to touch Protée's leg as he closes the drapes, he again maintains the status quo by silently pulling Aimée up to her feet, where she belongs, thus reminding her that the boundary between them will be respected. Protée understands that his employment depends on strict maintenance of appropriate relations, a task made even more difficult whenever the head of household, Marc, disappears to travel on business; as it becomes clear, Marc's presence guarantees adherence to "proper" behavior, while, when he is away, the job falls to Protée.

In realizing that his survival depends on the colonial family's stability, Protée proves much savvier than the homologous protagonist featured in Ferdinand Oyono's *Houseboy* (*Une vie de boy*), the 1956 novel that can be read as *Chocolat*'s "uncanny neighbor."[24] Both the novel and the film are set in Cameroon during French colonialism, and both explore power relations between a houseboy and his colonial family. Furthermore, in the book and the movie alike, the wife's boredom and transgressive inclinations lead inevitably to the banishment of the houseboy from the house; indeed, he knows too much about the behavior of the colonials, and his knowledge gives him a great deal of power, which makes the whites uncomfortable. However, while the movie shows him as a silenced "object" in the eyes of others, the novel makes him the subject of perception. In the book, he narrates his own thoughts about the events that unfold, and this difference in positioning allows the reader access to a perspective *Chocolat* silences *deliberately*, except for those places where it erupts without explanation and calls attention to itself most forcefully.

Oyono's *Houseboy* opens with a scene in which a mysterious narrator finds the dying houseboy Toundi, who utters the phrase that will serve as the philosophical underpinning of the entire novel: "What are we blackmen who are called French?"[25] His use of the word "what" instead of "who" hints that he has acquired, during the course of events depicted in the novel, an understanding of his positioning as object from the perspective of the colonizers. We discover, too, that Toundi has been keeping diaries ever since the missionaries taught him how to write, and now, by reading the journals, we are about to learn firsthand about Toundi's experience in a colonial family, including his reactions to those experiences. Thus, we have access to Toundi's thoughts as he gradually gets to the point where he begins to see through the façade of colonial power. Early on in the narrative, for instance, when he notices that his master is uncircumcised and thus not truly a man as defined by native standards, he concludes that his master is not powerful and wonders why he ever feared him. Similarly, he interprets the white man's inability to control his wife as signifying the husband's weaker status. As the novel continues, we follow Toundi's transformation into the wiser man who finally recognizes the extent to which his knowledge of the infidelities of his master's wife puts him, Toundi, in danger, precisely because it threatens existing master-servant power relations. Unfortunately, he does not heed the advice of the wiser chambermaid Kalisia, who urges him to flee before it is too late: "How can they go strutting about with a cigarette hanging out of their mouth in front of you—when you *know*. As far as they are concerned you are the one who has told everybody and they can't help feeling you are sitting in judgement on them. But that they can never accept. . . . If I were in your shoes, I swear I'd go right away. . . . I wouldn't even wait for my month's wages."[26] As tensions mount, Toundi eventually learns to fear for his life as the white couple becomes increasingly unpredictable and sadistic. Realizing that he knows too much and that his knowledge threatens their elevated view of themselves, he flees. At last, his rhetorical question, "What are we blackmen who are called French?" speaks to his understanding of the scapegoating leading to his death and, more generally, to colonial dehumanization.

So powerfully foregrounded in Oyono's novel, the houseboy's subjectivity is underemphasized in *Chocolat*, although, as already noted, Denis allows traces of it to emerge in the film's fabric. As a subject "under erasure," Protée proves an active participant in the film even though he is ultimately portrayed from the perspective of the isolated child seeking emotional interaction. The movie sustains its double focus on the silent houseboy and the quiet child all the way through the long flashback, with the result that we never know for sure what France or Protée is thinking because they say nothing for much of the time. No doubt, this challenges the spectators, for they are forced into an unfamiliar space that tests an audience's interpretative abilities. At the beginning of the flashback, for example, the child France does not yet know about racism or about the line separating colonizers from colonized, but the houseboy does. From her relatively innocent vantage point, Protée is her best friend; she even tries to play "house" with him, feeding him from a spoon. He obeys her command to eat, but when he licks a drop of food that falls on her hand and she instinctively giggles, his expression suddenly freezes. Denis leaves it to us to interpret what has just happened, putting us in the same position as France, who does not understand why he has become so serious. Protée, it seems, has suddenly realized that he has just crossed an important line.

This double focus on France, who casts Protée into the role of her playmate, and on Protée, aware of the dangers of any transgression (his own included), continues throughout the film. We again witness France's confusion about the houseboy's behavior in the scene where Luc Ségalen, a white man who has come to Africa for unknown reasons, shares an intimate moment in the garden with France's mother. Protée arrives with lemon drinks in an attempt to intervene and disrupt their growing intimacy, while Luc deliberately reads a passage about skin color from German officer Curt von Morgen's account of his 1891 Cameroon expedition. France and Aimée both look instinctively at Protée as if they have just been made aware of something for the first time, and Protée is turned into an object of curiosity. The scene is silent, so we have no access to anyone's thoughts. Spectators may surmise that Luc is deliberately trying to make everyone uncomfortable, but France cannot understand what has just taken place; she looks inquisitively from one adult to another. We are not privy to Protée's thoughts either. Something is taking shape in Protée's mind as well as in France's, but Denis declines to spell it out for us. Here, in this complex moment of relationality, the film seems ethical in its cinematic refusal to create the illusion that it possesses sufficient authority to "explain" the thoughts of colonialism's "others."

The twin narrative centering on France and Protée culminates in the powerful final scene between them in the garage, Protée's new work space after Aimée has him removed from the house because his presence reminds her of her own transgression. France has relied on Protée all along as companion, teacher, and emotional support, but now he asserts himself and, still silently, teaches her that they can no longer be friends in the colonial context. At great physical cost to himself, he tricks her into putting her hand on a hot pipe, which will scar her physically and emotionally. The eye contact between them speaks volumes but is indecipherable. Devastated, she does not understand why he has tricked her; her trusted companion has now become a stranger. For the first time, the child realizes that the houseboy is not there *for her*. Aptly named Protée (Proteus), he has changed beyond recognition. From the close-up of his pained but controlled expression, we understand that Protée knows that his premeditated act has broken her trust, and he walks away into the night, leaving France with her scars.

Representation, Authority, and Planetary Ethics

The scars are as individual as they are collective; France's name is, of course, also that of a nation. Thus, we can return to Bhabha's ideas about performativity and conclude that here, yet again, Denis's film stages colonialism's inability to fully assert its desire and authority over the colonized. In having allowed spectators to glimpse Protée's silenced subjectivity throughout, the film has been foreshadowing the site from which resistance to the totalizing discourse of colonialism emerges.

Extending the idea of the film's performativity, one can identify other kinds of instances in which *Chocolat* deliberately stages its own insufficiency as "authoritative" representation. The flashback section of the film, for instance, is supposed to feature the young woman's memories as a child in Cameroon, but critics have noticed several sequences in which the child could not have been present. They like to point, for instance, to the incident where Aimée reaches out to touch Protée's leg, but this takes place in the house, and France might have watched it. An episode France could not have witnessed, however, occurs inside the tribal chief's hut as the chief tells France's father his story about the face scar he received in an encounter with a lion. Since the young

France could not have been there, the question bears asking, what is the film performing in attributing this scene to France's memory? It is altogether possible that she imagined the hut scene after reading a description of it in her father's journals, which she carries with her upon her return to Cameroon as an older woman. In this respect, the older France occupies a double position as a subject with lived experience as well as a reader who accesses her colonial past through the writing of others. What she remembers, then, and what we see in the movie's flashback, combine both her own perceptions and those of her father, who has already represented them in his journal. The fact that France's memories appear seamlessly alongside material she could only have acquired indirectly through other people's accounts opens the door, of course, to a consideration of the film's ethical function as it purports, on the one hand, to represent "truth" *and* as it ostensibly performs, on the other hand, a questioning of its own truth-claims. In so doing, *Chocolat* draws attention to itself as an artistic intervention that resists any attempt to assert absolute authority, especially the authority associated with representation itself. Many critics have demonstrated how representation has functioned to construct "truths" about Europe's "others"—Edward Said's *Orientalism* still serves as the classic example[27]—but Denis's film is vigilant as it makes visible the fissures in any official representation of French colonization told from the perspective of the colonizer.

Chocolat introduces a new complexity when it moves out of the flashback and returns to the main narrative frame. Now an older France rides in the back seat of a car driven by the black man who has offered her a ride in contemporary Cameroon. He notes that she does not talk much, and, in fact, we realize in retrospect that she has said very little to the man since she has accepted the ride. He has tried to make polite conversation with her, but she has remained aloof and non-communicative. To pass the time, the man divulges a bit about his life, and it is now that the film reveals its surprising twist: the black man is not a native inhabitant of Africa, as both France and, most likely, the spectators also have imagined, but African American. "You're not disappointed?" he asks her, assuming that she has come to Africa to interact with indigenous Africans. Thus, it is not only *her* national home that is problematized by the film, but *his* as well; the assumptions made about what it means to be African are clearly being called into question here. From the moment France hears that this man is not an African who has endured the history of French colonization, her expression changes, her aloof manner disappears, and she indicates her desire to be friendly and talk. In other words, because he was not a French colonial subject, she feels she is not stepping over the line by entering into dialogue with him. In her childhood, Protée had taught her to keep her place by not befriending an African, and she has been living out that lesson, along with its metaphorical and physical scars, ever since. However, because French colonization is not part of this African American man's background, she feels at no risk of breaking any rules.

The crucial element for France, then, is not race but history. As she learns, the man is, like herself, a displaced person with cultural and historical connections in several spaces, in short, a transnational. Thus, she acknowledges their equality and invites him to share a drink, leaving the door open to further communication. But he is not interested; he has his own existential preoccupations ("Here, I'm nothing. . . . If I died now, I'd disappear totally"). He has relocated to Africa assuming that he would come back to his roots, to understanding and brotherhood, but he has found nothing of the kind. This is another indication that *Chocolat* is no nostalgic return to origins, nor is it a celebration of nomadism; it does not offer up vagrant postnationalism as a utopian space. Instead, it remains firmly embedded in what Lionnet and Shih have called "minor transnationalism," which deems particular historical context pertinent. The two critics stress, in fact, this important distinction between nomadism and their brand of transnationalism. "Flexible or nomadic subjects function," Lionnet and Shih maintain, "as if they are free-floating signifiers without psychic and material investment in one or more given particular geopolitical spaces. By contrast, minor transnational subjects are inevitably invested in their respective geopolitical spaces."[28] It is precisely because France is a transnational deeply marked by her own history that she is reluctant to pursue communication with this man until she discovers that he has not experienced French colonization and they are therefore equals.

However, while these two transnationals may share a space of non-dominance with respect to their individual historical realities, that shared space does not necessarily bind them together and guarantee their solidarity. Denis makes this point as well. Toward the end of *Chocolat*, before they part ways, the man reaches for France's hand to read her palm. Noticing the scar that has effaced her palm lines, his remarks—"No past, no future"—suggest that she is a nomad with no history and no direction. But *Chocolat* has not borne out this reading at all; on the contrary, the film has shown that she carries with her a very solid history wherever she travels. Like the native artifacts loaded into the cargo hold of the Cameroonian Airlines jet plane at the end of the film, she, too, has been exported to Europe from elsewhere, but she still maintains her status as a subject grounded in a specific historical time and place—as a human among other humans whose movement across the planet, as Dimock might gloss, is "weaving our history into our dwelling place," thus "making us what we are, a species with a sedimented imprint." "Honoring that imprint, and honoring also the imprints of other creatures evolving as we do," she goes on, "we take our place as one species among others, inhabiting a shared ecology, a shared continuum."[29]

In emphasizing a communal planetary environment here and elsewhere in her work, Dimock is gesturing toward a planetary ethics of relation. *Chocolat* moves in this direction as well. At the very end of the film, the camera follows neither France nor the African artifacts back to Europe. Instead, it stays in Cameroon and records, for an extended duration, the movements of three airline workers who take a break and carry on a relaxed, animated conversation (which we cannot hear) while the soundtrack of South African jazz artist Abdullah Ibrahim plays at full volume. In its closing gesture, *Chocolat* reaffirms once more its non-authoritative, ethical perspective by giving the last scene to the three native men in their own space and to the powerful music that seems to tell a story of its own, beyond the verbal and visual narrative of the film. Indeed, during the last few minutes of the film, its status as representation diminishes in importance as the music's performativity dominates. Here, as it has done throughout, the movie does not attempt to "formulate" or "possess" the other. Rather, it respectfully stages what Emmanuel Levinas has defined as an ethical dynamics of relationality, one in which, as the philosopher says, "such relation involves not striving to possess the other's freedom, but rather experiencing—and delighting in—the other's surpassing our cognitive 'grasp.' "[30] Denis lets us *see* that the three men enjoy life in their own space, but we do not have to *know* what they are saying by eavesdropping on their conversation.

Chocolat promotes and partakes of a planetary consciousness, too, in reminding us throughout about the reality of cultural, artistic, and political diffusion and influence. The image of traveling ships that Gilroy proposed in *The Black Atlantic* is now replaced by airplanes; Denis's film leaves us at the airport, where the aforementioned native workers load large African carved wooden objects into a plane's cargo hold. We know that these pieces are destined for export to places like France, where they will be reclassified as "artworks" to be displayed in museums or commodities to be sold in the marketplace, severed from their original function. With a Texaco gas station in the background in one scene, *Chocolat* reminds us that the colonizing countries and multinational corporations have made and continue to make enormous profits from the extraction of African oil. The film's critique of imperialism even extends to an arrogant French coffee grower who exploits the land as he wishes, treats everyone around him with disdain and disrespect, and assumes that by flashing his money he can have anything he wants. Colonialism guaranteed continued unequal social relations and economic expansion, so while our increasingly transnational world does, indeed, promote cultural relations and artistic influences, it also facilitates the exploitation of the planet's natural resources and populations as prosperous countries continue to form alliances and accumulate wealth at an unprecedented speed.

We live in a world of interconnections and relationality, but, given the geopolitical realities of transnational financial systems, profit-geared sharing of data banks, unfair and even predatory commercial practices, unequal distribution of natural resources, and increasing global warming, urgency demands an ethical intervention for the good of the planet. The interaction of geography, history, and empire has created hierarchies of power, and even an optimistic cosmopolitanism cannot guarantee that, as "citizens of the world," people will care about learning from others whose beliefs or cultures are different from their own; in effect, cosmopolitanism can still be, as it has been at various moments in its history, ethnocentric. Thus, an ethical relationality is desirable—the kind that overcomes inequality and instead honors, from the outset, equality-in-difference. Planetarity is thus an epistemological as well as an ethical project geared toward this relational ideal, a way of thinking that necessitates thinking-in-relation, where the terms themselves are not already marked in advance according to value or hierarchy. Here, we can return to the Foucauldian ideas summarized in the early pages of this chapter, especially to his critique of a philosophy of representation grounded, since Plato, in a system of dichotomies where one of the terms is already coded as positive and the other, relegated to its status as "other," as negative. This kind of thinking guarantees hierarchical thought and will never be able to value equality-in-difference. Walter D. Mignolo takes this point even further in "The Geopolitics of Knowledge and the Colonial Difference," where he highlights the importance of thinking not from the perspective of European philosophy but from the vantage point of "the colonial difference." The future of ethics, he notes, lies in "the densities of the colonial experience," which are also "the location of emerging epistemologies."[31] For an ethical planetarity to take shape, he contends, philosophy itself needs to be decolonized along the lines proposed by Enrique Dussel: "An Ethic of Liberation, with planetary scope ought, first of all, to 'liberate' (I would say decolonize) philosophy from Helenocentrism. Otherwise, it cannot be a future worldly philosophy, in the twenty-first century."[32] Incorporating the inherently relational, philosophical idea of equality-in-difference into the ethical project of planetarity, Mignolo coins the term "diversality." "An other logic (or border thinking from the perspective of subalternity) goes," he explains, "with a geopolitics of knowledge that regionalizes the fundamental European legacy, locating thinking in the colonial difference and creating the conditions for diversality as a universal project."[33] *Chocolat* seems to move in this direction as well, for Denis has offered us different kinds of new and provocative insights into French colonialism from the non-authoritative perspectives of a child and a houseboy, all the while questioning the truth-claims of authoritative representation itself.

Notes

1. Gayatri Chakravorty Spivak, *Death of a Discipline* (New York: Columbia University Press, 2003), 72, 73.

2. Kwame Anthony Appiah, *Cosmopolitanism: Ethics in a World of Strangers* (New York: W. W. Norton, 2006), 98–99.

3. Spivak, *Death of a Discipline*, 76, 82, 100.

4. See Françoise Lionnet and Shu-mei Shih, "Introduction: Thinking through the Minor, Transnationally," in *Minor Transnationalism*, ed. Françoise Lionnet and Shu-mei Shih (Durham, N.C.: Duke University Press, 2005), 1–23.

5. See Edouard Glissant, *Poetics of Relation*, trans. Betsy Wing (Ann Arbor: University of Michigan Press, 1997), originally published as *Poétique de la relation* (Paris: Gallimard, 1990); and Amin Maalouf, *In the Name of Identity: Violence and the Need to Belong*, trans. Barbara Bray (New York: Arcade, 2001), originally published as *Les identités meurtrières* (Paris: Grasset & Fasquelle, 1996).

6. Paul Gilroy, *The Black Atlantic: Modernity and Double Consciousness* (Cambridge, Mass.: Harvard University Press, 1993), 4, 19.

7. Maalouf, *In the Name of Identity*, 31.

8. Mary Louise Pratt, "Modernity and Periphery: Toward a Global and Relational Analysis," in *Beyond Dichotomies: Histories, Identities, Cultures, and the Challenge of Globalization*, ed. Elisabeth Mudimbe-Boyi (Albany: State University of New York Press, 2002), 32.

9. Homi K. Bhabha, "Introduction: Narrating the Nation," in *Nation and Narration*, ed. Homi K. Bhabha (London: Routledge, 1990), 1.

10. Homi K. Bhabha, "DissemiNation: Time, Narrative, and the Margins of the Modern Nation," in *Nation and Narration*, 292, 295, 297, 299 (emphasis in original).

11. Spivak, *Death of a Discipline*, 13.

12. Emily Apter, *The Translation Zone: A New Comparative Literature* (Princeton, N.J.: Princeton University Press, 2006), 92.

13. Wai Chee Dimock, "Introduction: Planet and America, Set and Subset," in *Shades of the Planet: American Literature as World Literature*, ed. Wai Chee Dimock and Lawrence Buell (Princeton, N.J.: Princeton University Press, 2007), 5.

14. See Michel Foucault, "Nietzsche, Genealogy, History," in *Language, Counter-Memory, Practice: Selected Essays and Interviews*, ed. Donald F. Bouchard, trans. Donald F. Bouchard and Sherry Simon (Ithaca, N.Y.: Cornell University Press, 1977), 139–64.

15. Michel Foucault, "Theatrum Philosophicum," in *Language, Counter-Memory, Practice*, 173, 177 (emphasis mine).

16. Ibid., 170, 171. I have found Foucault's ideas pertinent in interarts analysis; see my *Reading Relationally: Postmodern Perspectives on Literature and Art* (Ann Arbor: University of Michigan Press, 2000).

17. Claire Denis, dir., *Chocolat*, prod. Alain Belmondo and Gérard Crosnier, wr. Claire Denis and Jean-Pol Fargeau, perf. Giulia Boschi, Isaach de Bankolé, François Cluzet, Cécile Ducasse, Mireille Perrier, music Abdullah Ibrahim, Ciné-manuel, MK2 Productions, Cerito Films, La S.E.P.T., Caroline Productions, Le F.O.D.I.C. Cameroun, Wim Wenders Produktion Berlin, TFI Films Production, Orion Films, 1988.

18. For a discussion of three important films that revisit France's colonial past, see Alison Murray, "Women, Nostalgia, Memory: *Chocolat*, *Outremer*, and *Indochine*," *Research in African Literatures* 33, no. 2 (Summer 2002): 235–44. Unlike Murray, I do not read *Chocolat* as a "nostalgia film."

19. Gayatri Chakravorty Spivak, "Can the Subaltern Speak?" in *Marxism and the Interpretation of Culture*, ed. Cary Nelson and Lawrence Grossberg (Urbana: University of Illinois Press, 1988), 280.

20. Ibid., 285.

21. Wai Chee Dimock, *Through Other Continents: American Literature across Deep Time* (Princeton, N.J.: Princeton University Press, 2006), 155, 156 (emphasis in original).

22. Adam Muller sees the child France as an embodiment of moral cosmopolitanism and calls *Chocolat* a film with a "powerfully contemporary moral sensibility"; see Muller, "Notes toward a Theory of Nostalgia: Childhood and the Evocation of the Past in Two European 'Heritage' Films," *New Literary History* 37, no. 4 (Autumn 2006): 741. He reads *Chocolat* as an example of what Svetlana Boym has called "reflective nostalgia"; see Boym, "Reflective Nostalgia: Virtual Reality and Collective Memory," in *The Future of Nostalgia* (New York: Basic Books, 2001), 49–55.

23. Donald R. Wehrs has proposed a non-Western interpretation of this kind of self-regulating behavior in the context of maintaining an ethical relationship to the other: "The stress upon self-restraint and rational self-regulation integral to the moral traditions of Islam, Hinduism, and polytheistic sub-Saharan Africa (among others) may be accounted for as ethical modifications of freedom, not mere mechanisms of control"; see his article "Sartre's Legacy in Postcolonial Theory; or, Who's Afraid of Non-Western Historiography and Cultural Studies?" *New Literary History* 34, no. 4 (Autumn 2003): 772.

24. Ferdinand Oyono, *Houseboy*, trans. John Reed (London: Heinemann, 1990), originally published as *Une vie de boy* (Paris: Julliard, 1956). Borrowing from Kenneth Reinhard, Apter develops the concept of neighboring, a comparing of two texts that are "uncanny neighbor[s]" of each other, "determined by accidental contiguity, genealogical isolation, and ethical encounter" (*The Translation Zone*, 247). I have developed similar ideas about "relational reading" across the fields of literature and visual art; see Edson, *Reading Relationally*.

25. Oyono, *Houseboy*, 4.

26. Oyono, *Houseboy*, 100–101 (emphasis in original).

27. See Edward W. Said, *Orientalism* (New York: Pantheon, 1978).

28. Lionnet and Shih, "Introduction," 8.

29. Dimock, *Through Other Continents*, 6.

30. Quoted in Wehrs, "Sartre's Legacy," 771.

31. Walter D. Mignolo, "The Geopolitics of Knowledge and the Colonial Difference," *South Atlantic Quarterly* 101, no. 1 (Winter 2002): 67.

32. Quoted in Mignolo, "The Geopolitics of Knowledge," 70. Mignolo cites Enrique Dussel's work in "Beyond Eurocentrism: The World-System and the Limits of Modernity," in *The Cultures of Globalization*, ed. Fredric Jameson and Masao Miyoshi (Durham, N.C.: Duke University Press, 1998), 3–31.

33. Mignolo, "The Geopolitics of Knowledge," 91.

Gilgamesh's Planetary Turns

WAI CHEE DIMOCK

Can we understand the turn to "world literature"—as David Damrosch defines it—as a turn not to a designated canon but to a circulatory effect, "the *effective* life" of any text "whenever, and wherever, it is actively present within a literary system beyond that of its original culture"?[1] If so, then what are the consequences of thinking of literature in this way, that is, as a far-flung network of redistribution, recombination, and recontextualization? And is it possible to add another analytic layer, putting the emphasis less on the networks projected to come into being than on the ones already enjoined, feeding a stream of reusable material from earliest antiquity into an ever-growing body of work, sustaining a planetary ecology and bringing newness into the world through the turns of decomposition and recomposition?

In what follows, I experiment with this approach, looking at the epic not in isolation but as part of a recycling process unfolding on three continents, across a variety of genres and media, and over a period of several thousand years. The text being recycled is *Gilgamesh*, an epic originating from Mesopotamia and developing multiple variants even in 1700 B.C.E. The novel *Gilgamesh* (2001), by the Australian author Joan London, is the one of the most recent spin-offs from it. There are many others, including many from the United States, and in thinking about the "planetary ecology" of *Gilgamesh*, it is worth looking outside a strictly text-based medium to engage a distributive process that not only reuses the old but also spills over in all conceivable directions, into all conceivable venues.

Staging

I begin with a collaboration between dramaturge Chad Gracia and Pulitzer Prize-winning poet Yusef Komunyakaa. In 2006, these two teamed up for a stage adaptation of *Gilgamesh*. The text was published by Wesleyan University Press,[2] and the play was performed in New York, Chicago, Boston, and New Orleans, Komunyakaa's home for many years.

These were lean productions, with a small crew, no set to speak of, and about six actors doing double or triple duty, playing more than one role, and often serving as handy stage props. Making ingenious use of simple objects, actors produced a wealth of visual effects to make up for the bareness of the stage. In the Chicago performances by the Silk Road Theatre Project, the Goddess Ishtar, for instance, was shown only as a silhouette, a face in the moon, an effect accomplished with a flashlight and stretched cotton over a hula hoop. Humbaba, the guardian of the cedar forest and Gilgamesh's main adversary, was meanwhile represented by a bamboo frame covered with green and brown fabric and moved around by three actors. The Silk Road Theatre Project called this kind of theater "stylized and actor-driven." Another name for it would be poor man's theater: low-tech and low-cost, using nothing more than the primitive resources of the dramatic medium. However, this did not mean low-quality. The Silk Road Theatre Project is a respected company, receiving grants from Google, IBM, the MacArthur Foundation, and the National Endowment for the Arts. Their low-budget production is rather a point of pride, the signature style of a theater with a particular vision of itself. Founded in 2002 by Malik Gillani and Jamil Khoury as a response to the anti-Arab and anti-Islam sentiments sweeping across the United States after the 9/11 attacks, it set out to be a grassroots theater for the multi-faith and multiethnic communities that once flourished on the trade routes linking Asia to Africa and Europe. The Komunyakaa-Gracia adaptation of *Gilgamesh* is very much in that spirit.

I go into these details because these empirical circumstances are almost never mentioned in theories of the epic. While Mikhail Bakhtin draws on the language of theater to create an analytical vocabulary for the *novel*—for the "carnival" in Rabelais—the politics and pragmatics of stage adaptation are subjects that never come up when he discusses the *epic*, which he dismisses as a dead-end genre, ossified and moribund, with a past but no present or future.[3] What difference does it make to see the epic through an empirical lens, through specific instances of translation, citation, and stage adaptation, instances of recycling that bring it back, break it up, and redistribute it across a variety of locations and platforms? How do these activities, often happening at irregular intervals and at locations hard to predict, complicate our understanding of this particular genre and of "genre" as a planetary phenomenon, an evolving field spread across temporal as well as geographical coordinates?

The Komunyakaa-Gracia adaptation reaches back to the oldest known epic, a non-Western one, predating the *Iliad* and the *Odyssey* by a thousand years. It reminds us of the local and largely ungeneralizable contexts for recycling, some having to do with the quirks of on-site production and some much broader in scope, fueled by large-scale events such as global terrorism and the 9/11 attacks. How do these input networks—macro, micro, and any number of intermediaries—bear on the form of the epic, its morphological spectrum over the course of five thousand years, as well as the permutative possibilities of any particular moment? What is the typical scale of operation for the genre, and how much variation might we expect as we navigate within one work and among several works?

Mash-up

The case of *Gilgamesh* is especially instructive. Unlike the *Iliad* and the *Odyssey*, the Mesopotamian epic originated in written form, etched into clay tablets. It was not improvisationally composed by rhapsodes, who selectively rearranged the oral epics as they traveled. And yet, in its enormous range of variations—far more diverse than the Homeric epics—this epic stands as the earliest (and still most stunning) example of a text that was never integral to begin with, a text that upon its transcription was immediately translated and continued to flourish only through various turns of translation, combination, and recombination.

Gilgamesh was a historical king who ruled in the Mesoptamian city of Uruk around 2750 B.C.E. Legends about him probably arose shortly after his death; they were first written in Sumerian, a non-Semitic language with no relation to Akkadian, the Semitic language in which *Gilgamesh* would eventually be circulated across Mesopotamia. This earliest Sumerian material seems to have existed as five separate poems for about a thousand years, long after the Sumerian people were overrun by their Semitic neighbors; around 1700 B.C.E. the poems began to be collated and translated into the cuneiform script of the Babylonian language, a dialect of Akkadian. The best preserved were twelve tablets pieced together a bit later, probably around 1200 B.C.E. by the scholar-priest Sin-liqe-unninni, and eventually brought to the library of Ashurbanipal, king of Assyria (668–627 B.C.E.).

As is clear from this brief account, the making of *Gilgamesh* was long drawn out even in ancient Mesopotamia; the shape of the text and its basic features varied tremendously from one collator to another and one translator to another. These early efforts at collation, however, were nothing like the monumental labor performed in the nineteenth century by European scholars faced with hundreds and thousands of broken fragments of such clay tablets.[4] How to restore these to some legible order? Since the epic existed in so many different versions, put together by so many different scribes over such a long period of time, and since none of these had survived intact—even the most complete set, Sin-liqe-unninni's, is missing approximately one-third of its lines—guesswork was unavoidable in the nineteenth century, and it remains unavoidable in every modern translation. Stephen Mitchell's, one of the most readable, uses Sin-liqe-unninni's twelve-tablet "Standard Version" as the primary source, filling in the gaps with words or lines from some other tablets and from the Sumerian poems. Andrew George's 1999 Penguin edition and Benjamin Foster's 2001 Norton Critical Edition go even further. In the Penguin edition, Sin-liqe-unninni's "Standard Version" is presented along with four other versions: Babylonian texts from the early second millennium B.C.E.; Babylonian texts from the late second millennium B.C.E.; texts from the late second millennium B.C.E. but from outside Babylonia; and, finally, the Sumerian poems. In the Norton Critical Edition, four texts are offered: the "Standard Version"; the Sumerian poems; a late second-millennium B.C.E. translation of *Gilgamesh* into the Hittite language; and, finally, a parody called *The Gilgamesh Letter*. Both the Penguin and the Norton editions use square brackets and ellipses to indicate either conjectural inserts or unfilled gaps in the text.

What counts as the "text" of *Gilgamesh*—what is included and what is left out, how the gaps are filled and with what additional material—reflects an editor's preferences more than anything else. These preferences can go quite far in remaking the text, giving it an up-to-date purpose, an up-to-date agenda. Stephen Mitchell, for instance, translating *Gilgamesh* in the twenty-first century, cannot help seeing in the Mesopotamian epic an "eerie counterpoint to the recent American invasion of Iraq." In the poem, Gilgamesh's sudden announcement of epic purpose sounds in this context like the immemorial words of "the original preemptive strike": "where the fierce monster Humbaba lives. / We must kill him and drive out evil from the world."[5] Is this really a battle of good against evil, as Gilgamesh claims? "Everything in the poem argues against it," Mitchell says. "As a matter of fact, the only evil we are informed of is the suffering Gilgamesh has inflicted on his own people; the only monster is Gilgamesh himself." Humbaba, the targeted villain, "hasn't harmed a single living being": Mitchell explains that it is "impossible to see Humbaba as a threat to the security of Uruk or as part of any 'axis of evil.'" On the contrary, as the guardian of the Cedar Forest, he "is a figure of balance and a defender of the ecosystem. (Having a monster or two around to guard our national forests from corporate and other predators wouldn't be such a bad thing.)"[6]

Komunyakaa and Gracia do not claim for *Gilgamesh* quite this degree of contemporary relevance, although, as we will see, their play is not without topical accents of its own. Since theirs is not a translation but a stage adaptation venturing into an entirely different medium, the allowable deviations are also much greater. Komunyakaa took full advantage of these, not only inventing entirely new characters but also in some instances using the outline of the epic only as a loose-fitting shell to develop themes he had already been exploring elsewhere. The initial idea for the play had come not from him but from Gracia. Unlike Komunyakaa, a Pulitzer Prize-winning poet, and unlike Stephen Mitchell, celebrated translator of the *Bhagavad Gita*, the *Tao Te Ching*, and the *Book of Job*, among other works, Gracia is a dramaturge operating on a considerably lower level. (On his own website he is now listed as working in international trade and development, specializing in the Middle East.) It is fair to say that he is less the top dog in the theater world than a persevering fan of the Mesopotamian epic, determined to give it a contemporary staging.

Corruptible Body

Gracia was first introduced to *Gilgamesh* as a young reader of Will Durant's *Our Oriental Heritage*. It was the beginning of a lifelong attachment. For weeks after reading it, he could not get this line out of his head: "I too shall die, for am I not like Enkidu?"[7] The line is Gilgamesh's. He and Enkidu have been inseparable up to this point, their partnering not an issue. After the slaying of Humbaba, however, this inseparability suddenly becomes vexed. Gilgamesh does not want to be exactly like his friend at just this moment for Enkidu has been singled out for punishment by the gods: of the two, he is the one who must die. This differential outcome is in some sense the logical extension of the initial difference between the two friends: from the first we know that Gilgamesh is part God (through his mother, Ninsun, he is supposed to be "two-thirds divine, one-third human"), whereas Enkidu seems to be part animal: he is the "man-beast of the Steppe."[8] Both, it seems, are only fractionally human but fractional in opposite ways, pointing to two antithetical forms of identity. How do these get resolved? If humans are always going to be part-animal and part-god, which of these two gene pools will rise to the top, or, realistically, which will turn out to be the non-negotiable baseline, the most fundamental fact about us?

The death of Enkidu raises the question to a fever pitch. No longer fully human, is there enough humanity left for the corpse to resist being banished to the other side? How long can it put off that eventuality? How long can it hold on to its fractional species membership before being relegated once and for all to a much lower rung of the taxonomic hierarchy? Hanging in the balance seems to be the very nature of "humanness"—our place in the animate and inanimate world, our relations to other living things and to non-sentient organic matter. Who are our kin, our kind? Especially troubling here are the physicality of the body and its seemingly inexorable outcome. Does a body like that not doom us to being more animal-like rather than godlike? What exactly does it mean to be attached to, and coextensive with, a body that is perishable and corruptible?

Gilgamesh is unsparing on this point. Rather than giving Enkidu a dignified and ceremonious end, the Gilgamesh author(s) show him at the last as a corpse, a mound of dead flesh. Enkidu's deadness is accented by a small visual detail that has maximum shock effect, a revolting close-up from which we are not allowed to look away. It is this small detail that is stuck in Gracia's mind. We can think of it as a moment of "microcization": Gilgamesh hanging onto the corpse, not letting go, until

> a maggot
> drop[ped] from Enkidu's
> nose.[9]

Gracia was reading Ernest Becker's *The Denial of Death* at the same time as he was reading *Gilgamesh*, and it seemed to him that what Becker was saying about human beings—that we are "gods with anuses"—could have served as well as a motto for the Sumerian epic.[10] Gross physicality is, of course, a common sight in the epic; there are numerous instances in Homer's work, especially in the *Iliad*. But *Gilgamesh* is unique in putting the maggot at center stage, magnifying it far beyond its objective puniness. This is the less-than-human emblem of the less-than-human baseline of our species: it unites all of us, and it unites our species to all the others. As common denominators go, this one is exceptionally low, setting the bar for species membership at a level where there is in fact no sharp distinction between humans and nonhumans, nor between the so-called civilized and the so-called barbaric. Death seen up close, fear of dying oneself, the instant degradability of the physical body: these are the basic ingredients that make up the epic landscape shared by humans and animals. The genre is "primitive" in this sense: not only is *Gilgamesh* the oldest literature known to humans, but also the emotions provoked by it are raw, visceral, and primal. From the standpoint of evolution, they represent the most elemental brain processes, evolved in and robustly shared by a large number of animal species, having been there from the first and likely to be there till the bitter end.

Yet rather than being permanently stuck in the past and cut off from the living world, as Bakhtin contends, the epic *is* the genre of the living world. It is the genre that carries forward the most physically grounded, basic emotions known to humankind. The epic is a prehistoric continuum surviving into the twenty-first century, enunciating fears and hurts undiminished in strength and sway over the species. It is able to serve as this carrier mostly by remaining a "low" genre both in terms of its simple, death-driven narratives and in terms of the deflationary view of humanity that such narratives call up. This is a genre that constructs a spectrum of life forms—gods on the one end, worms on the other—and leaves little doubt about where we humans stand. "Mortals": this is the label that the epic reserves for our species. It sums us up. And, when the end arrives, as it is guaranteed to do, the epic quite often marks that occurrence with a formal spasm: simultaneously magnifying, contracting, and disorienting, it gives the end of life a hallucinatory intensity that fills every inch of space yet shrinks to a smaller and smaller point.

Macro and Micro

All of which is to say that the epic is doing active work on more than one scale, going back and forth between the large and the small and bringing these two into dialogue, bringing one to bear on the other, if not as an inverted prism, then as a persistent counterpoint. Aristotle is wrong, then, to associate the epic only with the vexingly large. The vexingly small is equally within its province.[11]

In fact, it probably does not make a lot of sense to maintain a strict separation between the epic and other genres simply on the basis of a text's own size or of the size of that which it examines, for the epic's operating coordinates are far from uniform, with a broad spectrum of variation linked to an alternating rhythm, often crossing over into the territory that is traditionally assigned to other genres.

In what follows, I would like to argue against a strict separation between epic and lyric. Rather than aligning the former only with the macro and the latter only with the micro, I would like to see these dimensional planes as up-and-down scalar variations that can be switched into and switched out of quite routinely, without too much fuss. Epic and lyric, in this view, are complementary registers, a functional duality allowing representational space to expand or contract as the need arises, to alternate when necessary between the technically neutral bird's-eye view and the deliberately charged close-up. While it still makes sense to think of lyric and epic as distinct genres, the "lyricization" of the epic is by no means oxymoronic but rather an important operational dimension of the genre, making it scale-rich, scale-variable.

For this reason, the otherwise localized phenomenon of death, happening inside just one body, can be both hidebound and world-destroying, both center and circumference. In *Gilgamesh* death is figured in both the concentrated repulsiveness of the maggot and the reproducible story of grief and fear, occasioned by the corruptibility of the body and expanding to include many spin-offs from the death event. It is a story populated by a host of gods and a host of unclassifiable creatures (such as Humbaba and the Scorpion People). All have some relation to humans, to the mortals that we are. The epic is a multi-scale, multi-species environment that stretches the bounds of representation far beyond the customary borders of the "real," turning unthinkably alien life forms into companionable creatures and interlocutors on life's journey.

It should come as no surprise, then, that one of the names the epic would adopt in the twentieth century is "science fiction." A modern mutation of the ancient genre, science fiction adds extraterrestrial species and interplanetary travel to the epic plot but otherwise sticks with the same death-driven and life-seeking narratives and the emotions they reproduce and reactivate. Intimation of mortality, the physical nature of the body, and the up-for-grabs definition of "humanness" itself: these basic ingredients of the Mesopotamian epic are also the basic ingredients of science fiction. One telling example illustrates this. Nearly five thousand years after *Gilgamesh*'s inception, the 102nd episode of the 1990s television series *Star Trek: The Next Generation* reaches back in self-conscious tribute to the ancient epic. The "Darmok" episode, well known among literary scholars, reinscribes the "epic DNA" of *Gilgamesh*—what made it so powerful and widely translated in ancient

Mesopotamia and also what makes it so eminently recyclable now. And yet, while this *Star Trek* episode does reenact the iconic scene of one companion dying and the other grieving, its overwhelming focus is not on the biological necessity of death but rather on the human determination to survive.[12]

This example, and numerous others like it, suggests that the epic is best explored as a cascading form, with a downstream textual field exploding in volume, energized by various projective arcs and increasingly scattered across a variety of genres and media. The *Star Trek* episode is indeed a striking example, a transcoding and redirecting of those cuneiform tablets onto a non-text-based (or at least not strictly text-based) platform that is mass-circulated and low in literary prestige but high in popular appeal, as measured in number of viewers. The ease with which the epic can make it onto the TV screen points to at least three possibilities. First, the genre seems to have an easily mobilized set of optics and a predisposition towards images, perhaps because humans have always been more visual than linguistic or because human emotions before the advent of language were triggered by visual cues.[13] Second, popular culture is not a problem for the epic. It is entirely at home there, its primitive griefs and fears and its easily visualizable plots comprehensible even to the unschooled and needing no exegesis. And finally, the frequency of recycling in the epic speaks to "lyricization" as one of the most important self-propagating mechanisms of the genre, since a very small group of words, and certainly not the entire epic, is selectively highlighted, extracted, and circulated anew, gaining new meanings and entering into new associations in entirely different environments. It is not the large size of the epic but the portability of a tiny fraction of it that allows it to spread far and wide, to be cited and embedded over and over again, in countless new updates and remakes.

But if this is true, portability would seem to rest on something like the *non-integrity* of the original text—the ease with which the latter can be broken up, pieces of it dislodged and taken elsewhere, and the ease with which it can be mixed in with new material, not only in contexts increasing far away in time and geography but also in registers often operating at a lower cultural elevation. As we have seen with *Gilgamesh*, the general tendency for the epic, in the thousands of years of its recycling, is to drift steadily downward, assimilating itself to more popular tastes, moving to more popular venues, speaking the street vernacular of the locals. The epic is eminently "corruptible" in this sense: random composting is natural to it, while fragmenting, fermenting, and disintegrating are its life-processes. Not only does the genre have a thematic interest in the degradability of matter, but it also is itself a part of that process, degrading with gusto and feeding the unsparing but microbially vital downward percolations that carry the process forward. From this perspective, the maggot is not only a repulsive detail; it is a counterintuitively *lyrical* detail, a close-up too gross for comfort but also life-giving in that grossness. It keeps the epic going, just as it keeps the planet's ecosystem turning.

The Maggot and the DNA of Epic

What would a play look like that gives pride of place to the maggot, a play dedicated to the twin concepts of corruptibility and renewability? Gracia started casting about for a playwright already thinking along those lines. Komunyakaa caught his attention right away, since the poet already has under his belt a poem entitled "Ode to the Maggot":

> Brother of the blowfly
> & godhead, you work magic
> Over battlefields,
> In slabs of bad pork
> & flophouses. Yes, you
> Go to the root of all things.
> You are sound & mathematical.
> Jesus Christ, you're merciless
> With the truth. Ontological & lustrous,
> You cast spells on beggars & kings
> Behind the stone door of Caesar's tomb
> Or split trench in a field of ragweed.
> No decree or creed can outlaw you
> As you take every living thing apart. Little
> Master of earth, no one gets to heaven
> Without going through you first.[14]

"Ode to the Maggot" was published in 2000 in *Talking Dirty to the Gods*. Komunyakaa was probably not thinking of *Gilgamesh* when he wrote this poem, and in fact its emotional orientation is significantly different. In *Gilgamesh*, the maggot is harsh, unstoppable, the voice of necessity from the biosphere. "Ode to the Maggot," on the other hand, is almost a fond tribute to the "little / Master of earth," finding something "ontological & lustrous" where most people would feel disgust. The poem employs a shift in perspective and in scale of attention that marks a shift from epic to lyric, recognizable even within a strict definition of those two genres. The shift is not too difficult, for the maggot in fact has the scalar flexibility that allows it to be at home in the alternating rhythm that links the two genres. On a lyrical note, Komunyakaa's poem reminds us that decomposing texts, like decomposing bodies, are the lifeblood of any generative process, a thought twined around the disintegration of matter that it executes on the epic stage. This modern-day maggot, in short, has enough in common with the ancient one in Mesopotamia to convince Gracia that Komunyakaa "had a *Gilgamesh* waiting inside him all along.[15]

It is an interesting idea, a theory of literature based on the virtual guarantee of cross-time reproduction. Even as the epic carries forward the evolutionary psychology of the human species on a large scale, it would seem itself to be enacting a micro-evolution on its own, long drawn out but apparently fairly dependable. What Gracia is proposing, in fact, is a special kind of textual genetics, based not on the replication of a DNA script but rather on the mutation and fragmentation of textual motifs, linguistic clusters, into smaller and smaller recombinable units. This would be a "lyricization" uniquely able to propagate, to produce new and altered assemblages at greater and greater distances. How do we otherwise account for the proven track record of *Gilgamesh*, for its history of being recycled over and over again, not always predictably, but not without some degree of regularity?

The environmental reason for this continuity is both simpler and more inexorable than we might think. For, to the extent that the death of physical organisms has remained a hard fact across time—in effect, one of the key constants of the biosphere—and to the extent that most of us have remained unreconciled to it, unconsoled in the face of its necessity, mortality might turn out to be the single most consequential human event on the planet, experienced to the full from one generation to another. The primitive devastations of *Gilgamesh* are no less devastating now than they were five thousand years ago. The potency and transmissibility of this particular bit of genetic material make the epic robust, durable, and adaptable.

As Komunyakaa's poem illustrates, however, the epic DNA reproduced throughout his corpus might not be mortality as a general condition but rather the smaller, grosser pressure point that is the maggot. This particular fascination no doubt has something to do with the author's background and the entwined coarseness and delicacy surrounding death in that particular environment. Son of a carpenter, Komunyakaa grew up in Bogalusa, Louisiana, forty miles north of New Orleans. He was given the name James William Brown, but later reclaimed the African name Komunyakaa, the name of his grandfather, a stowaway from the West Indies:

> My grandfather came from Trinidad
> Smuggled in like a sack of papaya
> . . . .
> The name Brown fitted him like trouble.[16]

The family was poor. One of the effects of that poverty was a kind of companionship with death, an accommodation to the act of killing and with what happens after the killing. In the "Meat" section of the long poem "A Good Memory," Komunyakaa writes:

> Folk magic hoodooed us
> Till the varmints didn't taste bitter
> Or wild. We boys & girls

Knew how to cut away musk glands
Behind their legs. Good
With knives, we believed
We weren't poor.

. . . .

Sometimes
We weighed the bullet
In our hands, tossing it left
To right, wondering if it was
Worth more than the kill.[17]

Someone who kills to eat every day is going to have a very different attitude than would well-to-do urbanites about meat consumption and about the edible nature of bodies. Hunger, a perennial problem in Bogalusa, would have been much worse if individual animal bodies were not so easily degradable, so easily absorbed back into the vital processes of the biosphere. This recycling-based aesthetics gives the maggot an honored place in Komunyakaa's poetry, assigning it the same ontological centrality (if a somewhat different emotional charge) that it carried in *Gilgamesh*. And, of course, it was this small, diligent, and easily portable bit of epic DNA that would also accompany the poet as he went to war.

For, in fact, Komunyakaa went to Vietnam. He was there from 1969 to 1970, working for the Army's newspaper, *The Southern Cross,* covering the military action and writing articles on Vietnamese history that won him a Bronze Star. He also published a volume of poems, *Dien Cai Dau,* perhaps the most memorable poetry to come out of the Vietnam War. In this volume, there is another poem, "We Never Know," also seemingly descended from *Gilgamesh*, that reenacts the same divided tableau of dying and surviving and once again puts flies and maggots at the center:

He danced with tall grass
for a moment, like he was swaying
with a woman. Our gun barrels
glowed white-hot.
When I got to him,
a blue halo
of flies had already claimed him.
I pulled the crumbled photograph
from his fingers.
There's no other way
to say this: I fell in love.
The morning cleared again,
except for a distant mortar

& somewhere choppers taking off.
I slid the wallet into his pocket
& turned him over, so he wouldn't be
kissing the ground.[18]

The dead man in the poem is a complete stranger, most likely an enemy combatant, someone the poet has just killed, someone he is supposed to kill. Yet this death is anything but routine. On the contrary, it is self-consciously lyrical: a spot of time special unto itself, luminous and overflowing with meaning, its smallness amplified into something much larger. It is fitting that this subjectively magnified event should be coupled with and offered in counterpoint to the larger narrative of war, here miniaturized in its turn. For death in combat is indeed a classic moment of scalar instability, oscillating between two or more phenomenal planes, between epic expanse and lyric compression, between the impersonal necessity of killing and the convulsiveness of death as bodily event.

The poem begins on a lyrical note, with a slightly blurred, almost hallucinatory image of the enemy combatant swaying and dancing. But it pulls back from that lyricization as it moves swiftly to the other end of the emotional spectrum, its descriptive lens zeroing in on the now-fallen body, with a "halo / of flies" already gathered. It is unsightly, grossly reductive and deflating, turning the dead soldier instantly into an abject corpse: edible flesh, food for worms. We could call this a moment of ecological realism; an impersonal, across-the-board recycling downward. Yet this particular form of recycling is one that acknowledges the subjectivity of each organism rather than erasing it completely. In fact, in a double-stranded structure almost like a double helix, the ecological realism is coupled here with an organism-based lyricism that counters it, a lyricism that grants the fallen soldier a degree of individuality. Startlingly, completely out of the blue, the poet announces that he has fallen in love. We do not know with whom he has fallen in love, whether it is the dead man or the person in the crumbled photograph pulled out of his wallet by the speaker just before the man dies. But that almost does not matter. The identity of the love recipient is less important than the fact that the sentiment is there, amplified, attended to, and given poetic life. Both epic and lyric are honored by this alternating rhythm, a scalar flexibility that unmakes and remakes, as tender as it is hard-nosed.

And the alternation persists. The poem's speaker now makes another gesture in the direction of lyric as he does two last things: he puts the wallet back into the dead man's pocket and turns him over, to face up. These gestures, each deliberate, each unexplained, and all non-trivial, do not change the fact that the dead man is organic matter. They do not have the power to fend off the "blue halo / of flies" that are most certainly there. On the contrary, it is the visceral proximity of those flies that makes the cross-stitched rhythm of epic and lyric so powerful, with two force fields intertwined and yet pulling in opposing directions, energized by that paradox, carrying forward both the non-negotiability of our physical end and the infinitely negotiable turns of textual reproduction.

Variation and Mutation

Since this alternating rhythm is so close to the expanding and contracting phenomenal planes of death in combat,[19] we should not be surprised that, in his more recent collection, *Warhorses* (2008), as Komunyakaa turns from Vietnam to Iraq and Afghanistan, the same genetic material from *Gilgamesh* and the same double-stranded structure would be brought along, put to work in these new environments. The cross-stitching of the large and the small is reflected this time in the very form of the poetry. In a long, fourteen-section poem called "Love in the Time of War," Komunyakaa devotes an entire section to the Sumerian epic, taking in the gods and the cosmos but also lyricizing the death of one particular individual, turning it into an arresting micro-phenomenon:

> Gilgamesh's Humbaba was a distant drum
> pulsing among the trees, a slave to the gods,
> a foreign tongue guarding the sacred cedars
> down to a pale grubworm in the tower
> before Babel. Invisible & otherworldly,
> he was naked in the king's heart,
> & his cry turned flies into maggots
> & blood reddened the singing leaves.[20]

The death of Humbaba is here given a context, a dense psychology, and a visceral immediacy. Once again, the maggots are impossible to miss, although this key signifier has now been transferred from Enkidu to Humbaba. This unexpected shift suggests that the epic is perhaps distinguished above all by its "mutating genes." Periodic shifts in its centers of gravity might turn out to be a crucial self-propagating mechanism, as important to the ongoing life of the epic form as anything that was written on the original clay tablets. This is another way of saying that, for the planet-wide continuum that is the epic, variation is the rule rather than the exception. Its ontology is the ontology of local input and local inflection: ever-multiplying, often randomly generated.

Humbaba is a case in point. As he appeared in the Mesopotamian texts, Humbaba was the guardian of the sacred Cedar Forest, restricted more or less to that sole function. He embodied a divine prohibition, and yet, strangely, he was also supposed to be evil. Stephen Mitchell, as we have seen, has seized upon this apparent contradiction and turned it into a fable for our own time. According to him, the supposed evil of Humbaba is largely projected by Gilgamesh, a preemptive name-calling to justify a preemptive first strike. Komunyakaa and Gracia do not go quite so far, but, like Mitchell, they are also struck by Humbaba less as a substantive entity than as a hollow sound. With no demonstrable physical might, he is merely a rumbling sound. The stage directions say, "The marching-rolling sound of Humbaba's approach is heard—circular. He is not seen. 'Humbaba' grows into a resounding echo." A creature of hearsay, Humbaba falls apart almost instantly in this stage adaptation. Enkidu says:

> Humbaba is no god.
> He is a small beast
> in a big forest.
> He is only a roar
> among the night trees.[21]

Humbaba as a small beast in a big forest is not strictly an invention by Komunyakaa and Gracia; the character is not an absolute departure from the Mesopotamian epic. This ambiguously unclassified creature has always been an agent, a proxy; he executes the will of the gods and serves at their pleasure. And the Mesopotamian gods are nothing if not treacherous. It is Shamash, after all, who unleashes the thirteen winds that blind Humbaba and pin him down, turning his imminent victory over Gilgamesh into a defeat. Still, it takes the stage adaptation and "Love in the Time of War" to turn the fate of Humbaba into a fully imagined story about a low-level functionary, quite far down on the totem pole, done in by the higher power he serves. He is not only "a slave to the gods" (which is more or less what we might expect) but, surprisingly, always "a foreign tongue" to them, meaningless as far as they are concerned, a tongue they never bother to learn.

But in what sense is Humbaba "a foreign tongue"? This is a manner of speaking, of course, since there is no evidence anywhere that Humbaba's actual language requires translation. His foreignness to the gods and his status as an alien come rather from the fact that, existentially and taxonomically, he belongs to a different level, a lower order: they are immortal, but he is not. Unlike the gods, and very much like Enkidu, Humbaba is perishable and corruptible, and the flies and maggots are there to prove it. These creatures are certainly nothing new: they have been with humans "before Babel." What is new, though, is that what is a given for humans is now a given for Humbaba as well. Not even remotely godlike, he is no better and no different from his supposed adversaries. The label "mortal" applies to him just it does to them, making him an eternal underling, "invisible and otherworldly" to the gods. If there had been any previous ambiguity about how to classify Humbaba and where he stood on the spectrum between gods and humans, the nature of his servitude and the nature of his death put that beyond doubt.

The "humanization" of Humbaba—here, effectively a demotion—is indeed a significant departure from the Sumerian epic, a recycling so radical that I would like to call it a *base modification*. In "Love in the Time of War," it is not through Gilgamesh, and not even through Enkidu, but rather through Humbaba, that "humanness" is being defined. And it is being defined in terms of its lowest common denominator, its physical degradation and psychological abjection. If the vitality of the epic comes in part from a downdrift, a channeling of its emotional charge toward the lower rungs of the hierarchy, in the hands of Komunyakaa that downward momentum reinvents the genre even as it redraws the boundaries between what is human and what is not. That impetus gives us a repopulated baseline that is increasingly the center of gravity, and it puts corresponding pressures on the shape of history told from that standpoint. Moreover, though "slave to the gods" could have been just a catchphrase, the word "slave," coming from Komunyakaa, is neither casual nor trivial. Nor is it casual or trivial that this particular layer of American history is being called up by the Iraq war, a military operation manned by those with no say in the process, "slaves" to higher powers who act as if they were gods. What results from this base modification is a radical redrawing of the epic map, a redefinition that loosens the criteria for species membership even as it turns over the most vital part of the story to the lower ranks.

Another Continent

This outcome, so striking in "Love in the Time of War," is not the only one possible, however. How would the epic map and its emotional baseline be modified again, when it is recycled on yet another continent and woven into the lives of other below-the-threshold groups? In her novel *Gilgamesh* (2001), the Australian author Joan London brings *Gilgamesh* to Nunderup, in southwestern Australia. However, remaining true to this epic's peregrinations over the course of the past five thousand years, she does not limit her action to one geographic or temporal location. Instead, her narrative is looped through major historical events of the twentieth century: World War I, the Armenian genocide, the Soviet invasion of Armenia, and the outbreak of World War II. It brings Edith Clark, a young Australian woman, and her young son, Jim, first to London and then to Yerevan, Armenia, and finally through Persia and Syria before returning to Nunderup.

What sets this planetary travel in motion is the arrival in Nunderup of two young men: Edith's cousin Leopold, who had been working on an archaeological dig not far from Baghdad, and Aram, his Armenian driver. The two companions had driven all across Mesopotamia, visiting ancient sites such as Ur, Nineveh, and Uruk. And now, in Australia's southwest, what they miss the most is the site of the royal libraries of Nineveh, where the clay tablets of *Gilgamesh* were first found. Leopold is never without this text: he "and

Aram spoke of Gilgamesh as if they knew him." They tell Edith about what great friends Gilgamesh and Enkidu were, and how "the two of them became so arrogant together that the gods decreed Enkidu must die and go to the Underworld."[22]

Once again, the stage is set for two companions and the death that awaits one of them. Who will it be? Edith's fate is intertwined with that of both men: it is Aram, the father of her child, whom she has set out to look for, but it is Leopold who shows up and escorts her on her return trip. It is also Leopold's jeep that hits a land mine not far from Aleppo. He has just left Edith and Jim there, in the safety of an orphanage; the explosion can be heard where they are. Yet he turns out to be alive and well at the end of the novel, sending a letter in his still-recognizable handwriting to let Edith know that he is in Baghdad once again, drinking coffee every day in a café, learning Arabic. There will be no reunion between him and Edith, but Jim is taking "the first ship out" to see for himself (256).

In this recycling, Gilgamesh dies and is resurrected. It seems that nobody has thought of this permutation before, just as nobody has thought of a young Australian woman as an epic protagonist or her lover as an Armenian who is able to survive several wars. The baseline population has shifted yet another way, and not in a way that anyone could have predicted. But we should not be too surprised, after all. Something new always happens when the old decomposes, as the epic is bound to do. Reaching back to several non-Western ancient languages, and mutating to incorporate countless local circumstances in a five-thousand-year-old recycling, these macro and micro networks of variants, at once finite and yet endlessly extendable, show that literature is above all a series of planetary turns.

Notes

1. David Damrosch, *What Is World Literature?* (Princeton, N.J.: Princeton University Press, 2003), 4 (emphasis in original).

2. See Yusef Komunyakaa and Chad Gracia, *Gilgamesh: A Verse Play* (Middletown, Conn.: Wesleyan University Press, 2006).

3. Mikhail Bakhtin, "Epic and Novel," in *The Dialogic Imagination: Four Essays*, ed. Michael Holquist, trans. Caryl Emerson and Michael Holquist (Austin: University of Texas Press, 1981), 3–40.

4. David Damrosch, *The Buried Book: The Loss and Rediscovery of the Great Epic of Gilgamesh* (New York: Henry Holt, 2007), 3.

5. Stephen Mitchell, introduction to *Gilgamesh: A New English Version*, trans. Stephen Mitchell (New York: Free, 2004), 26.

6. Ibid., 29–30.

7. Chad Gracia, "Collaborating with Komunyakaa: The Creation of *Gilgamesh*," *Callaloo* 28, no. 3 (Summer 2005): 542.

8. Komunyakaa and Gracia, *Gilgamesh: A Verse Play*, 27.

9. Ibid., 56.

10. Gracia, "Collaborating with Komunyakaa," 542.

11. While in *Poetics* the epic's bulk and breaking of dramatic unity are a challenge for Aristotle, the hexameter is able to turn the epic's extra mass into acceptable size, letting in all sorts of elements that would not have been admitted into a form such as tragedy. Here again we have a productive interchange between macro and micro at the level of form. In addition, Aristotle points to the presence of foreign words and metaphors in the epic, but the influx of foreignness—material coming from the outside, not there from the first and not there by invitation—would seem far more endemic than his isolated examples would suggest, its effects not incidental but fundamental to the genre. See Aristotle, *Poetics*, trans. Gerald F. Else (Ann Arbor: University of Michigan Press, 1970), sec. 22. For a longer discussion of this section of *Poetics*, see my *Through Other Continents: American Literature across Deep Time* (Princeton, N.J.: Princeton University Press, 2006), 81–82.

12. "Darmok," *Star Trek: The Next Generation*, season 5, episode 2, aired September 30, 1991.

13. Antonio R. Damasio and Jonathan H. Turner, among others, have argued that emotions evolved much earlier than language did, and that pre-linguistic affect was largely visual in nature. See, for instance, Antonio R. Damasio, *The Feeling of What Happens: Body and Emotion in the Making of Consciousness* (New York: Harcourt Brace, 1999); and Jonathan H. Turner, *On the Origins of Human Emotions: A Sociological Inquiry into the Evolution of Human Affect* (Stanford, Calif.: Stanford University Press, 2000).

14. Yusef Komunyakaa, "Ode to the Maggot," in *Talking Dirty to the Gods* (New York: Farrar, Straus and Giroux, 2000), 10.

15. Gracia, "Collaborating with Komunyakaa," 544.

16. Yusef Komunyakaa, "Mismatched Shoes," in *Magic City* (Hanover, N.H.: University Press of New England / Wesleyan University Press, 1992), 42.

17. Yusef Komunyakaa, "A Good Memory," in *Neon Vernacular: New and Selected Poems* (Hanover, N.H.: University Press of New England / Wesleyan University Press, 1993), 14–15.

18. Yusef Komunyakaa, "We Never Know," in *Dien Cai Dau* (Middletown, Conn.: Wesleyan University Press, 1988), 26.

19. In his classic meditation on historical method, Carlo Ginzburg argues that war is an occasion interweaving the "extreme long shots" of macrohistory with the extreme "close-ups" of subjective experience. See Ginzburg, *The Cheese and the Worms: The Cosmos of a Sixteenth-Century Miller*, trans. John Tedeschi and Anne Tedeschi (Baltimore, Md.: Johns Hopkins University Press, 1980).

20. Yusef Komunyakaa, "Love in the Time of War," in *Warhorses: Poems* (New York: Farrar, Straus and Giroux, 2008), 4.

21. Gracia and Komunyakaa, *Gilgamesh: A Verse Play*, 47, 50.

22. Joan London, *Gilgamesh: A Novel* (New York: Grove, 2001), 41–42. All references hereafter are to this edition and are noted parenthetically.

Writing for the Planet

Contemporary Australian Fiction

PAUL GILES

Interest among writers in conceptions of the planetary is far from a recent phenomenon. Srinivas Aravamudan, for instance, has discussed how "interplanetary reflections" were a staple of intellectual life during the Enlightenment, when astronomical attempts to explicate rotations of the planets worked as a corollary to the geographical exploration of distant lands that was also characteristic of this era.[1] Hester Blum has similarly emphasized how "theories of planetarity" are freighted with "a historical specificity" through her discussion of John Cleves Symmes's appropriation of Arctic space in his highly idiosyncratic geophysical inquiries of the 1820s, which involved attempts to discover a hollow interior to the Earth.[2] In this sense, there is a possibility that twenty-first-century debates around "a turn to the planet," in the title of a celebrated essay by Masao Miyoshi, may risk foreshortening complex cultural and historical perspectives by focusing so insistently on one irreducible, all-encompassing sphere, as if *the* planet were a fundamental trope, like the one true god. Miyoshi's 2001 essay does evoke specific material and political concerns: "global neoliberalism," the importance of class, the way the world is "deterritorialized" for the rich but "sectioned into nations and nationalities for those who cannot afford to move or travel beyond their home countries." Nevertheless, Miyoshi ultimately goes on to argue that in light of "the all-involving process of air pollution, ozone layer depletion, ocean contamination, toxic accumulation, and global warming," the very concept of "literary studies" has now been reduced to "one basis and goal: to nurture our common bonds to the planet—to replace the imaginaries of exclusionist familialism, communitarianism, nationhood, ethnic culture, regionalism, 'globalization,' or even humanism, with the ideal of planetarianism."[3] Along parallel lines, Wai Chee Dimock has suggested that, in relation to ecology and "the non-negotiability of our physical end," the idea of the "planetary" involves a sense of scale that challenges "the territoriality of the nation-state," bound as the latter customarily is to protectionist understandings of sovereignty.[4] Gayatri Chakravorty Spivak likewise distinguishes between the words "*planet*" and "*world*" or "*globe*," which latter terms are, in Spivak's account, more beholden to "the imposition of the same system of exchange everywhere," in "the gridwork of electronic capital."[5]

But if the planetary turn has fluctuated through time, it also fluctuates across space. One specific difficulty associated with this field is that the universalist and utopian proclivities woven into the very conception of what Miyoshi calls a "planet-based totality" frequently involve an extrapolation of much more localized perspectives.[6] Indeed, there is often an uneasy conjunction between the planetary and the parochial, a sense that the idealist rhetoric of planetarity serves to obfuscate narrower material or ideological interests. In his invocation of the Pacific Ocean as a site of epiphany and perpetual metamorphosis, to take one example, Rob Wilson effectively reconstitutes the American sublime in another form, drawing explicitly for the title of his book on a phrase taken from a 1640 sermon by Puritan elder Thomas Shepard, of the First Church of Cambridge, Massachusetts: "Be always converting, be always converted." Though Wilson's reading of Indigenous poetry as "lines of flight across the Pacific" works as an illuminating corrective to more land-based understandings of territorial formation, his aim "to remake the terms of a U.S. covenant as something *subject to poesis* and change" all too obviously involves dehistoricizing colonial formations and reimagining them in transcendental terms. From this perspective, the process of what he calls (following Paul Gilroy) "outer-national" self-formation becomes little more than a mirror image of internalized self-formation, where traditional U.S. values of spiritual apotheosis are projected upon the "Sea of Islands." In truth, such "Oceanic Kisses across Asia-Pacific" are poisoned darts, and this is the time-honored American missionary impulse in another guise.[7]

The conundrum here is that an oppositional politics of the planet so clearly informed by American perspectives has tended to critique what Chris Connery (writing from the University of California, Santa Cruz) described as the hegemonic values of U.S. market capitalism, while seeking instead to appropriate what Connery called the "geo-elemental" aspects of place as a way to escape "the ideological binds of continents or regions." Yet the irony endemic to such a position involves a transposition of the values of romantic independence traditionally ascribed to American literature and culture—an escape from "ideological binds"—and their reinscription within a wider planetary realm. Rather than addressing the more diffuse nature of colonial and geopolitical relations, American ecocritics sometimes lapse into a Manichaean polarity, as if the framework of the planet could be sustained by what Connery terms a geography of "resistance."[8] In truth, the politics of the planet are always more complicated and variegated than such unilateral forces of "resistance" can countenance, and planetary studies should rather take its cue from cultural geographers such as Edward W. Soja, who argued a decade ago that space should be seen as a "dialectical" phenomenon, or Doreen Massey, who has suggested more recently along the same lines that the "time-space compression" endemic to globalization needs to be differentiated socially and politically.[9] What is true of globalization is also true of planetarity: rather than being weighed down by a gravitational pull of uniform identity, whether emanating from environmentalist or other sources, it is necessary to modulate the rhetoric of the planet through an understanding of how its trajectory is always in earthly orbit. The most fundamental thing to say about a planet is not that it is a finite resource, a scientific hypothesis which may or may not be true, but that it is by definition always in rotation. A greater recognition of how planetary perspectives are inherently mutable and shifting might thus help to reorder the idea of the planet more within a material force field.

An uneasy consciousness of the planet as a disorienting phenomenon, a sphere of crosscurrents and crossovers, can be tracked back into the canonical narratives of nineteenth-century American literature. We find it, for example, in Melville's *Moby-Dick* (1851), which uses the watery nature of the planet to hollow out the conventional pieties of life on land, or in Edgar Allan Poe's *Narrative of Arthur Gordon Pym* (1838), whose phantasmagorical vision of the South Pole exposes as relative the magnetic needle of the mariner's compass. Poe's final representation of how cartographic direction slides away under the pressure of the blank Antarctic is reminiscent of his scientific exegesis in "Eureka: An Essay on the Material and Spiritual Universe" (1848), which considers Earth "in its planetary relations alone," choosing to disregard the "vanishing minutiae" of "exclusively terrestrial matters." Poe's emphasis here is on the vastness of the solar system, the incapacity of either the human mind or language to fathom "Infinity" other than as "the *thought of a thought*," and the concomitant impossibility of adducing "a fundamental First Cause" to explain the formation of the planets. Poe ridicules attempts on the part of "the empire of Philosophy" to establish the unity of the universe, humorously dismissing Kant as "the originator of that species of Transcendentalism which, with the change merely of a C for a K, now bears his peculiar name." He thereby punningly disparages Kantian transcendentalism as "cant," and seeks instead to explicate the universe in terms of a dynamic of attraction and repulsion, where the rotation and ellipses of "planetary orbits" are predicated upon the interaction of magnetic crosscurrents.[10] Given its discussion of specific astronomers—Herschel, Laplace, Lord Rosse, and others—and its specific focus on the position of Neptune, Uranus, and other planets, one might have expected Poe's extended essay "Eureka" to be a more foundational text in planetary studies than it actually is; yet Poe's marked skepticism about the extent to which the teleology of space can be conceptualized and his specific disavowal of any understanding of primary causes would make "Eureka" far too uncomfortable an experience for those who would prefer to understand the planet in terms of more emollient forms of biodiversity.

For Poe and Melville, then, the notion of the planet becomes above all a destabilizing phenomenon, one that interrogates landlocked horizons by revealing how conventional maps are always weighted in one manner or another. The oceanic dimensions of *Moby-Dick* explicitly take issue with the assumptions of Matthew Maury, cited by Melville in a footnote to chapter 44 of the novel ("The Chart"), about how a supposedly providential geography grants the Northern Hemisphere a divinely sanctioned hegemony over its southern counterpart. The assumption of Maury, an officer in the U.S. Navy, was that the oceanic sphere is readily susceptible to the laws of Manifest Destiny, and in *The Physical Geography of the Sea* (1855) he characteristically described the Southern Hemisphere as the "boiler" and the Northern Hemisphere as the "condenser of the steam-engine."[11] In Maury's eyes, this testified to a divine plan whereby the lower hemisphere had been designated as inherently subordinate, but in *Moby-Dick* and his other works, of course, Melville sports playfully with such received conceptions of the world through manifold images of inversion. Within the "gigantic involutions" of *Moby-Dick*, where the *Pequod* cruises across the Equator and round the Cape of Good Hope before heading across the Indian Ocean and crossing again into the Northern Hemisphere, the rotation of the planet betokens a relativizing impulse that reveals ways in which traditional maps have become ossified.[12]

Much more recently, New Zealand-born historian J. G. A. Pocock has described his own antipodean provenance as a factor in the tendency of his subsequent work to construe "the world as an archipelago of histories rather than a tectonic of continents." Though Pocock specifically disavows "the absurdity of imposing an antipodean framework on the history of the British kingdoms," what he calls his own "antipodean perception" does nevertheless "invite their inhabitants to see themselves as an association of insular and emigrant peoples, who had set going a diversity of histories in settings archipelagic, Atlantic and oceanic."[13] It is such an understanding of transnational fluidity and continuity as the abiding principle of social and political history, rather than the kind of apocalyptic regeneration more typical of an American missionary impulse, that has helped to shape the expansive planetary reach of Pocock's scholarship. In another version of planetarity similarly indebted to cultural materialism, Australian art historian Bernard Smith, writing in 1986, praised Peter Fuller for being, as Smith put it, "the first person to grasp the trans-national implications of the Antipodean intervention of 1959."[14] Smith was referring here to his "Antipodean manifesto," where he and seven modern painters argued they had a "natural" right to "see and experience nature differently in some degree from the artists of the northern hemisphere," a polemical gesture that foregrounded again the inherently politicized dimensions incumbent upon any recourse to the planetary sphere.[15] Smith's intellectual focus was not on the abstractions of false universalism, as he saw them, but on the unequal processes of cultural exchange across national and hemispheric space; he was thus, as Peter Beilharz has acutely remarked, "a theorist of peripheral vision," whose version of antipodes is best "understood as a *relation*, not a place." Whereas much American work on planetary space seeks to impose a universalist form of abstraction in a way all too redolent of the familiar rhetoric of U.S. empire, Smith's writing, with what Beilharz calls its "lifelong interest in unequal cultural exchange," produced a more hard-edged, "non-identitarian" account of planetary politics, countering the synthetic model of environmentalism with more Marxist and surrealist perspectives on how particular forms had achieved a global hegemony.[16]

Spherical Rotation: Winton, Jones, Tsiolkas, Wright

Following in the wake of the antipodean intellectual legacy charted by Smith and Pocock, I want here to sketch ways in which the activist aspects of planetary perspectives are playing themselves out in contemporary Australian fiction, so as to illustrate how the abstract universalism of U.S. critical discourse on the planet might usefully be countered by more robust engagements with the dynamics of spherical rotation. Tim Winton, for example, is a popular Australian writer whose 1991 novel *Cloudstreet*, a saga of two families growing up over several generations in Western Australia, was ranked in a poll conducted by the Australian Society of Authors as the top Australian book of all time.[17] Part of Winton's success involves his appeal to a middlebrow audience, with his committed Christianity being of a piece with his attachment to the protective bonds of community, nation, and family, and Winton's own public stances on environmental politics displaying similar kinds of investment, particularly in relation to his home state of Western Australia. This scenario is played out most explicitly in Winton's novel *Shallows* (1984), where Queenie Cookson's campaign to save the whales runs up against the more traditional class interests of local union leaders, whose priority is saving jobs rather than the environment. Yet despite the book's own deprecating references to questions of formal reflexivity—Queenie finds hardbound novels "were mostly about the writing of more novels, and the poetry concerned itself with itself," and she reads them simply to get to sleep—*Shallows* is itself highly self-conscious about its own belated position, both spatially and temporally, in relation to global culture.[18] Winton's narrative positions itself "on the southernmost tip of the newest and oldest continent, the bottom of the world," and it uses this antipodean starting point to interweave accounts of Western Australia in the nineteenth-century past and the twentieth-century present, thereby deliberately refurbishing Melville's *Moby-Dick* within a more postmodern context. Queenie's estranged husband, Cleveland Cookson, is actually said to be reading a "Penguin edition of *Moby-Dick*," and Winton's novel describes how whales in the vicinity of the Australian coast get trapped in shallow water, with the book's last section showing how they move "from one warm body of shallow water to the next" and end up as "huge, stricken bodies lurching in the shallows."[19] But the broader discursive marker here involves a more systematic inquiry into whether assumptions of profundity and depth can be sustained in what appears to be the ontologically flat environment of the late twentieth century. The novel thus turns on questions of fakery and authenticity—Cleve declares that Queenie's political campaign is "as dishonest as hell, as fake as this whole town"—and the outcome here, more ambiguous than it appears at first sight, involves a representation of how all the novel's dramatis personae, whales and activists alike, are "beached" in the "shallows" of a depthless country, from which the capacity of "exceptional grace" has been evacuated. Citing an 1831 journal by an American whaler, the book narrates how humans confronted their prey "looking very like Mr Swift's Lilliputians poring over Gulliver," and this intertextual dimension—going back through the fictitious journal to Melville and Swift—lends *Shallows* an explicitly self-referential quality, with its antipodean reversals indicating ways in which, formally as well as thematically, environmental issues are renegotiated within a contemporary Australian context.[20]

Winton's fiction thus uses a comparative structure to position his narratives in dialectical argument with European and North American cultural norms. *The Riders* (1994), set partly in Ireland and partly in France, has an explicitly comparative framework, juxtaposing the lingering smells of Australia's "burnt country" to the "hauteur and hubris" of Paris, as it plays off the hypothetical spaces of Fred Scully's native Australia against the storied landscapes of Europe: "Every field had a name, every path a stile. Everything imaginable had been done or tried out there. It wasn't the feeling you had looking out on his own land. In Australia you looked out and saw the possible, the spaces, the maybes."[21] In his most ambitious work, *Dirt Music* (2001), which took seven years to complete, Winton projects the landscapes of Western Australia in uncomfortable parallel to the synthetic space of American digital culture, so as to evoke a complex, multidimensional world where relations between "real" and "virtual" have become increasingly difficult to determine. *Dirt Music* does not just contrast the meretricious vulgarity of American popular culture with raw Australian authenticity; instead, it uses points of comparison as an epistemological axis to interrogate ways in which the native landscape may (or may not) be able substantially to signify through its own inherent presence. Thus, Luther Fox says on a road trip through Western Australia that he "feels like he's driving through a movie. A western," while Horne remarks sardonically that Western Australia is "like Texas. Only it's big."[22] Later in Fox's road trip, the novel juxtaposes maps of Western Australia, Ireland, and "multiples of France" as if to emphasize how the Australian territory exceeds conventional cartographic outlines. As with *Shallows*, the surrounding sea is described in *Dirt Music* as "flat," and the novel's idiosyncratic prose style—eliminating conventional syntax, so as to produce an illusion of stream of consciousness or what the novel calls "living in the present tense"—reinforces this sense of a postmodern world of depthlessness, from which traditional syntactic markers have been eliminated.[23] *Dirt Music* plays with the idea of a discrete environment, an isolated and autochthonous region, but it also discursively orients this antipodean country in relation both to romantic language—the novel starts with an epigraph from Emily Dickinson about "solitude of space" and goes on to cite Wordsworth, Blake, and Keats, among others—and to the musical culture that gives the novel its title. All kinds of music resound through the narrative—Roy Orbison, Ry Cooder, Arvo Pärt, J. S. Bach—and Winton's title flirts with an oxymoronic inclination whereby the ethereal quality of these harmonies becomes "dirty," with "bluegrass" parodically translated into "browngrass," as the music itself becomes an integral instrument of the life it describes.[24] This ultimately points toward a different order of being, more Platonic in its dimensions, where music is not so much created as already inherent within the sphere of creation, as in the model of bird life configured here as a counterpart to the human species: "Music wants to be heard . . . the world lives in him . . . He sings. He's sung."[25] *Dirt Music*'s last word is "real," and one of the key questions in the book is the ontological status of corporeal presence in a world dominated by media industries and associated forms of cultural displacement: "After weeks of the virtual, it was queer and almost painful to be completely present."[26] This idea of presence relates to local environments as well as to questions of human psychology and sexuality, although of course the myths of authenticity popularly associated with "the wide, brown land" are carefully framed within an ironic structure, with even the name of one of the book's fictional locales, Coronation Gulf, importing a Canadian place name into an Australian setting.[27]

This sense of the country as a site of planetary crossover and transposition also haunts the writing of Australian novelist Gail Jones, who draws explicitly on surrealist motifs to project her native territory as mapped incongruously in time and space. In *Black Mirror* (2002), which takes its title from Salvador Dali and its ambience from André Breton, Australia is represented visually as "a kind of stripey pattern," with "The Dead Heart of Australia" pointed out by a teacher with a ruler. In a scene set in Paris during the 1930s, Marcel Duchamp greets the artist heroine of this novel, Victoria Morrell, as "L'Australienne," whereupon she "felt herself suddenly endowed with symbolic accessories: bounding kangaroos, vistas of orange earth, spectral stringy eucalypts, empty dead centres, any number of odd and arresting Antipodean inversions." Within this framework, national identity itself becomes flattened into a fetishistic phenomenon, a collection of visual signs that flaunt their detachment from any connection with organic entities. True to the book's surrealist provenance, there is a play throughout *Black Mirror* between internal and external perspectives, with the love between a Jamaican man and an Australian woman being framed in terms of a cosmic geography, where the outside world is superseded and trumped by imaginative designs: "The earth's globe dissolves and is reformed to their design; in this upheaval both lovers become tropical and dark."[28] In Jones's later novel *Dreams of Speaking* (2006), the Australian passport itself comes to resemble a surrealist object, "a royal-blue square with the kangaroo and emu standing posed in the centre."[29] And in *Five Bells* (2011), the transnational sense of worlds merging and overlapping—Catherine feels that "Restlessness had caused her to move across the planet," while James senses that "Worlds were converging" and "Australia was Asian"—is framed within what this narrative calls "the surreal element of displacement," where the spectres of Dali, René Magritte, and Max Ernst preside over a story where time reverses and patterns flip over. On the final page of the novel, the Chinese character Pei Xing thinks of how "some of us walk backwards, always seeing what lies behind."[30]

This idea of a "backwards" motion, posterior to both the canonical centers of Western civilization and Australia's own Indigenous past, places contemporary Australian fiction once again in a self-consciously belated position, through which traditional narratives are remapped from a reverse, although not necessarily subsidiary, perspective. Imagery of planetary space, and of Australia introducing into narrow domestic enclosures a sense of cosmic distance, resonate powerfully throughout *Five Bells*. Catherine meditates on how "somewhere in America some poor bastard was thinking of Ireland, thinking of distance, and the turning planet, and of the sky sliding its twinkling diagrams through the dark, lonesome night," while Ellie, recalling a school lesson, contemplates how "birds curve around the planet," swooping in "speedy arcs" across the boundaries of nation and hemisphere as they pursue their migratory patterns.[31] In Jones's *Sorry* (2007), Stella similarly paints Australia as "the dark other-side of the planet," with the Aboriginal darkness coming to stand synecdochically for the relative darkness of Australia itself in relation to the planet as a whole. Here the "theories on human development and the diversity of cultures" propounded by a Cambridge anthropologist are deemed as "imperial and arrogant," and this text by a Western Australian novelist makes a point of describing instead the "fullness and detail" of the bush country, whose Indigenous specificity makes alien academic theories seem "irrelevantly abstruse."[32] There are also many allusions in this story of a lost daughter to Shakespeare's *Winter's Tale*, with the novel describing how the map of Europe "ripples and lifts" in the face of Aboriginal culture. In this way, the novel's evocation of a "parallel universe" works again both formally and thematically to encompass a wider world where the slanted, hegemonic nature of imperial interests are reimagined through an oppositional impetus of transnational disjunction and surreal juxtaposition.[33]

The point to emphasize here is how contemporary Australian fiction writers often engage with contemporary processes of globalization from a slanted perspective, addressing not only the conditions of migration and diaspora but also attributing to this planetary environment a distinctively politicized temper. In Christos Tsiolkas's first novel, *Loaded* (1995), the author remarks on how "a web of hatred connects the planet . . . The Serb hates the Croat who hates the Bosnian who hates the Albanian who hates the Greek who hates the

Turk who hates the Armenian who hates the Kurd who hates the Palestinian who hates the Jew who hates everybody."[34] Rather than being invested in any benign code of multiculturalism, the book uses its nihilistic, grunge ethic to inscribe a perverse code of postnationalism, within which national identity is hollowed out—"I'm not Australian. I'm not Greek. I'm not anything"—and replaced instead by a sexually oriented focus on the gay male body. Enjoying the "debasement" of "dark paths and silent alleyways," the narrator declares that "experiencing the body" becomes for him the highest good. By attributing his sense of well-being to a specifically Australian environment—he says that the "sea breeze of the southern ocean, the breeze that comes up from the end of the world, makes me strong"—Tsiolkas's character implicitly aligns his own reclamation of a proscribed gay sexual body with an environmentalist politics that appears to have been equally repressed.[35] Tsiolkas's later and more wide-ranging novel *Dead Europe* (2005) continues this brand of Australian exceptionalism, contrasting the moribund and "claustrophobic" landscape of Europe to the more expansive domain of his home in Melbourne: "It was only when I first travelled to Europe that I realised how rare was the profusion of space so close to my city." The global narrative is set in a post-9/11 world dominated by U.S. security interests, where the Stars and Stripes flying all over Prague send "a defiant fuck-you to the rest of the world."[36] However, the narrator contrasts this collective paranoia, along with the old ghosts of European hatred and vengeance where men are "still searching for the battles of long-forgotten wars," to the prospect of pastoral renewal and gay domestic bliss in "pure vast Australia where the air is clean, young." This is the Henry James international theme updated to an antipodean rather than transatlantic environment; indeed, Tsiolkas's Sula remarks in Paris that the Australians there "remind me of a character from Henry James, they have an innocence that the Americans have now lost." But, in its apocalyptic invocation of how a "fire, just and swift and magnificent, should rage through all of Europe," the novel also attests to the Protestant church influences carried over from Tsiolkas's own youth.[37] In a 2002 interview, the writer claimed he wanted to recuperate "notions of religious faith" by using them in a different kind of way, so as "to not exclude anyone from the social body"; and his subsequent work has been about transposing what he called in this interview the "shared responsibilities" of "communal forms of politics" to a more radical and utopian context, where the familial body of Australia becomes a site of provocative regeneration.[38]

In *Dead Europe*, the more obviously American and corporate forms of globalization—Visa cards, McDonald's, and so on—play only a background role. What Tsiolkas focuses on instead in this novel is a world interconnected through family migration and visceral hatreds, within whose toils an emphasis on the most perverse aspects of gay sex becomes paradoxically redemptive and regenerative. Sal Mineo is said to be attracted to the work of American fetish photographer Robert Mapplethorpe's "composition of a thick black cock emerging triumphantly out of an unzipped business suit," just as in Tsiolkas's subsequent novel *The Slap* (2008) the sense of Australian pastoral—"the dazzling sea, the brazen endless sky"—is bolstered by a pronounced emphasis in the book on physical health, albeit translated from its familiar Australian stereotype of rugged outdoor life into a more heterodox idiom, where the gay condition of a sexually active body becomes a paradoxical marker for the rude health of national culture as a whole.[39] By taking Australian civic and family norms in *The Slap* and rotating them on their axis—so that seeing a child being slapped becomes for Hector "electric, fiery, exciting," a form of sexual provocation, just as a racist "jolt of hatred" against a taxi driver whom she mentally berates as an "ignorant fundamentalist Muslim pig" is said to give Anouk "an illicit thrill"—Tsiolkas evokes a world somewhere between the suburban blandness of a John Cheever and the deviant cathexis of a Michel Houellebecq, where the tolerance of enlightened parents and guardians in Melbourne toward their sexually active teenagers reinscribes an alternative version of the Australian good life.[40] Tsiolkas admits to having been heavily influenced by Nietzsche—indeed, one of the chapters in *Dead Europe* is entitled "The Nietzschean Hotel-Porter"—and there is considerable emphasis throughout all of his fiction on questions of bodily well-being together with an implicit disgust at the idea of getting what Thanassis in *The Slap* calls "fat and lazy."[41] This represents a peculiarly sexualized version of more traditional conceptions of Australian nature, where the erotic integrity of the gay body comes to represent the health of the national body. In the last section of *The Slap*, the "young art-fag boy" Richie, who views gay sex and drugs as forms of liberation, comes across a boy wearing a black T-shirt across his chest, in which "the Union Jack had been replaced by the Aboriginal flag," and indeed Tsiolkas has explicitly linked Aboriginal history with ecological and gay politics, suggesting that all these movements have traditionally been "silenced and shunned in Australia."[42] The originality of Tsiolkas's work, however, involves crossing Christian conceptions of civic community with a Nietzschean emphasis on the strong human physique, thereby twisting familiar ethical conceptions in a new direction.

Such an interest in "silenced and shunned" pressure groups accords with the parallel contributions of Tsiolkas and Alexis Wright, a Waanyi Indigenous writer, to a "Sydney Three Writers Project" in 2007. Here Tsiolkas's explicit hostility to all forms of censorship—he is a champion of Pasolini's films, long a subject of contention in Australia, and asserted that writers and artists should be "*blasphemous*," beyond "bourgeois politeness"—runs alongside Wright's suggestion that Australians in general, who are "not fools about the country they love," have become more attuned to environmental issues. This is at least in part, says Wright, because of the way a legacy of Aboriginal philosophy that is inherently "holistic" and "tied to the land" has entered into mainstream Australian consciousness.[43] Libby Robin, thinking along similar lines, remarked in 2012 on how it was no coincidence that references to "ecologically sustainable" development were embedded at that time in no less than 129 pieces of Australian federal legislation.[44] Whereas Tsiolkas reimagines global landscapes in relation to the politics of the human body, Wright focuses on how Australia foregrounds the politics of the natural body, the environment of Earth; but for both writers there is an emphasis on using alternative scales to recalibrate relationships between mind and matter, playing off the abstractions of globalization against the physical exigencies of the planet. This accords with Nancy D. Munn's discussion of ways in which Aboriginal conceptualizations of space differ from the more established cartographies of Western mapmaking. In Aboriginal law, observes Munn, markers provide not "spatial boundaries" but "identifying *centers* from which a space with uncertain or ambiguously defined limits stretches out," and Aboriginal custom thus specifically "works against abstracting the problem of space from that of the body."[45] Such a conception of "mobile spatiosensual fields," in Munn's phrase, can be seen as structurally analogous to Tsiolkas's rejection of identity politics in favor of a more chameleonic conception of what Ben Authers calls "renegotiated subjectivities and contingent belongings."[46] What Aboriginal law asserts in relation to geographic space, in other words, Tsiolkas asserts in relation to human psychology, and in his eyes the key question for a rhetoric of national politics involves neither incorporation nor the reification of a communal state but, rather, the capacity within its borders to imagine queer difference.

Wright's own novel *Carpentaria* (2006) negotiates crosscurrents between history and myth through its account of ways in which global mining interests impact upon the fictional Aboriginal community of Desperance, located in northern Queensland. Yet the considerable imaginative power of this work derives in part from its multiple ambiguities, specifically, from the ways in which "outsider" and "inside knowledge" are constituted differently, with the tropes of tricksterdom displacing Indigenous legends into a realm of the surreal imagination.[47] Reluctant to abandon the spirit of one of his dead compatriots, Aboriginal activist Will Phantom keeps "speaking to and replying for Elias as though he was alive," and Wright's novel is similarly established around a complex aesthetic principle of echo and response, where the relationship between invocation and manifestation remains enigmatic. Such interactions between the collective dream-world and the purportedly "spirit world" are frequently given a comic turn, as in the way Norm Phantom recounts his own "sad stories" to a "huge, white cockatoo bird, named Pirate," who is granted by the "old people" the status of "an enchanter" with "psychic powers."[48] After Will has blown up part of the mining company's engineering apparatus, the scene weirdly appears on television with "bits of pipeline sticking out of the ground and throughout the surrounding bushland like an exhibition of postmodern sculpture outside the Australian National Gallery or Tate Modern in London"; and this sense of jarring and incompatible perspectives, where the "powerful spirituality" of Indigenous peoples and "the ancestral spirit who governed the land" consort incongruously with the "stuffed baby crocodiles" proudly displayed by Norm Phantom as among his "special works of local fish" on the walls of comfortable pubs, lends the novel its compelling, contemporaneous tone of indeterminacy.[49] This humorous and quirky idiom is underlined by the frequent allusions to surrealism—"the surreal fresco of fishermen coming to collect their trophies," a man on the beach with "the appearance of the surreal," and "the surreal stillness" after the fire—as if to highlight, as in Gail Jones's narratives, the fractured and disjunctive nature of this cultural landscape.[50]

Though Francis Devlin-Glass has suggested that *Carpentaria* "mobilizes the mythological in order to argue the interconnectedness of the Aboriginal sacred and political and ecological matters," it might conversely be argued that the remarkable force of Wright's novel derives from the way it problematizes such putative connections and abjures any kind of closure by holding competing possibilities always in tension.[51] There is also much discussion in *Carpentaria* of stars and planets, of how the Aboriginal community organizes its world with reference to the sea and "the world of the Milky Way," a scenario projected here as "the spirits of dead people twinkling as stars in the night ocean of the skies." Yet such an apotheosis is displaced again by metaphorical configuration into mere similitude: "the night droned away *as though* the whole planet was alive with the sound of Indian tubulas and clay drums" (my italics).[52] Just as the last word of Winton's *Dirt Music* is "real," so the last word of Wright's *Carpentaria* is "home"; yet this sense of planetary constellations upholding the idea of "the *Aborigine* people sitting at home in their rightful place" is held in check by the structural ironies within which this world of spirit is framed.[53] At the same time, Wright's focus on the uncanny, on Will Phantom being "like an animal sniffing the air and sensing danger approaching," or on how "the great creators of the natural world" produce gigantic cyclones that cause mere human "history" to be "obliterated," elucidates a world in which social designs of every kind are always in the shadow of planetary space.[54] While Wright's novel politicizes the planet, it also describes planetary perspectives as a corrective to the more limited economic positivism of corporate interests and the equally purblind conceptions of technological modernity.

View from the Bottom: The Planetary Turn and the Southern Hemisphere

All of this, in the context of the planetary turn, testifies to the pertinacity of Fredric Jameson's remark about how "one of our basic political tasks lies precisely in the ceaseless effort to remind the American public of the radical difference of other national situations." Jameson was writing back in 1986 about "third-world literature," but the same thing holds true for theories of the planetary: the "view from the top is epistemologically crippling," as Jameson put it, and what the planet signifies to those in the United States is not necessarily the same as what it signifies to those in Australia or, indeed, other parts of the Southern Hemisphere.[55] It is true that, in the wake of concerns about the potential havoc that might be wrought by climate change, the specter of the planet has introduced into Western consciousness a strange conceptual mix of the local and global, where vast environmental issues exist in uneasy juxtaposition with more narrowly focused domestic interests, but this has induced odd and at times grotesque anomalies between theory and practice rather than any consistent form of political action. The address to the United Nations in 2006 by Hugo Chavez, president of Venezuela, where he invoked the possibility of "the peoples of the South"—from Africa, Latin America, and Oceania—rising up against the northern empire of neoliberal globalization may remain, as any kind of active program, within the realms of hypothetical fantasy; but Chavez's intervention did nevertheless serve to give a distinctive political articulation to a perspective from the Southern Hemisphere, in its historically subordinate relation to the vested interests of the north.[56]

One of the structural ironies incumbent upon Indigenous perspectives of every kind is how they are intertwined, both socially and ontologically, with a rhetoric of modernity. On one hand, as David Morley and Kevin Robins argued, the recent interest in Indigenous rights across the globe has been interwoven symbiotically with reactions to the "psycho-geography" of displacement in an era of electronic media, since a nostalgic return to roots always tends to be the product of the "anxiety and fear" associated with a climate of alienation.[57] On a more abstract level, as Michael R. Dove has suggested, the relationship between "indigenous people and environmental politics" necessarily involves "a host of contradictions," since, through a characteristic back formation, it is the very concept of "modernity [that] makes indigeneity possible in the first place."[58] Without trying to reconcile such contradictions or to shoehorn contemporary Australian literature into any kind of uniform pattern, it might nevertheless be worth suggesting that this planetary dimension now forms as systematic a matrix for the production of Australian fiction at the beginning of the twenty-first century as did the postcolonial impetus during the last third of the twentieth century. Julian Murphet has argued that Australian literature was for most of the twentieth century "neo-colonial" in its knowingly subaltern relation to the cultural empires of Britain and the United States, and it was only "the remarkable sense of unmooring from a British centre of cultural gravity" in the 1960s, followed by the historic referendum granting full citizenship rights to Aboriginal Australians in 1967 and the turning away from America after Vietnam, that induced a more programmatic policy of "self-determination" from the 1970s onwards.[59] But if the institutional apparatus of the late twentieth century sought to enhance the status of Australian literature in relation to its British and American forebears, Australian literature of the twenty-first century might better be defined as a literature for the planet because it is predicated less upon old-style calls for national attention than upon a more subtle, nuanced recognition of ways in which the local and the global inevitably intersect across both an economic and an environmental axis.

In this sense, recent Australian literature, predicated as it is upon a cathexis of disorientation, typically projects the planet in a more disjunctive way than it appeared within the proselytizing agenda of Miyoshi, for whom the irreducible "totality" of the planet was its foremost claim on our critical attention. To be Australian is necessarily to have some recognition of the spherical shape of the planet, since, within our contemporary digital world of electronic instantaneity, the very days of the week and seasons of the year manifest themselves differently from the order in which they appear to denizens of the more crowded Northern Hemisphere. Such a hybridized model of affiliation, where Australian discourses are symbiotically linked to local spaces and transnational passages simultaneously, challenges more conventional understandings of what is meant by a "national" literature. Thinking again of the planet as a site of rupture and discord rather than unity, Dipesh Chakrabarty argued in 2012 that the fundamental "challenge" of climate change involves the dilemma "of having to think of human agency over multiple and incommensurable scales at once," a disorienting teleological shift that implies how "humans are now part of the natural history of the planet." Such a philosophical disturbance, noted Chakrabarty, effectively dismantles the "wall of separation between natural and human histories that was erected in early modernity and reinforced in the nineteenth century" by the human sciences.[60] In this sense, the cultural landscape of Australia, within whose geophysical formations questions of vast spatial and temporal scale have always been uppermost and where distinctions between natural and human history have never been so clear-cut, could be said to be ahead of the game. The most interesting Australian fiction writers in the twenty-first century tend to expose their narratives to the kind of jarring continuities between Indigenous and Western cultures that disrupt traditional understandings of social scale and, as a corollary, questions of human agency. It is their recognition of the implicitly loaded and potentially adversarial nature of such globalizing perspectives that makes the fiction of Winton, Jones, Tsiolkas, and Wright characteristic of contemporary Australian writing for the planet.

Notes

1. Srinivas Aravamudan, *Enlightenment Orientalism: Resisting the Rise of the Novel* (Chicago: University of Chicago Press, 2012), 118.
2. Hester Blum, "John Cleves Symmes and the Planetary Reach of Polar Exploration," *American Literature* 84, no. 2 (June 2012): 246.

3. Masao Miyoshi, "Turn to the Planet: Literature, Diversity, and Totality," *Comparative Literature* 53, no. 4 (Autumn 2001): 293, 292, 295.

4. Wai Chee Dimock, "Recycling the Epic: *Gilgamesh* on Three Continents," in *Scenes of Reading: Is Australian Literature a World Literature?*, ed. Robert Dixon and Brigid Rooney (Melbourne, Australia: Australian Scholarly Publishing, 2013), 12; Wai Chee Dimock, "Planetary Time and Global Translation: 'Context' in Literary Studies," *Common Knowledge* 9, no. 3 (Fall 2003): 488, 490.

5. Gayatri Chakravorty Spivak, *Death of a Discipline* (New York: Columbia University Press, 2003), 72.

6. Miyoshi, "Turn to the Planet," 295.

7. Rob Wilson, *Be Always Converting, Be Always Converted: An American Poetics* (Cambridge, Mass.: Harvard University Press, 2009), 20, 30, 120, 132.

8. Christopher L. Connery, "Ideologies of Land and Sea: Alfred Thayer Mahan, Carl Schmitt, and the Shaping of Global Myth Elements," *boundary 2* 28, no. 2 (Summer 2001): 175; Christopher L. Connery, "Pacific Rim Discourse: The U.S. Global Imaginary in the Late Cold War Years," *boundary 2* 21, no. 1 (Spring 1994): 56.

9. Edward W. Soja, *Postmodern Geographies: The Reassertion of Space in Critical Social Theory* (London: Verso, 1989), 78; Doreen Massey, "A Global Sense of Place," in *Reading Human Geography: The Poetics and Politics of Inquiry*, ed. Trevor J. Barnes and Derek Gregory (London: Arnold, 1997), 315.

10. Edgar Allan Poe, "Eureka: An Essay on the Material and Spiritual Universe," in *The Science Fiction of Edgar Allan Poe*, ed. Harold Beaver (London: Penguin, 1976), 213, 222, 297, 214, 261.

11. Matthew Fontaine Maury, *The Physical Geography of the Sea and Its Meteorology* (New York, 1855), 27–28.

12. Herman Melville, *Moby-Dick, or The Whale*, ed. Harrison Hayford, G. Thomas Tanselle, and Hershel Parker (Evanston, Ill.: Northwestern University Press, 1988), 455.

13. J. G. A. Pocock, *The Discovery of Islands: Essays in British History* (Cambridge, Eng.: Cambridge University Press, 2005), 19, 21.

14. Bernard Smith, foreword to *The Australian Scapegoat: Towards an Antipodean Aesthetic*, by Peter Fuller (Nedlands: University of Western Australia Press, 1986), xiii.

15. Bernard Smith et al., "The Antipodean Manifesto," in *The Antipodean Manifesto: Essays in Art and History*, by Bernard Smith (Melbourne: Oxford University Press, 1976), 166.

16. Peter Beilharz, *Imagining the Antipodes: Culture, Theory and the Visual in the Work of Bernard Smith* (Cambridge, Eng.: Cambridge University Press, 1997), xii, xiv (emphasis in original), 94, 188.

17. Robert Dixon, "Tim Winton, *Cloudstreet*, and the Field of Australian Literature," *Westerly* 50 (November 2005): 248.

18. Tim Winton, *Shallows* (1984; repr., Sydney: Allen and Unwin, 1985), 103.

19. Ibid., ix, 17, 222, 235.

20. Ibid., 192, 222, 114, 24.

21. Tim Winton, *The Riders* (Sydney: Pan Macmillan, 1994), 154, 260, 51.

22. Tim Winton, *Dirt Music* (Sydney: Pan Macmillan, 2001), 246.

23. Ibid., 295, 130, 53.

24. Ibid., viii, 418, 388.

25. Ibid., 415, 451.

26. Ibid., 461, 10.

27. Winton, *Dirt Music*, 414; and Brigid Rooney, *Literary Activists: Australian Writer-Intellectuals and Public Life* (St. Lucia: University of Queensland Press, 2009), 178.

28. Gail Jones, *Black Mirror* (Sydney: Pan Macmillan, 2002), 259, 29, 98.

29. Gail Jones, *Dreams of Speaking* (Sydney: Random House, 2006), 22.

30. Gail Jones, *Five Bells* (Sydney: Random House, 2011), 17, 38, 87, 171.

31. Ibid., 90, 136.

32. Gail Jones, *Sorry* (Sydney: Random House, 2007), 7, 551, 22.

33. Ibid., 125, 206.

34. Christos Tsiolkas, *Loaded* (1995; repr., London: Random House-Vintage, 1997), 64.

35. Ibid., 149, 132, 23, 133.

36. Christos Tsiolkas, *Dead Europe* (Sydney: Random House, 2005), 27, 139, 193.

37. Ibid., 159, 375, 282, 368.

38. Mary Zournazi, "On Believing—with Christos Tsiolkas," in *Hope: New Philosophies for Change* (Annandale, Australia: Pluto Press Australia, 2002), 99, 121, 109, 107.

39. Tsiolkas, *Dead Europe*, 213; and Christos Tsiolkas, *The Slap* (Crows Nest, Australia: Allen and Unwin, 2008), 123–24.

40. Tsiolkas, *The Slap*, 41, 62.

41. Zournazi, "On Believing," 100; Tsiolkas, *Dead Europe*, 329; and Tsiolkas, *The Slap*, 318.

42. Tsiolkas, *The Slap*, 428, 478; and Zournazi, "On Believing," 117.

43. Christos Tsiolkas, Gideon Haigh, and Alexis Wright, *Tolerance, Prejudice and Fear: The Sydney Three Writers Project* (Crows Nest, Australia: Allen and Unwin, 2008), 48, 149, 157.

44. Libby Robin, "Round Table" (paper, "Rethinking Invasion Ecologies: Natures, Cultures and Societies in the Age of Anthropocene," University of Sydney, June 19, 2012).

45. Nancy D. Munn, "Excluded Spaces: The Figure in the Australian Aboriginal Landscape," *Critical Inquiry* 22, no. 3 (Spring 1996): 453, 465 (emphasis in original).

46. Munn, "Excluded Spaces," 464; Ben Authers, "'I'm Not Australian, I'm Not Greek, I'm Not Anything': Identity and the Multicultural Nation in Christos Tsiolkas's *Loaded*," *Journal of the Association for the Study of Australian Literature* 4 (2005): 143.

47. Alexis Wright, *Carpentaria* (2006; repr., Artarmon, Australia: Giramondo, 2007), 59, 3.

48. Ibid., 176, 103.

49. Ibid., 416, 437, 407, 340.

50. Ibid., 213, 73, 412.

51. Francis Devlin-Glass, "Review Essay: Alexis Wright's *Carpentaria*," *Antipodes* 21, no. 1 (June 2007): 82.

52. Wright, *Carpentaria*, 251–52, 383.

53. Winton, *Dirt Music*, 461; Wright, *Carpentaria*, 519, 160. In *Carpentaria*, this structural irony is heightened by the acknowledgment on its final page of "the Australian government," through its "arts funding and advisory board," as a sponsor for the book's production.

54. Wright, *Carpentaria*, 461, 491–92.

55. Fredric Jameson, "Third-World Literature in the Era of Multinational Capitalism," *Social Text* 15 (Autumn 1986): 77, 85.

56. On Chavez, see Rob Wilson, "Afterword: Worlding as Future Tactic," in *The Worlding Project: Doing Cultural Studies in the Era of Globalization*, ed. Rob Wilson and Christopher Leigh Connery (Santa Cruz, Calif.: New Pacific; Berkeley, Calif.: North Atlantic Books, 2007), 209.

57. David Morley and Kevin Robins, *Spaces of Identity: Global Media, Electronic Landscapes and Cultural Boundaries* (London: Routledge, 1995), 197.

58. Michael R. Dove, "Indigenous People and Environmental Politics," *Annual Review of Anthropology* 35 (October 2006): 203, 193.

59. Julian Murphet, "Postcolonial Writing in Australia and New Zealand," in *The Cambridge History of Postcolonial Literature,* ed. Ato Quayson (Cambridge, Eng.: Cambridge University Press, 2012), 1:446, 1:452, 1:457.

60. Dipesh Chakrabarty, "Postcolonial Studies and the Challenge of Climate Change," *New Literary History* 43, no. 1 (Winter 2012): 1, 10.

The White Globe and the Paradoxical Cartography of Berger & Berger

A Meditation on Deceptive Evidence

BERTRAND WESTPHAL

We "climb above" and, voilà—we have just committed an ugly pleonasm. We say that evidence is "deceptive." That is another pleonasm. "Not so sure," would retort the purist. "Why should evidence be deceptive? Why should deceptive evidence be pleonastic?" And yet, is there evidence other than of the deceptive sort? The question makes sense if we consider, for example, the color white, which corresponds *evidently* to an absence of color. White is an empty space that seems to demand no more than to be filled. So be it. Let us agree on this. But let us also agree that we are caught in an illusion. So let us try a small experiment. Let us superimpose three circles—one red, another green, and yet another blue—so as to form a common intersection. What color will this intersection be? In the "subtractive colors" of paint and ink—it will be a false black. In additive colors—the colors of light—it will be a non-color, a white of sorts, which is the product of a combination of the three primary colors. All of this intersectional space is a "nothing," strictly speaking, for white results from a perception of an excess of color. Thus the evidence voids itself as the certainty inspired by the visible fades. Elementary as this evidence may appear, it turns out to be in no way evident. Which color is Henry IV's white panache? The famous question is less foolish than it may look.

Since 2006, Berger & Berger has been the manufacturing brand of two quasi-twin artists: Laurent P. Berger, a visual artist, and architect Cyrille Berger. The reputation of the two brothers has continued to grow in recent years.[1] Cyrille exhibited in the prestigious context of the Venice Biennales of Architecture, in 2008 and 2010. From October 7 to November 24, 2011, the artists' work was hosted by the Rosascape gallery, in the heart of Paris. This work subverts space, proposing—as the title of the exhibition suggests—"altered states."[2] Among the exhibition's "alterations" we find, pell-mell, *Parquet Vassivière*—an edge of flooring made from the wood of tree stumps showing through the surface of the artificial Lake Vassivière, in

Limousin—and a world map titled *Ghost Towns*, in which vanished towns cast their shadowy presence over a planet whose twentieth century saw such ghostly vestiges multiply *worldwide*. In addition, in this exhibition Berger & Berger have attempted, through their work *Astre blanc* (*White Star*), to provide their own answer to the question of the deceptive evidence of whiteness by employing the medium of a whitish globe made of porcelain and metal, with an irregular surface, and a diameter of some several decimeters.

In a manner evoking the negative map of *Ghost Towns*, Berger & Berger's globe points toward an uncertain cartography, a tricky representation of absent referents. It is about this cartography, remarkable even in its simplicity, that I wish to speak here.[3] For, indeed, what color exactly is the white star of Berger & Berger? To be sure, there is no easy answer to this and related questions prompted by things that otherwise may seem to be all too *evident*. The globe, for example, is too full of colors to be white. It is like the blood cell (*globule*), whose color would be white if it were not red. When it is terrestrial, which is primarily what I am thinking of, the globe would sooner be blue. In fact, that is what we have learned from the astronauts and other cosmonauts upon their return from their interstellar journeys. All in all, the globe is more round and more blue than an orange. "Ah," one might retort, "you have a surrealist penchant; have you read Eluard?"[4] Yes, I have. And yet this is where doubt creeps in. What if the earth's globe were at this point so saturated with color that, instead of being blue, it was actually white, dazzling us enough to prevent us from comprehending it? And, for good measure, what if it was not completely smooth and round, but quite dented? If this were so, then the work of Berger & Berger would be "realistic" and we would be among the few to "get" its realism. But—in reality—this is not the case, and so what makes the terraqueous globe a uniformly colored quasi-sphere is no more than a convention naturalized by a large number of observers held hostage by "evidence." We learn from this art that the size of an audience has never been a guarantor of the "truth" concerning reality, whatever that reality may be. We are made aware of this every Sunday in the stadiums, where all eyes are trained on a twirling globe, sometimes white, over which fight twenty-two athletic actors.

Berger & Berger do not in fact empty the globe; they return to it its excess of color and light. Thus, they empty the evidence. Their sincere regard for the globe's true nature, however, frustrates our expectations. For, after all, what could a white globe be? What *should* it be? This question is as slippery, as "round," as the artists' object. It does not give play to any hierarchy. To try to respond to it means groping in the dark endlessly, to propose a critical hypothesis, and no more than that, in the margins of all evidence. But perhaps one might offer a rejoinder, one obtaining somewhere between avoiding and acknowledging the evidence? Surely. Why not? Contributing to the emptying of the excessive plenitude of meaning by which the world is afflicted is not the worst course of action imaginable.

So here is the beginning of a critical proposition, of a non-evidential rejoinder.

The White of Deserts and Ice

At an altitude of a little less than three hundred meters, near Alamogordo, there is a gypsum desert whose whiteness sparkles under the deep blue sky of New Mexico. I briefly passed through the area in June 2005, but it could have been yesterday. The place looks almost lifeless except for the solitary yuccas holding court at the summit of dunes, like so many absurd artifacts placed there by a hand inclined to defy nature—the hand of a Frankenstein of the arid zones exhibiting a monster plant. With a little luck, you will also catch a glimpse of a lizard or two melting into the environment. Beyond that, nothing other than the empty splendor of the place. Even though the route is marked and the danger of getting lost is reduced, it is recommended to stock up on water before entering White Sands National Monument. This hazy stretch should inspire fear, but what it inspires, above all, is a feeling of liberty, of liberation, possibly the same emotion felt by the Mescalero Apaches who once wandered White Sands.

At sunset, the whiteness of the land is contrasted by the mauve shimmers of the setting sun amidst the shadows accentuating the sloping angles of the dunes. In the morning, the sun floods the gypsum crust and sparks reflections that slightly distort the contours of the meager vegetation. In the shadow of the dunes, somber rills moistened by the pink of sunrise break the white uniformity of the desert. The region is little visited by tourists, who have much to do elsewhere in New Mexico. Here, you can enjoy the beginning of solitude; you are seized by the desire to kick off your shoes and run across the miniscule gypsum crystals, more delicate than grains of sand. You actually do it.

Was it necessary to detour through the American Southwest to gambol in the gypsum dust? I am not sure. More people prefer to trample the white beaches of the seas, close or distant, in Sardinia, Malta, or under the tropical sun. There, the whiteness of the sand is highlighted by the turquoise burst of the waters or the fleeting reflection of a thousand colored fish. Sometimes, the reflected image is that of Ursula Andress's diving knife as she emerges from the waves to set foot on a Caribbean beach or that of Halle Berry as she replays the primordial scene in Cuba (we are told) several decades later, faced with another James Bond, under the eyes of other spectators. And so, again, we forget that white is a saturation of colors that lively colors decolor. We give in, as we say, to the "evidence." It is so easy to do so. But we realize right away that the situation is more complicated. We are too ready to forget where we actually are, that is, along the border between lands, in the grip of a misery that butts against the gold of the beach and the shiny façades of the hotels. We want, in other words, to associate the white sand of the beach with paradise; we really insist on it.

So what would the veritable paradise be, then? It would be the ideal sum of all the White Sands and all the white sand beaches, evidently, at the exclusion of everything else, too—*evidently*, alas. Paradise would be a white globe whose sparkling whiteness was born when the rays of a distant star, the sun—an other—washed over different kinds of powdered minerals. But this paradise, an idealizing, touristic reflection, would be emptied of all humanity. A globe of white sand would be as dry as the surface of the skull on a pirate flag that the absence of the seas would condemn to boredom.

It is true that this infernal paradise would be conceivable. For the sake of argument, let us imagine a moment when the water of the seven seas evaporated. Further, let us imagine that they left in their absence a planetary bed of white sand—for, without water, just like the depths of the sea, the surrounding green spaces would not survive very long, and not even the yuccas would be able to hold out. What would happen then? Would we have to deal with this situation in terms of scale, of a large scale, in effect, wherein too much white sand would suffocate, dehydrate, and shock? The questions are apt because any planetary paradise fades for lack of contrast; paradisiac is that which escapes hell or, on a more optimistic note, purgatory (a late creation, fruit of the sense of compromise and of a bottomless need for consolation). Bored to death in a space they think uniformly perfect, Adam and Eve begin to amuse themselves when the idea of a possible alternative space comes to them. And, after tasting the alternative, they become right away nostalgic for the kind of space that rejected them. So one can say that the world is badly made from the very beginning. No need to make a drawing either: a global White Sands would perhaps be the happiness of some lizards but not ours. Actually, if you think about it, and also about the aforementioned contrast, even the lizards would be depressed, for what is the point of remaining chameleonic when there is no one left to hide from?

In other words, *differentiation* is key; play with it, and you change the world. Let us alter the scale, then. Imagine a middle between nothing and everything (ah, Blaise Pascal . . .).[5] Say, a little scrap of white globe, just a little scrap, nothing more—a little, or much more, than White Sands, but not the planetary desert I evoked earlier. In imagining that place, I am toying with the idea of a Mediterranean space as deprived of the sea as other regions are deprived of their deserts. This playful notion would render the contours of the shores less brutally marked, a soft a priori, and would undo the sea's claim to a clearly demarcated space. The reliefs of the seabed would become visible. Cyprus, where Aphrodite was born, would be transformed into a *mons veneris*. The Mediterranean's southern and northern shores would move closer after the maritime currents had calmed down between the Columns of Hercules. (The student of Mediterranean history might reply that the columns support a heaven whose sense of ethics sags.) At any rate, there would be no inaccessible beaches any more. The vessels of fortune, too, would become obsolete, as would submarines. The *Nautilus* would no longer belong to science fiction but would be the vain offspring of a bygone past. No longer would there be capsizing, massive floods, or private dramas above the surface of crashing waves. We would move differently; we would get around better. Great! What a big deal! We would bump against new, lowered barriers. Schengen and its spirit would be always and everywhere present.[6] And, inevitably, newly erected walls would face the vast world in the places from which the waters had evaporated.

I write these lines in Portland, Maine, where water is everywhere. The tortilla curtain the states of the American Southwest have been raising to stop Latin American immigration, an influx they otherwise need so much, stands at the antipodes of Maine. I saw this hideous fence in Nogales, Arizona, while on my way to White Sands. I even crossed it involuntarily. It is crazy how easy it is to get to Mexico from the United States, at least from Nogales. All you have to do is take what becomes suddenly a one-way drive, then, once on the other side, ask yourself how to turn around. Of course, you forgot to bring all the mountainous paperwork needed to extinguish the bureaucratic thirst of sinister-looking U.S. customs agents.

And, far off, toward the northeast, in Portland, a fragment of the Berlin Wall is erected on a pier, supplemented by a wise commentary:

> The Berlin wall. Forget not the tyranny of this wall.
> Horrid Place.
> Nor the love of freedom that made it fall.

"Horrid, indeed," one hastens to agree. But there are walls whose fragments we still do not display. We justify them when, politically, they seem proper. It is no good! Draining the Mediterranean would not render its space less perilous. It would not make for one of those smooth spaces so much appreciated by Gilles Deleuze and Félix Guattari.[7] In fact, it would prompt a certain number of Mediterranean countries to go conquer the territory formerly covered by the high seas, which is what international right protects from the greed of nation-states. And this conquest would be done quickly, with tanks, planes, missiles, and discourse, with an arsenal of fire and incendiary words. Deterritorializing the sea and its waters would entail an aggressive and doubtlessly bloody reterritorialization that, in turn, would "update" our maps.

In my theory of geocriticism, the stable territory reconfigures itself according to a steady dynamic, for everything is here grasped consistently according to a productive in-between (*entre-deux*) model.[8] My 2007 book *Geocriticism* (*La Géocritique*) presented me with the opportunity to develop my understanding of this dynamic that more than one critic locates at the core of the postmodern approach to the world. Now, where Deleuze and Guattari reveal a line of escape that traverses all territory, others conceive of society—and modernity—as "fluid" (Zygmunt Bauman) and its "mobilization" as "infinite" in time as well as in space (Peter Sloterdijk).[9] Thus, common to a growing number of theories or even simple hypotheses exploring the "geophilosophic" surface of the planet (as Deleuze and Guattari would say) is a sense of a movement that delinks territory and stasis, identity and its anchorage in the singular, as well as the nation and its boundaries. Apropos of this movement, one thinks of the 2009 public debate in France, called upon to discuss the theme of its own national identity. The ensuing public debate came to a sudden end. It could not have been otherwise: in the twenty-first century, the concept of a national identity stated in the singular is a contradiction in terms. In my work, I have postulated that one of the driving principles of the geocritical approach is "transgressivity," which does not correspond to a "transgression" in the moral sense of the term (the only sense of the word that the French language knows), but to a state of cultural and social mobility.[10] Thus, in my account, the Latin *limes*—a kind of border considered to be absolutely impermeable—transforms itself into a *limen*, a porous border, or (when the latter is "stabilized" and unambiguously assumed) into a threshold destined to be crossed and thereby used to bring heterogeneous but in no way incompatible spaces into contact. The zones of contact are themselves particularly stimulating in that they shelter the constant emergence of the new. These zones of absolute contact are the *third spaces* that in work of the great geographer Edward Soja become "thirdspaces" and in my own work (and in French), *tiers espaces*. These spaces have been studied by several of the finest observers of today's cultural planet—in addition to Soja, one could mention Homi Bhabha, Michel Serres, Gloria Anzaldúa, and Salman Rushdie, a novelist who has often reflected on the creative processes behind his work.[11]

However, today's defenders of the national border are finding new allies. In their ranks, we notice the presence of Régis Debray who, in a recent essay, *Éloge des frontières,* remarks that Terminus, the Roman god of the confines who was honored at the edges of the fields, is beginning to regain his ancient power. "It is a big gap," Debray sighs. And he goes on: "Rarely have we seen, in the long history of Western credulity, such a hiatus between our spiritual state and the state of things."[12] Maybe so. And yet the question is whether it falls to the spiritual state to resign itself to a state of supposed things. Personally, I am not convinced. Culture has the right to imagine better and to propose it, even if, as the newspapers keep reminding us, in the political sphere the notion of State territory still exists. Culture does not kill. If it did, I would hope that it would cease to be called "culture." However, a politics without conscience turns lethal.

Consider the vast surfaces whitened when material is returned to chaos—we have seen some of those in recent years and have imagined others in the margins of recent artists' apocalyptic projections. We commemorated, in fact, the tenth anniversary of September 11, 2001 a little before the opening of the Berger & Berger exhibition; while I was traveling through Maine, preparations were well under way. Many Stars and Stripes flags, whose stars had been replaced by the inscription "9/11," were to be found in all the drugstores. Ten years ago, we all saw the terrible images of the attacks replayed in the media over and over again. Their flashes, no longer volatile, remain graven in our memories. Many of those, at least. One memory is of dazed people, whitened by ash, running through the streets of Manhattan, and scattered papers raining down from the burning towers. Other images, from another time and place, have shown the areas hit by the white phosphorus bombs condemned by the international conventions. These were fleeting pictures, strewn with corpses contorted by a fierce agony, bodies of innocents who found themselves at the wrong place at the wrong moment. The contour lines of these victims imprint themselves on that part of the globe whitened to phosphoric translucence. In the French vocabulary of photography, that which enlarges a negative is called a "shooter" (tireur) or "marksman." In this case, to the contrary, another shooter, who exercises a military craft, resists photography—and, for that matter, any form of publicity.

But let us come back to the world of fiction, which is sometimes supposed to maintain a looser rapport with the real world—with the world of a more material reality, a more solid one, a more evident one, and a more explosive one. Take, for instance, Cormac McCarthy, undoubtedly one of the great American novelists of the last generation. The man was born in Providence, Rhode Island. On this account, consider Chamfort too, who wrote that "someone said that Providence is the baptismal name of chance." It is certainly true that McCarthy ceaselessly baptizes chance in his books; it is true also that this task is daunting. But he left Providence quickly and moved to New Mexico, where he has lived ever since. He knows the desert. He certainly knows White Sands: he transformed the entire United States into a great desert in his novel *The Road*. What color are the post nuclear lands that have survived the "day after" and spread from one side of the country to the other, from the horizon to the road? The answer is, "every color and, therefore, white." In the book, a man and his son are survivors of what seem to be a nuclear attack or catastrophe. They leave their home, now ruined, and plot an erratic course through nothing. Their destination is the ocean shore, somewhere further southeast. In the middle of chaos, they scramble to find something to eat, all the while avoiding becoming the prey of survivors looking for sustenance and, lacking other food, human flesh. Ash is everywhere. It covers the globe entirely or in part, for we do not know the extent of the catastrophe. The ash is not black; it is white-grey. It reflects the vestiges of the world that has collapsed. It testifies to that which no longer is.

For McCarthy, White Sands have somehow scorched the human environment. They do not, however, provide any warmth. It is true that White Sands is not only a nature preserve crushed by the New Mexico sun. On July 16, 1945, the U.S. Army tested the first atomic bomb in a part of the desert bordering the preserve. Several weeks later, it dropped others on two Japanese cities. We know what happened. The code name for the desert operation was *Trinity*. Later, someone inquired of Robert Oppenheimer, director of the American atomic program, why he had chosen this religious reference. Oppenheimer did not recall the real reason. What he remembered, instead, were three lines from baroque poet John Donne:

> . . . As west and east
> In all flat maps—and I am one—are one,
> So death doth touch the resurrection.[13]

Taken from "Hymn to God, My God, in My Sickness," these lines are less enigmatic than they seem. Sick, the poet is stretched out in bed. Driven by scientific passion, his doctors have become cosmographers, examining the body laid out as if it were a map of the world. We must remember that on library globes, the east and the west touch, always relative and intermediate to one another: Donne lies at such an intersection. He hangs around the crossroads of death and resurrection. But what is the fragment's connection to the bomb? This link slips without doubt in the unsaid, for Oppenheimer forgot to cite the following line: "Is the Pacific Sea my home?" In August 1945, this question had taken on a special meaning. Oppenheimer was obsessed by the Empire of the Rising Sun, archipelago of the Pacific.

In New Mexico, Oppenheimer saw the explosion lead to, among other effects, a deluge of colors running from purple to green. But white was dominant. In 1966, the parts of White Sands containing the bomb crater and its environs were included in the official list of historic places of the United States of America. Today, the radioactivity level there is still ten times higher than the norm. In fiction, monitoring danger is more difficult. What are the radiation levels in McCarthy's novel, those striking the earth of the father and his son? The instruments of measurement, including thermometers, are absent. We know that in their ashen world, it is not warm. On the contrary, the cold astonishes them. The Atlantic coast is as frozen as the interior lands. The father and son's reasoning to get to the sea for protection proves, finally, to be flawed: as it turns out, the sea does not always warm tired bones. And the gypsum of the land, which is beautiful, is replaced by a viscous and glaucous matter. *Glauque*, the French word for "glaucous" (or "whitish"), derives, via the Latin *glaucus*, from the Greek *glaūkos*, which was a kind of white with a greenish tone, roughly similar to mucus. The swath of the white and frozen globe over which the man and his son flee has this consistency, for the world has got the flu. The man, whose respiratory tracts are damaged, passes away at the edge of a talus slope. His son hangs on. Hope is not dead. The flame of hope weakens, but, as always, McCarthy avoids blowing it out. Maybe the globe, white or glaucous, will reclaim its colors or, to the contrary, it will lose them, so as to be reborn. It all depends. But on what? The last paragraph of McCarthy's novel is quite beautiful, plunging us into a dense and brief interval between hope and sadness, evoking the trout that wriggled in the clear mountain torrents once upon a time or upon a future: "On their backs were vermiculate patterns that were maps of the world in its becoming. Maps and mazes. Of a thing which could not be put back. Not be made right again. In the deep glens where they lived all things were older than man and they hummed of mystery."[14] The mystery of living maps.

Too hot, then too cold. But what if the white globe received its excess of color (or its non-color) from the reflection of sun not on sand but on ice? Its whiteness then would result from the extension of the polar ice caps. This is unlikely, we are apt to retort, for the ice is melting everywhere. There are, however, those who evoke the dawn of a new glaciation: obviously, the faces of the apocalypse are shifting. But in Berger & Berger's *Astre blanc*, we see another possible world, one that asks only to be mentally visualized in a different way. So let us pose then an Arctic or Antarctic version of the White Sands hypothesis. To do so, let us think of several books: *White* by Marie Darrieussecq or *Arctic Dreams* by the great Barry Lopez. We would do well also to summon Jean Echenoz's *Je m'en vais* or Daniel Del Giudice's *Orizzonte mobile*, among so many others, some much older.[15]

The singularity of the Arctic or Antarctic adventure resides in how it challenges an extreme but well-demarcated environment. It starts in contrast with what the protagonist's life is in the daily universe of home, so stable and linear. The extreme cold and the ice it generates take their particularity from their deviation from a norm indispensable to human life. Something similar happens with extreme heat. The universal desert would be banal and unlivable, and so would be an ice cap as large as the world itself; unlivable, they would quickly be uninhabitable by mankind, in any case, by man and woman. Yes, the white globe of the hot or the cold apocalypse would not make sense by itself; it also would not present any interest in self as such, for it would come after life. At best, it would be the expression of a posthuman aesthetic in the most radical sense of the term. So let us switch perspective and approach our white, dented sphere from a different angle; leave the sand and ice where they are.

The White of Maps

The time has come to avail ourselves of the services of a search engine, and to ask it what might be meant by "white globe" in another possible world, a more commercial one than Berger & Berger's. Let us try Google; it might make us think of Globe. The response of Google's search engine is predictible. The keyword search of the French for "white globe" (*globe blanc*) turns up references to lamps, bulbs, chandeliers, and other light sources, and even a "white terrestrial globe for your desk." *Mehr Licht*! For the novice botanist that I am, still more surprising is the reference to "white globe" begonias, not to mention the "white globe" turnip. A search in English for "white globe" also sparks an utterly exuberant imaginary. Here, we discover quickly enough the existence of "white globe onions"; we could well conceive, I suppose, of a globe that would peel like an onion. But I am dead set on setting the apocalypse aside for now. In fact, Anglophone and especially American searches pull up more pictures of the earth as a white globe, pictures of the white earth in its geographic varieties, than do Francophone searches. One finds an array of images of globes.

The first image is beautiful and good: it is in white chocolate. A second is the logogram of a designer. A third interests me: it is of a perfectly round, white ball that bears a pithy but programmatic commentary: *a world without any discremenation"—Sic!* one might be tempted to add. (The multiple "i"s of "discrimination" are here "discriminated against," in a strange, perhaps George Perec-like manner.) There is indeed something to this idea of whiting out the world. I confess that something like this crossed my mind immediately when I saw Berger & Berger's white globe. Indeed, what would the world be, wondered the cartographer in me, if we were to re-whiten the maps?

Traditionally, maps were never white. Long ago we did not know the world at all, much less the universe. Even the principle of a globe was not *evident*. The more we learned about the world, the more we had to hide our ignorance or lack of awareness regarding the many things we did not know about it. And so we filled the void of the unknown with various figures drawn or painted on the borders of places known and nimbly mastered (or just stolen from others). We used and abused the recourse to goddesses and gods taken from familiar mythologies, to monsters, exotic animals, and men and women still more exotic. The more the globe demanded to be white and empty—the vaster the space of our ignorance—the more color it took on. And then our knowledge about the world reached its apex—above all, in the eyes of the West, whose appetite for conquest was insatiable. The globe then filled with place-names, and the silhouettes of the gods disappeared, useful no more for concealing a void.[16] We traced new and abundant borders. We formed territories, forgetting that they crossed spaces belonging to others. We transformed the globe into a puzzle whose different pieces were reduced to little, symbolic colors. Red was for the British Empire, as a general rule. Cecil Rhodes, who gave his name to Rhodesia, which later became Zimbabwe, Malawi, and Zambia, wanted to make the African map a red ensemble. G. K. Chesterton had summarized this vision in one of his "songs of education" consecrated to geography:

> The earth is a place on which England is found,
> And you find it however you twirl the globe round;
> For the spots are all red and the rest is all gray.[17]

Here, the globe is red and English or it is gray and void.

But the French Empire, which had meanwhile accelerated its own colonizing work, preferred a world map in a uniform blue; what was not red was no longer necessarily gray. The palette of colors served to fuel competition among the colonial powers. Other than red and blue, there was pink, orange, yellow, and green. Color-wise, there eventually remained few options to those charting the world. Of course, the actual inhabitants of the global puzzle board had not been asked for their chromatic choices. The white spots on maps did not exist prior to the second half of the eighteenth century, and they did not convey the mapmaker's helplessness or ignorance but a political objective. White indicated the direction in which the colonial power should turn. And it did turn, very quickly. Consequently, white spots disappeared from world maps and globes within a century. Everything was appropriated, with the exception of some corner of Antarctica or recess of the retreating jungle, so many crumbs left over from the opulence of the imperial feast. Joseph Conrad and Jules Verne were the last witnesses to this frenetic gorging.

After the Second World War, the puzzle board gained in subtlety and nuance. It was unmade and remade and continues to be so. The processes of colonization had given innumerable colors to the maps and to the globe. But the idea of cartographic saturation persisted. For there are only colors imposed by some on others. There are also lines, all those parallels, meridians, borders, and abstract demarcations that caused so much drama. The streaks that furrow the world are gaping wounds, today as yesterday. The walls that I have evoked are only one type of streak among others, visible and less so. In effect, sometimes these fences and borders are immaterial. They subtend the designs of the prejudiced. But their expression is always violent. Gilles Deleuze fought these streaks and striations; he wanted to "smooth out" space. Berger & Berger, for their part, have erased the dangerous symbols that, in connoting the planet, imprison its beings. They offer an alternative within anybody's reach, one that eshews measuring- and control-oriented lines and signposts. They give an alternative beyond discriminations and without a "message." To be sure, they are not naive. Their globe is lumpy like a skull that has taken a heavy blow. But their artistic solution allows for a new departure, a new hypothesis. Their white globe gives *carte blanche* to the freest spirits to do something other than nourish the apocalypse, the advance of white sands, the glaciation of ideas.

I must say that I rather like the idea of this deliberately imperfect sphere that inspires reflection and imposes nothing. Here, whiteness suggests the effacement of any landmark. It exempts the earth from a task that the planet has sometimes assigned itself and that has proven to be the source of many conflicts: the quest for a center and thus the establishment of a hierarchy of gazes and viewpoints, referents and references—the very hierarchy of colors that the maps have reproduced. As we know, the West and its cultures have not ceased to promote this quest, which, in many respects, resembles a very Proustian "search for lost time." We have, however, arrived at the point where we should at last ask what cultural universality might signify for this West, indeed, for this *nostalgic* West. What would a planetary cultural space be today, a space that would connect the world's grand narratives, the *mythoi*, which were already "grand narratives" for the ancient Greeks? While working on a piece[18] about the anthropological structures described by Gilbert Durand in the wake of Mircea Eliade, Gaston Bachelard, and several other great specialists of world mythology, I came to the conclusion that we should not subsume under the same scheme or "system" myths originating from different cultures—for instance, from Dravidian India, central Europe, or Brazilian Amazonia. For what would this "system" be other than one that would replicate the West's colorfully mapped contours? Orbiting around this self-proclaimed center would suddenly appear innumerable mythic satellites ("narrative units") whose consistency would stem from the dynamic relations formed around the referential "node" that would be the West and, in particular, Europe. In France, François Jullien has raised the question in *De L'Universel: De l'uniforme, du commun et du dialogue entre les cultures* (2008). Jullien, a philosopher and a Sinologist, was taken to task for distinguishing too neatly between the great cultures, for instance between the West and China. At the very least, however, he does pose a question quite pertinent, even a little . . . impertinent: "Is the universal not derived from a composite, not to say chaotic dynamic? And does the universal's prestige, in Europe, not rest precisely on this universal's contribution to holding together the heterogeneous by serving as the latter's ideological keystone?"[19]

Yes, it does, but in what terms would it be possible to escape ethnocentrism? The answer calls for patient reflection. One should give oneself, as I have tried here, some time to meditate on this question. It would be the kind of moment that Václav Havel—great thinker, Czechoslovakian dramaturge, and, after the fall of the Berlin Wall, first president of the Czech Republic—recommended that Europe take a break to reflect in order to better confront the challenges of tomorrow, as do the wise at sunset before going to bed. Havel was not heard. He died not long ago, and Europe is not doing well either. As for the rest of the globe, it is not much better off. Indeed, it is precisely the kind of reflexive exercise that Václav Havel submitted to our (in) attention that Berger & Berger invite through the spectacle of their sculpture. The globe is battered but, ideally, it can be rethought, emptied of its nonsense. *Vox clamantis in deserto candido*? (The voice of him that crieth in the wilderness?) Without a doubt—and not to offend Régis Debray—the spiritual state is often a prelude to the state of things. This idea is refreshing, and, given our present circumstances, not at all negligible. Undoubtedly, a white globe—an intersection of suppressed or excessive colors—represents all but "evidence."

Translated from the French by Darren Jackson

Notes

1. To learn more on Berger & Berger's work, one can consult their website: http://www.berger-berger.com.

2. See the exhibition's website at http://www.rosascape.com/site/expo-berger berger2011-us.html.

3. In a different version, this text, written in French, accompanied the exhibition where it was presented in the form of a pamphlet.

4. This is a reference to one of the most famous lines in French surrealist poetry: "The earth is blue like an orange" (my translation). The line is taken from Eluard's poem "The Earth Is Blue," included in *L'amour la poésie* (*Love, Poetry,* 1929) (Paris: Gallimard, 1929), republished as *Love, Poetry: L'amour la poesie*, trans. Stuart Kendall (Boston: Black Widow Press of Commonwealth Books, 2007).

5. "For at last, what is man in nature? A nothing faced with infinity, an everything faced with nothing, *a middle between nothing and everything*." See Blaise Pascal, *Pensées* (1670 [par. 72]), in *Oeuvres complètes* (Paris: Gallimard, 1954), 1106 (my translation and emphasis).

6. Schengen is a village in Luxembourg where several European accords (1985, 1990) have been signed. Thus, the agreements constituted what is called the "Schengen space," which is to say a zone of (relatively) free circulation at the heart of the European Union, whose customs borders are now located at the exterior limits of the participating states.

7. "Sedentary space is striated, by walls, fences, and paths between fences, while nomadic space is smooth, marked only by 'traits' that fade and move with the trajectory." Gilles Deleuze and Félix Guattari, *Capitalisme et Schizophrenie 2: Mille Plateaux* (Paris: Minuit, 1980), 472, my translation.

8. See my *La géocritique: Réel, fiction, espace* (Paris: Minuit, 2007), trans. Robert T. Tally Jr. as *Geocriticism: Real and Fictional Spaces* (New York: Palgrave Macmillan, 2011); and my *Le monde plausible: Espace, lieu, carte* (Paris: Minuit, 2011). On geocriticism, see also Robert T. Tally Jr., ed., *Geocritical Explorations: Space, Place, and Mapping in Literary and Cultural Studies* (New York: Palgrave Macmillan, 2011); and Laurence Dahan-Gaida, ed., "Numéro special Géocritique," special issue, *Epistémocritique* 9 (Fall 2011), http://www.epistemocritique .org/spip.php?rubrique60&lang=fr.

9. See Zygmunt Bauman, *Liquid Modernity* (Cambridge, Eng.: Polity, 2000); and Peter Sloterdijk, *Eurotaoismus: Zur Kritik der politischen Kinetik* (Berlin: Suhrkamp, 1989).

10. Geocriticism posits "spatio-temporality," the notion that space is in time and vice versa. This is seized in a permanent movement (transgressivity) and is articulated as a link between the real and its fictional representations (referentiality). The notion also implies that these representations activate a phenomenon of global legibility (the referential space deploys itself in a fictional manner in the text or in the image that in turn informs space).

11. For other treatments of this issue and for a selective bibliography, one can consult Westphal, *Geocriticism*, 69–74.

12. Régis Debray, *Éloge des frontières* (Paris: Gallimard, 2010), 20 (my translation).

13. John Donne, "Hymn to God, My God, in My Sickness," in *Poems of John Donne*, ed. E. K. Chambers (London: Lawrence and Bullen, 1896), 1:211–12.

14. Cormac McCarthy, *The Road* (London: Picador, 2006), 307.

15. Marie Darrieussecq, *White* (Paris: P.O.L., 2003); Barry Lopez. *Arctic Dreams* (New York: Charles Scribner's Sons, 1986); Jean Echenoz, *Je m'en vais* (Paris: Minuit, 1999); Daniel Del Giudice, *Orizzonte mobile* (Turin: Einaudi, 2009).

16. On these questions, see chapter IV, "L'invention du lieu," in my essay *Le monde plausible*, 156–204.

17. Gilbert Keith Chesterton, "Geography," in *The Collected Poems of G. K. Chesterton*, ed. Gilbert Keith (New York: Dodd, Mead, 1946), 93.

18. Bertrand Westphal, "Une lecture géocritique des structures anthropologiques de l'imaginaire," *Iris* 43 (2012). The referenced text is Gilbert Durand, *Les structures anthropologiques de l'imaginaire* (1960; reprinted, Paris: Dunod, 1992).

19. François Jullien, *De l'universel: De l'uniforme, du commun et du dialogue entre les cultures* (2008; reprinted, Paris: Seuil, 2011), 14.

Comparing Contemporary Arts; or, Figuring Planetarity

TERRY SMITH

The nature of our present contemporaneity and how the various arts practiced today manifest it have become hot topics in many spheres, from the arcane to the popular. In the *New York Times Book Review* of March 11, 2012, writer and visual artist Douglas Coupland opened his review of Hari Kunzru's book *Gods without Men* (2011) by reflecting that one marker of how rapidly, and recently, times have changed is that, on 9/11/2001, people did not have smartphones to record the events of the day.[1] From this observation Coupland leapt to a generalization: "It has been only in the past decade that we appear to have entered an aura-free universe in which all eras coexist at once—a state of possibly permanent atemporality given to us courtesy of the Internet. No particular era now dominates. We live in a post-era era without forms of its own powerful enough to brand the times. The zeitgeist of 2012 is that we have a lot of *zeit* but not much *geist*."

Coupland is a writer and visual artist, a Canadian (and, unsurprisingly, an expert on McLuhan) best known as the coiner—in the title of his 1991 novel—of the term "Generation X." To his credit, he followed the above by declaring: "I can't believe I just wrote that last sentence, but it's true; there is something psychically sparse about the present era, and artists of all stripes are responding with fresh strategies." Then he goes on to identify "a new literary genre" that, he believes, responds in a fresh way to the current situation: "Translit novels cross history without being historical; they span geography without changing psychic place. Translit collapses time and space as it seeks to generate narrative traction in the reader's mind. It inserts the contemporary reader in other locations and times, while leaving no doubt that its viewpoint is relentlessly modern and speaks entirely of our extreme present . . . Translit's precursors are, say, 'Winesburg, Ohio' and 'Orlando,' and the genre's twenty-first century tent poles are Michael Cunningham's novel 'The Hours' and David Mitchell's 'Cloud Atlas.' "[2]

As it happens, each of these texts has led to a film, and in the instances of *Orlando* (Sally Potter, 1992) and *The Hours* (Stephen Daldry, 2002), very good ones. *Cloud Atlas*, directed by the Wachowski brothers, was released in October 2012. Is this an example of one of the arts—or, more accurately, one tendency within one of the arts—developing in a way that happens to influence another, or are certain artists in both forms responding, in parallel ways, to the same set of changing cultural, social, and political conditions? If it is the latter, what are these conditions, on what scale (or scales) do they operate, and how do they shape such responses?

Despite his flip style, I believe that Coupland was on to something. I want to suggest that what amounts to an epochal change—or, more accurately, a change from historical development understood as a sequence of periods to conditions in which not atemporality but multiple, antinomial cotemporalities prevail—is playing itself out across the arts, in forms particular to each but also somewhat shared. To put it in terms that read as if they are naming successive versions of the same kind of thing but, in fact, are signs of splitting, we are living through a movement from modernity through postmodernity to contemporaneity and planetarity. These developments occur unevenly, at different times and at different rates, and do so distinctly in each place. Some are already historical; others are in their early stages. Overall, as Coupland's remarks attest, this situation is experienced as an all-at-once coincidence of different temporalities and spatialities. In its immediacy, multiplicity, and dispersive spread, it feels as if all structures have evaporated, as if historical continuity has disappeared from human affairs and the ongoingness of natural phenomena has melted away. The paradox of contemporaneity, however, is not that human and natural continuity has suddenly expired and that incipience prevails in everything, everywhere, and everywhen. It is, rather, as climate change among other indicators tells us, that these two continuities—which separated during modernity—are not only reintegrating but also changing places as drivers of planetary destiny. In these circumstances, works of art are diminished if they are treated primarily as evolutionary additions to their own art form, as testimony to the expressive needs of their creators, as instances of the aspirations of the artists' society or nation, or as embodiments of the creativity inherent in the human spirit. They will of course be one or more of these, but in contemporary circumstances, they are much else besides. In their specificity—by virtue of their actual location in a set of interlocked worlds-within-the-world—and in their potential universality—by virtue of the (in principle) unlimited imaginative scope that inspires them—works of art are integral to both localized and wide-scale change in the workings of this world.

San Diego-based artists Newton and Helen Mayer Harrison exemplify this complex positioning. With roots in conceptual, performance, and land art, they have been pioneers since 1969 in seeking direct and usable solutions to actual problems in particular settings. They continue to pursue the goal of "ecosystemic well-being." Each of their projects is conceived from its beginnings as a trigger to the imagination of the residents of a particular place, who are the only people actually able to bring projects to realization. The projects are, therefore, developed in a totally cooperative manner. Typically, the artists are invited to an area by an arts or activist organization, work with it to identify an environmental problem, consult with local experts, and then present a display in a public venue that visualizes the circumstances that led to the problem; propose what the artists call a visual "metaphor" that suggests a viable solution; and provoke discussion of how that solution might be brought about in actuality. Projects have ranged from sewage filtration ponds in parks in rust belt cities in the United States (for example, Braddock, Pennsylvania) through lagoon reclamation in Thailand, to some that are national and even continental in scale.

Presented at various venues in Europe between 2000 and 2003, the Harrisons' *Peninsula Europe I: Bringing Forth a New State of Mind* envisaged the European landmass as a single, coherent environmental whole, oblivious of national borders, and organized according to the best use of its waterways, mountains, and other natural resources. Through reconfigurations of maps, and displays of information about water flows, land use, and nonpolluting industries such as green farming, the artists showed that the ideal of Europe so contested by national political rivalries could be envisaged—indeed, that the region was once, and could be again, integrated by "biodiversity ribbons." To the authors, these metaphorical ribbons become icons: lynxlike configurations, as if the land were a living creature, like one of the ancient animals it used to support. While their grand vision for Europe as a whole remains an ideal, various smaller-scale projects based on the same values have been pursued, notably in Holland, where their *Green Heart* concept—which proposes the removal of housing from central Holland and its concentration in the areas close to the nation's borders—has influenced national planning since 1994.[3]

If the work of the Harrisons is a particularly striking instance of a successful practice in contemporary circumstances, it is not alone in the specifics of its response, nor is it by any means the only kind of visual art that matches the complexity of the current situation. There are many others, and others within the other arts. My aim in this two-part chapter is to sketch a framework for understanding how artists working in a variety of mediums are tackling these challenges. I will explore first the question of how the various arts have undergone the shift from modern to contemporary worlds. Working primarily from a cinematic example—Terrence Malick's 2011 film, *The Tree of Life*—the second half of my intervention will take up the larger issues of the nature of our present contemporaneity and the consequent need to figure planetarity.

The Contemporary Arts Compared

Comparing the arts is absolutely no longer (if it ever was) a matter of identifying the main thrust, the driving direction, and the distinctive achievements of one art form and then measuring it against those of another that is contemporaneous with it. If, for most of the modern era, commentators could point to a body of mainstream work that moved steadily forward by distinguishing itself from its accumulating traditions, rendering them past, while at the same time being frequently disrupted by avant-garde experimentation on its other flank, in contemporary circumstances the situation for each of the arts has become rather more like that described by John Cage in 1992: "We live in a time I think, not of mainstream, but of many streams or even, if you insist upon a river of time, that we have come to [a] delta, maybe even beyond [the] delta to an ocean which is going back to the skies."[4] This is a striking metaphor for the diversity experienced at every level, in every aspect, of the contemporary arts. How did this come about? Exactly what is happening at present? Where might it be going? To answer, let me set the scene for how we might see structure within this flowing diversity by offering a summary of three key ideas underlying my work, since around 2000, on late modern and contemporary visual art.[5]

From Modern to Contemporary

The core art-historical idea is the claim that a worldwide shift from modern to contemporary art was prefigured in the major movements in late modern art of the 1950s and 1960s in Euro-America and became explicit in art world discourse by the 1980s. Postmodern aesthetic practice was an important signal of this change; postmodern theory, its first analysis. A market phenomenon in the major centers during the 1990s, contemporary art was at the same time divided, and expanded, by art emergent from the rest of the world. Since then, contemporary art everywhere has engaged more and more with spectacle culture—with image-saturated commerce, globalized lifestyle, and social media—and with anxieties caused by political volatility and climate change. These developments flow through the present, thus shaping art's imaginable futures—at least in the short term.

These changes from modern to contemporary art do not, however, constitute a monopolizing phenomenon that spread from a predominant center, as did the great art styles of the nineteenth and twentieth centuries. Rather, the changes occurred at different times and in distinctive ways in each cultural region and in each art-producing locality. I believe that the histories specific to each place should be acknowledged, valued, and carefully tracked alongside recognition of their interaction with other local and regional tendencies, and with the waxing and waning of more powerful regional and international art-producing centers. Applied retrospectively, under the banner of "alternative modernities," this approach has led to enriched histories of art throughout the world during the modern period.[6] They are the grounds of the diversity that we now see flowing through the present. Yet this diversity is not, as some claim, best understood as a "global art," a "world art," or a "geoaesthetics."[7] Each of these terms certainly highlights a key aspect of contemporary art. Nevertheless, however loosely defined or critically intended, each of them echoes the metropolitan-provincial models that obtained during the age of empires and thus is dating fast. Worse, they falsely suggest an overarching coherence, an inclination toward hegemony that, while present within parts of them, is, I argue, residual within the whole ensemble. Rather, we note now the contemporaneousness of distinct kinds of contemporary art, each of which, if it has an "aesthetic," has its own, internally diversified one. From the perspective of worlds-within-the-world, we can see that each is, at once and in distinctive ways, local, regional, *and* international—that is to say, *worldly*—in character.[8]

Contemporaneous Currents

Antinomial difference is the most striking feature of relationships within this multiplicitous, scaled, and intensely interactive flow. What are these distinct kinds of contemporary art? As another major art critical idea, I argue that three strong currents may be discerned in art made since around 1989. Remodernist, retro-sensationalist, and spectacularist tendencies fuse into one current, which continues to predominate in Euro-American and other modernizing art worlds and markets, with widespread effect both inside and outside those constituencies. Against these, and giving rise to a second current, is art created according to nationalist, identarian, and critical priorities. This art has emerged especially from previously colonized cultures. It came into prominence on international circuits such as biennials and traveling temporary exhibitions: this is the art of transnational transitionality. For many of the artists, curators, and commentators involved, it has evolved through at least three discernable phases: a reactive, anti-imperialist search for national and localist imagery followed by a rejection of simplistic identarianism and corrupted nationalism in favor of a naive internationalism and then by a broader search for an integrated cosmopolitanism, or worldliness, in the context of the permanent transition of all things and relations. The third current cannot be identified as a style, a period, or a tendency. It proliferates below the radar of generalization. It results from the great increase in the number of artists worldwide and the opportunities offered by new informational and communicative technologies to millions of users. These changes have led to the viral spread of small-scale, interactive, DIY (Do It Yourself) art (and art-like output) that is concerned less with high art style or confrontational politics and more with tentative explorations of temporality, place, affiliation, and affect—the ever-more-uncertain conditions of living within contemporaneity on a fragile planet.

In view of these considerations, the comparative questions become: Can arts other than visual be understood in terms of two, three, or more contemporaneous currents? Did modern architecture, cinema, literature, and music, say, become contemporary in similar kinds of ways? Can contemporaneous currents be discerned in their present disposition?

Retromania: Currents across the Arts

Toward the end of their thoughtful review of *What Is Contemporary Art?* (2009), Anthony Gardner and Huw Hallam make the following observations:

> It seems likely that his triumvirate of spectacularism, postcolonialism and practices engaging in the critical interrogation of contemporaneity itself will be observable in other areas of cultural production and [therefore be] of great interdisciplinary value. These categories may even prove to harbour their greatest analytic power when faced with phenomena posing as exceptions. If used to examine the situation of contemporary music, for instance, Smith's categories are quickly recognizable in several fairly stereotypical forms of production. "Spectacularism" is again split: into "remodernism," easy enough to spot in most of the world's leading publicly sponsored concert halls, where it can often be caught straining to hold onto cultural formats inherited from the nineteenth century; and into the pop industry's "retro-sensationalism," working, as the labels that dominate the sector do, to ensure that "of the people" means ever increasing corporate profit according to an all too familiar geographic patterning. Jazz, Tropicalism, or the myriad redressings of hip-hop across the globe can all lay claim to having shaped postcolonial struggle, and this is not unconnected to strong traditions of the kinds of "do-it-yourself-with-friends" engagements with music (from politically motivated improvisation collectives, to garage band jamming, to LGBT community orchestras) that Smith argued characterized his third stream of contemporary art practice.[9]

These are fertile suggestions for further inquiry. Taking up just one of them, we might note that the account offered by Simon Reynolds in *Retromania: Pop Culture's Addiction to Its Own Past* (2011) parallels my read of retro-sensationalism in the art of Damien Hirst, the Young British Artists, Takashi Murakami, and many, many others. To Reynolds, the essence of popular music, pop culture, and "pop" itself as a quality of experience is that it is a pure event, utter eventuality, which he calls "future-rush."[10] Is this the quintessential modernist value: the shock of the new? Or is he evoking contemporaneity as it is experienced in every first, or immediate, encounter with newness in any and all of the arts, whatever other distinctions might apply? In any event, it is no surprise that he despairs of the all-pervasive retro character of popular music: "In the 2000s the pop present became even more crowded out by the past, whether in the form of archived memories of yesteryear or retro-rock leeching off ancient styles. Instead of being about itself, the 2000s have been—so far—about every other previous decade happening at once: a simultaneity of pop time that abolishes history while nibbling away at the present's own sense of itself as an era with a distinct identity and feel."[11]

In stark contrast to Coupland's awed acceptance of atemporality as an opportunity for new kinds of artistic response, Reynolds sees the "pulse of the NOW" weakening in pop music, not only in its ordinary forms (band reformations and reunion tours, reissues, remakes, and mash-ups), but also, most egregiously, among its outstanding practitioners. Lady Gaga's performances and videos are stunning, but sonically not a lot is happening. To Reynolds, still the modernist, this is an abuse of "the artistic imperative to be original," leading him to despair that "there has never been a society in human history so obsessed with the cultural artifacts of *its own immediate past*."[12] "What happens," he asks in a related interview, "when we run out of past[s]?"[13] In this sense, today's popular music is not contemporary in any interesting sense: it is a noisy fading away from the heights of the 1960s and 1970s, when this form of music, like the economic system that provoked it and sustained it, reached its peak. It bears noting that Reynolds is also alert to the fact that the greatest change in all forms of music in the past ten years has not occurred in the writing or performance of music itself but in the technical means of its production and distribution. Napster and the iPod are the change agents in what he calls "the macro-structure of how music is made," not any one musician, or ensemble, or band, or scene, nor any aggregation of them, however "good" they may be to listen to on a one-to-one basis. Reynolds cites remix band Gonjasufi: "I talk about Gonjasufi in the book—there's lots of interesting things there, in that the mix is drawn from the past as well as from contemporary things. They've listened to grime and dubstep but they've also listened to a huge array of music from history and from across the globe, but you don't get that pure, hard hit of futurism, hardly ever."[14]

This observation applies even to outstanding musicians among those with world-picturing ambitions, such as DJ Spooky That Subliminal Kid (my example, not his) in, for example, his *Terra Nova: Sinfonia Antarctica*, 2009. In an article written to accompany the launch of *Retromania*, Reynolds was more precise about the experience of time during the analogue era, as being structured around "delay, anticipation[,] and the Event," whereas within what he calls digiculture, "time is lateral, recursive, spongiform, riddled with wormholes," and is marked by "a paradoxical combination of instantaneity and permanence, speed and stasis."[15] These analyses resonate with those I will discuss in the second part of this chapter.

Retromania is sourced to the negative narrowness of monopolizing distributive companies: it is they who are the powerhouses of contemporary cultural consumption; it is they who treat music from elsewhere as "xenomania." Like all other forms of postmodernism, he suggests, retromania is symptomatic of the creative vacuity at the heart of late capitalism, a mode that remains inventive at the level of building desire for commodities, reproducing them in viable numbers, and distributing them everywhere. Since the 1970s, music from outside Euro-America (and from the immigrant communities within it) has been cataloged as "world music."[16] On its own grounds, however, much of this music works powerfully, and resonates elsewhere throughout the world, enough for it to constitute a second current on my model. It, too, has been around long enough to have its version of recent past nostalgia. I leave it to those more knowledgeable to assess whether this taste for self-reference amounts to retromania and whether or not more subtle kinds of musical remembering are typically in play in classical music contexts, though I believe that they are, and that that is their main point, even in the small portion of attention that they devote to contemporary compositions.

To return now to my opening reference, Coupland locates his generalization about a present possibility for literature within a global optic, but his view, too, is primarily from the Euro-America centers outwards. This perspective has, in the recent past, given us comparative literature (the West vis-à-vis the Rest), Commonwealth literature (English literature vis-à-vis Anglophone writing from the former colonies), and French literature and writing in French (French versus Francophone writing), among many other similar Orientalisms. None of these were entirely a matter of one-way traffic dispensed from the metropolitan centers outwards and downwards. But it was clear until recently where most of the enabling power lay.

Arguably, "magical realism" in South American writing was, however, a construct of regional consciousness vis-à-vis West European and North American literatures. This signaled a shift. Perhaps the emergence of a second current in the world's writing about itself? One that, after four decades of diversification that has blasted apart each of the disciplinary categories just listed, Coupland wishes to name "Translit"?

Dwelling on this shift in her *Death of a Discipline* (2003), Gayatri Chakravorty Spivak urged students of writing to "cross borders under the auspices of a Comparative Literature supplemented by Area Studies" by imagining themselves as "planetary rather than continental, global, or worldly." In words that appear more than once in the *Planetary Turn* collection, she announced:

> I propose the planet to override the globe. Globalization is the imposition of the same system of exchange everywhere. In the gridwork of electronic capital, we achieve that abstract ball covered with latitudes and longitudes, cut by virtual lines, once the equator and the tropics and so on, now drawn by the requirements of Geographical Information Systems. To talk planet-talk by way of an unexamined environmentalism, referring to an undivided "natural" space rather than a differentiated political space, can work in the interests of this globalization in the mode of the abstract as such. (I have been insisting that to transmute the literatures of the global South into an

> undifferentiated space of English rather than a differentiated political space is a related move.) The globe is on our computers. No one lives there. It allows us to think that we can aim to control it. The planet is in the species of alterity, belonging to another system; and yet we inhabit it, on loan. It is not really amenable to a neat contrast with the globe. I cannot say "the planet, on the other hand." When I invoke the planet, I think of the effort required to figure the (im)possibility of this underived intuition.[17]

I will return to the implications of her comments on this effort of imaginative figuring in the second part of this chapter, which examines this third major current in the arts today. In this section, I have proposed that macro-level changes in the arts in recent decades have constituted, and in some centers continue to constitute, a general movement from modern to contemporary forms. I have further maintained that these changes have occurred, and in some places are still occurring, differentially yet concomitantly, according to a structure that I dub the "three current model." I hope that these suggestions are of some value to those wishing to track the flow of the arts of the present.

Figuring Planetarity: The Problem of Visuality

Let us now shift gears, as Spivak's invocation requires us to do, up through the scales of the psychic, social, economic, and political worlds-within-the-world that, layered together, constitute our planetary sphere. The cross-artistic currents I have been exploring are, I submit, manifestations of the great changes that have occurred since the mid-twentieth century in the distribution of power within and between these scales. On the political and economic levels, it is now a commonplace to observe that, while the era of the European and North American colonizers seems to be in decline, their enormous influence persists and is taking new forms. Some, in the years after 1989, believed that the United States stood alone as the world's "last remaining superpower," as the only "hyperpower." However, its failures in international policy and national governance since 2001 are clear evidence that no nation retains the kind or extent of geopolitical influence once wielded by the advanced countries of the modern period. The economic rise of China, India, Brazil, and others is everywhere acknowledged, but it remains to be seen whether their efforts at global and regional influence will be of the same kind.

Furthermore, in the twenty-first century, nation-states no longer align themselves according to the four-tier system of First, Second, Third, and Fourth Worlds. Multinational corporations based in the Euro-American centers control only a significant portion, instead of the entire, world economy, for new global corporations are located in South, East, and North Asia. Manufacturing, distribution, and services are themselves dispersed around the globe, and linked to delivery points by new technologies and old-fashioned labor. Some would argue that, with globalization, capitalism has achieved its pure form. Certainly, the living standard of millions has been lifted, but only at enormous cost to social cohesion, peaceful cohabitation, and natural resources. Most national and local governments, as well as many international agencies, seek to regulate this flow and assuage its worst side effects—so far without conspicuous success. The institutions that drove modernity appear, to date, incapable of dealing with the most important unexpected outcome of their efforts: the massive disruptions to natural ecosystems that now seem to threaten the survival of the Earth itself. Awareness of this possibility has increased consciousness of our inescapably shared, mutually dependent existence on this fragile planet.

In such circumstances, how is planetarity being figured, in visual terms? I see planetary figuration occurring on a number of levels simultaneously, and, to clarify, I will choose examples from three: world-scale regimes of seeing, such as those made possible by new technologies of vision and visualization; the aesthetics of disappearance in contemporary visual art; and the configuration, in certain movies, of worlds within the World.

Regimes of Vision

"Visuality," to begin with, was a term much in currency during the postmodern 1980s, where it was widely taken to mean the social circulation of images, including mental images and projections in the imagination of peoples as much as individuals. A distinction was drawn between it and "vision," understood as the physical processes of seeing common to us all. Hal Foster's collection *Vision and Visuality* (1988) built on this differentiation as a basis for exploring the connected character of all forms of visualization, high and low, within Western modernity, along with their history. Martin Jay, following Foucault, called them "scopic regimes."[18] But the usage was vague then, and has remained so since. A few attempts to historicize broad-scale changes in "ways of seeing" in Western societies have been made, but with little success. Exceptions include Régis Debray, whose theory of "mediology" features interesting schemas of visualization that are seen as components of significant political change.[19]

In *The Right to Look: A Counterhistory of Visuality* (2011), Nicholas Mirzoeff substantially advances our thinking about these issues. Struck by Thomas Carlyle's use of the word "visuality" in 1840 to characterize the capacity of heroic individuals to take broad views of the sweep of history and to act within it, Mirzoeff looked for similar competencies on the part of other leaders. When battlefields became too large to be seen with the naked eye or the telescope from a single position, generals such as Napoleon and Wellington developed the ability to visualize dispersed but connected domains and to anticipate and initiate actions across them in a coordinated way toward the overall end of victory. As European nations pursued their colonizing ambitions, they developed complex structures of visuality that ruled at home and abroad. Mirzoeff names this the "Imperial Complex" and dates its dominance to the years 1860–1945. He acknowledged that this ability was first developed in plantation economies throughout the world, where overseers controlled complex, sequential processes of production and large numbers of workers primarily by means of oversight—always, of course, backed up by the exercise of extreme violence. The "Plantation Complex" was dominant from around 1660 to 1860. Following President Dwight D. Eisenhower in his farewell address to the nation in 1954, Mirzoeff dubs the third phase the "Military-Industrial Complex." If we add entertainment and information to military and industrial, we recognize it as having prevailed from 1945 through the present.

Against these regimes Mirzoeff posits a set of matching counter-visualities, that is, resistances to their dominance that also took strong but distinct visual forms. The oversight visuality that held sway during the plantation years was opposed by "revolutionary realism" in Europe, and, in Haiti especially, by what he calls "abolition realism." Similarly, he suggests, various forms of indigenous counter-visuality were developed to evade imperial visuality, and, when imperialism took on fascist dimensions during much of the mid- and later twentieth century, by "antifascist neorealism," a battle still being waged in parts of the world. If the military-industrial complex favored "aerial visualization" during its earlier phase, it was opposed by what Mirzoeff calls "decolonial neorealism." Since 1989, this complex has entered a more intensive phase: "post-panoptic visuality." Opposition to it, he believes, must take the form of an environmentally alert "planetary visualization," which brings us to the current situation.[20] At the time of writing (up to late 2010), Mirzoeff could at least allude on his final page to the significance of the Arab Spring as harbinger of a contemporary counter-visuality: "The everyday form created in Tahrir Square, Cairo, has been the best example to date of the possibilities of a praxis of the everyday that is not found but made."[21] Eruptions such as these ever since have thrown into confusion what he identifies in *The Right to Look* as the latest mechanism of military-industrial control: the deliberate creation and maintenance of conditions in which militarized counterinsurgency becomes the overriding task of government. While focused at present in Middle East hot war zones, this strategy has every potential to be used against the citizens of even overtly democratic states. Reviewing the world picture as of 2010, he concludes: "Several outcomes seem possible from this swirling crisis: a new authoritarianism, a perpetual crisis, or, just possibly, a time in which my claim to the right to look is met by your willingness to be seen."[22]

Like almost everyone else, Mirzoeff failed to foresee the spread of Tahrir Squares throughout the Middle East, nor their appearance, in distinct forms, throughout the West—in the streets of Spain, Greece, and even Israel, and in the squares of cities throughout the United States. He has not hesitated to become deeply involved in this unanticipated movement. Indeed, he maintains a blog that is itself a kind of occupying: he devotes a given part of each day to "Occupy 2012: A Daily Observation on Occupy," producing a short text that reflects on the potentials and possibilities of occupying as an absolutely contemporary kind of countervisuality.[23]

Contemporary Visual Art: The Aesthetics of Disappearance

In a recent single-screen, continuous loop video work, *Shadow Sites II* (2011), Iraqi artist Jananne Al-Ani takes viewers through a sequence of zooms from aerial distance in to framed landscapes that show residual traces of natural forms and man-made structures (ancient, modern, and contemporary). The video combines archaeological techniques of searching for sites through cast shadows with unusual regularities with digital and satellite mapping technologies used by the military. In this way, it alerts us to the operation of "aerial visuality" as defined by Mirzoeff. Yet, because we soon see that each formation was made using plaster, ambiguity and imprecision actually are shown to prevail at this level. The ideals of informational exactitude and precision targeting that military and governmental surveillance claim are shown to be false. The God's-eye camera keeps zooming close to a ground zero that insists on fading to another place, closing in to a surface that it cannot penetrate. Al-Ani is responding to the prevalence of surveillance technologies in warfare and civil life as well as to the critiques of them offered by theorists such as Paul Virilio.[24] At the same time, she works very much from her own perspective as an Iraqi artist, which position is made clear by one of her recent statements:

> My early work focused on orientalist representations of the Middle East in western visual culture and particularly of enduring myths and fantasies surrounding the veil. Since 2007, I have been developing a new body of work, *The Aesthetics of Disappearance: A Land Without People*, which explores the disappearance of the body in the contested and highly charged landscapes of the Middle East. The project includes single screen films *Shadow Sites I* (2010) and *Shadow Sites II* (2011). Frequently depicted as a desert, an exotic place with no history and no population, the Middle Eastern landscape has become familiar to westerners as the blank backdrop to military action. In response to the use of aerial reconnaissance and satellite navigation devices in the 1991 Desert Storm campaign and the 2003 Gulf War, both films adopt the vantage point of such missions, while taking an altogether different viewpoint of the land surveyed. Scanning the surface or burrowing into the earth, the films excavate what cannot otherwise be seen on the ground. Landscapes disappear and reappear

> as one image slowly dissolves into another, like a mineshaft tunneling deep into a substrate of memories preserved over time.[25]

We see in her work the pursuit of a critical distance from dominant regimes of visuality, distance, or interval that is, on the one hand, a necessary but by no means sufficient component of what Mirzoeff calls "planetary visuality" and, on the other hand, an example of what Spivak identifies as the pressing need to "figure planetarity."[26] It is to this need that I turn in conclusion.

Worlds-within-the-world and Filmic Visuality

Many other artists working today imagine the physical conjunction of a number of different kinds of world: the intimate, personal sense of "my world"; the close neighborhood of the local; further worlds, increasingly distant beyonds, until a sense of the World in general is reached; then the transitory, "no-places" in between. Such a conception evokes the co-temporality of these worlds, their differential movement through time. As a contribution toward the task of imagining planetarity, let me take this spatial idea of simultaneous worlds and, in an effort to envisage the structure of the world as we experience it today, marry that idea to the notion that these worlds share temporal contemporaneousness.

Beginning spatially, we might imagine four planes, surfaces, fields, arenas, or domains that stand to each other as layers—"orders" in an older parlance, or "levels" in a more recent one. Let us call them "worlds" in the sense of worlds-within-the-World. They could be represented as follows:

WORLD/WORLDS: PLANES, LAYERS
Earth, planet, natural histories, evolution, information
Sentient interiority (human, animal, things? machinic?)
Societies, social relations, cultures, local economies, nation-states
Geopolitics and economics, international arrangements, NGOs, civilizations

I have been inspired to this (tentative) proposal partly in reaction against the somewhat simplistic modeling of worlds-within-the-World recently, and very influentially, advanced by theorists of globalization and government such as Samuel P. Huntington and Joseph Nye Jr.[27] Nye suggests that we envisage the distribution and play of power throughout the world as a chess game played on multiple boards at once, in which actors moving pieces on one board (say, the geopolitical) impact on another (say, the cultural). He urges that, if the United States is to retain its preeminence, it must act in awareness of the effects of power across all relevant domains and do so in a planned way, within frameworks of conscious policy (hence his concept of "soft power," avidly adopted as a tool of foreign policy by governments around the world today, not least the Chinese government). Being actually more concerned with coercive power, having forgotten their Foucault, and being unconcerned about climate change, both Nye and Huntington pay little attention to interiority and the planetary. But their models do have the virtue of highlighting the fact that we form perspectives on the world at large according to the forces in play within the world, or worlds, in which we mostly act, or most immediately need to act, and that we are often unaware, or unable to envisage, the nature of the relationships that connect them.

With these cautions in mind, let me complicate the diagram with some suggestions as to the kinds of ties that are commonly held to link up these planes. I indicate only some of the most prominent *forms* that these relationships take, through the *names* that they have attracted:

WORLD/WORLDS/WORLDING: PLANES & RELATIONSHIPS
Earth, planet, natural histories, evolution, information
<Indigeneity, ecology, virtuality>
Sentient interiority (human, animal, machinic? things?)
<art, language, sexualities, belief, humanities, sciences, media>
Societies, social relations, local economies, nation-states, cultures
<diplomacy, war, criminality, cooperation>
Geopolitics and economics, international arrangements, NGOs, civilizations
<modernity, globalization, globality, planetarity>

To "complete"—to the degree that *that* is possible—this tentative sketch of the world picture, I would posit that a host of actions, difficult to diagram, actually weave the connections within this model, where they constitute the *substance* of relationships. I would call them "connectivities." These include the imagination, feeling, projection, identification, communication; producing, consuming, prosuming; warring, surging, peace-making, reconciling, deterring, negotiating; searching, networking, flocking; and many others, both shared and specific to particular practices. Imagine them as threads weaving through these layers and forms of connection, thus giving us a three-dimensional matrix. This overall activity, this weaving of connectivities, is what I would term "world-making" or "worlding." Please notice too what we might call the *rounding* of the model, its return to itself, such that our taking of the Earth itself as *the* grounding matches, at world-scale, a planetary consciousness rather than a globalizing thirst for dominance and hegemony. One ambition here is to enable a conception of the world that does not begin from the image of the globe, or that of a map of continents, but of course includes them within a broader pictorial imagining of worlds-within-the-World that now stretches through more space and more time and in more differentiated ways than hitherto imaginable.[28]

Furthermore, if something like this connective layering represents the structure of our intersecting worlds, how might we understand it to have changed throughout time?[29] Debray, Mirzoeff, and others have proposed frameworks for following the movement of visual imagining across some centuries. Tracking the movement of the entire scalar structure is rather more daunting. Yet certain artists have let their imaginations enter this space.

We have seen in our cinemas recently one such example: Malick's film, *The Tree of Life*. For all of its obvious flaws, New Age overreaching, and quasi-Creationist banalities, this is an extraordinary effort to imagine visually the world-historical dynamic of something like the structure I have just sketched. *New York Review of Books* writer Geoffrey O'Brien gives us a concise description of the movie and offers what is, in my view, an accurate judgment of it:

> Malick has never shied from grandiosity, and in *The Tree of Life* more than ever before he risks the humorless and overblown. Into what might in other hands have been the small-scale, melancholy tale—too elliptical even to be called a tale—of the not unusually eventful childhood of a boy in Texas, his two brothers, and his father and mother, he has managed to incorporate the creation of the universe, the origins of life on earth, the age of dinosaurs, and the prospect of future dissolution, with musical accompaniment by the powerful tonalities of Berlioz's *Requiem Mass*. But he has made an audacious and magnificent film.[30]

O'Brien goes on to make many useful observations, to me the most pertinent of which narrate the film as an extended evocation of the adult architect's memories of his childhood, a postmodern one in Houston, the third largest city in the United States. O'Brien's glosses turn on the fact of the accidental death of a beloved younger brother at nineteen. "The whole film," the critic points out, "might be a poem of deep grief diffused over a lifetime."[31] No heroes here. In contrast to the "spooky fears" of teenage Goth movies, O'Brien notes, Malick "proposes the existential dread of cosmology. He can't show the life of this boy unless he shows you his parents; and the time and place where the parents lived; and the planet on which that era unfolded; and the universe in which that planet came into existence, and within which it will meet its end."[32]

O'Brien makes this sound like a personal compulsion of the filmmaker and the film itself an elaborate act of representation, on a par, perhaps, with Proust's *Remembrance of Things Past*. However grand a comparison this is—and there is no greater, in literature—I believe that it limits understanding what has been put before us. For are we not moved to ask: Is not something like what is glimpsed in these flowing stagings that which the world—quite literally, the planet—is asking us to imagine more fully? Is the movie not asking us to see beyond the proximities within which we normally live, with so little regard for realities more distant in space and for those more powerfully pushing through from other times? If *The Tree of Life* is a representation, it is one of the world remembering itself, the world unfolding from now to then, and then to now, a representation of The Tree of Life itself—that is, of the "way of nature" and the "way of grace" combined.

In view of the questions before us, we can conclude only by asking some more. Is Malick toying with the ambition—however flawed, partial, hubristic, and at times banal—to represent the world remembering itself or, more accurately, to show a set of world memories that run from those that are absolutely specific to one living being to those that are, absolutely, of the universe? Does not such a quest uncover to us the structure of worlds-within-the-World, its processes of layering and unraveling, its violent disjunctions and its affiliative connectivities? Is this not a picturing of a kind of planetary consciousness operating along, across, and between the scales of the world-picture? Is this not what we might hope art can do for us all?

Notes

1. Not to spoil a good story, but, in the interests of historical accuracy, it should also be recalled that the thousands of media workers living nearby—a concentration unequaled elsewhere on the planet—had many other modes of recording what was happening to them. Thus the plethora of images and sound records of the event, at least from the second strike forward, which generated a repertoire that fed its highly mediated resonance.

2. Douglas Coupland, "Convergences," review of *Gods without Men*, by Hari Kunzru, *New York Times*, March 8, 2012, Sunday Book Review, http://www.nytimes.com/2012/03/11/books/review/gods-without-men-by-hari-kunzru.html?pagewanted=all.

3. A full description of projects since 1970 may be found at http://www.theharrisonstudio.net. The *Peninsula Europe* project is described in detail by the artists in "Public Culture and Sustainable Practices: Peninsula Europe from an Ecodiversity Perspective, Posing Questions to Complexity Scientists," *Structure and Dynamics* 2, no. 3 (2007): 1–38, http://escholarship.org/uc/item/9hj3s753.

4. Quoted in the epigraph to David W. Bernstein, introduction to *Writings through John Cage's Music, Poetry, and Art*, ed. David W. Bernstein and Christopher Hatch (Chicago: University of Chicago Press, 2001), 1.

5. See Terry Smith, *What Is Contemporary Art?* (Chicago: University of Chicago Press, 2009); and Terry Smith, *Contemporary Art: World Currents* (Upper Saddle River, N.J.: Prentice Hall, 2011). Art historians interested in historiography and methodology might like to consult Terry Smith, "The State of Art History: Contemporary Art," *Art Bulletin* 92, no. 4 (December 2010): 366–83. Contemporaneity is discussed in Terry Smith, Okwui Enwezor, and Nancy Condee, eds., *Antinomies of Art and Culture: Modernity, Postmodernity, Contemporaneity* (Durham, N.C.: Duke University Press, 2008).

6. See Kobena Mercer, ed., *Cosmopolitan Modernisms* (London: Institute of International Visual Art; Cambridge, Mass.: MIT Press, 2005).

7. See, for example, Peter Weibel and Andrea Buddenseig, eds., *Contemporary Art and the Museum: A Global Perspective* (Ostfildern, Ger.: Hatje Cantz, 2007); Hans Belting and Andrea Buddenseig, eds., *The Global Art World: Audiences, Markets and Museums* (Ostfildern, Ger.: Hatje Cantz, 2009); and Kitty Zijlmans and Wilfred van Damme, eds., *World Art Studies: Exploring Concepts and Approaches* (Amsterdam: Valiz, 2008).

8. Discussed in more detail in Terry Smith, "Currents of World-Making in Contemporary Art," *World Art* 1, no. 2 (2011): 171–88.

9. Anthony Gardner and Huw Hallam, "On the Contemporary—and Contemporary Art History," review of *What Is Contemporary Art?* by Terry Smith, *Journal of Art Historiography*, no. 4 (June 2011): 6–7. The full review can be found at http://arthistoriography.files.wordpress.com/2011/05/gardnerhallam.pdf.

10. See Simon Reynolds, *Retromania: Pop Culture's Addiction to Its Own Past* (London: Faber and Faber, 2011), 20.

11. Ibid., x–xi.

12. Ibid., 176, xiii (emphasis in original).

13. Colin McKean, "Is Pop Culture Consuming Itself? Simon Reynolds Discusses Retromania," *The Quietus*, June 8, 2011, http://thequietus.com/articles/06386-simon-reynolds-retromania-interview.

14. Quoted in McKean, "Is Pop Culture Consuming Itself?"

15. Simon Reynolds, "Excess All Areas," *The Wire*, no. 328 (June 2011): 32. For an excellent appraisal, see James Parker, "Simon Reynolds, Retromania, and the Atemporality of Contemporary 'Pop,' " review of *Retromania: Pop Culture's Addiction to Its Own Past*, by Simon Reynolds, *Discipline*, no. 2 (Autumn 2012): 156–64.

16. Tower.com still includes this category within its "Music Style Map," defining it interchangeably with the category "International General." See the map at http://www.tower.com/browse.cfm?div_id=2.

17. Gayatri Chakravorty Spivak, *Death of a Discipline* (New York: Columbia University Press, 2003), 72.

18. See Hal Foster, ed., *Vision and Visuality* (Seattle: Bay, 1988); and Martin Jay, *Downcast Eyes: The Denigration of Vision in Twentieth-Century French Thought* (Berkeley: University of California Press, 1994).

19. See Régis Debray, *Vie et mort de l'image: Une histoire du regard en Occident* (Paris: Gallimard, 1992); Régis Debray, "The Three Ages of Looking," trans. Eric Rauth, *Critical Inquiry* 21, no. 3 (Spring 1995): 529–55; Régis Debray, "Socialism and Print," *New Left Review*, no. 46 (July–August 2007): 5–28; and Régis Debray, *Transmitting Culture*, trans. Eric Rauth (New York: Columbia University Press, 2000).

20. See the summary diagram in Nicholas Mirzoeff, *The Right to Look: A Counterhistory of Visuality* (Durham, N.C.: Duke University Press, 2011), 35.

21. Ibid., 309.

22. Ibid.

23. See http://www.nicholasmirzoeff.com/O2012/.

24. Paul Virilio, *The Aesthetics of Disappearance*, trans. Philip Beitchman (New York: Semiotext(e), 1991).

25. Quoted in Catherine de Zegher and Gerald McMaster, eds., *All Our Relations: 18th Biennale of Sydney* (Sydney: Biennale of Sydney, 2012), 258; see also www.janannealani.net.

26. On page 73 of her *Death of a Discipline*, Spivak rightly draws attention to the priority of indigenous peoples in the figuring of planetarity. I take up this important topic in "Worlds Pictured in Contemporary Art: Planes and Connectivities," in *The World and World-Making in Art*, ed. Caroline Turner (Canberra: ANU e-Press, 2012).

27. See Samuel P. Huntington, *The Clash of Civilizations and the Remaking of the World Order* (New York: Simon and Schuster, 1997); Joseph S. Nye Jr., *The Future of Power* (Cambridge, Mass.: PublicAffairs, 2011); and Joseph S. Nye Jr., *Soft Power: The Means to Success in World Politics* (Cambridge, Mass.: PublicAffairs, 2004).

28. Just how difficult it is to move from this limited repertoire of models can be seen from recent surveys of modes of data visualization. See, for example, Manuel Lima, *Visual Complexity: Mapping Patterns of Information* (New York: Princeton Architectural Press, 2011); and Martin W. Lewis and Kären E. Wigen, *The Myth of Continents: A Critique of Metageography* (Berkeley: University of California Press, 1997).

29. A comparable approach to these questions may be found in David Christian, *Maps of Time: An Introduction to Big History* (Berkeley: University of California Press, 2004). On the history of conceptions of time, see, among many others, Norbert Elias, *Time: An Essay* (Oxford: Oxford University Press, 1992); and David Christian, "History and Time," *Australian Journal of Politics and History* 57, no. 3 (September 2011): 353–65.

30. Geoffrey O'Brien, "The Variety of Movie Experience," review of *The Tree of Life*, directed by Terrence Malick, *New York Review of Books*, July 14, 2011, 30.

31. O'Brien, "The Variety of Movie Experience," 30. See also Anthony Lane, "Time Trip," review of *The Tree of Life*, directed by Terrence Malick, *New Yorker*, May 30, 2011, http://www.newyorker.com/arts/critics/cinema/2011/05/30/110530crci_cinema_lane.

32. O'Brien, "The Variety of Movie Experience," 32.

Beyond the Flaming Walls of the World

Fantasy, Alterity, and the Postnational Constellation

ROBERT T. TALLY JR.

> The planet is in the species of alterity, belonging to another system; and yet we inhabit it . . .
>
> —Gayatri Chakravorty Spivak, *Death of a Discipline*

In his influential 1827 essay "On the Supernatural in Fictitious Composition," Sir Walter Scott extols the beauty and power of E. T. A. Hoffmann's writing but criticizes "the wildness of Hoffmann's fancy," declaring that the German romantic's taste and temperament have "carried him too far 'extra moenia flammantia mundi,' too much beyond the circle not only of probability but even of possibility." Scott is concerned that the "fantastic" mode is only acceptable to the degree that "it tends to excite agreeable and pleasing ideas."[1] In his use of the Latin phrase (borrowed from Lucretius), Scott invokes a spatial metaphor to make a broader point. By venturing "beyond the flaming walls of the world," the fantasy author indulges, in Scott's view, in an extravagant aesthetic that evokes horror or even disgust by conjuring up a radical alterity that defamiliarizes the habitus and aggrandizes the horrible. Not stated directly by Scott but implied in his mild critique is the degree to which this *outré* sensibility disrupts the conventions and expectations of a national literature. In addition to providing a nationally circumscribed space for a particular country's authors, such a literature, we gather, must somehow represent the recognizably national character of or in its narratives, a character that must above all be familiar to readers. Extravagant fantasy subverts, however, nationalistic standards of beauty by becoming "grotesque" and "Arabesque." Such fiction undermines the national vocation of literature through its techniques of estrangement, that is, by its imaginative flights away from familiar landscapes, customs, and events; it tends to domesticate the strange elements and represent them in a comfortable, recognizable pattern.[2] A romantic realism of the sort found in Scott's own historical novels offers a fitting mode for such a national narrative, as the foundational legends and myths can be incorporated into a calm, more quotidian, and rather familiar culture. In contrast, by positing a radical alterity from the outset, the fantastic mode exceeds national and cultural boundaries, drawing the narrative out into the world and beyond.

Today's planetary turn in literary and cultural studies may be associated with a number of interrelated historical phenomena that have forcefully inserted the intertwined matters of spatiality, fantasy, and postnationality into the critical discussion. Above all, the multiform processes now aggregated under the rubric of globalization, including those practices in the aesthetic or cultural spheres sometimes called postmodern, have occasioned the diminution of the national in favor of the global, the elevation of space above (or at least to the level of) time, and the interrogation of representational protocols linked to the nation-state. In sum, most of the formerly recognizable hermeneutics are deemed no longer suitable for making sense of the present, dynamic world-system. As numerous artists, critics, philosophers, and social scientists have observed, the revolutionary social transformations throughout the world in the postwar era have fundamentally altered the effectiveness of sense-making systems of past epochs, be they scientific, religious, or, as is my concern here, literary-cultural. Narrative fiction, for example, may no longer operate as it had in Scott's day, when the "form-giving form" of the historical novel (to use Georg Lukács's expression) could organize an ostensible totality (*Lebenstotalität*) through which the individual could locate him- or herself within a cognizable world-system.[3] Scott's historical novels attempted to shape the diffuse passions, partisan interests, and different spaces into a distinctively national imaginary geography, and, as Jonathan Arac has pointed out, these novels were essential precursors to national narrative in American literature.[4] However, in the twentieth century, the postmodern predicament of representation is part and parcel of an existential crisis akin to being lost in space; it is an utterly alienating experience, evoking an anxiety that Martin Heidegger had associated directly with the uncanny, the *unheimlich* or "unhomely," the *Nicht-zu-hause-sein* ("not-being-at-home").[5] But, then, the loss of a sense of "home" is also a recognition of the disruptions of "domestic" or national space caused by forces of globalization. Fredric Jameson's highlighting of "cognitive mapping on a global scale" as both a partial solution to the crisis of representability and a vocation of postmodern art emphasizes the spatial anxiety and postnationality of such a cartographic project.[6]

I would propose, in my turn, that such mapping is incomplete unless it is also speculative, figurative, and, in a broad sense, *fantastic*. Unlike the naively mimetic maps of an earlier epoch, the literary cartography of the postnational world-system has to be, in some ways, otherworldly. Such, at least, is my argument here. Although there is no question about the value of myth, folklore, or "national fantasy" in establishing national narrative,[7] I would submit that, in the present world-historical moment, the radical alterity of fantasy is well positioned to foster a postnational and thus planetarily oriented literary perspective. I am not speaking of fantasy as a genre, although I am interested in the potential of what Jameson has called "generic discontinuities" in narratives as part of the overall undertaking of literary cartography.[8] Rather, I am thinking of fantasy as a discursive modality, one that is marked by its fundamental attention to otherness or otherworldliness. Fantasy, of which science fiction and utopia may be considered subsets, enables a figurative mapping of the (so-called) real world while using the (so-called) unreal or impossible as its means. In theory and in practice, the alterity of fantasy makes possible new ways of seeing—and, by the same token, of interpreting and perhaps changing—the world-system forming the untranscendable horizon of all thinking today.[9] Somewhat as it did for earlier local, regional, or national space, but far more so, thinking planetary space in the age of globalization requires cognitive abstraction and imagination that makes "the literature of estrangement," to use China Miéville's phrase, the form potentially best suited to our postmodern and postnational condition. As Miéville asserts pointedly, "the fantastic . . . is *good to think with*."[10] For, to be sure, the fantastic allows us, among other things, to see the planet anew, to visualize our world in novel ways, and to imagine different approaches to representing and otherwise engaging the world-system. In "constellating" and working through the various intersecting forces affecting the existential experience of life on the planet at this historical moment, we may venture—like the wayward imagination of Hoffmann in Scott's analysis—beyond the flaming walls of the world in order to discover, in a more meaningful sense, the real world after all. In this "postnational constellation," to recall the phrase Jürgen Habermas used in a different context,[11] the principal vocation of literary and cultural work may be to project novel cartographies and alternative trajectories by which to navigate this increasingly unrepresentable, even unrecognizable, *Lebenswelt*. After the planetary turn and in the context of an increasingly visible world literature whose representative space is neither regional nor national but global, the postnational constellation may be an apt figure for the present world-system itself, and a fantastic mapping of the planetary space we occupy may constitute an urgent project for contemporary theorists and critics.

Imagining the Planet

Widely known as "Earthrise," one of the past century's most famous photographs depicts a distinct, blue-and-white planet emerging in the distance over the barren grey-white surface of the moon. Taken by Apollo 8 astronauts in lunar orbit on December 24, 1968, the iconic image became a worldwide sensation when it appeared on TV sets and in newspapers on Christmas morning. Humans have been using their vision and imagination to make sense of the world throughout their history, and yet never before had such a vista been available to them, as, for the first time, they ventured beyond the boundaries of the terraqueous globe and looked back upon it as outsiders. From this new perspective, viewers of the "Earthrise" photograph were repositioned in the universe. Now able to achieve a critical distance from their planet, they were no longer cosmopolites comfortably at home in the world but saw the latter as a strange *otherworld*, as if for the first time. Arguably, in the contemplation of this image and of its ramifications, a planetary consciousness emerged.[12]

This is certainly how American poet Archibald MacLeish envisioned the import of the event. Writing in the *New York Times* only hours after the first appearance of the photograph, MacLeish considered the moment an epochal shift in humankind's relationship to the world. Referring first to Dante's geocentric universe, then to its waning and ultimate collapse after the Copernican Revolution and modern physics, which had rendered the earth a metaphysically meaningless ensemble of violent forces that could bring about the slaughter of millions in absurd world wars and nuclear destruction, MacLeish announced that "now, in the last few hours, the [planet] notion may have changed again. For the first time in all of time men have seen it not as continents or oceans from the little distance of a hundred miles or two or three, but seen it from the depth of space; seen it whole and round and beautiful and small." As MacLeish explained on that Christmas day,

> The medieval notion of the earth put man at the center of everything. The nuclear notion of the earth put him nowhere—beyond the range of reason even—lost in absurdity and war. This latest notion may have other consequences. Formed as it was in the minds of heroic voyagers who were also men, it may remake our image of mankind. No longer that preposterous figure at the center, no longer that degraded and degrading victim off at the margins of reality and blind with blood, man may at last become himself.
>
> To see the earth as it truly is, small and blue and beautiful in that eternal silence where it floats, is to see ourselves as riders on the earth together, brothers on that bright loveliness in the eternal cold—brothers who know now they are truly brothers.[13]

This somewhat grandiose interpretation of an astronaut's timely snapshot indicates the extent to which a kind of planetary turn, in poetry, philosophy, and the arts and sciences as a whole was not only already under way but also deeply longed for by so many of the inhabitants of that "small and blue and beautiful" orb.[14]

The image of the planet captured in and promoted by "Earthrise," which functioned simultaneously as an aesthetic, scientific, ideological, and utopian work of art, occasions a powerful rethinking of the relations among space, narrative, geopolitics, and the world-system. Ironically perhaps, the repercussions of the "Earthrise" phenomenon led not to the extension or intensification of the space age, but to a "return to earth," as it were, with more scientific and humanities-based attention being paid to this planet and far less to Mars, Jupiter, and the great beyond. As Robert Poole observes in *Earthrise: How Man First Saw the Earth*, the postwar period had been dominated by rockets and space travel whose proponents could proclaim, with Wernher von Braun, that the party who conquered space would control the planet. This notion certainly inspired a great deal of military and political enthusiasm for space research. Along the same lines, science fiction depicting space exploration would dominate popular culture in various media throughout the 1950s and 1960s. Obviously, astrophysics, technology, science fiction, and interplanetary expeditions remain salient today—witness the recent burst of interest in the *Curiosity* rover's Mars landing on August 6, 2012, for example—but they have no longer the cultural cachet they had achieved in the early 1960s. After "Earthrise," the fevered imaginations of the populace turned back to the planet Earth. As Norman Cousins put it, "the significance of the lunar expeditions was not that men set foot on the Moon, but that they set eye on the Earth."[15]

Time magazine used the photograph as the cover of its final issue of 1968, with the one-word caption ("Dawn") as if to emphasize the image's liminal and inaugural role in marking the transition to a new stage of world history. Given the turbulence of that year—what with the assassinations, riots, and political turmoil in the United States; the upheavals and repressions in Prague, Paris, and elsewhere in Europe; and the warfare and violence of Vietnam, South America, and Africa—the "Earthrise" image, when couched as a "dawn," acquired a poignant, optative, and utopian nuance. Where the future had previously been determined as a "space race" among antagonistic, destructive superpowers, this austere, beautiful vision of a small, fragile, and isolated planet reoriented the very idea of spatiotemporal progression. For many like MacLeish, this image was itself a sign that national boundaries and ideological differences were no longer of any great importance. The time had come to view the Earth and its inhabitants as a single people occupying a single global space.

What I want to suggest in dwelling on these pictures is that the moment of this global self-image constitutes a nexus where several important aspects of the planetary turn in the arts, sciences, and humanities intersect. Significantly, this literal turn back toward the planet from the outermost reaches of human space exploration is representative of an aesthetic planetary turn whereby the entire Earth is for the first time seen in its global totality.[16] This moment coincides with tumultuous geopolitical events, most spectacularly visible in the wars of Southeast Asia and the Middle East, in the anticolonial national movements in Africa, in the revolutions in Latin America, and in the internal conflicts throughout Europe and the United States. Also, although this would come into focus more clearly only later, with the collapse of the Bretton

Woods agreement, the rise at this time of multinational capital and transnational economies was making the older colonial and mercantile financial systems obsolete, paving the way to widespread financialization and other forms of cultural-economic globalization.[17] The boom in "Third World" literature complements and supplements the innovations in fiction and poetry in the West, while a burgeoning aesthetic of postmodernism in fiction, cinema, visual art, and especially architecture alters the way space and culture are perceived. Thus the widely distributed "Earthrise" image of the planet emerged at a time of radical transformation worldwide.[18] Amid so much real-world activity, something quite otherworldly—the earth itself—appeared.

To be sure, this "Earthrise" photograph conveyed a striking reality; indeed, its photographic realism was literal, and grasping its import is crucial to understanding its influence and effect in imagining the planet anew. But the image was also the stuff of the most extremely *outré* science fiction: the fantastic voyage beyond the moon. Parodied in Lucian's *True History* and celebrated by Georges Méliès in *Le voyage dans la lune*, with hundreds of lunar fantasies occupying the spectrum in between, this sort of cosmic travel made possible the discovery of hitherto unknown or unimagined realities. The fantastic nature of the worldview afforded from outer space might be said to have inspired a wholly different way of thinking on the surface of the little green-blue sphere. National, regional, and local concerns and conflicts, for instance, suddenly may have looked trivial in the face of an abruptly more salient global space. The rivalries that animated the geopolitical *Weltanschauungen* of the era may have seemed petty and absurd from this postnational and supracontinental perspective. This was indeed the case for the more optimistic of commentators who dared to imagine a united and harmonious future that formerly only the most wide-eyed dreamers could envision. As Poole points out in a reference to the Apollo 8 mission that produced the "Earthrise" photograph, "the mightiest shot in the Cold War turned into the twentieth century's ultimate utopian moment."[19] And utopia, like the planet itself, is a figure of radical alterity. As Gayatri Chakravorty Spivak has put it in her discussion of planetarity and world literature, the planet's "alterity, determining experience, is mysterious and discontinuous—an experience of the impossible."[20]

A Meditation on the Impossible

Utopia is currently a favored topic among many spatially oriented critics, including Jameson and David Harvey.[21] In some respects, it represents a paradigmatically modern genre or discursive form, with major literary works (including Thomas More's 1516 genre-establishing *Utopia*) coming about during the Age of Discovery and the European voyages to the "New World"[22] and another wave of utopianism finding its voice and audience amid the nineteenth century's Industrial Age uncertainties with Charles Fourier's phalansteries, Edward Bellamy's "nationalism," and William Morris's "news from nowhere." But, as I have argued elsewhere,[23] a sort of utopian mode has reasserted itself most strenuously in the postmodern world of our globalization era, paradoxically a world in which utopian alternatives to the status quo seem utterly impossible, even inconceivable. Jameson has famously observed that it appears easier today to imagine the end of the world than the breakdown of late capitalism; often forgotten, however, is Jameson's indispensable follow-up to this remark: "perhaps that is due to some weakness in our imaginations."[24]

An *empowered* imagination, one that would set out to map a planetary space rather than limiting itself to its local or national subsets, would need to come to grips with the radical alterity of the world, specifically with the fantastic otherworldliness emerging in conjunction with an altogether unfamiliar perspective, such as the view from outer space. Obviously, this imaginative project would have to exceed the limits of the real and the known; it would involve not only a consideration of the possible but also "a meditation on the impossible."[25] This meditation on the impossible seems in fact to be part of the cartographic efforts of fantasy, as the projection of imaginary spaces becomes an essential aspect of our engagement with the all-too-real world-system after the spatial or planetary turn.

Yet the term "*fantasy*" itself presents a problem. Numerous spatial critics have embraced utopian discourse as a means of conceiving radical alternatives to the status quo, but many of these commentators have been openly hostile to fantasy as a mode or genre on the grounds that fantasy is an escapist, politically reactionary, and backward-looking art form. A case in point is Darko Suvin's groundbreaking 1979 science fiction study, which dismissed fantasy as anti-rational and metaphysical.[26] Another is Jameson himself, who, in his own extensive statement on utopia, condemns any confusion between fantasy and science fiction ("We must now lay this misunderstanding to rest"), referring to their distinction as "The Great Schism."[27] Nor does it help that the most inescapably popular figure in fantasy literature, J. R. R. Tolkien (who, incidentally, was politically conservative), actively defended fantasy precisely as a kind of "escapist" practice. Complaining that anti-fantasy critics have confused "the Escape of the Prisoner with the Flight of the Deserter," Tolkien asks, "Why should a man be scorned if, finding himself in prison, he tries to get out and go home. Or if, when he cannot do so, he thinks and talks about other topics than jailers and prison-walls?"[28] Indeed, Tolkien goes so far as to claim that the world outside this prison is just as "real," whether the prisoner can see it or not, which suggests a view of fantasy as an imaginative method for apprehending the "real world" rather than a means of escaping from it.

It is perhaps ironic, then, that a similar argument has been made by Miéville in his spirited defense of the genre against charges brought by Marxists and utopian critics. Miéville has said some rather mischievous things about Tolkien, most famously that the Oxford professor's influential presence was "a wen on the arse of fantasy literature," although he has repented of this view a bit in recent years.[29] As a Marxist, Miéville represents, of course, nearly the political antipode of Tolkien. Yet, even though he comes from such a different perspective, Miéville contends that fantasy is superior to realism when it comes to getting at the truth of "'the real world.'" After discussing Marx's own analysis in *Capital* of the fetishism of the commodity and the hidden social relations embedded in it, Miéville offers that "'real' life under capitalism *is a fantasy*: 'realism,' narrowly defined, is therefore a 'realistic' depiction of 'an absurdity which is true,' but no less absurd for that. Narrow 'realism' is as partial and ideological as 'reality' itself."[30] Further, Miéville insists, "the apparent epistemological radicalism of the fantastic mode's basic predicate," namely "that the impossible is true," makes it well suited to the task of an oppositional or critical project.[31] As Miéville concludes, "the fantastic might be a mode peculiarly suited to and resonant with the forms of modernity. . . . Fantasy is a mode that, in constructing an internally coherent but actually impossible totality—constructed on the basis that the impossible is, for this work, *true*—mimics the 'absurdity' of capitalist modernity."[32]

Tolkien's and Miéville's positions respond to the perception that fantastic literary works are not only inferior to more realistic stories but also morally or politically suspect. Tolkien famously quarreled with fellow conservative C. S. Lewis over whether it was immoral for a Christian to embrace myth, which Lewis disparaged as "lies breathed through silver."[33] And, as a practicing fantasist as well as a socialist activist in his own right, Miéville is forced to defend fantasy from those on the Left who have objected to its escapism, nostalgia, or ideological incorrectness. Thus, even when the opposition to fantasy is less morally or politically charged, the prevailing view of political critics is that realism, with its familiar and recognizable world presumably shared by reader and writer, is the preferred mode.

This is, after all, Sir Walter Scott's rejoinder to Hoffmann in "On the Supernatural in Fictitious Composition." In finding Hoffmann's work both *grotesque* and *Arabesque*—the very terms Edgar Allan Poe gleefully adopted to refer to his collected stories, although it is noteworthy that Poe had intended to name the revised and expanded collection *Phantasy Pieces*—Scott does not hide a certain disdain for the otherworldly, which here covers the merely exotic (as the term "Arabesque" makes clear) as well as the twisted or horrible. His essay offers a foundational text for the debate about the suitable proportion of fantasy and reality in literature during the nineteenth century. This polemic also famously includes Nathaniel Hawthorne's *apologia* for "romance" as opposed to the more strictly realistic "novel," which "is presumed to aim at a very minute fidelity, not merely to the possible, but to the probable and ordinary course of man's experience."[34] And, as we have seen, this argument about how much fantasy is acceptable in serious literature—what Kathryn Hume has succinctly named the "fantasy versus mimesis" controversy[35]—continues to elicit heated responses.

Yet again, it is important to reiterate that it is Scott who casually delineates the contours of the battlefield. To do so, he first quotes a paragraph of Hoffmann's *The Entail*, in which a frightfully supernatural occurrence culminates with a calm, somewhat revelatory, but still eerie explanation. Scott then elaborates as follows:

> The passage which we have quoted, while it shows the wildness of Hoffmann's fancy, evinces also that he possessed power which ought to have mitigated and allayed it. Unfortunately, his taste and temperament directed him too strongly to the grotesque and fantastic—carried him too far "extra moenia flammantia mundi," too much beyond the circle not only of probability but even of possibility, to admit of his composing much in the better style which he might easily have attained. The popular romance, no doubt, has many walks, nor are we at all inclined to halloo the dogs of criticism against those whose object is merely to amuse a passing hour. It may be repeated with truth, that in this path of light literature, "tout genre est permis hors les genres ennuyeux," and of course, an error in taste ought not to be followed up and hunted down as if it were a false maxim in morality, a delusive hypothesis in science, or a heresy in religion itself. Genius too, is, we are aware, capricious, and must be allowed to take its own flights, however eccentric, were it but for the sake of experiment. Sometimes, also, it may be eminently pleasing to look at the wildness of an Arabesque painting executed by a man of rich fancy. But we do not desire to see genius expand or rather exhaust itself upon themes which cannot be reconciled to taste; and the utmost length in which we can indulge a turn to the fantastic is, where it tends to excite agreeable and pleasing ideas.
>
> We are not called upon to be equally tolerant of such capriccios as are not only startling by their extravagance, but disgusting by their horrible import.[36]

Neither a naive realist nor an advocate of a strictly mimetic narrative art, Scott is willing to forgive literature that extends "beyond the flaming walls of the world" so long as it can "excite agreeable and pleasant ideas." Thus, he introduces a pragmatic and moral dimension into the discussion of literary aesthetics. That is, the question is less about what constitutes fantasy and more about the consequences of using such fantastic elements.

The French maxim that Scott paraphrases is Voltaire's assertion that "all genres are good except boring genres." However, he cribs the Latin expression not from literary fiction, whether fantastic or realistic, but from philosophy, specifically from Lucretius's first century B.C.E. treatise *De Rerum Natura* (*On the Nature of Things*). In the original, the expression *extra moenia flammantia mundi* does not carry a negative connotation. On the contrary, in fact, for Lucretius the phrase signifies a great achievement, a sign of the intellectual courage of the scientific or philosophical mind willing to go beyond the superstitious chimeras of religion in order to seek the truths that lie "beyond the flaming walls of the world." The famous line refers to Epicurus, the atomist and materialist Greek philosopher whose "victory," according to Lucretius, brought religion down under our feet and placed human beings on a level with heaven.[37] It is also worth noting that, in this original Epicurean context, the movement "beyond the flaming walls of the world" is not considered an attempt to escape from the real world into a false one but rather a brave discovery of precisely that more truly real world that had been hidden and veiled by the false realities of superstition and religion. In its oddly tortuous philological journey from the first century B.C.E. to the nineteenth century, the phrase as used by Scott had developed a meaning nearly opposite to what Lucretius had intended. However, in what might be considered one more turn of the screw or yet another dialectical reversal, one can argue that Scott's own use of the expression as a means of criticizing fantasy actually reveals the power of fantasy as a device for social and literary critique.

Indeed, one could suggest that Lucretius's defense of the materialist thought of Epicurus against the superstitions of religious belief finds modern and postmodern counterparts in Jameson's pro-utopian argument against so-called practical thinking and also in Miéville's defense of fantasy against its Marxist detractors (including, of course, such science fiction enthusiasts as Jameson himself). In both cases, a theorist inveighs against the prejudices and barriers to thinking that predominate in his place and time. For example, in *Marxism and Form*, Jameson acknowledges the anti-utopian positions of Marx and Engels in the nineteenth century. Referring in particular to the reemergence of utopian discourse in Herbert Marcuse's critical theory, Jameson argues, however, that by the 1960s another "dialectical reversal" had occurred. He contends that while

> in the older society (as in Marx's classic analysis) Utopian thought represented a diversion of revolutionary energy into idle wish-fulfillments and imaginary satisfactions, in our own time the very nature of the Utopian concept has undergone a dialectical reversal. Now it is practical thinking which everywhere represents a capitulation to the system itself, and stands as a testimony to the power of that system to transform even its adversaries into its own mirror image. The Utopian idea, on the contrary, keeps alive the possibility of a world qualitatively distinct from this one and takes the form of a stubborn negation of all that is.[38]

Along similar lines, utopian theorist Russell Jacoby has maintained that "any effort to escape the spell of the quotidian . . . is the sine qua non of serious thinking about the future—the prerequisite of *any* thinking."[39] In this sense, the more realistic, practical, or feasible position becomes antithetical to the necessarily fantastic, critical project of meditating upon the impossible.

But, again, this is the very crux of Miéville's defense of fantasy. In his "Cognition as Ideology," Miéville questions the supremacy of Suvin's influential characterization of science fiction as a form of cognitive estrangement, with the corollary that the estrangements of fantasy or myth are fundamentally non-alienating, metaphysical, mystifying, or anti-rational.[40] Miéville decries the attitude that has allowed "generations of readers and writers to treat, say, faster-than-light drives as science-fictional in a way that dragons are not, despite repeated assurances from the great majority of physicists that the former are no less impossible than the latter."[41] Against the anti-fantasy sentiments of the spaceship enthusiasts or dragon detractors, Miéville files all genres—science fiction, utopia, and fantasy—under the label "the literature of alterity." This intensive regard for *otherness*, whether presented in terms of the past or future, the earthly or the interstellar, the monstrous or the alien, is shared by all forms of the fiction of estrangement, including some, like *Moby-Dick*, that are inexpressibly "strange" even while featuring absolutely realistic (or, at least, possible) persons and events. Miéville's terminology thus enables the fantastic to exceed or even invert tightly circumscribed genre boundaries. For Miéville, science fiction or utopia are mere subsets of the broader category of fantasy, which allows a meditation on the impossible that can enable a radically different vantage point from which to view the "real world." As Miéville puts it, "we need fantasy to think the world, and to change it."[42]

Change and form go hand in hand here. What Jameson has said of the dynamic of form and world transformation in utopian thought applies equally well to the notion of fantasy as the literature of radical alterity: "utopia as a form is not the representation of radical alternatives; it is rather simply the imperative to imagine them."[43] Truly radical alterity would, in a somewhat literal sense, be unrepresentable since, in the apprehension of the novel otherworld and in its incorporation into our own mental databases, this representation *refamiliarizes* this otherness and, in one way or another, domesticates estrangement. As Jameson notes elsewhere, "insofar as the Utopian project comes to seem more realizable and more practical, it turns into a practical political program in our world, in the here-and-now, and ceases to be Utopian in any meaningful sense."[44] Or, on the flip side of the same argument, "the more surely a given Utopia asserts its radical difference from what currently is, to that very degree it becomes, not merely unrealizable but, what is worse, unimaginable."[45] Hence, we are left once more with a tenebrous conception of radical alterity as a meditation on the impossible rather than as a viable otherworld to dwell in.

Nevertheless, the value of this fantastic effort seems to be confirmed in the imaginative endeavor involved in mapping our own "real world," particularly the postmodern world-system in which the traditional guideposts are no longer trustworthy or desirable. "Happy are those ages when the starry sky is the map of all possible paths," writes Lukács of the centuries dominated by the epic. "The world is wide and yet it is like a home."[46] In our world-system, the celestial cartography is not so reliable or *heimlich*, and the existential and critical paradigm coming on the heels of the planetary turn may require the speculative or fantastic extension beyond the world's flaming walls in order to chart, albeit provisionally and tentatively, both our location and our available courses of action.

"Shall I Project a World?"

The planetary space and fantastic mode of apprehending it find their nexus in a speculative critical activity I have been associating with literary cartography and geocriticism. I have been particularly interested in the ways narratives map a postnational space that cannot easily fold itself into the ideological and geographical atlases of an earlier configuration.[47] I do not mean to say that the existential mapping of one's *Lebenswelt* (à la Heidegger and Sartre, or even with Lukács's "transcendental homelessness" as a model) emerges only with the postmodern condition, but rather that this kind of cartography reflects the profoundly different spatial and cultural anxieties of a postnational world-system in which former certainties are made uncertain and familiar codes lose their meaning. Ironically, in the postnational constellation, the insights of a pre-national *Weltanschauung* might offer clues to a speculative, fantastic geocriticism adapted for the critical exigencies of the current moment of globalization.

The "pre-national" view I have in mind is a variation of the medieval conception of the world, a vision described by Erich Auerbach in "Philology and *Weltliteratur*" in the immediate aftermath of World War II, at what might be thought of as the incipient stage of postmodernity. In this essay, Auerbach maintains that the national (and nationalist) traditions of literary study, however valuable in the past two centuries, were no longer suitable for understanding the world. "To make men conscious of themselves in their own history," the critic reflects, "is a great task, yet the task is small—more like a renunciation—when one considers that man not only lives on earth, but that he is in the world and in the universe."[48] Auerbach asserts that "our philological home is the earth: it can no longer be the nation. . . . We must return, in admittedly altered circumstances, to the knowledge that prenational medieval culture already possessed: the knowledge that the spirit [*Geist*] is not national." Auerbach then quotes the words of a medieval thinker, Hugh of St. Victor, who taught that "the man who finds his homeland sweet is still a tender beginner; he to whom every soil is as his native one is already strong; but he is perfect to whom the entire world is as a foreign land." By invoking this "*mundus totus exilium est*" as his motto, Auerbach turns on its head the wisdom of a medieval Christian, who cautions against attaching oneself to the earthly world; as Auerbach explains, "Hugo intended these lines for one whose aim is to free himself from a love of the world. But it is a good way also for one who wishes to earn a proper love for the world."[49]

The perspective of the exile, of one who *cannot* be "at home" in the world, is embraced by Edward Said in his reading of Auerbach and in his own work. In "Reflections on Exile," Said argues that "seeing 'the entire world as a foreign land' makes possible originality of vision."[50] This originality of vision or critical distance is, I would add, not altogether dissimilar from that which obtains through a fantastic or otherworldly vantage, such as the one achieved by the Apollo 8 photographers who witnessed the planet Earth rising above the horizon of the moon. Both Auerbach's plea for a postnational approach to world literature and Said's conviction that the condition of exile affords one a paradoxically privileged position as an observer suggest that the exile is the exemplary figure for the critic in the age of globalization.[51] This is not to say that the perspective of the exile, even if it captures the situation of the contemporary critic, is a comfortable one.[52] The new vista afforded by finding oneself in an unfamiliar situation is more likely to be bewildering than liberating. Amid the spatial anxieties and temporal confusions of the postnational condition, the artist or critic is called upon to come to grips with things as best as one can. As I have proposed, this may require an exercise in the fantastic, a speculative and perhaps even unrealistic practice, but one that can produce a map, albeit a provisional one, by which to make sense of the world-system.

Lending itself to such mapping or reading is, to take just one example, a key scene in Thomas Pynchon's 1966 novel *The Crying of Lot 49*. The protagonist, Oedipa Maas, finds herself inexplicably entangled within a global conspiracy, surrounded by bizarre characters, and lost in the confusion of competing, often inscrutable interests, while she is attempting to sort out the complex details of a dead man's estate. At her wit's end and thoroughly frustrated by her predicament, Oedipa resolves to reread Pierce Inverarity's will in an effort to gain a clearer sense of things. Thus, she imagines herself as a "dark machine in the center of the planetarium" that can "bring the estate into pulsing stelliferous Meaning" and writes the following in her memorandum book: "*Shall I project a world?* If not project then at least flash some arrow on the dome to skitter among the constellations and trace out your Dragon, Whale, Southern Cross. Anything might help."[53]

"Projecting a world" seems a perfectly appropriate task for both the artist and the critic after the planetary turn, and Pynchon's astronomical metaphor offers another intriguing trope for aesthetic and critical maneuvers. The constellation is at once utterly fantastic, inasmuch as the tracings drawn in the night sky are thoroughly imaginary, and also terrifically real, insofar as travelers and navigators have been able to reliably locate themselves and chart courses in the world based upon these fantastic celestial drawings. With few exceptions, constellations are completely artificial, human-made, and even arbitrary. As anyone who has tried to identify and memorize the constellations will concede, their names are not particularly descriptive and rarely fit the images purportedly sketched in the skies. *Canis minor*, for instance, which comprises only two stars, looks more like a line than a small dog. In a recent, only somewhat tongue-in-cheek article titled "Starry Blight: How a Bunch of Peasants from Mesopotamia Ruined the Night Sky," Daniel Engber refers to these constellations as "a smog of Bronze Age graffiti."[54] Yet, in antiquity as in the modern world, such imaginary lines, fantastically projected from human stargazers situated on the surface of this planet, have helped one make sense of one's place in the world, serving as points of reference in a broadly defined terrestrial cartography, as well as operating in a quite practical way to help humans navigate the "real world" below the heavens. This is a clear example, among many others, of the real-world effects of fictions produced in a fantastic mode.

If the present world-system lacks traditional guideposts or reveals such markers to be less than helpful, then it may be fitting to advocate the fantastic project of "projecting a world"—of "constellating" the various forces, places, and events in the global space in new ways so that we can better understand and engage with the world. One of the formerly indispensable "guideposts" to be challenged or superseded in this effort is the nation-state itself. Although this spatio-political ensemble retains immense power even in the postnational constellation, and even though it tenaciously maintains its influence over literary and cultural studies (particularly in university curricula), its effectiveness is waning amid the overwhelming, trans- or supranational forces of the world-system.[55] With the term "*postnationality*," I might add, I refer specifically to the current condition, in the era of globalization, in which the nation-state is no longer the *locus classicus* or *primum mobile* of culture, of the economy, or even of politics. As Habermas has observed, in the past, "the phenomena of the territorial state, the nation, and a popular economy constituted within national borders formed a historical constellation in which the democratic process assumed a more or less convincing institutional form. . . . Today, developments summarized under the term 'globalization' have put this entire constellation into question."[56] Under the auspices of globalization, the national models, including those employed in the study of literature and culture, are no longer reliable or even desirable. The "historical constellation" in which the nation-state constituted the dominant force in social, political, economic, and spatial organization of the world-system is as much an imaginative projection as other constellations. However, just as the ideological comes to appear natural, the national paradigm has seemed so constitutive of human sociality that it is harder to imagine alternatives. The radical alterity of fantasy or of the fantastic mode broadly conceived enables and promotes a projection of a world that can, if only provisionally, be mapped.

Therefore, it is not surprising that literary and cultural critics such as Walter Benjamin and Theodor Adorno (or their Frankfurt School successor Habermas) should find the figure of the constellation so useful for theory. In organizing the swirling, vicissitudinous elements of modern culture and society, the critic draws imaginary lines *not* to fix such phenomena in place as a way of determining once and for all their true meaning or of constraining their mobile diversity but to arrange them in a cognizable pattern for further use. Amid the disorienting and dynamic phenomena of the postmodern condition, one may wish to "project a world," in other words, to create patterns that, while obviously artificial, provisional, and imaginary, can aid us in conceptualizing and navigating the planetary space we inhabit. As Oedipa Maas knowingly concluded, "Anything might help."

Along these lines, a fantastic, postnational criticism may enable a new way of seeing and mapping this planetary space that now provides the ultimate ground or horizon of thought in the age of globalization. Like those Apollo 8 astronauts who ventured into the universe and beyond the moon—quite literally "beyond the flaming walls of the world"—a critical practice such as geocriticism, operating as it does in a fantastic mode, may thereby achieve novel vistas, look back on the worldly world from our radically otherworldly perspective, project new constellations and maps, and maybe just see things a bit differently. In navigating the planetary space of a postnational constellation geocritically, we may thus embrace the strangeness of the contemporary world-system, imagine radical alternatives, and descry—if only in uncertain, tentative, and momentary glimpses—the features of other worlds.

Notes

1. Sir Walter Scott, "On the Supernatural in Fictitious Composition; and Particularly on the Works of Ernest Theodore William Hoffmann," in *Sir Walter Scott on Novelists and Fiction*, ed. Ioan Williams (London: Routledge and Kegan Paul, 1968), 348.

2. See, for example, Wai Chee Dimock, "Planet as Duration and Extension," in *Through Other Continents: American Literature across Deep Time* (Princeton, N.J.: Princeton University Press, 2006), 1–6.

3. See Georg Lukács, *The Theory of the Novel*, trans. Anna Bostock (Cambridge, Mass.: MIT Press, 1971); see also Georg Lukács, "The Classical Form of the Historical Novel," in *The Historical Novel*, trans. Hannah Mitchell and Stanley Mitchell (Lincoln: University of Nebraska Press, 1983), 19–88.

4. See Jonathan Arac, *The Emergence of American Literary Narrative, 1820–1860* (Cambridge, Mass.: Harvard University Press, 2005), 6–8.

5. Martin Heidegger, *Being and Time*, trans. John Macquarrie and Edward Robinson (New York: Harper and Row, 1962), 233.

6. See Fredric Jameson, *Postmodernism, or, the Cultural Logic of Late Capitalism* (Durham, N.C.: Duke University Press, 1991), 51–54.

7. In addition to the relatively obvious uses of national myths or legends, and just to mention works pertaining to U.S. culture, I include here the "fantasy" that underlies and promotes nationalism, as discussed in Lauren Berlant, *The Anatomy of National Fantasy: Hawthorne, Utopia, and Everyday Life* (Chicago: University of Chicago Press, 1991); Wai Chee Dimock, *Empire for Liberty: Melville and the Poetics of Individualism* (Princeton, N.J.: Princeton University Press, 1989); and, more recently, Donald E. Pease, *The New American Exceptionalism* (Minneapolis: University of Minnesota Press, 2009).

8. See Fredric Jameson, "Generic Discontinuities in SF: Brian Aldiss' *Starship*," in Jameson, *Archaeologies of the Future: The Desire Called Utopia and Other Science Fictions* (London: Verso, 2005), 254–66.

9. As Fredric Jameson has put it, "all thinking today is *also*, whatever else it is, an attempt to think the world system as such." See *The Geopolitical Aesthetic: Cinema and Space in the World System* (Bloomington: Indiana University Press; London: British Film Institute, 1992), 4 (emphasis in original).

10. China Miéville, "Editorial Introduction," in "Symposium: Marxism and Fantasy," ed. China Miéville, special issue, *Historical Materialism* 10, no. 4 (2002): 46 (emphasis in original).

11. See Jürgen Habermas, *The Postnational Constellation*, trans. and ed. Max Pensky (Cambridge, Mass.: MIT Press, 2001).

12. Indeed, as a number of environmentalist and ecocritics have noted, the "Earthrise" photo may have sparked the environmentalist movement and led to Earth Day, partially ended the "Space Age" by recalling attention to the planet Earth itself, and transformed humanity's attitude toward the planet, confirming a "Spaceship Earth" vision that reimagines the global space not as an empty backdrop for human activity but as a dynamic and affective geographical domain. See Robert Poole, "From Spaceship Earth to Mother Earth," in *Earthrise: How Man First Saw the Earth* (New Haven, Conn.: Yale University Press, 2008), 141–69.

13. Archibald MacLeish, "Riders on Earth Together, Brothers in Eternal Cold," *New York Times*, December 25, 1968.

14. Similar in spirit to MacLeish's conclusion, Arthur C. Clarke declared that the Apollo 8 mission constituted "a second Copernican revolution" and speculated that the children born that year might one day "live to become citizens of the United Planets." Quoted in Poole, *Earthrise*, 5–6.

15. Quoted in Poole, *Earthrise*, 3.

16. Although subsequent missions would achieve lunar landing and other milestones of the space program, the Apollo 8 astronauts traveled the furthest from the Earth's surface, going beyond the moon, hence gaining the vantage from which to capture the "earthrise."

17. See David Harvey, "Time-Space Compression and the Postmodern Condition," in *The Condition of Postmodernity: An Enquiry into the Origins of Cultural Change* (Oxford: Blackwell, 1990), 284–307; Giovanni Arrighi, "Epilogue: Can Capitalism Survive Success?" in *The Long Twentieth Century: Money, Power, and the Origins of Our Times* (London: Verso, 1994), 325–56; and my "Meta-Capital: Culture and Financial Derivatives," *Works and Days* 30, no. 2 (2012): 231–47.

18. For a rather different analysis focusing on environmental criticism in its assessment of globalization and cosmopolitanism, see Ursula K. Heise, *Sense*

of Place and Sense of Planet: The Environmental Imagination of the Global (Oxford: Oxford University Press, 2008).

19. Poole, *Earthrise*, 11.

20. Gayatri Chakravorty Spivak, *Death of a Discipline* (New York: Columbia University Press, 2003), 102.

21. See, for example, Jameson, *Archaeologies of the Future*; and David Harvey, *Spaces of Hope* (Berkeley: University of California Press, 2000).

22. Significantly, in Thomas More's *Utopia*, the utopian island is discovered on one of Amerigo Vespucci's transatlantic voyages. See More, *Utopia*, trans. Paul Turner (New York: Penguin, 2003).

23. See my "Radical Alternatives: The Persistence of Utopia in the Postmodern," in *New Essays on the Frankfurt School of Critical Theory*, ed. Alfred J. Drake (Newcastle upon Tyne, Eng.: Cambridge Scholars, 2009), 109–21; and my *Utopia in the Age of Globalization: Space, Representation, and the World-System* (New York: Palgrave Macmillan, 2013).

24. Fredric Jameson, *The Seeds of Time* (New York: Columbia University Press, 1994), xii.

25. Jameson, *Archaeologies of the Future*, 232.

26. See Darko Suvin, *Metamorphoses of Science Fiction: On the Poetics and History of a Literary Genre* (New Haven, Conn.: Yale University Press, 1979).

27. Jameson, *Archaeologies of the Future*, 56. See also "The Great Schism," in *Archaeologies of the Future*, 57–71.

28. J. R. R. Tolkien, "On Fairy-Stories," in *The Tolkien Reader* (New York: Ballantine Books, 1966), 60.

29. See China Miéville, "There and Back Again: Five Reasons Tolkien Rocks," *Omnivoracious* (blog), June 15, 2009, http://www.omnivoracious.com/2009/06/there-and-back-again-five-reasons-tolkien-rocks.html.

30. Miéville, "Editorial Introduction," 42 (emphasis in original).

31. Ibid., 42–43. Note, however, that Miéville quite rightly does not claim that fantasy is itself a revolutionary mode or "acts as a guide to political action" (46). The value of fantasy lies less in its politics—which could lie anywhere on the political spectrum—than in its imaginative encounter with radical alterity itself.

32. Miéville, "Editorial Introduction," 42 (emphasis in original).

33. J. R. R. Tolkien, "Mythopoeia," in *Tree and Leaf* (New York: Harper Collins, 2001), 85.

34. Nathaniel Hawthorne, *The House of the Seven Gables*, ed. Michael Davitt Bell (Oxford: Oxford University Press, 1991), 1. In the prefatory remarks to his other novels, *The Scarlet Letter*, *The Blithedale Romance*, and *The Marble Faun*, Hawthorne includes similar statements justifying his use of fanciful or unrealistic matter and methods.

35. See Kathryn Hume, *Fantasy and Mimesis: Responses to Reality in Western Literature* (New York: Methuen, 1984).

36. Scott, "On the Supernatural," 348.

37. See Lucretius, *The Nature of Things*, trans. A. E. Stallings (New York: Penguin, 2007), 29.

38. Fredric Jameson, *Marxism and Form: Twentieth-Century Dialectical Theories of Literature* (Princeton, N.J.: Princeton University Press, 1971), 110–11.

39. Russell Jacoby, *Picture Imperfect: Utopian Thought for an Anti-Utopian Age* (New York: Columbia University Press, 2005), xvii (emphasis in original).
40. See China Miéville, "Cognition as Ideology: A Dialectic of SF Theory," in *Red Planets: Marxism and Science Fiction*, ed. Mark Bould and China Miéville (Middletown, Conn.: Wesleyan University Press, 2009), 231–48. For more on Suvin's characterization of science fiction as a form of cognitive estrangement, see *Metamorphoses of Science Fiction*, 7–9.
41. Miéville, "Cognition as Ideology," 234.
42. Miéville, "Editorial Introduction," 48.
43. Jameson, *Archaeologies of the Future*, 416.
44. Fredric Jameson, "A New Reading of *Capital*," *Mediations* 25, no. 1 (Fall 2010): 13.
45. Jameson, *Archaeologies of the Future*, xv.
46. Lukács, *The Theory of the Novel*, 29.
47. See, for example, my "On Geocriticism," in *Geocritical Explorations: Space, Place, and Mapping in Literary and Cultural Studies*, ed. Robert T. Tally Jr. (New York: Palgrave Macmillan, 2011), 1–9; and my *Spatiality* (London: Routledge, 2013).
48. Erich Auerbach, "Philology and *Weltliteratur*," trans. Maire Said and Edward Said, *Centennial Review* 13, no. 1 (Winter 1969): 16–17.
49. Ibid., 17. For the translation of the Latin, see *The Didascalicon of Hugh of St. Victor: A Medieval Guide to the Arts*, trans. Jerome Taylor (New York: Columbia University Press, 1961), 101.
50. Edward Said, "Reflections on Exile," in *Reflections on Exile and Other Essays* (Cambridge, Mass.: Harvard University Press, 2000), 186.
51. See, for example, my "*Mundus Totus Exilium Est*: Reflections on the Critic in Exile," *Transnational Literature* 3, no. 2 (May 2011): 1–10.
52. For a much more nuanced critical reading of the new cosmopolitanism in the age of globalization, see Timothy Brennan, *At Home in the World: Cosmopolitanism Now* (Cambridge, Mass.: Harvard University Press, 1997).
53. Thomas Pynchon, *The Crying of Lot 49* (New York: Harper and Row, 1966), 82.
54. Daniel Engber, "Starry Blight: How a Bunch of Peasants in Mesopotamia Ruined the Night Sky," *Slate*, July 12, 2012, http://www.slate.com/articles/health_and_science/a_fine_whine/2012/07/against_constellations_why_are_we_stuck_with_bronze_age_graffiti_.html.
55. On the postnational approach to American literature in the world today, see Wai Chee Dimock and Lawrence Buell, eds., *Shades of the Planet: American Literature as World Literature* (Princeton, N.J.: Princeton University Press, 2007); Paul Giles's fascinating trilogy, *Transatlantic Insurrections: British Culture and the Formation of American Literature, 1730–1860* (Philadelphia: University of Pennsylvania Press, 2001), *Virtual Americas: Transnational Fictions and the Transatlantic Imaginary* (Durham, N.C.: Duke University Press, 2002), and *Atlantic Republic: The American Tradition in English Literature* (Oxford: Oxford University Press, 2006); and Yunte Huang, *Transpacific Imaginations: History, Literature, Counterpoetics* (Cambridge, Mass.: Harvard University Press, 2008).
56. Habermas, *The Postnational Constellation*, 60.

Decompressing Culture

Three Steps toward a Geomethodology

CHRISTIAN MORARU

> Everything begins with Houses, each of which must join up its sections and hold up compounds—Combray, the Guermantes' house, the Verdurins' salon—and the houses are themselves joined together according to interfaces, but a planetary Cosmos is already there, visible through the telescope, which ruins or transforms them and absorbs them into an infinity of the patch of uniform color.
>
> —Gilles Deleuze and Félix Guattari, *What Is Philosophy?*

> The world has moved back to [the] centre of political consciousness, not in the traditional sense of the "earth as garden," but as new technologically worlded and pneo-stoic cosmopolitical percept of the "earth-as-planet" . . .
>
> —Neil Turnbull, "The Ontological Consequences of Copernicus"

> Let us remain masters of the mystery that the earth breathes.
>
> —Emmanuel Levinas, *Difficult Freedom*

"The face of the earth": have you ever pondered the idiom? If thousands of years of use have worn it thin, the dawn of the third millennium is witnessing the old chestnut's semantic reset. This makes you wonder what the phrase is conveying nowadays. Tying some of us down to exploit, disenfranchise, and otherwise "expe[l] from the narratives of futurity,"[1] globalization is also drawing more and more of the earth's denizens farther and farther afield, and so it bears asking: How is our historically unmatched familiarity with the beyond-the-familial rekindling the syntagm in casual conversation, in popular media, and in the humanities? How might we defamiliarize its all-too-familiar words privately and publicly, colloquially and academically, as we chat, fantasize, roam the biennales, write, or cuddle up with our favorite books? Conversely, while windows are opening wider and wider onto the world—whether in Microsoft or, no less innovatively, in Frédéric Beigbeder's 2003 9/11 best-selling *Windows on the World*—what kind of figures are the earth's places cutting in our digital and fictional frames?[2] And, along the lines of the global-planetary imbrications and tensions tackled throughout this collection, what is the tired locution's awakening teaching us as techno-economic, sociopolitical, and cultural trends of unprecedented magnitude impact on and are impacted by those places? How is the earth's face revealing us, in and across those locales, something that globalization often obfuscates and stymies while planetarization forefronts and nourishes?

Undoubtedly timely, the questions boil down to a critical act, to interpretation. Generally speaking, they all invite renewed scrutiny of the earth's fast-changing figure in the aftermath of the planet's latest, themselves multi-faceted reconfigurations. More specifically, more practically, and thus more closely to our private homes and disciplinary abodes, the sheer *existence* of the socioeconomic layout, saliently interconnective logic, and *courte* or *longue durée* etiology of the in-progress world-system are not at issue here, or not in the first place. As far as I am concerned, the overall global narrative is legible enough both diachronically, as an evolutionary rationale, and synchronically, as a present if still evolving "form." In plainer English, whereas the roots of the geocultural framework contextualizing the planetary visions—the primal scenes of planetarity—adduced later in this essay admittedly push deep into the early Renaissance's transcontinental travels, "discoveries," and redistributions of territory, community, affect, and capital, this framework, this worldly form of the present, remains no less unparalleled for that; the historical uniqueness of this "physiognomy" strikes me as hard to ignore. I call it *macroscopic* because it breaks forth and *appears* accessible, not to say obvious, from above or afar—from technologically enabled, spatial-evaluative positions and postures—but also because of its scope, of its scalarity. Indeed, it implies and often is a distant judgment, a large-scale representation, image, or photo. This is the proverbial bird's- or, more accurately, astronaut's-eye view; the interval-informed approach *and* what this yields; what "appears" and what one makes out from the physical-intellectual distance that brings into relief, without always rendering "evident," the cross-territorial, integrative-interlinking, and world-systemic operations coming loosely under the heading of "planetarization."

The Infinite and the Infinitesimal

Yet again, the issue at hand is not, or is solely in part, the macroscopic. Our problem, or at least the problem my intervention is wrestling with, falls chiefly under the *microscopic*. It is of the order of the infinitesimal. This is where the rubber meets the road and the material landscape the road runs through. But, as I shall reiterate, the micro focus does not involve a complete shift away from the macro, from the cosmic perspective of the NASA ("Apollonian") "gaze" and the "infinite" it gestures toward while paradoxically construing Earth as one, limited "unit."[3] The macro and the micro work—must work, of necessity—as the two arms of the analytical scissors.

Consequently, in the era of the "big picture," of a picture taken by a see-it-all—and see-it-*as*-all—eye-in-the-sky, the challenge to the discerning observer is the indiscernible or, better still, the planet's unsettlingly ambiguous encryption in it, the macro's murmur in the vernacular of the micro, in the tiny, the local, and the humble. For, fraught with distinctions and codifications of planetarity, the indistinguishable is or looks so only at first glance. To pick up the gauntlet, therefore, is to try and ascertain what entails to work out cultures' fine print with this planetary configuration, figure, or face as master framing device; what it takes to attend geoaesthetically to the enduringly enticing arabesque of "small things" alongside and through their godly and human handlers, venues, and styles; in brief, what it means to us, now, to *read "with" the planet*: to read it, namely, not as a reductive totality—a wrongheaded, unethical, and futilely globalist undertaking—but, in reading *against* that ominous oneness, to read the planet *with* and ultimately *for* the myriad of places, archives, and artifacts of which its fragile, pluricentric, and makeshift whole consists.

My premise, in other words, is that the planet is swimming into the critic's ken. On a less Keatsian tone, the earth's face is coming into view in its fully tangible dispensations and cultural-intellectual affordances complete with their sometimes uneven, contradictory, and plainly deleterious upshots. Controversially complex, this development is nevertheless bringing about a "discontinuity" in how we understand ourselves and others and, in that, has all the makings of an event.[4] As such, it is an occasion not so much for uncritical cheering as for earnest and sustained interrogation. For instance, does the earth have a face to begin with? Has it ever had one, and, if so, how visible was or is that face? Of course, our earth does have a *surface*. It has had one all along, if not a solid one *ab ovo*. This is not what I am talking about, though. Primarily a matter of geometry, geodesy, and, more basically, geology—after all, "earth" supplies here a geological synecdoche for "planet"—the earth as surface is, so to speak, sur-facial, hence culturally superficial, impassive. This blank, faceless face is pre-figurative, as geological vastness, or post-figurative, as one big riverbed for liquidities. Either way, it is aesthetically "asleep," as Michael Ondaatje might say.[5] Less an expression than sheer expanse, this unmarked flatness—this "undented" plane, Bertrand Westphal might gloss—lacks in cultural volume as it does in variety.[6] Thus, the mysteries it harbors are either hollow or redundant. Depthless, smooth, and uniform, this is not a face proper but a geographical façade, indifferent theater for the drama of difference rather than the "semiosphere" in which discourse is engendered and exchanged.[7] And, since this a-, proto-, or post-semiotic superficiality, quantifiable as it is, does not feature a topology, it makes no provisions for a typology or principle of classification either, that is, for a language, for a locus-minded logos; the face of the earth so conceived is scarcely a site of meaning.

Turn of the Planet, Turn to the Planet

However, it may turn into one. After all, as several critics in this book remind us, turning is what the earth does as a planetary body, in both senses. It turns (*planā*, in Ancient Greek) to gyrate, concomitantly around other celestial objects and its own axis. But, by the same movement quite literally, it also turns *to* change, turning in order to change and thus into a changed world order itself, the earth's revolutions bound up with the twists and turns in human history, revolutionary or less so. On one side, then, the earth's whirling through space as the planet physically revolves and evolves, and as space on earth itself stretches out, shrinks, is redistributed, and is mapped out in step with the systoles and diastoles of human civilization; on the other side, our own pirouettes, swerves, and about-faces, marking how we shuffle around the world, how we transform it, how we ourselves change in the wake of worldly changes, and how the latter call on us to revisit our *Anschauungen* of the spinning *Welt* and of ourselves in it: all these turns matter a great deal. What is more, they do so together, for they have been demonstrably intertwined through the ages. If geography—the earth's human writing into cartographic as well as topo-material visibility, the planet's life within and without disciplines and human practices—is subject to becoming, then "the becoming" of such fields, discourses, and the culture they speak to "is geographical" too according to Deleuze's tribute to the "Superiority of Anglo-American Literature."[8] On this ground, no anthropology or ethnography without a geophysical chapter is ever complete; no cultural history or paradigm shift account that overlooks the earth's own motions, cycles, and crises passes muster; no posthumanism still treating the planetary as inert context or backdrop to the human text or figure fulfills its promise; and, more broadly, no philosophy that does not operate "geophilosophically" is worth its salt.[9]

As Deleuze and Guattari posit, not only is thought's measure the ability to "create" its concepts, but this creation also requires an "earth or deterritorialization" as its "foundation."[10] Note too that, for the two thinkers, the earth and its historical de-, re-, and, we shall discover, underterritorializing dynamics are mere figures of speech neither ontologically, "out there" in the world, nor philosophically, inside the reasoning apparatus of the "Geophilosophy" chapter of *What Is Philosophy?* Or they are figures etymologically, as it were, inasmuch as they designate *aspects* in a fairly palpable, phenomenological fashion, ways in which the earth and thought *look and should be looked at*, once again, correlatively, together. Equally significant is that this togetherness, this mutuality of planetary complexion and thought's complexities, fluctuates across time. Thus, while the illuminating codependence of the earthly and the philosophical has always been in play, the post–Cold War years have enhanced and foregrounded it spectacularly. No other chapter in history, I contend, has literalized the planet's figure so extensively, making it so ineludible in its ubiquitous physical immediacy, so non-figurative in its concrete, geocultural presence, and so productive conceptually, so consequential for how one thinks—for how "immanent" to thinking *thinking with the planet* has become of late across disciplines.

This "immanence," this philosophical instrumentality of the planet, derives, as Deleuze and Guattari also comment on Martin Heidegger, from a planetary turn, given that "by virtue of its structure," Being "continually turns away when it turns toward," to the point that "the history of Being or of the earth is the history of its turning away."[11] For one thing, this movement is to no negligible degree trans- (and, some might add, post-) statal; arguably, Henri Lefebvre has guessed wrong when, back in 1975, he assured his readers that planetarity—*la mondialité*—would be a "planetary extension of the State."[12] For another thing, this has been a turn away from, and accompanied by the subsequent opening up of, territorial units, polities, policies, patrimonies, and paradigms heretofore neatly circumscribed—"territorialized" in terms of administration, coverage, and meaning—by national jurisdictions, nationalist mythologies, and related epistemological claims and descriptive models, or just so advertised. These complex turns trace the ambivalently distancing or "deterritorializing" by which the planet de facto draws closer to us, to the little places of our lives but also to that hub of human reflexivity where it becomes effectively "immanent" to thought or becomes thought *tout court* so as to involve thought itself in the "double becoming" that would make it planet-like—"earth," write Deleuze and Guattari—and thereby transform it radically.[13]

In the multimillennial, interweaving histories of the world and thought, we stand, as Kostas Axelos would probably alert us, at the decisive juncture at which the coextension and co-implication of planetary spatiality and thought—the "devenir-pensée du monde" and "devenir-monde de la pensée"—render how the world shapes representation and how representation plays out planetarily in scope, structure, and content two faces of the same coin.[14] For, if the planet turns away, it does so only to return, turning back toward us ontologically and analytically, as existential grit and interpretive grid, working itself into the everyday and its material heterologies at the same time that it turns into the pivot or "plane" around which thought and comprehension themselves gravitate. This way, the planet's turn lays out, still in Deleuze and Guattari's lingo, a "plane of immanence." "Clearly not a program, design, end, or means," this plane nonetheless "constitutes," today more than ever, "the absolute ground of philosophy," the foundation on which, in accord with the planet's cycles, thought warrants re-founding.[15] The sciences and the arts too, I suggest, are responding to these challenges, making similar moves on their own thinking planes and in their discourse-specific languages.[16] Thus, the planet serves, increasingly and with historically unrivaled force, as a level, matrix, or condition of possibility for a *forma mentis* whose purview covers the conceptual (philosophical), the referential (scientific), as well as the aesthetic (imaginative).

This is how the planet is turning to us to *concern* us all, thinkers and artists, specialists and laypersons, irrespective of where and what we are, to sponsor novel forms of world writing and reading, of imagining, figuring, and figuring out the world-as-world. Otherwise put, this concern works both ways. We are concerned, "looked at" by the planet as it is turning to us so we can see the earth's face, but this turn invites ours; we ourselves have to turn to the planet. The earth has entered the picture as planet and, in the geocultural dimension of planetarity, shows its face to us. This face is meaningful, but it will not be *readable*—it will remain fairly meaningless for us—unless we too face it. Because the turn *of* the planet subsumes thought itself, it calls for an intellectual turn *to* the planet; the reciprocity of planetarization and thought—of thinking on the planet and of thinking of the planet as planet—presupposes apposite "concerns," a certain planetary consideration on *our* part. This is as much as saying that, besides the world cast variously identified as multitude (Antonio Negri), Crowd (Alain Badiou), "global soul" (Pico Iyer), cosmopolitan (jet-setting or not), and, if somewhat disconcertingly, "nowhere man" (Iyer, Alexandar Hemon), the planet affords itself a receptive consciousness.[17] In turning to the planetary spectacle of meaning, this consciousness takes in the world homologically, availing itself of a methodology germane to its planetary object, moment, and environment. In that, this methodology is a *geomethodology*. In it, objective and subjective concerns, context and text dovetail. Its major constitutive steps and tightly interrelated thrusts are as follows:

The first is principally topological. As such, it latches onto planetarization as spatialization of the world and of aesthetic routines alike.

The second is, in the main, structural or relational. It homes in on a segment, locus, or facet of one or more artworks to tease out—to "decompress" analytically—their *planetary inscription*, namely, the "here"-"there," "we"-"they," "part"-"whole" relatedness structure folded into them. This "folding," I submit, is the common denominator of emerging planetary culture. Otherwise, "planetary culture" is far more befitting because there is no one-size-fits-all folding or compressing mechanism but only folding or compressing codes, which differ a great deal from one cultural site, practice, or agent to another. In decoding cultures, in showing how "here" is *co-imagined*—pictured inside, alongside, and more broadly "with" "there," and vice versa—geomethodology proceeds as a reverse engineering of sorts, characteristically activating a *reading-with* or a *with-reading*: it reads these works and their subsequent topo-cultural "*part*ialities" *with* the planetary "whole."

The third is predominantly ethical. Building on the previous two, it reaches beyond the descriptive by retooling the "with" as a twofold critical-deontological "for": geomethodology is not only geared toward tracing symptoms of planetarity "in territory," in this film or that novel; it also reads *for* the planet, on its behalf. This is where planetary interpretation and planetary stewardship become one and also where, at its most exhortative, my intervention comes closest to the rhetorical vivacity of a manifesto.

Below, I walk us through these three geomethodological components in this order.

The Space of Method

This methodology is a *geomethodology* first and foremost insofar as the earth's planetary becoming—the turn *of* the planet—is spatial. As Lefebvre, David Harvey, and others have noticed, one way or the other, planetarization works through, brings about, and, once more, "appears" as a trans-territorialization—dislocation, reallocation, and novel aggregation—of space and its meanings on earth. Felt by the planet, carved into the earth's body in the form of late twentieth and early twenty-first-century boundaries, passageways, itineraries, and geopolitical units of exchange, discourse, communality, and contestation, this turn cannot be thought of independently from the planet's geophysical shifts even though its logistics remain largely anthropological. Seemingly a natural category, a given (to us, humans), space has been, in reality, as Lefebvre would also insist, subject to well-defined production technologies. Occurring in and through human history, the planet's turn is thus inseparable from our spatial footprint on earth.

As Westphal maintains in *Le monde plausible*, the historical scene of this turn is postmodernity[18] or, in my estimation, whatever postmodernity we have left—or, better still, whatever post-postmodernity may have arisen—after the Cold War. If the "spatial imagination"—across the humanities as well as across the world "out there"—is older than postmodernism, the "spatial turn" has undeniably and dramatically picked up speed during the Cold War's last years to culminate, inside the academy, with a "hyperspatialization" of postmodern theory through interventions by topo-theorists, ecocritics, and literary cartographers such as Michel Foucault, Harvey, Marc Augé, Edward W. Soja, Lawrence Buell, Ursula K. Heise, Franco Moretti, and Brian Jarvis, and, outside, with a planetary spatialization of the postmodern paradigm itself.[19] Postmodernism's planetarization was a Pyrrhic victory: the postmodern went places only to self-displace and eventually dissipate through dissemination, creolization, and failure after failure to meet non-Western exigencies. Noteworthy here is what made it possible—what helped postmodernism travel—in the first place: its "place fixation" itself (if you indulge the pun) or perhaps the opposite, that is, postmodernism's bottomless appetite for unfixing and loosening, for setting things adrift and for deferral, the transgressive, intertextually digressive *furor topologicus* that bows to neither center nor inside because the marginal and the outside, along with the "outside the text" (*hors-texte*), have lost their contours on its maps. In this light, postmodernism's anti-logocentrism is a "lococentrism";[20] a pleonastic yet insatiable "fixation" on *locus* makes it, indeed, twice *loco*. But the postmodern's re-centering around space rests on a core-periphery dialectic redolent of Pascal's *Pensées*, where the stable, "rooted" center-circumference dichotomy gives way to multiple, ubiquitous, shifty, and "rhizomic" spatialities. This plural and fluid topology has been—*was*, some might rejoin—postmodern, terminally postmodern perhaps, before becoming not only a theoretical-aesthetic but also a geocultural "dominant" of planetarity. In response to this topology, authors from Don DeLillo, Andrei Codrescu, Paul Auster, Joseph O'Neill, Iyer, Orhan Pamuk, Mircea Cărtărescu, Michel Houellebecq, and Teju Cole to David Hollinger, Thomas L. Friedman, Jean-Luc Nancy, Masao Miyoshi, Michael Hardt, and Negri—all fiction writers, critics, and philosophers representative of both paradigms or, more accurately, of the *transition* from one to another—dwell on the "disappearance of the outside" and of those "hiding" places where territory-bounded and culturally "cloistered" individuals and groups struggle to opt out of one of our time's sea change scenarios.[21]

Imperfectly accommodated by the spatial-discursive model of postmodernism, new kinds of painting, moviemaking, writing, reading, and thinking are made possible, and the world they conjure up becomes intellectually, ethically, and aesthetically "plausible" once the planetary turn has been completed or, more realistically for now, has reached a point of no return. As I have expounded in my book on cosmodernism, in carrying us past this moment the contemporary is taking us beyond the postmodern,[22] for it weaves the present and those present in it into a chronotopically novel fabric. Marking the fast-evolving structure of presentness temporally, this quasi-ecumenical *fuite en avant, this rush forward of the world itself,* shrinks the playground of "now" also known as contemporaneousness down to a more modest interval: the time lapsed since the end of the Cold War. Spatially, one registers, at the same time, a compensatorily amplifying and juxtaposing "positional" pathos that unpacks the historically discontinuous category of "here" and the attendant notion of self so as to set forth the effective presence "in our midst," in the immediate proximity, or in the mediate, at-distance propinquity of those once upon a time "out there," not "from around here," or not like "us."[23] My point is not simply that Harvey's "time-space compression" model covers just a slice of a more complex world reality subject to a range of simultaneous, spatiotemporal contractions and expansions, but that what sets our epoch apart is a radical geosocialization of places and of place generally. Even though its intensity and cultural markers shift from one place to another, this process obtains on a scale as conspicuous as it is planetary. In this respect, as a "trend," the cosmodern is to the United States and most Euro-Atlantic cultures what the planetary is to the entire world, including the late postcolonial. Put differently, the Western cosmodernization of the postmodern represents a world-fractal phenomenon, is part and parcel of a development or turn of planetary proportions. This turn comes down to a planetarization of world places.

Granted, there are exceptions to this phenomenon. But because what I want to point up is the worldwide, documentably topocultural dominant, it is worth stressing that this planetarization or planetary spatialization stands out as a defining reality of the third millennium. What our hyperconnected world has been "specializing" in, and also what distinguishes it, is worldly spatialization itself, which bears on how we are in this world, what we do in it, and what we make of it. A perennial attribute of Heidegger's *Da-sein*, being-in-the-world, with others, has been heightened by the accelerated "de-distancing" of the world's places, people, and cultural practices.[24] Thus, as previously disconnected or loosely connected regions have brought closer together modernity's world *en miettes*, the spatiality (*Räumlichkeit*) tied into Being *ab origine* has now become planetary spatiality. Already instituted—rendered present—by the Heideggerian *Welt*, presence sets itself off and is legible in planetary co-presence.

Getting the Picture: Rationality and Relationality

Spatialization works by way of an ample repertoire of cultural sites, vectors, and materials; planetary spatialization operates, via the same arenas and socio-aesthetic rites, planetarily. The ever-expanding contiguity and co-articulation on a planetary scale of formerly stand-alone—or so imagined—agents, discourses, and settings are hallmarks of our *worlding world*.[25] But, to reemphasize, what "worlds" (*weltet*, in Heidegger) this world, and what "welds" its "independent" statements and clauses into a worldly syntax, is a world picture (*Weltbild*) that must be grasped both objectively (empirically) and subjectively (cognitively). Reflective of the world's "worlded" form or "built," this *Weltbild* facilitates reflection *on* this world, helps us "get the picture" of the world. It is in this multiple sense that the planet has entered the picture: topologically, as spatial extension of the human; historically, as a certain point in time when the planetary picture comes about—the time of the planet or the Heideggerian "age of the world picture";[26] and "spatiologically," in Lefebvre's terminology, or, in mine, geomethodologically—as a planetarily minded approach in the humanities and beyond.[27]

Critical of the interpretive arsenal and sociocultural aggregation model of "methodological nationalism," this approach cuts across traditionally territorialized—territorially bounded or pictured—societies.[28] Its algorithm works out readings through strategies of *semiotic spatialization*, namely, through *telescoping*, meaning-making associations that, besides the unavoidable if cautious at-distance ratiocinations, also venture, as I will momentarily, semantically microscopic *decompressions*—self-distancing interpretations—of local and proximal spaces and of their aesthetic renditions. Not completely unwarranted, the Heideggerian qualms about our attempts to reterritorialize our purchases on particular places and occurrences therein by bridging the distances and divides between them and otherwise transterritorializing their locations and significations do not capture our present historical circumstances. What Heidegger did not factor in is a crucial mutation distance as concept and world spatial habitus has undergone over the last half a century: due to the planetary spatialization of places, distance itself has been so thoroughly displaced and placed, territorialized, *inside* places, territories, and cultural microdomains that dwelling on distance, on this kind of structural or structure-embedded distance, no longer means throwing your lot with globalist-totalist ideologies. To the contrary—and on this ground—"distant" reading can play out as close reading, "thick description" of spatial and aesthetic distance-laden sites. In "The Age of the World Picture" and elsewhere, the German philosopher is taken aback by the anthropocentric arrogance behind wide-sweeping, culturally-politically coopting, and technologically assisted "calculations" about remote objects, their positions, meanings, and our physical-intellectual access to them. No doubt, thinks Heidegger, there is something to be said about the "gigantism" ("Americanist" or not) of our "distant" topo-interpretive élans.[29] But, as Gayatri Chakravorty Spivak and others have proposed, the planet and the reading model based on it may override the "globe" and the globalist claims that assimilate the far-flung and its others into the selfsameness makeup of the world's political and cultural centers.[30] Where globality *rationalizes* to shrink the earth's topo-epistemological interspaces by a "top-heavy" comparison that "impos[es] the same system of exchange everywhere,"[31] planetarity *relationalizes* to link up and read side by side, as well the worldly insides of, non-interchangeable entities and thus allow for the Heideggerian "incalculable," the aesthetically immeasurable, and the culturally asymmetrical.[32] Typically geomethodological, this relational—correlational and intrarelational—move overcomes the local-global "theoretical stalemate"—and Spivak's North-South antinomy no less—by crossing the gap of difference without annulling it; much like the planetarity that makes it both "necessary" and "impossible," the move delineates an analytical back and forth between either spatially distinct, though connectable, meaning units (works, genres, authors, movements) or from one meaning level to another *within* the same unit or cluster of adjacent, partially overlapping, or wholly coextensive units.[33]

Not infrequently, critics who have taken the former road have assumed that those units are not only external to each other but also organized into a self-evident hierarchy of space ("centers" vs. "margins"), culture ("origins"/"originals"/"sources" vs. "imitations"/"replicas"/"echoes"), and power ("capitals"/"metropolises" vs. "provinces"/"colonies"). Rearing its head even in a more democratically run world republic of letters such as Pascale Casanova's, this geoaesthetic pecking order antedates the planetary turn.[34] With a long disciplinary history behind it, the modus operandi underpinning it has yielded notoriously mixed results especially within the "influence studies" variety of comparative literature. Eminently driven by a "macro" kind of logic—in fact, excessively "macrological" at times—it risks shortchanging the micro; wielded from afar or above, and habitually from unacknowledged hubs and heights of political and cultural capital, this panoramic view of the faraway and the atypical provides for a "distant reading" where distance is not only a "condition of knowledge" but also its stumbling block.[35] If the cavalier dismissal of "close reading" is license for playing fast and loose with the idiomatic richness of the infinitesimal, then whatever planetary picture the "distant" critical procedure paints may not differ significantly from the "totalistic" brushstrokes of the globalist model.[36]

The Telescopic, the Microscopic, and the Planetary

More picturesque, planetarily speaking, is the latter road. Less traveled and more recently cut, it is better marked not only with the usual road signs but also with the planet's lush and variegated ontosemiotics—with meaningful life. What with its high speed, uniformly designed ramps, exits, rest areas, express tollgates, and lookout points over distant if awe-inspiring scenery, the other road is an autobahn. The critical traffic it fosters remains geared toward covering the distance physically rather than uncovering the geocultural minutia of the in-between locales. The highway is just that, a high road to—at times even a bypass around—the problematics of the planetary trivia, the horizontal counterpart of a telescopy exclusively and unambiguously sold on the ideology of *tēle* ("at distance," in Ancient Greek). No less necessary, it must be treaded carefully, as thinkers from Heidegger to Deleuze and Guattari to Paul Virilio counsel. At the very least, planetary critics must supplement it with the long-winded detour whose critical microscopy may help us better descry the planet's face—the roar of the bigger world—in the wrinkles of the apparently isolated, in the cultural grimaces, historical modes, and stylistic mood of unambitious, "cosmically" shy, or politically disenfranchised topographies. Thus, not only does this critical itinerary prove analytically safer sometimes—for we risk missing less as we stop by, look out the window, or take pictures—but it also is more emphatically ethical because it encourages us to "relate" to those we meet along it. To continue in the same Frostian vein, this road can literally make all the difference. Here, the journey pulls the world together and draws out spatially and intellectually the planet's togetherness by zooming in on the different, the off-the-beaten path, and the small. The distance is neither absent nor purely figurative. Its geographical dimension is still in play. But this expanse has been encoded discursively as the interstice between the work's outer and deeper layers, and then critically, as the scopic-interpretive gap between a first and second glance, between what we have in sight as we turn to look and as our gaze caresses the work's surface, and what comes into clearer focus as we complete our turn and inspect deeper, that is, the kind of planetary picture we might be able to come away with as we develop, quasi-photographically, the cultural negative of the novel or painting in question.

The highway, the astronaut, the satellite, the GPS, and their maps and vistas are elevated both attitudinally and altitudinally. In their more mechanical applications, they betray a twofold hauteur of standpoint, a perspectival loftiness of geopositioning and topography as well as of judgment. Quite high on their macro agenda is the barely disguised ambition to corral the infinite into various distant readings, measurements, and conjectures, whereas the back road is, less assumingly, a portal to the infinitesimal. A dromological version of the microscope, this route runs more emphatically—to paraphrase Gregory Bateson—through a geography of the mind before trekking across the planet's terraqueous body. In other words, it is predicated on a geoaesthetic order, on a homological, world and artwork model alike in which the Stoic, macro universe of ever-expanding circles of belonging of the Stoic, macro universe slide into one another and, together, into the particular, into the "located" work, and into the micro as their generic category.

It is in this sense that the micro telescopes—shrinks down to size to compress and encapsulate—the macro, which makes the opposition far less cut-and-dried. For, in this sense too, the microscope is an epistemological telescope, a *sense-making machine*. Harnessing its magnifying capabilities, the microscopic reading technique subsequently decompresses meaning, spreads out the world's bigger canvas folded inside the little picture, holds up to view the whole in the fragment, the planetary curled around or nestling *inside* the *omphalós* of the indigenous, the dialectal, and the place-bound. The idea behind this compression-cum-decompression reading optics is not to abolish or transcend distance in order to annex the destination. As noted earlier, the classical telescope—a variety of the hegemonic, rationally ordering "Enlightenment eye"—skips over places to cover, in hopes of canceling out, great distances. Instead, the microscopic connects vastly separated cultural dots by affirming and "working through" place after place, beginning with that starting point into which worlds seem to have collapsed. In tarrying with it diligently—in tracking the cultural specimen's Brownian motion closely—the critical microscope pursues the planetary spatialization of the geocultural sample under scrutiny, thus setting forth the "inherently relational" constitution of that place or locus as intersectional communality or trans-communitarian *locus communis*.[37] An aesthetic site where "here" and "ours" are spatialized into "distant kinship" with "there" and "theirs," this place and its cultural *haecceity*—this individual place or aesthetic locus and their *this-ness*—are no longer opposed to planetarity but apposite to it, a scaled-down *with-world*.[38] Characteristically, this site cites ("telescopes") the planet spatially and intertextually, "sites" (situates) and quotes—with one word, embodies—worldly relationality in ways that may or may not be right away noticeable. Watermarked with the planet's figure, this "sitational," textual-spatial formation lends itself, accordingly, to a reading with this figure, across the panoply of local figurations serving as the figure's cypher and vehicle. This reading is, to invoke Westphal again, a *lecture du monde* in the strong sense of the world as worlded or relational *mundus*, in short, a with-reading poised to face and shed light on the "with-ness" makeup of this world.[39] To that effect, planetary reading turns to the latter's relational structure—to the planet's "mondiality"—microscopically, scanning the micro for signs of the macro.

If the close reading handed down to us by the New Critics all too often purports to "resolve" the contradictory by simplifying the complex, planetary close (or micro)reading seeks to complicate the illusorily simple. More to the point, this kind of interpretation does the planet's bidding epistemologically—and thus instantiates what Axelos pinpointed as the planet's "thought-becoming"—by spotting the worldly multiplicity of place, time, and discourse in the deceptively monistic, the distant relatives, the exogenous, and the incoherent genealogies placed under erasure by institutionalized culture and officially endorsed by the nation-state's endogenous fantasies. In this form, *culture is a cover-up operation*. Therefore, simulation is hardly the issue here, Jean Baudrillard's variously rehearsed case notwithstanding; to the contrary, dissimulation is the problem. "Streamlined" culture does not so much simulate as it dissimulates, conceals, disregards, or shortshrifts the many that have gone into the cobbling together of the one, of the same, of the nation, and the like. Countercultural *because* cross-cultural, reading with the planet exposes, first, the compilation itself, the outsourcing of nativist mythologies, and the heteroclite underbelly of the putatively all-of-a-piece, and second, the worldliness of the *bricolage*. Whistleblowers of sorts, planetary critics leak culturally classified information about the recycled material's planetary provenance or, conversely, about the worldly affiliation of presumably discrete traditions and autonomous identities by laying bare the worldly relationality the fast-expanding planetary imaginary has threaded into descriptions of allegedly self-subsistent singularities. What these critics enact, then, is a protocol of perusal driven by a fractal logic. They look, that is, for the *totum in parte*, contemplate the "all"'s face *in filigree*, in that which seems to be facing no one else but itself. Does this mean that they rely too much on a reading against the grain? Not quite. In practice, their reading is also one *with* the grain. What is more, this reading often fleshes out the insights of worldliness turning up in U.S. and other literatures with symptomatically increased frequency since the late 1980s. Post–Cold War narrative stages so insistently the retraining of the gaze on the planetary all carved into the apparently second-fiddle, minuscule, cloistral, ingrown, and otherwise unworldly that some of the most emblematic fictions of our time can be read as geomethodological blueprints.

Intimations of Cosm*all*ogy

Mircea Cărtărescu's *oeuvre* is a case in point. If Hungarian author George Konrád confesses in his 1984 book *Antipolitics* that "the world is one; and it is more interesting than Budapest,"[40] the Romanian writer feels, around the same time and a few hundred miles east of Konrád's Budapest, the pull of worldly oneness *in situ*: not only does this oneness exist, but it can be *lived out* locally, in and *as* his hometown. "I truly love my world, the world of Bucharest," he declares elsewhere, "yet I am fully aware that Bucharest is concomitantly *all*, the Aleph."[41] To get a grip on the many-sided Borgesian allusion, it is important to remember that, at the time, the regime was seeking to expunge Romania's capital from the world's cultural and political script and turn it, along with the rest of the country, into what the dissidents were calling "internal exile." Pushing back against this agenda, the "cultural resistance" movement (*rezistenţa prin cultură*) of the Romanian 1980s marked one of the most cosmopolitan periods in East European history.

In the vanguard of this struggle, Cărtărescu fights off the twin incarceration of his beloved city and of himself in it by opening it out onto what his 1985 poetry volume calls the "All" (*Totul*).[42] Drawing from this and other earlier works, his 1993 novel *Nostalgia* sketches an astoundingly holistic vision of planetarity.[43] Forlorn and dilapidated, plagued by shortages and blackouts, late Cold-War Bucharest is, literally and allegorically, written by the book back into the wider world and thereby made "interesting," into a site of and argument for worldly belonging. In Cărtărescu's work, the city and its people reclaim their seat in the bigger world. They are, we gather, part and parcel of this world; they spend their lives in its nurturing embrace, although not out in the open, for politics and policies of cultural lockdown have all but deterritorialized the greater outside—or, more exactly, have *under*territorialized it. But, from beneath the defaced surface of Ceauşescu's "golden-age" Bucharest, the writer summons strange faces and the very face of worldly strangeness: the face of the planet, the figure of that incoherent and raucous oneness, of the planetary being-with or worldly *Mitsein* fractured by the Berlin Wall, by the country's heavily militarized borders, and more generally by the disjunctive geopolitics of the Cold War. From within the maze of concrete housing projects, the author conjures up cosmic panoramas by bridging physical and metaphysical gaps. In dialogue with E. T. A. Hoffmann, Franz Kafka, Gabriel García Márquez, Jorge Luis Borges, Thomas Pynchon, and other modern and postmodern masters of the fantastic, the absurd, and magical realism, Cărtărescu unearths a maimed metropolis whose heart throbs in the world's wider body and whose idiosyncratic mix of squalor and "Paris of the Balkans" charm he flips over to display unsuspected depths and gateways into the hidden, the elsewhere, and the otherwise—into the world's larger assemblage. Where the Western mindset relegates his city to an alien geography overrun by strays and ruled by vampiric dictators razing entire neighborhoods to make room for their sepulchral headquarters, Cărtărescu unfolds a borderless dreamland.

The oneiric politics of *Nostalgia*'s urban imaginary was lost on Cărtărescu's readers neither when the book first came out in spring 1989, under the title *Visul* (*The Dream*) and butchered by censorship, nor a few years later, when it was reissued in unabridged form. Its staggeringly world-relational toposophy went head-on against officially upheld "tradition," an exceptionalist-solipsistic notion redolent of early twentieth-century, agrarian-Orthodox and nationalist-chauvinist doctrines, on which the Communist Party was falling back in the late 1980s to ward off perestroika. The novel symbolically liberates the city's body politic by linking it with other urban bodies and bodies of work, with other places, *topoi*, styles, texts, and contexts. An *other* to the city and its officially sanctioned corporeality thus coalesces beyond the closed-off self, community, and place, an other into whose capaciously agglutinating texture *Nostalgia*'s main first-person narrator weaves himself and his kin.

The weaving spider is, in fact, Cărtărescu's signature *mise en abyme*. A motif *in* the story, it also designates, metafictionally, the novel's multiply intertextual fabric and, inside it, the web of Kabbalah-like copulas between stages and layers of existence where the individual brain is plugged into other brains and their projections into other worlds and the worlds behind those, *ad infinitum*. As in one of the novel's sections, the narrating writer-in-the-novel plays the spider sliding up and down the threads of various plot lines. He gets in and out of the minds of his dramatis personae, transforming into his characters while telling us about their own changes into others. At the same time, he shows how the phylogeny of these metamorphoses (another Cărtărescu trademark) rehearses cosmic ontogeny by recapping a whole cosmology—an entire cosm*all*ogy. Indeed, what he ultimately puts up is a planetary spectacle of the All and of those without whom this whole's wholeness would fall short, a performance of self and—and as necessarily *with*—others (*álloi* in Ancient Greek).[44]

People's bodies; Bucharest's crumbling body; the nation's hyperterritorialized bulk; and the world's geocultural corpus: these are *Nostalgia*'s concentric circles, the network-*mundus*. Whatever takes place in this planetary web must take place first topologically and, we will see before long, ethically, to wit, must take *its* place from another place and place-giver "not here." For, explains Giorgio Agamben, no matter where it happens, what ontological seat in the planetary amphitheater gets assigned to it, this place-taking occurs as one "eases" into a place, into a residential "easement" that is both one's own lawfully and "always-already" an adjacency *within* the private property in which the proprietorial and the exclusive are consequently premised on an other's presence, on the shared, and the communal right-of-way. Owners and the finite space where their ownership is exercised are founded, as Emmanuel Levinas and Jacques Derrida press home ever so often, on hospitality, its guests (others), and the luminous infinity bathing the face-to-face of hosting. Innately *ek-static*, beings thus depend on—rest on and have "always-already" internalized—a literally vital outside. Their realm *and* modality is a horizontally as well as vertically spatialized relation. A priorily adjacent, traversed by visible and invisible "easements," here-ness only apparently takes hold just "here," on one level of existence.[45] What happens on one level unfolds or can unfold Kabbalistically on the rest as a drama of All-ness, of quasi-mystical partaking of the All. Everything—this very All—is a matter of scale, scope, and perspective. Matter itself is no exception because what defines it is extension and "situation" in a space where all locations communicate and so make up a continuum. How and what things are hinges on where they are, but they can mutate abruptly because their places are (or are not) theirs insofar as these are spliced together or border on other places across, near, inside, beneath, or above them.

Ontology *is* topology, then; position, an inherently relational spatial coordinate, ultimately turns into an ontological category while ontology too becomes, as Soja would say, spatialized.[46] Therefore, one can shuttle back and forth between different levels of life. One can "overcome" ontological difference, run the whole gamut of being and thus be in "other" ways and worlds topologically: here, one changes by simply changing one's place, status, or classification. By the same token, this ontology is political. *Nostalgia*'s planetary imagination marshals beings polemically by reshuffling the segregationist-insular biogeography of Cold War Romania along the lines of flight of a two-pronged onto-spatial rhetoric. On one side, this rhetoric is metonymic; it sets people and objects next to people and objects in whose vicinity they have neither been nor are supposed to be. On the other side, it is synecdochic. Treating individuals and locales as subsets of greater units stretching above and athwart the Party-State's immediate, totalitarian totality and ossified taxonomies, this *pars pro toto* planetary figuration only reformulates, from the vantage point of the part, the *totum in parte* of fractal reading. Thus, either way, Cărtărescu's characters act out a drama of being—they *are*—as they are in relation to others, thence de-termined, at the same time bounded and freed by the proximity to others and their modes of being. Propinquity, the terminus that both limits and assigns the self a contiguous meaning, also liberates it, brings it forth and across. Political through and through, topological and cultural relatedness is thus *Nostalgia*'s *modus essendi*. Bucharest's "little context"' reflects the shape of bigger places and units or feeds into them without warning. Unlike the more jejune constructions of "local" and "global," the micro and macro worlds are similarly built but neither repetitious nor opposed. In broader bodies, venues, and sequences, the self does not run into versions of itself but into others. An ontological alloy—made of *álloi*—the All's structure is non-*allergic*, cosm*al-lo*gic. This constitution features others and calls upon the self to acknowledge them both outside and inside itself. Further, if the All is indeed the Alpha and Omega of "little" existential forms and, further, if these forms mirror the whole's own form, then they are its microcosm; further still, because the levels of this ontology interface and overlap, the microcosm is not only isoform and juxtaposed to the macrocosm but also a portal to it, an *Aleph*.

"Mondializing" the City: Blueprints and Constellations

In calling the small, the finite, the shut-in, the incarcerated, the city and its bodies Alephs, the Romanian writer also calls out to Borges, interpellates and interpolates his "Aleph." Another homology comes into play here via the Argentine author's holistic ("*All*istic") model of intertextuality: the Babel Library. In it, literature and place are limitless in number and extent and so coextensive, one. Therefore, the universal library and the universe overlap too. In "The Library of Babel," "The Book of Sand," "The Total Library," and other Borgesian *ficciones*, the library, the book, and the textual show off the universe qualitatively, best illustrate its fabric, its "textile" makeup. Conversely, they also hint that, if the cosmos is like a book, all books are infinite. That means that every book holds the rest of the holdings, is an Aleph, "one of the points in space that contains all points."[47] What de-fines "bookness" is in-finitude as well as inter-textuality, cosmic boundlessness *and*/inside boundedness. Underlying the latter is, fundamentally, otherness, the others and their books' presence in a particular book. This book, which *Nostalgia* emulates, does not only "put up" with a "parasitic" other to it within itself; the book simply cannot have a self, an identity, cannot be "original," in short, cannot be what it is without that "alien" presence inside it, without having its roots, its origin, somewhere else, in another text. It follows that the Aleph is not just unlimited and intertextual—and intertextual because unlimited, transgressive, liable to cross over to the other side time and time again—but also "alterial," a repository of alterity. It is being that *is* while also being what it is not, its other, much like the Aleph includes its "counterpart," the Zahir, and everything else between the A (Alpha) and Z (Omega) of existential, cultural, and political "alternatives."[48]

Borges's "Aleph" is not only the novel's primary intertextual ingredient but also the Kabbalistic-cosmological trope and cultural stratagem through which Cărtărescu reveals his cosmology as cosm*allogy* and Bucharest as an Aleph, a site of astonishing otherness and size locked *inside* the nation-state's paranoically policed borders.[49] A carceral space, the Romanian capital is also "*une ville devenue monde*,"[50] a city made into world—"mondialized"—by the writer's planetary imaginary. Describing Los Angeles as the "epitomizing world-city" and utmost sample of postmodern urban geography, Soja notices that the metropolis is a cosmopolis because it "reproduc[es] *in situ* the customary colours and confrontations of a hundred different homelands." A microcosm of the illimitable and itself without limit, bursting with "fulsome" heterogeneity, Soja's LA is, in his own formulation, a Borgesian "LA-leph," at once "everywhere" and "the only place on earth where all places are." And they are there because, as the critic implies apropos, again, of Borges, the Aleph is a "radical[ly] open," "all-inclusive simultaneity" sheltering a whole panoply of otherness.[51] This makes the Californian Aleph so mind-bogglingly "global" that it defies critical survey.[52] Instead, Cărtărescu's Aleph stimulates and entices, leading on and out of the all-too-limited. Not the Balkans' Paris any more, Bucharest has yet to become their LA. The stakes of its planetary projections are different. If in Pynchon's *The Crying of Lot 49* Oedipa Maas follows real roads, signs, and maps to famously "project a world," [53] in Cărtărescu the geoimaginary blueprint of Bucharest is jarringly at odds with the plans drawn by the city's rulers. De facto, their world picture does not include Bucharest, and, truth be told, there is no world picture to speak of either. Not so in *Nostalgia*'s camera obscura. Here, a world picture slowly forms, one in which Bucharest registers.

More memorable yet is the other image, which the writer develops "microscopically" from the city's negative: the world's own face across and amidst the faces, facets, and petals on Bucharest's wet, black bough. But this is not just the by now banal view from above. Nor is it the view from nowhere, as critics of "universalist" cosmopolitanism might quip. A view from within, inside, or underneath a temporally and spatially anchored locale, this is a "consideration" of place that takes in and honors this place as "situated" or *placed planetarity*, an effort to account for the world relationality intrinsic to place and subsequently to do away with the pseudo-disjunctions of place and planet, micro and macro, and so forth. For, as Tariq Jazeel echoes Doreen Massey, "place is not opposed to the planet. It is instead an ongoing assemblage, constellation, and agonistic coming together of narratives and trajectories that are in themselves insufficiently conceptualized as either local or global." Thus, "the spatialization of place, in this sense, provides the sphere of the possibility of existence of multiplicity. . . . The negotiation of difference in place is always a process of, and invitation to, reconstellate the 'we,' and place's geographical challenge thought this way is precisely that it is never closeable."[54] To "reconstellate" this "we"—the spatialized communality of the polis—the critic must look not only around and over the nation-state's fences, horizontally, but, as Robert T. Tally Jr. acknowledges in his *Planetary Turn* essay, also over the horizon, up, where the constellations turn and the earth itself turns into Earth by trading its topographical surfaciality for geosemiotic voluminousity. A triangulation of place *in the micro mode* susceptible to withstand parochial, clannish, and authoritarian attempts at cordoning off cultural sites, the critical maneuver likely to redraw, à la David Hollinger, the Theophrastian circle of "we"[55] for the twenty-first century actually depends on macro ("Apollonian") vistas and their "mondial" mental pictures. To be more exact, this dependence is an interdependence. For the macro itself collapses, Aleph-like, into the micro, but, upon geomethodological "decompression," it becomes readable in the culture's "small print" as much as the Stoics' innermost circles of selfhood and family present themselves as ripple or butterfly effect—outer circles—of far-off, incongruous, and "eccentric" "we"-constellations.

Snowflakes: The Imagination as Geopositioning Technology

Amplifying exponentially across the post–Cold War novel, the thematization of the dialectic of micro and macro world pictures becomes more transparently political in Cărtărescu's later work (*Orbitor* [*Blinding*]), but also in DeLillo (*Underworld*, *Cosmopolis*, *Falling Man*, and *Point Omega*), Chang-rae Lee (*Native Speaker*, *A Gesture Life*, *Aloft*, and *The Surrendered*), Cole (*Open City*), Gish Jen (*World and Town*), Jonathan Safran Foer (*Extremely Loud and Incredibly Close*), Nicole Krauss (*The History of Love*), Hemon (*Nowhere Man*), Gary Shteyngart (*The Russian Debutante's Handbook* and *Absurdistan*), Bharati Mukherjee (*The Holder of the World*, *Desirable Daughters*, and *Miss New India*), Jhumpa Lahiri (*Namesake*), Colum McCann (*Let the Great World Spin*), O'Neill (*Netherland*), Ondaatje (*The English Patient*), Houellebecq (*Les particules élémentaires* [*The Elementary Particles*], *Plateforme* [*Platform*], *La possibilité d'une île* [*The Possibility of an Island*], and *La carte et le territoire* [*The Map and the Territory*]), Alexandru Mușina (*Nepotul lui Dracula* [*Dracula's Nephew*]), Zadie Smith (*White Teeth*, *On Beauty*, and *NW*), Ian McEwan (*Saturday*), Dubravka Ugrešić (*The Ministry of Pain*), Christos Tsiolkas (*Dead Europe*), Brian Chickwava (*Harare North*), and Orhan Pamuk (*Kar* [*Snow*]), to list only a few of the Romanian writer's kindred spirits.

In Pamuk's 2002 novel, for example, contemporary Istanbul, a mere three hundred miles south of Cărtărescu's Bucharest, then, farther away, eastern Anatolia's town of Kars, and entire Turkey with them claim "accessions" to wider geopolitical aggregates such as EU and are simultaneously reclaimed by forces of religious, regional, and separatist entrenchment dead set on rescinding Mustafa Kemal Atatürk's secularist legacy. Historically between a rock and a hard place, Pamuk's country finds itself trapped between incompatible options: the greater world of NATO (since 1951) and Europe (an increasingly conflicted aspiration), for which the Young Turks' modernity-bent reformism had paved the way, and, pulling in the opposite direction, Iran-backed Islamists and, yet in another, radical Kurdish autonomists (PKK). Turkey's predicament, Pamuk hints, lies in what might be called the extraneous fallacy: the assumption that, first, such options, positions, affiliations, and the cultural-religious models derived from or attributed to them are indomitably external to each other, following as they allegedly do distinct trajectories in space and time; and second, that they are mutually exclusive as a matter of course. Nowhere is this antinomic worldview more ingeniously refuted than in the "telescoping" episode where Ka, the protagonist, tells us about "All Humanity and the Stars," the "constellating" poem he composes in reaction to his companion's comment that "the history of the small city [of Kars] has become as one with the history of the world."[56] "In the notes he made afterward," we learn, "Ka described [the poem's] subject"

> as the sadness of a city forgotten by the outside world and banished from history; the first lines followed a sequence recalling the opening scenes of the Hollywood films he had so loved as a child. As the titles rolled past, there was a faraway image of the earth turning slowly; as the camera came in closer and closer, the sphere grew and grew, until suddenly all you could see was one country, and of course—just as in the imaginary films Ka had been watching in his head since childhood—this country was Turkey; now the blue waters of the Sea of Marmara and the Bosphorus and the Black Sea and the Nişantaş of Ka's childhood, with the traffic policeman on Teşvikiye Avenue, the street of Niğar [*sic*] the poetess, and trees and rooftops (how lovely they looked from above!); then came a slow pan across the laundry hanging on the line, the billboard advertising Tamek canned goods, the rusty gutters and the pitch-covered sidewalks, before the pause at Ka's bedroom window. Then a long tracking shot through the window of rooms packed with books, dusty furniture, and carpets, to Ka at a desk facing the other window; panning over his shoulder, the camera revealed a piece of paper on the desk and, following the fountain pen, came finally to rest on the last letters of the message he was writing, thus inviting us to read:
>
> ADDRESS ON THE DAY OF MY ENTRANCE
> INTO THE HISTORY OF POETRY: POET KA,
> 16/8 NIGÂR THE POETESS STREET,
> NIŞANTAŞ, ISTANBUL, TURKEY

As the narrator adds in a reference to the snowflake-shaped cosmic diagram he comes across in one of Ka's notebooks, "discerning readers will already have guessed" that Ka's address "is located on the Reason axis but positioned to suggest the power of the imagination."[57] Intersecting Reason and Memory,[58] the Imagination re- or geo(-)positions Ka(r[s])—the artist, the place, and Turkey with them—planetarily, across worlds, rationalities, and individual-collective memories. By a mix of zoom-in and zoom-out scenes, Pamuk and his authorial alter ego both locate their places in the outside worlds and make out these worlds in the Turkish quotidian, lying inside one another like so many Chinese boxes, overlapping, or crisscrossing each other to weave the Alephic fractality—the "snowflake"—of planetarity. Ka does not have to invent the "little things" that his compatriots live and die for, for these things are already there, in the Universal Studio picture of the turning planet. But he needs to turn to the picture an eye trained for this kind of planetary "detail." The magnifying-glass workings of the microanalysis also makes possible the macroanalytic flip side, which helps him detect the world's multitudinal footprints in snowy Kars. It is, arguably, all a matter of scale, of a revisionary scalarity no longer wedded to national-linguistic territoriality but willing to take the risk of another mapping. Both imaginary and real, so vivid in Kars's Turkish-Kurdish-Iranian-Armenian-Russian-West-European urban potpourri and so subtly reinforced by Pamuk's Brechtian-Pirandellian intertextual games, this is a complex cartography in which place, affect, faith, gender, ethnicity, and governance "crystalyze" to gel, snowflake-like, into aggregates of culture inside, outside, and astride statal and sectarian turfs.

"Where the print is finest"

One of the more heartening points O'Neill drives home in his 2009 Pen/Faulkner Award-winning *Netherland* is that this cultural meteorology might bring about social climate change in the post-9/11 United States by way of everyday community practices as leisurely and unassumingly plebeian as sports.[59] For cricket, the Turkish-Irish-American author teaches us through his Dutch protagonist Hans van der Broeck and especially Hans's West Indian friend, Chuck Ramkissoon, is more than a pastime. It is not in the past either. Its time has not passed. Or, if it has, so has the exceptionalist-autonomist temporality in which American communality has sometimes pictured itself. As a community, Chuck believes, the United States still has to pass the geopolitical and cultural-demographic test of the planetary present. Popular with Americans since the early eighteenth century but gradually elbowed aside by baseball's modern "hegemony," the game of cricket is thus more than a trope or fictional ploy. It is a concrete, athletically embodied modality of presentifying or updating an America that, in the September 11, 2001 aftermath, must reconstellate itself as community so as to work through the meanings of not only the World Trade Center tragedy but also of the planetarization without which the traumatic event would remain meaningless. A community driven to the limit by the violently worlding world, the United States cannot afford *not* to use its new, liminal position to think through its communal cultural-ethical limits and spatio-political limitations. Cricket, implies Faruk Patel, one of the rumored financial backers of Chuck's New York Cricket Club project, uniquely brings together liminality, Americanness, and understanding, or, less redundantly, simply *brings together*. Chuck's basic idea was to build a team, a field and its facilities, and socialize with teammates, opponents, fans, and the cricketers' families, in a nutshell, to deploy cricket as a twenty-first-century ritual of American togetherness. There may be, as Faruk opines, "a limit to what Americans understand," and that "limit" may well be, as he goes on, "cricket" itself. But if that is true, then the game ceases to be trivial. Instead, it takes on a sociocultural and, we shall see, political "consequentiality" beyond the inconsequentially ludic because it opens up the agonistic venue where Americans might recontest *practically* the meaning of being in the world.[60] Accordingly, in this space, they may not limit themselves to theoretical de- and re-limitations of territory, culture, and identity inside somewhat less rigid boundaries and categories, to mere reconceptualizations of what it means to be in the world; here, they may and in a sense must also "experiment" with worldliness, that is, with being-in-the-world as a *community-fostering* modality of being.

Hans and others are aware of the "laboratory experiment" underway.[61] But the laboratory, Chuck maintains, is not limited to the cricket field because the latter's liminal condition necessarily marks and unmarks this terrain as a strict enclosure, *ad quem* limit or terminus. Thus, the field and surrounding grounds set themselves up as an American microcosm. Or, with another metaphor pressed into service by my geomethodological reading, the laboratory is also a photo lab—better yet, a socio-photo lab. In it, not only "developers" like Chuck but also Americans at large, players, crowds, and the whole body of *socii* give themselves another chance to learn or relearn how to develop, from the ludic negative of the cricket community, a new picture of the United States and of the world inside and outside the country.

"The bigger you think, the crappier it looks. . . . So this is going to be my motto—think small," Theo announces in McEwan's 2005 novel *Saturday* as the world's "big things" are encroaching on his private world and concerns.[62] "My motto is, Think fantastic," Chuck lets Hans know with one of the novel's frequent nods at *The Great Gatsby*.[63] As logicians might note, this is a one-way contradiction because Chuck's plan is not to import, from the outside, worldly "bigness" into cricket-reconstellated American smallness. He just does not envision worldliness as an outside; not an optional, flavor-enhancing additive to the American melting pot, the world is neither external nor supplemental to the United States. He has two goals. The first is to flesh out the big already tightly packed within the small, the history burrowed inside our seemingly ahistorical contemporaneity, the potential future with which the flat present is thus interleaved, the macro within the micro. The second is to help Americans *visualize* this multilayered structure, picture their home as, with, and of the world and the world as and deep inside it, in brief, turn to the planet by turning meaningfully, self-analytically and ethically, to each other, their country, and its renewed hospitality. As he tells Hans, if "you ask people to agree to complicated rules and regulations," the sport might just be the answer because, in spite of its colonial history, it has served and can serve again as a "crash course in democracy. Plus—and this is key—the game forced [players from the warring tribes of Papua New Guinea] to share a field for days with their enemies, forced them to provide hospitality and places to sleep." "Hans," he carries on, "that kind of closeness changes the way you think about somebody. No other sport makes this happen."[64] When Hans wonders if his friend thinks of Americans as "savages," Chuck rejects the implication by bolstering not only his "fantastic" vision's import as a world-communal picture but also the planetary relationality over whose filigree, specifically and deliberately, the world picture is laid palimpsest-like. "I'm saying," he elaborates, "that people, all people, Americans, whoever, are at their most civilized when they're playing cricket. What's the first thing that happens when Pakistan and India make peace? They play a cricket match. Cricket is instructive, Hans. It has a moral angle. I really believe this. Everybody who plays the game benefits from it. So I say, why not Americans?" The question is timely because, as the 9/11 attacks proved to Chuck and others, "Americans cannot really see the world. They think they can, but they can't. I don't need to tell you that. Look at the problems we're having. It's a mess, and it's going to get worse. I say, we want to have something in common with Hindus and Muslims? Chuck Ramkissoon is going to make it happen. With the New York Cricket Club, we could start a whole new chapter in U.S. history. Why not? Why not say so if it's true? Why hold back? I'm going to open our eyes."[65]

To open our American eyes in order to see and "get" the world picture is thus to "fulfill [our] destiny,"[66] in other words, to re-become the hospitable community for which cricket can provide a model morally urgent, practical, and plausible. This plausibility is to be taken once again in Westphal's sense and, beyond it, in the sense in which, as Deleuze and Guattari postulate, "the other is a possible world as it exists in a face that expresses it and takes shape in a language that gives it a reality."[67] The community, what it is and can possibly be, in its present or plausible future, shines through the faces of others. The only "white man [he] saw on the cricket fields of New York," Hans is surrounded by "teammates" who "variously originated from Trinidad, Guyana, Jamaica, India, Pakistan and Sri Lanka," with "Hindus, Christians, a Sikh, and four Muslims" drawing together "into a circle for prayer" before the match.[68] In this circle of "we," a new communality becomes readable at long last. "I've heard," Hans confesses,

> that social scientists like to explain such a scene—a patch of America sprinkled with the foreign-born strangely in play—in terms of the

> immigrant quest for subcommunities. How true this is: we're all far away from Tipperary, and clubbing together mitigates this unfair fact. But surely everyone can also testify to another, less reckonable kind of homesickness, one having to do with unsettlements that cannot be located in spaces of geography or history, and accordingly it's my belief that the communal, contractual phenomenon of New York cricket is underwritten, there *where the print is finest*, by the same agglomeration of unspeakable individual longings that underwrites cricket played anywhere—longings concerned with horizons and potentials sighted or hallucinated and in any event lost long ago, tantalisms that touch on the undoing of losses too private and reprehensible to be acknowledged to oneself, let alone to others. I cannot be the first to wonder if what we see, when we see men in white take to a cricket field, is men imagining *an environment of justice*. (italics added)[69]

The passage draws the fine distinction between immigrant "*sub*communities" and communities that could be called planetary—sodalities in which planetarization can be "experienced" and witnessed socially, but also experienced with, observed as if under a microscope. Typical of earlier, postcolonial diasporas, the former cohere around ethnos, more specifically, around effectively or imaginarily separate and competing *ēthne*, where "competition" tends to be disjunctive and topoculturally exclusionary, further prying the competing bodies apart and spacing them out literally or figuratively across intervals of territory, faith, feeling, belonging, and cultural practice. What matters is ethnos-as-*gamesmanship*; the communality game is played on a field athletically and socially finite, limited as to what the players might do and mean together. Gathering around one, trans-ethnical ethos—the ethos of cricket—the latter group category is cross- or supra-communal, integrative. In its finitude of time, space, skill, and membership, an infinite, because infinitely definable, communality awaits.[70] An agonistic protocol of togetherness, its ludus is multiply ethical, in fact: it relies on cricket's civic behavior injunction and play-by-the-rules principle; it works as a language conveying "others," playfully, quasi-ineffable emotional states ("tantalisms") that, by the same movement, can be either sublated or "mined" for bonding purposes; and, since it is inclusive of winners and losers, hosts and guests, Americans and "foreigners," main actors and family extras alike, it is also, if not already just, then a template for justice. At premium in this playful zone is ethics-as-*sportsmanship*; here, the contest is not primarily a face-off but a face-to-face preamble. While the tiny relational community of cricket is not and cannot substitute itself to the world, this world's face is legible in Chuck's contractual vision, where the contract's "print is finest"—where, in making sense of the Van Cortland Park cricket "picture" ("it looks like a Brueghel," exclaims Hans's wife), one makes sense of the planet.[71]

Reading for the Planet: Criticism and Stewardship

Face the world's face. This is what Chuck urges us, if not in so many words. Let us do so. Popping up among the players' faces, the planet's Arcimboldian face also shows itself in all its confounding hodgepodge, unflagging shiftiness, and self-contradictory mien around Cărtărescu's Bucharest, Ugrešić's Amsterdam, Foer's New York, Houellebecq's Paris, and Zadie Smith's northwest London, as well as in Muşina's Braşov, Pamuk's Kars, and Mukherjee's Gauripur—in the world, its cities, its less glamorous towns, and everywhere in between them; indeed, this face has become a "world and town" staple, as Jen suggests in her 2010 Chinese-Cambodian-New Englander Riverlake saga.

Ubiquitous as this enigmatic profile may be, it is also a fragile one, anguished, unstable, precariously balanced. O'Neill has no illusions about it. His take on things, American and otherwise, is hardly Pollyannish. As we seek and perhaps recognize this face, let us remember that Chuck's handcuffed body gets dumped in the Gowanus Canal. The inevitable question, then, is whether his vision ends up in the same place. My answer is that, although Hans leaves New York to join his family in the United Kingdom, the reunion with his son Jake, his estranged British wife Rachel, her parents and his former colleagues, Londoners, strangers, and even with his own past and long-passed mother, farther and farther away spatially, temporally, and empathically from the inner circle of "we," enacts what Chuck describes as cricket's "lesson in civility."[72]

This lesson is important. But no less important is this: as in Cărtărescu, whose characters keep climbing up on the roofs of their apartment complexes to hug the world, or in Jen, whose small town has its own observation ("twin") towers, or in Lee's *vol d'oiseau* surveys from *Aloft*, the at-distance, macro pedagogy of aerial-theoretical planetary togetherness and empathy can only do so much. But what it does do, the onto-scopic opening that it marks, matters. Its distant self-positioning sows, dialectically, the perspectival "micro" seeds of nearness, closeness, intimacy, and being-with. We shoot up and above in space to draw near and see our place anew, but then we pull back to come back, enlightened: with Cole, McCann, and the later Pynchon (*Against the Day*), we uncover the world, rise to bask in the planet's aura above cities, above the horizon, so we can recover our humanness on the ground and in ways that may also reground us; with DeLillo's earlier "Human Moments in World War III" story, we ascend to our "orbital" stations to reconceptualize the big things, to de- and re-think them so we can "talk about small things, routine things";[73] with Lee's Hector (*The Surrendered*), we screen, from such intellectual altitudes, "tumultuous world history" for also small but intensely private moments;[74] we temporarily and tactically decouple so we can recouple, rejoin, regroup and "reunite," relate and endure in our relations. True, with McCann, we get reports that the "ontological glue" is thin up there. But this is why that is where we must walk first, alone on our tightropes, in our Skylabs, in our space suits, or, with Joseph McElroy's cyborg hero Imp Plus (*Plus*), in our hi-tech space bodies: so we can fight the gravity-like pull of trite notions and navel-gazing whims and walk the earth with others again, "feel" what it truly takes to be a couple, with the loved ones and family, but also with those who are not relatives, not from "around here" and yet related to us.[75]

As Houellebecq jokes in *The Map and the Territory*, the "satellite image" may not be God's viewpoint. To be sure, the reasons to doubt the picture's divine provenance abound.[76] Think only about how the world's spatial technology-enhanced visual availability has led to increased vulnerability to surveillance, control, space weaponization, and military "targeting."[77] Authors like O'Neill do want us to think about the world panopticon. So let us do this too. But they also push us to envisage a world *demotikón*, a world of multitudes. They prompt us to follow the dialectical ontology of the macro and micro all the way to its ethical end, where the world's face turns—and turns us as well—to the faces of those around us and to the problematic of care "in" or, better still, across "territory," to a responsibility idea and practice notionally and nationally reterritorialized, extended conceptually and physically to other spaces and people. This is where the geomethodology dramatized by planetary fiction should take us: to the point at which reading with the planet turns itself into reading *for* the planet and criticism into a "moral" enterprise, into planetary stewardship. "Decompressed" along these lines, *Netherland*'s final pages decline to work like Deleuzian-Guattarian uniformity-inducing, picture-"ruining," "bad"-infinity-keyed telescopy.[78] If they telescope the world, they do so in the term's opulent, fundamental amphibology. That is, they simultaneously condense and enlarge a world. They bring it closer and spread it out so we can contemplate its dazzling gallery of faces.

The romantic sublime of at-distance contemplation bounced the aloof gaze back to itself. This is what happens to Caspar David Friedrich's solitary hero in the 1818 canvas *Chalk Cliffs on Rügen*, and this is what Friedrich Nietzsche fancies we see as we stare into the famous abyss of *Beyond Good and Evil*: the depths reflecting our look straight back to us.[79] Instead, the planetary sublime is refractive rather than sterilely reflective. If the planetary gaze comes back to its origin, it does so ethically, not by reinforcing the self-same's epistemological cocoon through a scopically self-centered, repetitive pantomime, but through a detour. The "alternative" route is just that: an alternate trajectory optically and ethically, an itinerary across alterity that acknowledges others and their faces. It may start out in a telescopically distancing mode, as does one of the "Google scenes" in O'Neill's book, with the "satellite image" of the earth's a-semiotic crust, on which "a human movement is a barely intelligible thing . . . no signs of nations, no sense of the work of man."[80] Or it may begin, also in a classically telescopic fashion, up in a gondola of the befittingly named London Eye, where Hans, Jake, Rachel, and their German and Lithuanian companions—the world's ambassadors to Hans's private moment—climb higher and higher to the zenith so that once again the city and the world of humans with it "becom[e] . . . less recognizable." But the episode is part of an act that comprises a second scene, which the novel's ending both directs (builds, shapes theatrically) and directs *us* to it, "denudes" and places under the microscope for us.

Thematically and structurally, the stage for this scene is laid by another "telescopy," that of the human dramas stratified in the season's texture. "The English summer," writes O'Neill on the previous page, "is actually a Russian dolls of summers, the largest of which is the summer of unambiguous disaster in Iraq, which immediately contains the destruction of Lebanon, which itself holds a series of ever-smaller summers that led to the summer of Monty Panesar and, smallest perhaps, the summer of Wayne Rooney's foot."[81] And so, inside the Ferris Wheel ride lies, in other time and space, another (Staten Island) ferry ride, which Hans took with his mother one September evening years before. On the deck, after admiring the "world lighting up" in front of them as the Manhattan sunset was "concentrating" that "world" in the "lilac acres of two amazing high towers going up above all others," Hans and his mother instinctively turned their smiling faces to each other. Back on the Ferris following this quick flashback and after his capsule "reach[es] the top of our celestial circuit . . . to a point where [we] can see horizons previously unseen, and the old earth reveals itself," Hans "come[s] to face his family with the same smile" while "Lithuanian ladies" ask about London landmarks and Jake "befriends a six-year-old boy who speaks not a word of English."[82]

This instant is, as Deleuze and Guattari would probably call it, aesthetic in that it ultimately "create[s] the finite," the little situation, the tiniest "Russian doll" of human life, or the infinitesimal that "rediscovers," "restores," and shows off the "infinite."[83] Neither the infinite nor the infinitesimal is anterior/posterior or superior/inferior to the other, and, one more time, this non-hierarchical chronology and axiology is anything but the centerpiece of the local-global debate. "The town," the philosophers stress, "does not come after the house, nor does the cosmos after the territory. The universe does not come after the figure, and the figure is an aptitude of the universe."[84] They are telescoped inside each other, available—reluctantly perhaps—to our geomethodological microscopy. The figure figures a universe because there is a universe to be figured and figured out, and the universe itself is a figure, a representation and a face of many faces, all alongside one another and oftentimes all in one or in one place.

Let us be mindful of this because it sums up geomethodology's basic tenet, from which the decompressing technique of reading follows. It is the kind of distancing-cum-de-distancing technology Levinas welcomed in his "Heidegger, Gagarin, and Us" essay against Heidegger's apprehensions about the fast-growing human capabilities of "measuring and executing, for the purpose of gaining mastery over that which is as a whole."[85] As Michael Lang explains in a 2003 essay on Heidegger's "planetary discourse," for the German thinker the new, de-distancing technologies wind up supplanting human relationships. The only relationships left are technological or, in the more extreme, Pynchonian formulation from *Gravity's Rainbow*, *téchne*'s relation to itself. In the Heidegger-Harvey line of thought, Lang demonstrates, this de-distantiaton is tantamount to circumventing the human and its undergirding relatedness. Eventually, this leads to a "compression," congealing, and preordaining of everything in this world, including the material texture and the meanings of the post-Enlightenment West and of the whole globe with it, now seized mechanically and "totalistically" as a passive reflection ("globalization") of the Western model.[86] Not only does Heideggerian technology de-spatialize; it does so unethically. The resulting *Weltbild* globalizes the planet and its understandings.

What Levinas admires in the astronaut's "feat" is a completely different technology. This technology *spatializes* ethically. It "redistricts" place planetwide to help both the comfortably placed and the displaced to relate and come together in potentially countless ways. Less "dangerous than the spirits [*génies*] of the *Place*" that, throughout history, have placed so as to include, shelter, and help thrive, but also to exclude, control, and enslave by "splitting . . . humanity into native and strangers," this is a distancing technology liable to renew the earth as a common home. "What counts most of all, Levinas says, is that [Gagarin] left the Place," the Earth as Place. In Levinas's assessment, the Soviet cosmonaut rose "beyond any horizon" but only to open up new horizons, within which the planet's mystery, its many facets, and the faces and relations in which they are all necessarily entangled in the world at large and in the world's Kars and Riverlakes are reaffirmed and cared for rather than fatuously mastered.[87]

Or, perhaps a mastery of sorts is in play here, after all. It is the more subdued mastery of the mystery that fleetingly brushes our faces when we turn to the planet's face and to the countless faces glued together, mosaic-like, in neighborhoods, cantinas, and playgrounds, at bar mitzvahs, in Ferris wheel cabins, and in other little places. Advancing critically on the trail blazed by this technological breakthrough, geomethodology allows that this mystery, the enigma of the planet's others, may—and in effect must—persist as such, in plain sight and undefaced, protected by the very "nudity" of the face in which it comes forth. As Levinas never tires of reminding us, we are with those others in the world so that we ourselves can be. This is the core precept of his ethics-before-ontology argument and also the reason reading *with* the planet is or ought to be not only an analytical scenario but also a model of exemplary sociability. For, if we turn to the planet's face right, "with" follows suit, turning into "for."[88]

Notes

1. Mary Louise Pratt, "Planetary Longings: Sitting in the Light of the Great Solar TV," in *World Writing: Poetics, Ethics, Globalization*, ed. Mary Gallagher (Toronto: University of Toronto Press, 2008), 211.

2. Before providing the title of Frédéric Beigbeder's novel (Paris: Grasset, 2003), *Windows on the World* was a restaurant on the top floor of the North World Trade Center Tower. The English version of the French original came out in 2004 in Frank Wayne's translation (New York: Hyperion, 2004).

3. In his article "Spatializing Difference beyond Cosmopolitanism: Rethinking Planetary Futures" (*Theory, Culture & Society* 28, no. 5 [2011]), Tariq Jazeel relies on Denis Cosgrove's 2001 book *Apollo's Eye: A Cartographic Genealogy of the Earth in the Western Imagination* to claim that photos of the Earth such as those taken by Apollo 17 in 1972 attest to an "Apollonian gaze" (81), which, Jazeel would have us believe, betrays an imperial, culturecentric, and totalizing "reverie" redolent of cosmopolitanism's "one-worldist" thrust (87). As it turned out, NASA pictures are no different from those taken since the 1970s by hundreds of other space missions, shuttles, orbiting stations, and satellites belonging to a steadily growing number of countries, Western and non-Western. While the meaning of these images has shifted somewhat in the post–Cold War era, it would be safe to say that even back in the 1970s they meant and suggested much more than what Cosgrove and others thought or think they did. Equally reductive is Jazeel's grasp of cosmopolitanism. Finally, the scalar synergy of the macro and micro categories also plays out in the argument Wai Chee Dimock makes in her own *Planetary Turn* essay.

4. On the "event" as discontinuous and ambiguous occurrence, see Alain Badiou's *Handbook of Inaesthetics*, trans. Alberto Toscano (Stanford, Calif.: Stanford University Press, 2004), 118, 132.

5. Where "there is no expression," the face is "asleep," writes Michael Ondaatje in *The English Patient* (New York: Vintage, 1993), 28.

6. See, in this collection, Bertrand Westphal's essay "The White Globe and the Paradoxical Cartography of Berger & Berger: A Meditation on Deceptive Evidence."

7. Youri Lotman, *La sémiosphère*, trans. Anka Ledenko (Limoges, France: Presses Universitaires de Limoges, 1999), 9–20.

8. Gilles Deleuze and Claire Parnet, *Dialogues*, trans. Hugh Tomlinson and Barbara Habberjam (New York: Columbia University Press, 1987), 37.

9. Gilles Deleuze and Félix Guattari, *What Is Philosophy?* trans. Hugh Tomlinson and Graham Burchell (New York: Columbia University Press, 1994), 95.

10. Ibid., 41.

11. Ibid., 95.

12. Henri Lefebvre, *State, Space, World: Selected Essays*, ed. Neil Brenner and Stuart Elden, trans. Gerald Moore, Neil Brenner, and Stuart Elden (Minneapolis: University of Minnesota Press, 2009), 96.

13. Deleuze and Guattari, *What Is Philosophy?* 109.

14. Kostas Axelos, *Vers la pensée planétaire: Le devenir-pensée du monde et le devenir-monde de la pensée* (Paris: Minuit, 1984), 29–31.

15. Deleuze and Guattari, *What Is Philosophy?* 41.

16. In their essay on Deleuze and Guattari's "plan d'immanence" from *Le vocabulaire de Gilles Deleuze* edited by Robert Sasso and Arnaud Villani (Nice, France: Les Cahiers de *Noesis*, 2003), Maurice Élie and Arnaud Villani observe that "distinct from the *plane of reference*, which characterizes science, consists of 'actuals' [*actuels*], and gives up on the infinite, and also distinct from the *plane of consistence*, which characterizes art, consists of affects and percepts, and brings about the finite so as to regain the infinite, the *plane of immanence* consists of concepts and recovers the infinite [directly]" (272) (my translation).

17. On "multitude," see Antonio Negri, *Art and Multitude: Nine Letters on Art, Followed by Metamorphoses: Art and Immaterial Labour*, trans. Ed Emery (Cambridge, Eng.: Polity, 2011), 7, 75; on "Crowd," Badiou's *Handbook of Inaesthetics*, 31–32. See also Pico Iyer, *The Global Soul: Jet Lag, Shopping Malls, and the Search for Home* (New York: Random House, 2000) and "The Nowhere Man," *Prospect* 30, no. 3 (February 1997): 30–33; and Alexandar Hemon's novel *Nowhere Man* (New York: Random House, 2002). Also, as pointed out in the introduction to this collection, Masao Miyoshi was among the first to draw attention to, but also to argue for, a turn *to* the planet in a sense that he determined as enabling culturally, politically, and otherwise. On this topic, see, one more time, his article "Turn to the Planet: Literature, Diversity, and Totality," in *Comparative Literature* 53, no. 4 (Fall 2001): 283–97.

18. Bertrand Westphal, *Le monde plausible: Espace, lieu, carte* (Paris: Minuit, 2011), 12–15.

19. On postmodernism's "spatial imagination," see also Julian Murphet, "Postmodernism and Space," in *The Cambridge Companion to Postmodernism*, ed. Steven Connor (Cambridge, Eng.: Cambridge University Press, 2004), 116–35.

20. On "lococentrism," see the "Place" chapter in Lawrence Buell's *The Environmental Imagination: Thoreau, Nature Writing, and the Formation of American Culture* (Cambridge, Mass.: Belknap Press of Harvard University Press, 1995), 252–79.

21. "Out is over," variously proclaims, among others, Thomas L. Friedman in *Longitudes and Attitudes: Exploring the World after September 11* (New York: Farrar, Straus and Giroux, 2002), 22, and elsewhere in his books. On the disappearance of the planet's traditional "hiding places," see David Hollinger, *Cosmopolitanism and Solidarity: Studies in Ethnoracial, Religious, and Professional Affiliation in the United States* (Madison: University of Wisconsin Press, 2006), xxii.

22. Christian Moraru, *Cosmodernism: American Narrative, Late Globalization, and the New Cultural Imaginary* (Ann Arbor: University of Michigan Press, 2011), 2.

23. Ibid., 307–16.

24. Martin Heidegger, *Being and Time*, trans. Joan Stambaugh (Albany, N.Y.: SUNY Press, 1996), 97.

25. For the evolving meaning of "world" as verb (*welten*) in Heidegger, with particular emphasis on the philosopher's early work, see Françoise Dastur, "Heidegger's Freiburg Version of the Origin of the Work of Art," in *Heidegger toward the Turn: Essays on the Work of the 1930s*, ed. James Risser (Albany, N.Y.: SUNY Press, 1999), 129, 140.

26. Martin Heidegger, *The Question concerning Technology and Other Essays*, trans. and with an introduction by William Lovitt (New York: Garland, 1977), 129.

27. Lefebvre, *State, Space, World*, 196.

28. Ulrich Beck, "Toward a New Critical Theory with a Cosmopolitan Intent," *Constellations* 10, no. 4 (2003): 453.

29. Heidegger, *The Question concerning Technology*, 135.

30. Gayatri Chakravorty Spivak, *Death of a Discipline* (New York: Columbia University Press, 2003), 72.

31. Ibid., 30, 72.

32. Heidegger, *The Question concerning Technology*, 135.

33. Spivak, *Death of a Discipline*, 82, 92. On the local-global "theoretical stalemate," see Ursula K. Heise's groundbreaking *Sense of Place and Sense of Planet: The Environmental Imagination of the Planet* (Oxford: Oxford University Press, 2008), 7–13. Heise's "eco-cosmopolitan" solution to the impasse is to look, in contemporary culture and thinking, for "ways of imagining the global that frame localism from a globalist environmental perspective" (9). While sticking to my stronger distinctions between the global and the planetary, I am sympathetic to the critic's attempt to salvage at least some of the global paradigm's terminology and content. I also second her plea "for an increased emphasis on a sense of planet" (59). A major contribution to ecocriticism, Heise's argument reads, repeatedly and proficiently, local manifestations of culture against the backdrop of the global scenarios in which they are "imbricated" (59). At least during its initial stages, the cultural telescopy on which my own argument rests tends to do the opposite by X-raying the local for planetary "engravings."

34. See Pascale Casanova, *The World Republic of Letters*, trans. M. B. DeBevoise (Cambridge, Mass.: Harvard University Press, 2004).

35. On "distant reading" and its problematic procedure, see Franco Moretti, "Conjectures on World Literature," *New Left Review* 1 (January-February 2000): 56–58.

36. Moretti also makes his rather unpersuasive and, to my mind, unnecessary case against close reading in "Conjectures on World Literature," 57. N. Katherine Hayles has recently argued, in a different context, for an integration of close and distant reading into a synthetic model apropos of Foer's experimentalism ("Combining Close and Distant Reading: Jonathan Safran Foer's *Tree of Codes* and the Aesthetic of Bookishness," *PMLA* 128, no. 1 [January 2013]: 226–31).

37. On the relationality of place and the need to "work through" the latter, see Jazeel, "Spatializing Difference beyond Cosmopolitanism," 92. On the "Enlightenment project" in terms of time, space, and their "collapse," see David Harvey, *The Condition of Postmodernity: An Inquiry into the Origins of Cultural Change* (Cambridge, Mass.: Blackwell, 1990), 240–59.

38. On distant kinship, see Wai Chee Dimock, *Through Other Continents: American Literature across Deep Time* (Princeton, N.J.: Princeton University Press, 2009), 144–45.

39. Westphal uses the phrase "world reading" (*lecture du monde*) in *Le monde plausible*, 15.

40. George Konrád, *Antipolitics: An Essay*, trans. from the Hungarian by Richard E. Allen (San Diego, Calif.: Harcourt Brace Jovanovich, 1984), 179.

41. Mircea Cărtărescu, "Realismul poeziei tinere" ("Young Poets' Realism"), in *Competiția continuă: Generația 80 in texte teoretice* (*The Race Goes On: Theoretical Texts on the 1980s Generation*), ed. Gheorghe Crăciun, 183 (Pitești, Romania: Editura Vlasie, 1994).

42. Mircea Cărtărescu, *Totul* (*All*) (Bucharest: Cartea Românească, 1985).

43. *Visul* (Bucharest: Cartea Românească, 1989) was republished in complete form in 1993 (Bucharest: Humanitas) and has been translated into a number of languages. For the English version, see *Nostalgia*, trans., with an afterword, from the Romanian by Julian Semilian, introduction by Andrei Codrescu (New York: New Directions, 2005). Later prose works such as novels like *Travesti* (*Disguise*) (Bucharest: Humanitas, 1994), the *Orbitor* (*Blinding*) three-volume series (Bucharest: Humanitas, 1996–2007), and the short pieces gathered in the best seller *De ce iubim femeile* (*Why We Love Women*) (Bucharest: Humanitas, 2005) detail *Nostalgia*'s description of Bucharest.

44. *Állos* (masculine plural *álloi*) is "another" in Ancient Greek. It may designate either another *like* the self (by and large an other of the same sort) or an other *to* this self, in which case its meaning is closer to *héteros*. "The other of two," the latter marks the other's otherness more emphatically. In Latin, *alius* and *alter* enact roughly the same distinction. While unquestionably significant, the difference between *állos* and *héteros* is not instrumental to my argument.

45. On the spatial ethics of taking place and the *ek-static* outside, see Giorgio Agamben, *The Coming Community*, trans. Michael Hardt (Minneapolis: University of Minnesota Press, 2009), 13–15, 23–25, and 67–68.

46. Edward W. Soja, *Postmodern Geographies: The Reassertion of Space in Critical Social Theory* (New York: Verso, 1989), 131–37.

47. Jorge Luis Borges, "The Aleph," in *Collected Fictions*, trans. Andrew Hurley (New York: Penguin, 1999), 280.

48. On the Zahir as "an unbearable symbol of the infinite, painful circularity, an[d] obsessive counterpart of the elusive Aleph," see Matei Calinescu's *Rereading* (New Haven, Conn.: Yale University Press, 1993), 12, 11–16.

49. On Borges, the Aleph, the Kabbalah, and Judaic tradition in general, see Jaime Alazraki, *Borges and the Kabbalah and Other Essays on His Fiction and Poetry* (New York: Cambridge University Press, 1988); Edna Aizenberg, *The Aleph Weaver: Biblical, Kabbalistic and Judaic Elements in Borges* (Potomac, Md.: Scripta Humanistica, 1984). In Edna Aizenberg, ed., *Borges and His Successors: The Borgesian Impact on Literature and the Arts* (Columbia, Mo.: University of Missouri Press, 1990), see especially its fifth section, "Hebraism and Poetic Influence," 249–84, which features two lectures by Borges on the Book of Job and Spinoza, respectively. Worth mentioning is also Evelyn Fishburn's article "Reflections on the Jewish Imaginary in the Fictions of Borges," in *Variaciones Borges: Journal of the Jorge Luis Borges Center for Studies and Documentation* 5 (1998): 145–56. On Borges's own thoughts on the Kabbalah, see "The Kabbalah," in *Seven Nights*, trans. Eliot Weinberger, introduction by Alasdair Reid (New York: New Directions, 1984), 99.

50. Soja, *Postmodern Geographies*, 223.

51. Edward W. Soja, *Thirdspace: Journeys to Los Angeles and Other Real-and-Imagined Places* (Cambridge, Mass.: Blackwell, 1996), 54–57.

52. Soja, *Postmodern Geographies*, 222–23.

53. "Shall I project a world?" asks Pynchon's Oedipa Maas in *The Crying of Lot 49* (New York: HarperCollins, 1999), 64.

54. Jazeel, "Spatializing Difference beyond Cosmopolitanism," 92.

55. David Hollinger, *Cosmopolitanism and Solidarity*, 73, 36.

56. Orhan Pamuk, *Snow*, translated from the Turkish by Maureen Freely (New York: Vintage, 2005), 306.

57. Ibid., 306–7.

58. See Ka's cosmic "snowflake" in Pamuk, *Snow*, 283.

59. I thank Jeffrey J. Williams and John McGowan for pointing out to me the divergent readings to which O'Neill's *Netherland* lends itself. Williams touches on this issue briefly in his article "The Plutocratic Imagination," which came out in *Dissent* (Winter 2013), http://www.-dissentmagazine.org/article/the-plutocratic-imagination.

60. O'Neill has also broached the unapparent and multiple relevance of the game in his review of C. L. R. James's 1963 cricket book *Beyond a Boundary*, "Bowling Alone," published in *The Atlantic Monthly* on September 11, 2007, http://www.powells.com/review/2007_09_11. I thank John Protevi for mentioning O'Neill's piece to me.

61. Joseph O'Neill, *Netherland* (New York: Vintage, 2009), 12.

62. Ian McEwan, *Saturday* (New York: Random House, 2005), 35.

63. O'Neill, *Netherland*, 80.

64. Ibid., 211.

65. Ibid.

66. Ibid., 210.

67. Deleuze and Guattari, *What Is Philosophy?* 17.

68. O'Neill, *Netherland*, 10–11.

69. Ibid., 120–21.

70. Jean-Luc Nancy, *Verité de la démocratie* (Paris: Galilée, 2008), 30–32.

71. O'Neill, *Netherland*, 10. My comments on this place in *Netherland* also allude to Heise's *Sense of Place and Sense of Planet*.

72. O'Neill, 15.

73. Don DeLillo, *The Angel Esmeralda: Nine Stories* (New York: Scribner, 2011), 25, 29.

74. Chang-rae Lee, *The Surrendered* (New York: Riverhead, 2010), 102.

75. Colum McCann, *Let the Great World Spin* (New York: Random House, 2009), 325.

76. Michel Houellebecq, *The Map and the Territory* (New York: Knopf, 2012), 46–47.

77. Rey Chow, *The Age of World Target: Self-Referentiality in War, Theory, and Comparative Work* (Durham, N.C.: Duke University Press, 2006), 31, 41.

78. Deleuze and Guattari, *What Is Philosophy?* 189.

79. Friedrich Nietzsche, *Beyond Good and Evil: Prelude to a Philosophy*, trans. R. J. Hollingdale, with an introduction by Michael Tanner (London: Penguin, 1990), 102.

80. O'Neill, *Netherland*, 252.

81. Ibid., 252–53.

82. Ibid., 254–56.

83. Deleuze and Guattari, *What Is Philosophy?* 197.

84. Ibid., 196.

85. Heidegger, *The Question concerning Technology and Other Essays*, 132.

86. Michael Lang, "Mapping Globalization or Globalizing the Map?: Heidegger and Planetary Discourse," *Genre* 36 (Fall/Winter 2003): 239–44.

87. Emmanuel Levinas, *Difficult Freedom: Essays on Judaism*, trans. Seán Hand (Baltimore: Johns Hopkins University Press, 1990), 233–34. On the complex interplay of the Levinasian face and technology, see the entire issue of *Transformations*, no. 18 (2010).

88. On relational art as a "model of sociability," see Nicholas Bourriaud, *Relational Aesthetics* (Dijon, France: Les Presses du réel; New York: Idea Books, 2002), 109.

BIBLIOGRAPHY

Adamson, Joni. "American Literature and Film from a Planetary Perspective: Teaching Space, Time, and Scale." *Transformations* 21, no. 1 (2010): 23–41.

Agamben, Giorgio. *The Coming Community*. Translated by Michael Hardt. Minneapolis: University of Minnesota Press, 2009.

Ahmed, Sara. *Queer Phenomenology: Orientations, Objects, Others*. Durham, N.C.: Duke University Press, 2006.

Aizenberg, Edna. *The Aleph Weaver: Biblical, Kabbalistic and Judaic Elements in Borges*. Potomac, Md.: Scripta Humanistica, 1984.

———, ed. *Borges and His Successors: The Borgesian Impact on Literature and the Arts*. Columbia: University of Missouri Press, 1990.

Alazraki, Jaime. *Borges and the Kabbalah and Other Essays on His Fiction and Poetry*. Cambridge, Eng.: Cambridge University Press, 1988.

Albrow, Martin. *The Global Age: State and Society beyond Modernity*. Stanford, Calif.: Stanford University Press, 1997.

———. "Who Rules the Global Rule Makers?" *La Vie des idées* (November 3, 2011). Available in English at mirror site "Books and Ideas," http://www.booksandideas.net/Who-Rules-the-Global-Rule-Makers.html.

Amin, Samir. *Re-Reading the Postwar Period*. New York: Monthly Review, 1994.

Anderson, Amanda. "Cosmopolitanism, Universalism, and the Divided Legacies of Modernity." In *Cosmopolitics; Thinking and Feeling beyond the Nation*, edited by Pheng Cheah and Bruce Robbins, 265–89. Minneapolis: University of Minnesota Press, 1998.

Anderson, Chris. *The Long Tail: Why the Future of Business Is Selling Less of More*. New York: Hyperion, 2006.

Appadurai, Arjun. "Patriotism and Its Futures." *Public Culture* 5 (1993): 411–29.

Appiah, Kwame Anthony. *Cosmopolitanism: Ethics in a World of Strangers*. New York: W. W. Norton, 2006.

Apter, Emily. *The Translation Zone: A New Comparative Literature*. Princeton, N.J.: Princeton University Press, 2006.

———. "Untranslatables: A World System." *New Literary History* 39, no. 3 (2008): 581–98.

Arac, Jonathan. *The Emergence of American Literary Narrative, 1820–1860*. Cambridge, Mass.: Harvard University Press, 2005.

Aravamudan, Srinivas. *Enlightenment Orientalism: Resisting the Rise of the Novel*. Chicago: University of Chicago Press, 2012.

Aristotle. *Poetics*. Translated by Gerald F. Else. Ann Arbor: University of Michigan Press, 1970.

Arrighi, Giovanni. *The Long Twentieth Century: Money, Power, and the Origins of Our Times*. London: Verso, 1994.

Ashford, Nicholas A., and Ralph P. Hall. *Technology, Globalization, and Sustainable Development: Transforming the Industrial State*. New Haven, Conn.: Yale University Press, 2011.

Auerbach, Erich. "Philology and *Weltliteratur*." Translated by Maire Said and Edward Said. *Centennial Review* 13, no. 1 (1969): 1–17.

Authers, Ben. "'I'm Not Australian, I'm Not Greek, I'm Not Anything': Identity and the Multicultural Nation in Christos Tsiolkas's *Loaded*." *Journal of the Association for the Study of Australian Literature* 4 (2005): 133–45.

Axelos, Kostas. *Vers la pensée planétaire: Le devenir-pensée du monde et le devenir-monde de la pensée*. Paris: Minuit, 1984.

Axtell, Robert L. "The Emergence and Evolution of Institutions of Self-Governance on the Commons." Working Paper, Department of Computational Social Science, George Mason University, Fairfax, Va., 2013.

Badiou, Alain. *Ethics: An Essay on the Understanding of Evil*. Translated by Peter Hallward. London: Verso, 2001.

———. *Handbook of Inaesthetics*. Translated by Alberto Toscano. Stanford, Calif.: Stanford University Press, 2004.

———. *St. Paul: The Foundation of Universalism*. Translated by Ray Brassier. Stanford, Calif.: Stanford University Press, 2003.

Bakhtin, Mikhail. *The Dialogic Imagination: Four Essays*. Edited by Michael Holquist. Translated by Caryl Emerson and Michael Holquist. Austin: University of Texas Press, 1981.

Balibar, Etienne. "Ambiguous Universality." *differences* 7, no. 1 (1995): 48–74.

Bauman, Zygmunt. *Globalization: The Human Consequences*. New York: Columbia University Press, 1998.

———. *Liquid Modernity*. Cambridge, Eng.: Polity, 2000.

BBC News Technology. "Sweden Tops Tim Berners-Lee's Web Index." September 5, 2012, http://www.bbc.co.uk/news/technology-19478298.

Beck, Ulrich. "Toward a New Critical Theory with a Cosmopolitan Intent." *Constellations* 10, no. 4 (2003): 453–68.

———. *What Is Globalization*? Translated by Patrick Camiller. Cambridge, Eng.: Polity, 2000.

———. *World Risk Society*. Cambridge, Eng.: Polity, 1999.

Beck, Ulrich, and Edgar Grande. "Varieties of Second Modernity: The Cosmopolitan Turn in Social and Political Theory and Research." *British Journal of Sociology* 61, no. 3 (2010): 409–43.

Beigbeder, Frédéric. *Windows on the World*. Paris: Grasset, 2003. Trans. Frank Wayne. New York: Hyperion, 2004.

Beilharz, Peter. *Imagining the Antipodes: Culture, Theory and the Visual in the Work of Bernard Smith*. Cambridge, Eng.: Cambridge University Press, 1997.

Belting, Hans, and Andrea Buddenseig, eds. *The Global Art World: Audiences, Markets and Museums*. Ostfildern, Ger.: Hatje Cantz, 2009.

Benhabib, Seyla. *Another Cosmopolitanism*. New York: Oxford University Press, 2008.

———. *Situating the Self: Gender, Community and Postmodernism in Contemporary Ethics*. New York: Routledge, 1992.

Berger, Laurent P., and Cyrille Berger. *Altered States*. ROSASCAPE*, Paris, October 7–November 24, 2011. Exhibition archives online at http://www.rosascape.com/site/expo-bergerberger2011-us.html.

———. Berger & Berger. Artists' website. http://www.berger-berger.com.

Bergermann, Ulrike, Isabell Otto, and Gabriele Schabacher, eds. *Das Planetarische. Kultur—Technik—Medien im postglobalen Zeitalter.* Munich: Wilhelm Fink, 2010.

Berlant, Lauren. *The Anatomy of National Fantasy: Hawthorne, Utopia, and Everyday Life.* Chicago: University of Chicago Press, 1991.

———. *Cruel Optimism.* Durham, N.C.: Duke University Press, 2011.

———. "Intuitionists: History and the Affective Event." *American Literary History* 20, no. 4 (2008): 845–60.

———. "A Properly Political Concept of Love: Three Approaches in Ten Pages." *Cultural Anthropology* 26, no. 4 (2011): 683–91.

Bernstein, David W. Introduction to *Writings through John Cage's Music, Poetry, and Art,* edited by David W. Bernstein and Christopher Hatch, 1–6. Chicago: University of Chicago Press, 2001.

Bhabha, Homi K. "DissemiNation: Time, Narrative, and the Margins of the Modern Nation." In *Nation and Narration,* edited by Homi K. Bhabha, 291–322. London: Routledge, 1990.

———. "Introduction: Narrating the Nation." In *Nation and Narration,* edited by Homi K. Bhabha, 1–7. London: Routledge, 1990.

———. *The Location of Culture.* London: Routledge, 1994.

Bisley, Nick. *Rethinking Globalization.* New York: Palgrave Macmillan, 2007.

Bleicher, Thomas. "Novalis und die Idee der Weltliteratur." *Arcadia* 14, no. 3 (1979): 254–70.

Blum, Hester. "John Cleves Symmes and the Planetary Reach of Polar Exploration." *American Literature* 84, no. 2 (2012): 243–71.

———. "The Prospect of Oceanic Studies." *PMLA* 125, no. 3 (2010): 670–77.

Bollier, David. *Viral Spiral: How the Commoners Built a Digital Republic of Their Own.* New York: New, 2008.

Borges, Jorge Luis. *Collected Fictions.* Translated by Andrew Hurley. New York: Penguin, 1999.

———. *Seven Nights.* Translated by Eliot Weinberger. Introduction by Alasdair Reid. New York: New Directions, 1984.

Bourriaud, Nicolas. *The Radicant.* Translated by James Gussen and Lili Porten. New York: Lukas and Sternberg, 2009.

———. *Relational Aesthetics.* Dijon, France: Les Presses du réel; New York: Idea Books, 2002.

Boyle, James. *The Public Domain: Enclosing the Commons of the Mind.* New Haven, Conn.: Yale University Press, 2008.

———. "The Second Enclosure Movement and the Construction of the Public Domain." *Law and Contemporary Problems* 66, no. 33 (Winter/Spring 2003): 33–74.

Boym, Svetlana. *The Future of Nostalgia.* New York: Basic Books, 2001.

Braidotti, Rosi. *The Posthuman.* Cambridge, Eng.: Polity, 2013.

Brennan, Teresa. *The Transmission of Affect.* Ithaca, N.Y.: Cornell University Press, 2004.

Brennan, Timothy. *At Home in the World: Cosmopolitanism Now.* Cambridge, Mass.: Harvard University Press, 1997.

Brooks, Neil, and Josh Toth, eds. *The Mourning After: Attending the Wake of Postmodernism.* Amsterdam: Rodopi, 2007.

Brown, Marshall. "Globalism or Globalization?" *Modern Language Quarterly* 68, no. 2 (2007): 137–43.

Buck, Susan J. *The Global Commons: An Introduction*. Washington, D.C.: Island, 1998.

Buell, Lawrence. *The Environmental Imagination: Thoreau, Nature Writing, and the Formation of American Culture*. Cambridge, Mass.: Belknap Press of Harvard University Press, 1995.

Butler, Judith. "For a Careful Reading." In *Feminist Contentions: A Philosophical Exchange*, edited by Linda Nicholson, 35–58. New York: Routledge, 1995.

Butler, Judith, and Athena Athanasiou. *Dispossession: The Performative in the Political*. Cambridge, Eng.: Polity, 2013.

Butler, Judith, Ernesto Leclau, and Slavoj Žižek. *Contingency, Hegemony, Universality: Contemporary Dialogues on the Left*. New York: Verso, 2000.

Butler, Judith, and Gayatri Chakravorty Spivak. "A Dialogue on Global States, 6 May 2006." *Postmodern Culture* 17, no. 1 (2006).

Calinescu, Matei. *Rereading*. New Haven, Conn.: Yale University Press, 1993.

Callinicos, Alex, ed. "Europe on the Edge." Special issue, *International Socialism* 63 (1994).

Calvino, Italo. *If on a Winter's Night a Traveler*. Translated by William Weaver. 1980. Reprint, New York: Everyman's Library, 1993.

Cărtărescu, Mircea. *De ce iubim femeile*. Bucharest: Humanitas, 2005.

———. *Nostalgia*. Translated by Julian Semilian. Introduction by Andrei Codrescu. New York: New Directions, 2005.

———. *Orbitor*. 3 vols. Bucharest: Humanitas, 1996–2007.

———. "Realismul poeziei tinere" ("Young Poets' Realism"). In *Competiția continuă: Generația 80 in texte teoretice* (*The Race Goes On: Theoretical Texts on the 1980s Generation*), edited by Gheorghe Crăciun, 183. Pitești, România: Editura Vlasie, 1994.

———. *Totul*. Bucharest: Cartea Românească, 1985.

———. *Travesti*. Bucharest: Humanitas, 1994.

———. *Visul*. Bucharest: Cartea Românească, 1989. Republished Bucharest: Humanitas, 1993.

Casanova, Pascale. *The World Republic of Letters*. Translated by M. B. DeBevoise. Cambridge, Mass.: Harvard University Press, 2004.

Castells, Manuel. *The Rise of the Network Society*. Vol. 1, *The Information Age: Economy, Society, and Culture*. Oxford, Eng.: Blackwell, 1996.

———. *The Power of Identity*. Vol. 2, *The Information Age: Economy, Society, and Culture*. 2nd ed. Hoboken, N.J.: Wiley-Blackwell, 2009.

———. *End of Millennium*. Vol. 3, *The Information Age: Economy, Society, and Culture*. Hoboken, N.J.: Wiley-Blackwell, 1998.

Chakrabarty, Dipesh. "Postcolonial Studies and the Challenge of Climate Change." *New Literary History* 43, no. 1 (2012): 1–18.

Chaunu, Pierre. *Histoire, science sociale: La dureé, l'espace et l'homme à l'époque moderne*. Paris: Société d'édition d'enseignement supérieur, 1974.

Cheah, Pheng, and Bruce Robbins, eds. *Cosmopolitics: Thinking and Feeling Beyond the Nation*. Minneapolis: University of Minnesota Press, 1998.

Chesterton, Gilbert Keith. *The Collected Poems of G. K. Chesterton*. Edited by Gilbert Keith. New York: Dodd, Mead, 1932.

Chocolat. Film. Directed by Claire Denis. 1988. Distributed by Impuls and Orion Classics.

Chow, Rey. *The Age of World Target: Self-Referentiality in War, Theory, and Comparative Work*. Durham, N.C.: Duke University Press, 2006.

Christian, David. "History and Time." *Australian Journal of Politics and History* 57, no. 3 (2011): 353–65.

———. *Maps of Time: An Introduction to Big History*. Berkeley: University of California Press, 2004.

Clifford, James. "Traveling Cultures." In *Cultural Studies*, edited by Larry Grossberg, Cary Nelson, and Paula A. Treichler, 96–116. New York: Routledge, 1992.

Cochrane, Allan, and Kathy Pain. "Chapter 1: A Globalizing Society?" In *A Globalizing World? Culture, Economics, Politics*, edited by David Held, 5–46. New York: Routledge in association with the Open University, 2000.

Connery, Christopher L. "Ideologies of Land and Sea: Alfred Thayer Mahan, Carl Schmitt, and the Shaping of Global Myth Elements." *boundary* 2 28, no. 2 (2001): 173–201.

———. "Pacific Rim Discourse: The U.S. Global Imaginary in the Late Cold War Years." *boundary* 2 21, no. 1 (1994): 30–56.

Coupland, Douglas. "Convergences." Review of *Gods without Men*, by Hari Kunzru. *New York Times*, March 8, 2012. Sunday Book Review. http://www.nytimes.com/2012/03/11/books/review/gods-without-men-by-hari-kunzru.html?pagewanted=all.

Dagan, Hanoch, and Michael A. Heller. "The Liberal Commons." *Yale Law Journal* 110, no. 4 (2001): 549–623.

Dahan-Gaida, Laurence, ed. "Numéro special Géocritique." Special issue, *Epistémocritique* 9 (Fall 2011). http://www.epistemocritique.org/spip.php?rubrique60&lang=fr.

Damasio, Antonio R. *The Feeling of What Happens: Body and Emotion in the Making of Consciousness*. New York: Harcourt Brace, 1999.

Damrosch, David. *The Buried Book: The Loss and Rediscovery of the Great Epic of Gilgamesh*. New York: Henry Holt, 2007.

———. *What Is World Literature?* Princeton, N.J.: Princeton University Press, 2003.

"Darmok," *Star Trek: The Next Generation*, season 5, episode 2, aired September 30, 1991.

Darrieussecq, Marie. *White*. Paris: P.O.L., 2003.

Dastur, Françoise. "Heidegger's Freiburg Version of the Origin of the Work of Art." In *Heidegger toward the Turn: Essays on the Work of the 1930s*, edited by James Risser, 119–44. Albany, N.Y.: State University of New York Press, 1999.

Davis, Heather, and Paige Sarlin. "'On the Risk of a New Relationality': An Interview with Lauren Berlant and Michael Hardt." *Reviews in Cultural Theory* (2008): 7–27.

Debray, Régis. *Éloge des frontiers*. Paris: Gallimard, 2010.

———. "Socialism and Print." *New Left Review*, no. 46 (2007): 5–28.

———. "The Three Ages of Looking." Translated by Eric Rauth. *Critical Inquiry* 21, no. 3 (1995): 529–55.

———. *Transmitting Culture*. Translated by Eric Rauth. New York: Columbia University Press, 2000.

———. *Vie et mort de l'image: Une histoire du regard en Occident*. Paris: Gallimard, 1992.

Deleuze, Gilles. *Cinema 2: The Time-Image*. Translated by Hugh Tomlinson and Robert Galeta. Minneapolis: University of Minnesota Press, 1989.

Deleuze, Gilles, and Claire Parnet. *Dialogues*. Translated by Hugh Tomlinson and Barbara Habberjam. New York: Columbia University Press, 1977.

———. *Dialogues II*. Translated by Hugh Tomlinson and Barbara Habberjam. Revised edition. New York: Columbia University Press, 2007.

Deleuze, Gilles, and Félix Guattari. *Capitalisme et schizophrenie 2. Mille Plateaux*. Paris: Minuit, 1980.

———. *A Thousand Plateaus: Capitalism and Schizophrenia*. Translated by Brian Massumi. Minneapolis: University of Minnesota Press, 1987.

———. *What Is Philosophy?* Translated by Hugh Tomlinson and Graham Burchell. New York: Columbia University Press, 1994.

Del Giudice, Daniel. *Orizzonte mobile*. Turin: Einaudi, 2009.

DeLillo, Don. *The Angel Esmeralda: Nine Stories*. New York: Scribner, 2011.

Denby, David. "The New Disorder: Adventures in Film Narrative." *The New Yorker*, March 5, 2007, 80–85. http://www.newyorker.com/arts/critics/atlarge/2007/03/05/070305crat_atlarge_denby.

Derrida, Jacques. *The Politics of Friendship*. Translated by George Collins. New York: Verso, 1997.

———. *Specters of Marx: The State of the Debt, The Work of Mourning & the New International*. Translated by Peggy Kamuf. London: Routledge, 1994.

Devlin-Glass, Francis. "Review Essay: Alexis Wright's *Carpentaria*." Review of *Carpenteria*, by Alexis Wright. *Antipodes* 21, no. 1 (2007): 82–84.

Dharwadker, Vinay, ed. *Cosmopolitan Geographies: New Locations in Literature and Culture*. New York: Routledge, 2001.

Dibble, Julian. "A Rape in Cyberspace: How an Evil Clown, a Haitian Trickster Spirit, Two Wizards, and a Cast of Dozens Turned a Database into a Society." *Village Voice*, December 23, 1993. http://www.villagevoice.com/2005-10-18/specials/a-rape-in-cyberspace/full/.

Dimock, Wai Chee. *Empire for Liberty: Melville and the Poetics of Individualism*. Princeton, N.J.: Princeton University Press, 1989.

———. "Gilgamesh on Three Continents." Paper presented at "Scenes of Reading: Is Australian Literature a World Literature?" University of Sydney, May 25, 2012.

———. "Introduction: Planet and America, Set and Subset." In *Shades of the Planet: American Literature as World Literature*, edited by Wai Chee Dimock and Lawrence Buell, 1–16. Princeton, N.J.: Princeton University Press, 2007.

———. "Literature for the Planet." *PMLA* 116, no. 1 (2001): 173–88.

———. "Planetary Time and Global Translation: 'Context' in Literary Studies." *Common Knowledge* 9, no. 3 (2003): 488–507.

_____. "Recycling the Epic: Gilgamesh on Three Continents." In *Scenes of Reading: Is Australian Literature a World Literature?*. Edited by Robert Dixon and Brigid Rooney, 3–15. Melbourne, Australia: Australian Scholarly Publishing, 2013.

———. "Scales of Aggregation: Prenational, Subnational, Transnational." *American Literary History* 18, no. 2 (2006): 219–28.

———. *Through Other Continents: American Literature across Deep Time*. Princeton, N.J.: Princeton University Press, 2006.

Dimock, Wai Chee, and Lawrence Buell, eds. *Shades of the Planet: American Literature as World Literature*. Princeton, N.J.: Princeton University Press, 2007.

Dixon, Robert. "Tim Winton, *Cloudstreet*, and the Field of Australian Literature." *Westerly* 50 (November 2005): 245–60.

Donne, John. *Poems of John Donne*. Edited by E. K. Chambers. London: Lawrence and Bullen, 1896.

Dortch, Marlene H. "Federal Communications Commission." FCC 05–151, September 25, 2005. http://hraunfoss.fcc.gov/edocs_public/attachmatch/FCC-05-151A1.pdf.

Dove, Michael R. "Indigenous People and Environmental Politics." *Annual Review of Anthropology* 35 (October 2006): 191–208.

Durand, Gilbert. *Les structures anthropologiques de l'imaginaire*. 1960. Reprint, Paris: Dunod, 1992.

Dussel, Enrique. "Beyond Eurocentrism: The World-System and the Limits of Modernity." In *The Cultures of Globalization*, edited by Fredric Jameson and Masao Miyoshi, 3–31. Durham, N.C.: Duke University Press, 1998.

Earl, Jennifer, and Katrina Kimport. *Digitally Enabled Social Change: Activism in the Internet Age*. Cambridge, Mass.: MIT Press, 2011.

Echenoz, Jean. *Je m'en vais*. Paris: Minuit, 1999.

Edson, Laurie. *Reading Relationally: Postmodern Perspectives on Literature and Art*. Ann Arbor: University of Michigan Press, 2000.

Eisenstein, Zillah. *Empire: Feminisms, Racism, and the West*. New York: Zed Books, 2004.

Elias, Amy J. "The Dialogical Avant-Garde: Relational Aesthetics and Time Ecologies in *Only Revolutions* and *TOC*." *Contemporary Literature* 53, no. 4 (2012): 738–78.

———. "Interactive Cosmopolitanism and Collaborative Technologies: New Foundations for Global Literary History." *New Literary History* 39, no. 3 (2008): 705–25.

Elias, Norbert. *Time: An Essay*. Oxford: Oxford University Press, 1992.

Élie, Maurice, and Arnaud Villani. *Le vocabulaire de Gilles Deleuze*. Edited by Robert Sasso and Arnaud Villani. Nice, France: Les Cahiers de Noesis, 2003.

Elster, Ernst. "Weltlitteratur und Litteraturvergleichung." *Archiv für das Studium der neueren Sprachen und Litteraturen* 107 (1901): 33–47.

Éluard, Paul. *Love, Poetry: L'Amour la poesie*. Translated by Stuart Kendall. Boston: Black Widow Press of Commonwealth Books, 2007.

Engber, Daniel. "Starry Blight: How a Bunch of Peasants in Mesopotamia Ruined the Night Sky." *Slate*, July 12, 2012. http://www.slate.com/articles/health_and_science/a_fine_whine/2012/07/against_constellations_why_are_we_stuck_with_bronze_age_graffiti_.html.

Eshelman, Raoul. *Performatism, or the End of Postmodernism*. Aurora, Colo.: Davies Group, 2008.

———. "Transcendence and the Aesthetics of Disability: The Case of *The Curious Incident of the Dog in the Night-Time*." *Anthropoetics* 15, no. 1 (2009). http://www.anthropoetics.ucla.edu/ap1501/1501eshelman.htm.

Ferguson, Frances. "Planetary Literary History: The Place of the Text." *New Literary History* 39, no. 3 (2008): 657–84.

Fishburn, Evelyn. "Reflections on the Jewish Imaginary in the Fictions of Borges." *Variaciones Borges: Journal of the Jorge Luis Borges Center for Studies and Documentation* 5 (1998): 145–56.

Foster, Hal, ed. *Vision and Visuality*. Seattle: Bay, 1988.

Foucault, Michel. *Language, Counter-Memory, Practice: Selected Essays and Interviews*. Edited by Donald F. Bouchard. Translated by Donald F. Bouchard and Sherry Simon. Ithaca, N.Y.: Cornell University Press, 1977.

———. "Of Other Spaces." Translated by Jay Miskowiec. *Diacritics* 16, no. 1 (1986): 22–27.

Friedman, Susan Stanford. "Planetarity: Musing Modernist Studies." *Modernism/Modernity* 17, no. 3 (2010): 471–99.

Friedman, Thomas L. *The Lexus and the Olive Tree: Understanding Globalization*. New York: Farrar, Straus and Giroux, 1999.

———. *Longitudes and Attitudes: Exploring the World after September 11*. New York: Farrar, Straus and Giroux, 2002.

———. *The World Is Flat 3.0: A Brief History of the Twenty-First Century*. 3rd ed. New York: Farrar, Straus and Giroux, 2007.

Gans, Eric. *Signs of Paradox: Irony, Resentment, and Other Mimetic Structures*. Stanford, Calif.: Stanford University Press, 1997.

Gardner, Anthony, and Huw Hallam. "On the Contemporary—and Contemporary Art History." Review of *What Is Contemporary Art?* by Terry Smith. *Journal of Art Historiography*, no. 4 (2011): 1–9. http://arthistoriography.files.wordpress.com/2011/05/gardnerhallam.pdf.

Germain, Randall D. *Globalization and Its Critics: Perspectives from Political Economy*. Basingstoke, Eng.: Palgrave Macmillan, 2000.

———. *Global Politics and Financial Governance*. Basingstoke, Eng.: Palgrave Macmillan, 2010.

Gibson, William. *Neuromancer*. New York: Ace Books, 1984. Reprinted by Ace Trade Paperback, 2000.

Gilder, George. "Feasting on the Giant Peach." *Forbes ASAP*, August 26, 1996.

Giles, Paul. *Atlantic Republic: The American Tradition in English Literature*. Oxford: Oxford University Press, 2006.

———. *Transatlantic Insurrections: British Culture and the Formation of American Literature, 1730–1860*. Philadelphia: University of Pennsylvania Press, 2001.

———. *Virtual Americas: Transnational Fictions and the Transatlantic Imaginary*. Durham, N.C.: Duke University Press, 2002.

Gilroy, Paul. *The Black Atlantic: Modernity and Double Consciousness*. Cambridge, Mass.: Harvard University Press, 1993.

———. "Planetarity and Cosmopolitics." *British Journal of Sociology* 61, no. 3 (2010): 620–26.

Ginzburg, Carlo. *The Cheese and the Worms: The Cosmos of a Sixteenth-Century Miller*. Translated by John Tedeschi and Anne Tedeschi. Baltimore, Md.: Johns Hopkins University Press, 1980.

Girard, René. *Things Hidden since the Foundation of the World*. Translated by Stephen Bann and Michael Metteer. Stanford, Calif.: Stanford University Press, 1987.

Glissant, Édouard. *Poetics of Relation*. Translated by Betsy Wing. Ann Arbor: University of Michigan Press, 1997. Originally published as *Poétique de la relation*. Paris: Gallimard, 1990.

Glotfelty, Cheryll, and Harold Fromm, eds. *The Ecocriticism Reader: Landmarks in Literary Ecology*. Athens: University of Georgia Press, 1996.

Goethe, Johann Wolfgang. *Gedenkausgabe der Werke, Briefe und Gespräche*. Edited by Ernst Beutler. 24 vols. Zurich: Artemis, 1948–54.

Görner, Rüdiger. "Goethe's Cosmopolitanism." In *Cosmopolitans in the Modern World: Studies on a Theme in German and Austrian Literary Culture*, edited by Suzanne Kirkbright, 33–40. Munich: Iudicium, 2000.

Gracia, Chad. "Collaborating with Komunyakaa: The Creation of *Gilgamesh*." *Callaloo* 28, no. 3 (2005): 541–44.

Greco, Gian Maria, and Luciano Floridi. "The Tragedy of the Digital Commons." *Ethics and Information Technology* 6 (2004): 73–81.

Grusin, Richard. *Premediation: Affect and Mediality after 9/11*. London: Palgrave Macmillan, 2010.

Guattari, Félix. *Chaosmose*. Paris: Galilée, 1992.

Guertin, Carolyn. *Digital Prohibition: Piracy and Authorship in New Media Art*. London: Continuum, 2011.

Guillén, Claudio. *The Challenge of Comparative Literature*. Translated by Cola Franzen. Cambridge, Mass.: Harvard University Press, 1993.

Habermas, Jürgen. *The Postnational Constellation: Political Essays*. Translated and edited by Max Pensky. Cambridge, Mass.: MIT Press, 2001.

Hamm, Heinz. *Goethe und die französische Zeitschrift Le Globe: Eine Lektüre im Zeichen der Weltliteratur*. Weimar: Böhlau, 1998.

Hands, Joss. *@ Is for Activism*. London: Pluto, 2011.

Hardin, Garrett. "The Tragedy of the Commons." *Science* 162, no. 3859 (December 13, 1968): 1243–48.

Hardt, Michael. "For Love or Money." *Cultural Anthropology* 26, no. 4 (2011): 676–82.

Hardt, Michael, and Antonio Negri. *Commonwealth*. Cambridge, Mass.: Belknap Press of Harvard University Press, 2009.

———. *Multitude: War and Democracy in the Age of Empire*. New York: Penguin, 2004.

Harrison, Helen Mayer, and Newton Harrison. "Public Culture and Sustainable Practices: Peninsula Europe from an Ecodiversity Perspective, Posing Questions to Complexity Scientists." *Structure and Dynamics* 2, no. 3 (2007): 1–38. http://escholarship.org/uc/item/9hj3s753.

The Harrison Studio. Website of Newton and Helen Mayer Harrison. http://www.theharrisonstudio.net.

Harvey, David. *The Condition of Postmodernity: An Enquiry into the Origins of Cultural Change*. Oxford: Blackwell, 1990.

———. *Spaces of Hope*. Berkeley: University of California Press, 2000.

Hassapopoulou, Marina. "*Babel*: Pushing and Reaffirming Mainstream Cinema's Boundaries." *Jump Cut: A Review of Contemporary Media* 50 (Spring 2008). http://www.ejumpcut.org/archive/jc50.2008/Babel/index.html.

Hawthorne, Nathaniel. *The House of the Seven Gables*. Edited by Michael Davitt Bell. Oxford: Oxford University Press, 1991.

Hayles, N. Katherine. "Combining Close and Distant Reading: Jonathan Safran Foer's *Tree of Codes* and the Aesthetic of Bookishness." *PMLA* 128, no. 1 (2013): 226–31.

Heidegger, Martin. *Being and Time*. Translated by John Macquarrie and Edward Robinson. New York: Harper and Row, 1962.

———. *The Question concerning Technology and Other Essays*. Translated by William Lovitt. New York: Garland, 1977.

Heise, Ursula K. *Sense of Place and Sense of Planet: The Environmental Imagination of the Global*. New York: Oxford University Press, 2008.

Held, David, ed. *A Globalizing World? Culture, Economics, Politics*. New York: Routledge in association with the Open University, 2000.

Held, David, and Anthony McGrew, eds. *The Global Transformations Reader: An Introduction to the Globalization Debate*. 2nd ed. Cambridge, Eng.: Polity, 2003.

Heller, Michael A. *The Gridlock Economy: How Too Much Ownership Wrecks Markets, Stops Innovation, and Costs Lives*. New York: Basic Books, 2008.

Heller, Michael A., and Rebecca S. Eisenberg. "Can Patents Deter Innovation? The Anticommons in Biomedical Research." *Science* 280, no. 5364 (1998): 698–701.

Hemon, Aleksandar. *Nowhere Man*. New York: Nan A. Talese / Random House, 2002.

Hess, Charlotte, and Elinor Ostrom. *Understanding Knowledge as a Commons*. Cambridge, Mass.: MIT Press, 2007.

Higgins, Charlotte. "The Birth of Twitter Art." *The Guardian*, July 8, 2009. http://www.guardian.co.uk/commentisfree/2009/jul/08/fourth-plinthy-antony-gormley.

Hildebrandt, Kurt. *Goethe: Seine Weltweisheit im Gesamtwerk*. 2nd ed. Leipzig: Philipp Reclam, 1942.

Hirst, Paul, and Grahame Thompson. *Globalization in Question*. 2nd ed. Cambridge, Eng.: Polity, 1999.

Hobbes, Thomas. *Leviathan, with Selected Variants from the Latin Edition of 1668*. Edited by Edwin Curley. Indianapolis, Ind.: Hackett, 1994.

Hoberek, Andrew, ed. "After Postmodernism: Form and History in Contemporary American Fiction." Special issue, *Twentieth-Century Literature* 53, no. 3 (2007).

———. "Introduction: After Postmodernism." *Twentieth-Century Literature* 53, no. 3 (2007): 233–47.

Hoberek, Andrew, et al. "Twentieth-Century Literature in the New Century: A Symposium." *College English* 64, no.1 (2001): 9–33.

Hofmokl, Justyna. "The Internet Commons: Towards an Eclectic Theoretical Framework." *International Journal of the Commons* 4, no. 1 (2010): 226–50.

Hollinger, David A. *Cosmopolitanism and Solidarity: Studies in Ethnoracial, Religious, and Professional Affiliation in the United States*. Madison: University of Wisconsin Press, 2006.

———. *Postethnic America: Beyond Multiculturalism*. New York: Basic Books, 1995.

Hoogvelt, Ankie. *Globalization and the Postcolonial World: The New Political Economy of Development*. 2nd ed. Baltimore: Johns Hopkins University Press, 2001.

Houellebecq, Michel. *The Map and the Territory*. New York: Knopf, 2012.

Huang, Yunte. *Transpacific Displacement: Ethnography, Translation, and Intertextual Travel in Twentieth-Century American Literature*. Berkeley: University of California Press, 2002.

———. *Transpacific Imaginations: History, Literature, Counterpoetics*. Cambridge, Mass.: Harvard University Press, 2008.

Hugh of St. Victor. *The "Didascalicon" of Hugh of St. Victor: A Medieval Guide to the Arts*. Translated by Jerome Taylor. New York: Columbia University Press, 1961.

Hume, Kathryn. *Fantasy and Mimesis: Responses to Reality in Western Literature*. New York: Methuen, 1984.

Hunter, Dan. "Cyberspace as Place and the Tragedy of the Digital Anticommons." *California Law Review* 91, no. 2 (2003): 439–519.

Huntington, Samuel P. *The Clash of Civilizations and the Remaking of World Order*. New York: Simon and Schuster, 1996.

Huyssen, Andreas. *Die frühromantische Konzeption von Übersetzung und Aneignung: Studien zur frühromantischen Utopie einer deutschen Weltliteratur*. Zürcher Beiträge zur deutschen Literatur-und Geistesgeschichte 33. Zürich: Atlantis Verlag, 1969.

Interdependence Movement. "Declaration of Interdependence." http://www.interdependencemovement.org/declaration_form.php.

Iriye, Akira, and Jürgen Osterhammel, eds. *Global Interdependence: The World after 1945*. Cambridge, Mass.: Belknap Press of Harvard University Press, 2013.

Irr, Caren. "Toward the World Novel: Genre Shifts in Twenty-First-Century Expatriate Fiction." *American Literary History* 23, no. 3 (2011): 660–79.

Iyer, Pico. *The Global Soul: Jet Lag, Shopping Malls, and the Search for Home*. New York: Alfred A. Knopf, 2000.

———. "The Nowhere Man." *Prospect* 30, no. 3 (1997): 30–33.

Izzard, Eddie. "Stripped, Live." DVD. Directed by Sarah Townsend. UK: Universal, November 23, 2009. 104 min.

Jacoby, Russell. *Picture Imperfect: Utopian Thought for an Anti-Utopian Age*. New York: Columbia University Press, 2005.

Jameson, Fredric. *Archaeologies of the Future: The Desire Called Utopia and Other Science Fictions*. London: Verso, 2005.

———. *The Geopolitical Aesthetic: Cinema and Space in the World System*. Bloomington: Indiana University Press; London: British Film Institute, 1992.

———. *Marxism and Form: Twentieth-Century Dialectical Theories of Literature*. Princeton, N.J.: Princeton University Press, 1971.

———. "A New Reading of *Capital*." *Mediations* 25, no. 1 (2010): 5–14.

———. *Postmodernism, or the Cultural Logic of Late Capitalism*. Durham, N.C.: Duke University Press, 1991.

———. *The Seeds of Time*. New York: Columbia University Press, 1994.

———. "Third-World Literature in the Era of Multinational Capitalism." *Social Text* 15 (Autumn 1986): 65–88.

Jameson, Fredric, and Masao Miyoshi. *The Cultures of Globalization*. Durham, N.C.: Duke University Press, 1998.

Jay, Martin. *Downcast Eyes: The Denigration of Vision in Twentieth-Century French Thought*. Berkeley: University of California Press, 1993.

Jay, Paul. *Global Matters: The Transnational Turn in Literary Studies*. Ithaca, N.Y.: Cornell University Press, 2010.

Jayaraman, Karthik. "Tragedy of the Commons in the Production of Digital Artifacts." *International Journal of Innovation, Management and Technology* 3, no. 5 (2012): 625–27.

Jazeel, Tariq. "Spatializing Difference beyond Cosmopolitanism: Rethinking Planetary Futures." *Theory, Culture & Society* 28, no. 5 (2011): 75–97.

Johnson, Steven. *Future Perfect: The Case for Progress in a Networked Age*. New York: Riverhead, 2012.

Jones, Gail. *Black Mirror*. Sydney: Pan Macmillan, 2002.

———. *Dreams of Speaking*. Sydney: Random House, 2006.

———. *Five Bells*. Sydney: Random House: 2011.

———. *Sorry*. Sydney: Random House, 2007.

Jowitt, Ken. *New World Disorder: The Leninist Extinction*. Berkeley: University of California Press, 1992.

Jullien, François. *De l'universel: De l'uniforme, du commun et du dialogue entre les cultures*. 2008. Reprint, Paris: Seuil, 2011.

Kellner, Douglas. *From 9/11 to Terror War: The Dangers of the Bush Legacy*. Lanham, Md.: Rowman and Littlefield, 2003.

———. "Globalization, Terrorism and Democracy: 9/11 and Its Aftermath." In *Frontiers of Globalization Research: Theoretical and Methodological Approaches*, edited by Ino Rossi, 243–68. New York: Springer, 2008.

———. *Media Spectacle and Insurrection, 2011: From the Arab Uprising to Occupy Everywhere*. London: Bloomsbury Academic, 2012.

Kennedy, Clare. *Paradox, Aphorism and Desire in Novalis and Derrida*. London: Maney, 2008.

Kintisch, Eli. *Hack the Planet: Science's Best Hope—or Worst Nightmare—for Averting Climate Catastrophe*. Hoboken, N.J.: Wiley, 2010.

Kirby, Alan. "The Death of Postmodernism and Beyond." *Philosophy Now* 58 (November/December 2006): 34–37.

———. *Digimodernism: How New Technologies Dismantle the Postmodern and Reconfigure Our Culture*. New York: Continuum, 2009.

Kollmeyer, Christopher J. "Globalization, Class Compromise, and American Exceptionalism: Political Change in 16 Advanced Capitalist Countries." *Critical Sociology* 29, no. 3 (2003): 369–91.

Komunyakaa, Yusef. *Dien Cai Dau*. Middletown, Conn.: Wesleyan University Press, 1988.

———. *Magic City*. Hanover, N.H.: University Press of New England / Wesleyan University Press, 1992.

———. *Neon Vernacular: New and Selected Poems*. Hanover, N.H.: University Press of New England / Wesleyan University Press, 1993.

———. *Talking Dirty to the Gods*. New York: Farrar, Straus and Giroux, 2000.

———. *Warhorses: Poems*. New York: Farrar, Straus and Giroux, 2008.

Komunyakaa, Yusef, and Chad Gracia. *Gilgamesh: A Verse Play*. Middletown, Conn.: Wesleyan University Press, 2006.

Konrád, George. *Antipolitics: An Essay*. Translated by Richard E. Allen. San Diego, Calif.: Harcourt Brace Jovanovich, 1984.

Kristeva, Julia. *Nations without Nationalism.* New York: Columbia University Press, 1993.

Kunzru, Hari. "Postmodernism: From the Cutting Edge to the Museum." Review of "Postmodernism" exhibition at the Victoria and Albert Museum, London. *The Guardian*, September 15, 2011. http://www.guardian.co.uk/artanddesign/2011/sep/15/postmodernism-cutting-edge-to-museum.

Kuzniar, Alice A. *Delayed Endings: Nonclosure in Novalis and Holderlin.* Athens: University of Georgia Press, 1987.

Lal, Kaushalesh. *Information and Communication Technologies in the Context of Globalization: Evidence from Developing Countries.* Basingstoke, Eng.: Palgrave Macmillan, 2007.

Lane, Anthony. "Time Trip." Review of *The Tree of Life*, directed by Terrence Malick. *New Yorker*, May 30, 2011. http://www.newyorker.com/arts/critics/cinema/2011/05/30/110530crci_cinema_lane.

Lang, Michael. "Mapping Globalization or Globalizing the Map? Heidegger and Planetary Disocurse." *Genre* 36 (Fall/Winter 2003): 239–50.

Lanier, Jaron. *You Are Not a Gadget: A Manifesto.* New York: Alfred A. Knopf, 2010.

Lechner, Frank J., and John Boli. *The Globalization Reader.* 4th ed. Malden, Mass.: Wiley-Blackwell, 2012.

Lee, Chang-rae. *The Surrendered.* New York: Riverhead, 2010.

Lefebvre, Henri. *State, Space, World: Selected Essays.* Edited by Neil Brenner and Stuart Elden. Translated by Gerald Moore, Neil Brenner, and Stuart Elden. Minneapolis: University of Minnesota Press, 2009.

Lessig, Lawrence. *The Future of Ideas: The Fate of the Commons in a Connected World.* New York: Random House, 2001.

Levander, Caroline Field, and Robert S. Levine, eds. *Hemispheric American Studies.* New Brunswick, N.J.: Rutgers University Press, 2007.

Levinas, Emmanuel. *Difficult Freedom: Essays on Judaism.* Translated by Seán Hand. Baltimore: Johns Hopkins University Press, 1990.

Lewis, Martin W., and Kären E. Wigen. *The Myth of Continents: A Critique of Metageography.* Berkeley: University of California Press, 1997.

Lima, Manuel. *Visual Complexity: Mapping Patterns of Information.* New York: Princeton Architectural Press, 2011.

Lionnet, Françoise, and Shu-mei Shih. "Introduction: Thinking through the Minor, Transnationally." In *Minor Transnationalism,* edited by Françoise Lionnet and Shu-mei Shih, 1–23. Durham, N.C.: Duke University Press, 2005.

Lipovetsky, Gilles. *Hypermodern Times.* Translated by Andrew Brown. Cambridge, Eng.: Polity, 2005.

London, Joan. *Gilgamesh: A Novel.* New York: Grove, 2001.

Lopez, Barry. *Arctic Dreams.* New York: Charles Scribner's Sons, 1986.

Lotman, Youri. *La sémiosphère.* Translated by Anka Ledenko. Limoges, France: Presses Universitaires de Limoges, 1999.

Lovink, Geert. *Networks without a Cause: A Critique of Social Media.* Cambridge, Eng.: Polity, 2011.

Lucretius. *The Nature of Things.* Translated by A. E. Stallings. New York: Penguin, 2007.

Luhmann, Niklas. *The Reality of the Mass Media*. Translated by Kathleen Cross. Stanford, Calif.: Stanford University Press, 2000.

Lukács, Georg. *The Historical Novel*. Translated by Hannah Mitchell and Stanley Mitchell. Lincoln: University of Nebraska Press, 1983.

———. *The Theory of the Novel*. Translated by Anna Bostock. Cambridge, Mass.: MIT Press, 1971.

Maalouf, Amin. *In the Name of Identity: Violence and the Need to Belong*. Translated by Barbara Bray. New York: Arcade, 2000. Originally published as *Les identités meurtrières*. Paris: Grasset & Fasquelle, 1996.

———. *Le dérèglement du monde*. Paris: Grasset & Fasquelle, 2009.

Machan, Tibor R. "Introduction: The Commons." In *The Commons: Its Tragedies and Other Follies*, edited by Tibor R. Machan, xiii–xxii. Stanford, Calif.: Hoover Institution, 2001.

Macherey, Pierre. *Hegel or Spinoza*. Translated by Susan M. Ruddick. Minneapolis: University of Minnesota Press, 2011.

MacLeish, Archibald. "Riders on Earth Together, Brothers in Eternal Cold." *New York Times*, December 25, 1968.

Maloney, Suzanne. "The Economic Dimension: The Price of Freedom." In *The Arab Awakening: America and the Transformation of the Middle East*, edited by Kenneth Pollack et al., 66–75. Washington, D.C.: Brookings Institution, 2011.

Manning, Susan, and Andrew Taylor, eds. *Transatlantic Literary Studies: A Reader*. Baltimore: Johns Hopkins University Press, 2007.

Marion, Jean-Luc. *Being Given: Toward a Phenomenology of Givenness*. Translated by Jeffrey Kosky. Stanford, Calif.: Stanford University Press, 2002.

Marx, Karl, and Friedrich Engels. *Werke*. Vol. 4. Berlin: Dietz, 1959.

Massey, Doreen. "A Global Sense of Place." In *Reading Human Geography: The Poetics and Politics of Inquiry*, edited by Trevor J. Barnes and Derek Gregory, 315–23. London: Arnold, 1997.

Massumi, Brian. "The Future Birth of the Affective Fact: The Political Ontology of Threat." In *The Affect Theory Reader*, edited by Melissa Gregg and Gregory J. Seigworth, 52–70. Durham, N.C.: Duke University Press, 2010.

Maury, Matthew Fontaine. *The Physical Geography of the Sea and Its Meteorology*. New York, 1855.

McCann, Colum. *Let the Great World Spin*. New York: Random House, 2009.

McCarthy, Cormac. *The Road*. London: Picador, 2006.

McEwan, Ian. *Saturday*. New York: Random House, 2005.

McGowan, Todd. "The Contingency of Connection: The Path to Politicization in *Babel*." *Discourse* 30, no. 3 (2008): 401–18.

McHale, Brian. "What Was Postmodernism?" *ebr: electronic book review* (2007): 2007-12-20. http://www.electronicbookreview.com/thread/fictionspresent/tense.

McKean, Colin. "Is Pop Culture Consuming Itself? Simon Reynolds Discusses *Retromania*." *The Quietus*, June 8, 2011. http://thequietus.com/articles/06386-simon-reynolds-retromania-interview.

McLaughlin, Robert L. "Post-Postmodern Discontent: Contemporary Fiction and the Social World." *symploke* 12, nos. 1–2 (2004): 53–68.

Melville, Herman. *Moby-Dick; or, The Whale*. Volume 6 of *The Writings of Herman Melville*. Edited by Harrison Hayford, Hershel Parker, and G. Thomas

Tanselle. Evanston, Ill.: Northwestern University Press; Chicago: Newberry Library, 1988.

———. *Pierre; or, The Ambiguities*. Volume 7 of *The Writings of Herman Melville*. Edited by Harrison Hayford, Hershel Parker, and G. Thomas Tanselle. Evanston, Ill.: Northwestern University Press; Chicago: Newberry Library, 1971.

Mendovi, Leerom. "'Terminal Crisis?' From the Worlding of American Literature to World-System Literature." *American Literary History* 23, no. 3 (2011): 643–59.

Mercer, Kobena, ed. *Cosmopolitan Modernisms*. London: Institute of International Visual Art; Cambridge, Mass.: MIT Press, 2005.

Meyer-Kalkus, Reinhard. "World Literature beyond Goethe." Translated by Kevin McAleer. In *Cultural Mobility: A Manifesto*, edited by Stephen Greenblatt, 96–121. Cambridge, Eng.: Cambridge University Press, 2010.

Miéville, China. "Cognition as Ideology: A Dialectic of SF Theory." In *Red Planets: Marxism and Science Fiction*, edited by Mark Bould and China Miéville, 231–48. Middletown, Conn.: Wesleyan University Press, 2009.

———. "Editorial Introduction." In "Symposium: Marxism and Fantasy," edited by China Miéville. Special issue, *Historical Materialism* 10, no. 4 (2002): 39–49.

———. "There and Back. Again: Five Reasons Tolkien Rocks." *Omnivoracious* (blog), June 15, 2009. http://www.omnivoracious.com/2009/06/there-and-back-again-five-reasons-tolkien-rocks.html.

Mignolo, Walter D. "The Geopolitics of Knowledge and the Colonial Difference." *South Atlantic Quarterly* 101, no. 1 (2002): 57–96.

Mirrlees, Tanner. *Global Entertainment Media: Between Cultural Imperialism and Cultural Globalization*. New York: Routledge, 2013.

Mirzoeff, Nicholas. *Occupy 2012: A Daily Observation on Occupy*. http://www.nicholasmirzoeff.com/O2012/.

———. *The Right to Look: A Counterhistory of Visuality*. Durham, N.C.: Duke University Press, 2011.

Mitchell, Stephen. Introduction to *Gilgamesh: A New English Version*. Translated by Stephen Mitchell, 1–64. New York: Free, 2004.

Miyoshi, Masao. "Turn to the Planet: Literature, Diversity, and Totality." *Comparative Literature* 53, no. 4 (2001): 283–97.

Moïsi, Dominique. *The Geopolitics of Emotion: How Cultures of Fear, Humiliation, and Hope Are Reshaping the World*. New York: Doubleday, 2009.

Moraru, Christian. *Cosmodernism: American Narrative, Late Globalization, and the New Cultural Imaginary*. Ann Arbor: University of Michigan Press, 2010.

———. "The Global Turn in Critical Theory." *symploke* 9, no. 1–2 (2001): 74–82.

———. "Thirteen Ways of Passing Postmodernism: Introduction to Focus." *American Book Review* 34, no. 4 (May-June 2013): 3–4.

More, Thomas. *Utopia*. Translated by Paul Turner. New York: Penguin, 2003.

Moretti, Franco. "Conjectures on World Literature." In *Debating World Literature*, edited by Christopher Prendergast, 148–62. London: Verso, 2004.

Morley, David, and Kevin Robins. *Spaces of Identity: Global Media, Electronic Landscapes and Cultural Boundaries*. London: Routledge, 1995.

Moya, Paula M. L., and Ramón Saldívar, eds. "Fictions of the Trans-American Imaginary." Special issue, *Modern Fiction Studies* 49, no. 1 (2003).

Mukherjee, Bharati. *The Tree Bride*. New York: Hyperion, 2004.

Muller, Adam. "Notes toward a Theory of Nostalgia: Childhood and the Evocation of the Past in Two European 'Heritage' Films." *New Literary History* 37, no. 4 (2006): 739–60.

Munn, Nancy D. "Excluded Spaces: The Figure in the Australian Aboriginal Landscape." *Critical Inquiry* 22, no. 3 (Spring 1996): 446–65.

Murphet, Julian. "Postcolonial Writing in Australia and New Zealand." In vol. 1, *The Cambridge History of Postcolonial Literature,* edited by Ato Quayson, 446–83. Cambridge, Eng.: Cambridge University Press, 2012.

———. "Postmodernism and Space." In *The Cambridge Companion to Postmodernism*, edited by Steven Connor, 116–35. Cambridge, Eng.: Cambridge University Press, 2004.

Murphy, Timothy S. "To Have Done with Postmodernism: A Plea (or Provocation) for Globalization Studies." *symploke* 12, nos. 1–2 (2004): 20–34.

Murray, Alison. "Women, Nostalgia, Memory: *Chocolat*, *Outremer*, and *Indochine*." *Research in African Literatures* 33, no. 2 (2002): 235–44.

Nancy, Jean-Luc. *Verité de la démocratie*. Paris: Galilée, 2008.

National Research Council (Committee on Intellectual Property Rights and the Emerging Information Infrastructure, Computer Science and Telecommunications Board Commission on Physical Sciences, Mathematics, and Applications). *The Digital Dilemma: Intellectual Property in the Information Age*. Washington, D.C.: National Academy, 2000.

Nealon, Jeffrey T. *Post-Postmodernism or, The Cultural Logic of Just-in-Time Capitalism*. Stanford, Calif.: Stanford University Press, 2012.

Negri, Antonio. *Art and Multitude: Nine Letters on Art, Followed by Metamorphoses: Art and Immaterial Labor*. Translated by Ed Emery. Cambridge, Eng.: Polity, 2011.

———. *Insurgencies: Constituent Power and the Modern State*. Translated by Maurizia Boscagli. With a new foreword by Michael Hardt. Minneapolis: University of Minnesota Press, 2009.

Ngai, Sianne. *Our Aesthetic Categories: Zany, Cute, Interesting*. New Haven, Conn.: Harvard University Press, 2012.

———. *Ugly Feelings*. New Haven, Conn.: Harvard University Press, 2005.

Nicolescu, Basarab. *Théorèms poétiques*. Preface by Michel Camus. Paris: Rocher, 1994.

Nietzsche, Friedrich. *Beyond Good and Evil: Prelude to a Philosophy*. Translated by R. J. Hollingdale. Introduction by Michael Tanner. London: Penguin, 1990.

Ning, Wang, and Brian McHale, eds. "Postmodernist Fiction: East and West." Special issue, *Narrative* 21, no. 3 (2013).

Nixon, Rob. "Neoliberalism, Genre, and 'The Tragedy of the Commons.' " *PMLA* 127, no. 3 (May 2012): 593–99.

Noonan, Douglas S. "Internet Decentralization, Feedback, and Self-Organization." In *Managing the Commons*, edited by John A. Baden and Douglas S. Noonan, 2nd ed., 188–94. Bloomington: Indiana University Press, 1998.

Novalis. *Schriften*. Edited by Paul Kluckhohn and Richard Samuel. 2nd ed. Stuttgart: Kohlhammer, 1960–75.

Nussbaum, Martha. "Patriotism and Cosmopolitanism." *Boston Review* 19, no. 5 (1994): 3–34.

Nye, Joseph S., Jr. *The Future of Power*. Cambridge, Mass.: PublicAffairs, 2011.

———. *Soft Power: The Means to Success in World Politics*. Cambridge, Mass.: PublicAffairs, 2004.

O'Brien, Geoffrey. "The Variety of Movie Experience." Review of *The Tree of Life*, directed by Terrence Malick. *New York Review of Books*, July 14, 2011. http://www.nybooks.com/articles/archives/2011/jul/14/variety-movie-experience/.

Ondaatje, Michael. *The English Patient*. New York: Vintage, 1993.

"110 Best Books: The Perfect Library." *The Telegraph*, April 6, 2008. http://www.telegraph.co.uk/culture/books/3672376/110-best-books-The-perfect-library.html.

O'Neill, Joseph. "Bowling Alone." *The Atlantic Monthly*. September 11, 2007. http://www.powells.com/review/2007_09_11.

———. *Netherland*. New York: Vintage, 2009.

Osterhammel, Jürgen, and Niels P. Petersson. *Globalization: A Short History*. Translated by Dona Geyer. Princeton, N.J.: Princeton University Press, 2009.

Ostrom, Elinor. "Analyzing Collective Action." In "Issue Supplement s1," *Agricultural Economics* 41, no. S1 (November 2010): 155–66. DOI: 10.1111/j.1574-0862.2010.00497.x.

———. *Governing the Commons: The Evolution of Institutions for Collective Action*. Cambridge, Eng.: Cambridge University Press, 1990.

Ostrom, Elinor, Roy Gardner, and James Walker. *Rules, Games, and Common-Pool Resources*. Ann Arbor: University of Michigan Press, 1994.

Oyono, Ferdinand. *Houseboy*. Translated by John Reed. London: Heinemann, 1990. Originally published as *Une vie de boy*. Paris: Julliard, 1956.

Palumbo-Liu, David, Bruce W. Robbins, and Nirvana Tanoukhi, eds. *Immanuel Wallerstein and the Problem of the World: System, Scale, Culture*. Durham, N.C.: Duke University Press, 2011.

Pamuk, Orhan. *Snow*. Translated by Maureen Freely. New York: Vintage, 2005.

Parker, James. "Simon Reynolds, Retromania, and the Atemporality of Contemporary 'Pop.'" Review of *Retromania: Pop Culture's Addiction to Its Own Past*, by Simon Reynolds. *Discipline*, no. 2 (2012): 156–64.

Parmett, Helen Morgan. "Community/Common: Jean-Luc Nancy and Antonio Negri on Collective Potentialities." *Communication, Culture & Critique* 5 (June 2012): 171–90.

Pascal, Blaise. *Oeuvres complètes*. Paris: Gallimard, 1954.

Pease, Donald E. *The New American Exceptionalism*. Minneapolis: University of Minnesota Press, 2009.

Perloff, Marjorie. *Unoriginal Genius: Poetry by Other Means in the New Century*. Chicago: University of Chicago Press, 2010.

Phillips, Anne. *Multiculturalism without Culture*. Princeton, N.J.: Princeton University Press, 2007.

Pizer, John. "Cosmopolitanism and *Weltliteratur*." *Goethe Yearbook* 13 (2005): 165–79.

Pocock, J. G. A. *The Discovery of Islands: Essays in British History*. Cambridge, Eng.: Cambridge University Press, 2005.

Poe, Edgar Allan. "Eureka: An Essay on the Material and Spiritual Universe." In *The Science Fiction of Edgar Allan Poe*, 205–309. Edited by Harold Beaver. London: Penguin, 1976.

Poole, Robert. *Earthrise: How Man First Saw the Earth*. New Haven, Conn.: Yale University Press, 2008.

Poster, Mark. "Global Media and Culture." *New Literary History* 39, no. 3 (2008): 685–703.

Poteete, Amy R., Marco A. Janssen, and Elinor Ostrom. *Working Together: Collective Action, the Commons, and Multiple Methods in Practice*. Princeton, N.J.: Princeton University Press, 2010.

Pratt, Mary Louise. "Modernity and Periphery: Toward a Global and Relational Analysis." In *Beyond Dichotomies: Histories, Identities, Cultures, and the Challenge of Globalization*, edited by Elisabeth Mudimbe-Boyi, 21–47. Albany: State University of New York Press, 2002.

———. "Planetary Longings: Sitting in the Light of the Great Solar TV." In *World Writing: Poetics, Ethics, Globalization*, edited by Mary Gallagher, 207–23. Toronto: University of Toronto Press, 2008.

Pynchon, Thomas. *The Crying of Lot 49*. New York: Harper and Row, 1966.

Ramazani, Jahan. *A Transnational Poetics*. Chicago: University of Chicago Press, 2009.

Rancière, Jacques. *On the Shores of Politics*. Translated by Liz Heron. London: Verso, 1995.

———. *The Politics of Aesthetics: The Distribution of the Sensible*. Translated by Gabriel Rockhill. London: Continuum, 2004.

Rantanen, Terhi. *The Media and Globalization*. London: Sage Publications, 2004.

Raulet, Gérard. *Critical Cosmology: On Nations and Globalization—A Philosophical Essay*. Lanham, Md.: Lexington Books, 2005.

Raymond, Eric S. *The Cathedral & the Bazaar: Musings on Linux and Open Source by an Accidental Revolutionary*. Sebastopol, Calif.: O'Reilly, 1999.

Reagle, Joseph Michael, Jr. *Good Faith Collaboration: The Culture of Wikipedia*. Cambridge, Mass.: MIT Press, 2010.

Reynolds, Simon. "Excess All Areas." *The Wire*, no. 328 (June 2011): 32.

———. *Retromania: Pop Culture's Addiction to Its Own Past*. London: Faber and Faber, 2011.

Robbins, Bruce. *Secular Vocations: Intellectuals, Professionalism, Culture*. New York: Verso, 1993.

Robertson, Roland. "Glocalization: Time-Space and Homogeneity-Heterogeneity." In *Global Modernities*, edited by Mike Featherstone, Scott M. Lash, and Roland Robertson, 25–44. London: Sage Publications, 1995.

———. "Social Theory, Cultural Relativity and the Problem of Globality." In *Culture, Globalization and the World-System: Contemporary Conditions for the Representation of Identity*, edited by Anthony D. King, 69–90. Minneapolis: University of Minnesota Press, 1997.

Robin, Libby. "Round Table." Paper presented at "Rethinking Invasion Ecologies: Natures, Cultures and Societies in the Age of Anthropocene," University of Sydney, June 19, 2012.

Robins, Kevin, and Frank Webster. *Times of the Technoculture: From the Information Society to the Virtual Life*. London: Routledge, 1999.

Rooney, Brigid. *Literary Activists: Australian Writer-Intellectuals and Public Life*. St. Lucia: University of Queensland Press, 2009.

Royal Swedish Academy of Sciences. "The Prize in Economic Sciences 2009." Press release. October 12, 2009. http://www.nobelprize.org/nobel_prizes/economics/laureates/2009/press.pdf.

Saco, Diana. *Cybering Democracy: Public Space and the Internet*. Minneapolis: University of Minnesota Press, 2002.

Said, Edward W. *Orientalism*. New York: Pantheon, 1978.

———. *Reflections on Exile and Other Essays*. Cambridge, Mass.: Harvard University Press, 2000.

Samuels, Robert. *New Media, Cultural Studies, and Critical Theory after Postmodernism: Automodernity from Žižek to Laclau*. New York: Palgrave Macmillan, 2009.

Samuelson, Paul A. "The Pure Theory of Public Expenditure." *Review of Economics and Statistics* 36, no. 4 (1954): 387–89.

Sassen, Saskia. "Neither Global nor National: Novel Assemblages of Territory, Authority, and Rights." *Ethics and Global Politics* 1, no. 1–2 (2008): 61–79.

———. *A Sociology of Globalization*. New York: Norton, 2007.

Scholte, Jan Aart. *Globalization, Second Edition: A Critical Introduction*. 2nd ed. New York: Palgrave Macmillan, 2005.

Schweik, Charles M. "Free/Open-Source Software as a Framework for Establishing Commons in Science." In *Understanding Knowledge as a Commons: From Theory to Practice*, edited by Charlotte Hess and Elinor Ostrom, 277–310. Cambridge, Mass.: MIT Press, 2007.

Scott, Sir Walter. "On the Supernatural in Fictitious Composition; and Particularly on the Works of Ernest Theodore William Hoffmann." In *Sir Walter Scott on Novelists and Fiction*, 222–51. Edited by Ioan Williams. London: Routledge and Kegan Paul, 1968.

Shaviro, Steven. *Connected, or What It Means to Live in the Network Society*. Minneapolis: University of Minnesota Press, 2003.

Shirky, Clay. *Cognitive Surplus: How Technology Makes Consumers into Collaborators*. New York: Penguin, 2010.

"61 Essential Postmodern Reads: An Annotated List." *Los Angeles Times*, July 16, 2009. http://latimesblogs.latimes.com/jacketcopy/2009/07/the-mostly-complete-annotated-and-essential-postmodern-reading-list.html.

Slater, Don. *New Media, Development and Globalization: Making Connections in the Global South*. Cambridge, Eng.: Polity, 2013.

Sloterdijk, Peter. *Bubbles: Spheres Volume I: Microspherology*. Translated by Wieland Hoban. Los Angeles: Semiotext(e), 2011.

———. *Eurotaoismus: Zur Kritik der politischen Kinetik*. Berlin: Suhrkamp, 1989.

Smith, Bernard. *The Antipodean Manifesto: Essays in Art and History*. Melbourne: Oxford University Press, 1976.

———. Foreword to *The Australian Scapegoat: Towards an Antipodean Aesthetic*, by Peter Fuller. Nedlands: University of Western Australia Press, 1986.

Smith, Katie. "Gayatri Chakravorty Spivak (1942–)." In *Glossary of Globalization and Autonomy/Mondialisation et Autonomie*. http://www.globalautonomy.ca/global1/glossary_pop.jsp?id=PR.0024.

Smith, Terry. *Contemporary Art: World Currents*. Upper Saddle River, N.J.: Prentice Hall, 2011.

———. "Currents of World-Making in Contemporary Art." *World Art* 1, no. 2 (2011): 171–88.

———. "The State of Art History: Contemporary Art." *Art Bulletin* 92, no. 4 (2010): 366–83.

———. *What Is Contemporary Art?* Chicago: University of Chicago Press, 2009.

———. "Worlds Pictured in Contemporary Art: Planes and Connectivities." In *The World and World-Making in Art*, edited by Caroline Turner. Canberra: ANU e-Press, 2012.

Smith, Terry, Okwui Enwezor, and Nancy Condee, eds. *Antinomies of Art and Culture: Modernity, Postmodernity, Contemporaneity*. Durham, N.C.: Duke University Press, 2008.

Snediker, Michael D. *Queer Optimism: Lyric Personhood and Other Felicitous Persuasions*. Minneapolis: University of Minnesota Press, 2008.

Social Sciences and Humanities Research Council. "Globalization and Autonomy / Mondialisation et autonomie." *Globalization and Autonomy Online Compendium*, 2002. http://globalautonomy.ca/global1/index.jsp.

Soja, Edward W. *Postmodern Geographies: The Reassertion of Space in Critical Social Theory*. London: Verso, 1989.

———. *Thirdspace: Journeys to Los Angeles and Other Real-and-Imagined Places*. Cambridge, Mass.: Blackwell, 1996.

Song, Min Hyong. "Becoming Planetary." *American Literary History* 23, no. 3 (2011): 555–73.

Spivak, Gayatri Chakravorty. *An Aesthetic Education in the Era of Globalization*. Cambridge, Mass.: Harvard University Press, 2011.

———. "Can the Subaltern Speak?" In *Marxism and the Interpretation of Culture*, edited by Cary Nelson and Lawrence Grossberg, 271–313. Urbana: University of Illinois Press, 1988.

———. *A Critique of Postcolonial Reason: Toward a History of the Vanishing Present*. Cambridge, Mass.: Harvard University Press, 1999.

———. *Death of a Discipline*. New York: Columbia University Press, 2005.

Steger, Manfred. *Globalization: A Very Short Introduction*. 3rd ed. Oxford: Oxford University Press, 2013.

Stiglitz, Joseph. *Globalization and Its Discontents*. New York: W.W. Norton, 2003.

Strich, Fritz. *Goethe und die Weltliteratur*. Bern: Francke, 1946.

———. "Weltliteratur und vergleichende Literaturgeschichte." In *Philosophie der Literaturwissenschaft*, edited by Emil Ermatinger, 422–41. Berlin: Junker und Dünnhaupt, 1930.

Suvin, Darko. *Metamorphoses of Science Fiction: On the Poetics and History of a Literary Genre*. New Haven, Conn.: Yale University Press, 1979.

Tabachnick, David, and Toivo Koivukoski. *Globalization, Technology, and Philosophy*. Albany: State University of New York Press, 2004.

Tally, Robert T., Jr., ed. *Geocritical Explorations: Space, Place, and Mapping in Literary and Cultural Studies*. New York: Palgrave Macmillan, 2011.

———. "Meta-Capital: Culture and Financial Derivatives." *Works and Days* 30, no. 2 (2012): 231–47.

———. "*Mundus Totus Exilium Est*: Reflections on the Critic in Exile." *Transnational Literature* 3, no. 2 (May 2011): 1–10.

———. "On Geocriticism." In *Geocritical Explorations: Space, Place, and Mapping in Literary and Cultural Studies*, edited by Robert T. Tally Jr., 1–9. New York: Palgrave Macmillan, 2011.

———. "Radical Alternatives: The Persistence of Utopia in the Postmodern." In *New Essays on the Frankfurt School of Critical Theory*, edited by Alfred J. Drake, 109–21. Newcastle upon Tyne, Eng.: Cambridge Scholars, 2009.

———. *Spatiality*. London: Routledge, 2013.

———. *Utopia in the Age of Globalization: Space, Representation, and the World-System*. New York: Palgrave Macmillan, 2013.

Taussig, Michael. *The Nervous System*. New York: Routledge, 1992.

Tawada, Yōko. *Sprachpolizei und Spielpolyglotte*. Tübingen: Konkursbuch Verlag Claudia Gehrke, 2007.

Thies, Sebastian. "Crystal Frontiers: Ethnicity, Filmic Space, and Diasporic Optic in *Traffic*, *Crash*, and *Babel*." In *E Pluribus Unum? National and Transnational Identities in the Americas / Identidades nacionales y transnacionales en las Américas*, edited by Sebastian Thies and Josef Raab, 205–28. Münster: LIT Verlag; Tempe, Ariz.: Bilingual, 2008.

Thoreau, Henry David. *Walden; or, Life in the Woods*. In *A Week, Walden, The Maine Woods, Cape Cod*, edited by Robert F. Sayre, 321–588. New York: Library of America, 1985.

Thrift, Nigel. *Non-Representational Theory: Space, Politics, Affect*. London: Routledge, 2007.

Todorov, Tzvetan. *Le nouveau désordre mondial: Réflexions d'un Européen*. Paris: Robert Laffont, 2003.

Tolkien, J. R. R. "Mythopoeia." In *Tree and Leaf*. New York: Harper Collins, 2001.

———. "On Fairy-Stories." In *The Tolkien Reader*. New York: Ballantine Books, 1966.

Tower Records. "Music Style Map." http://www.tower.com/browse.cfm?div_id=2.

Tsiolkas, Christos. *Dead Europe*. Sydney: Random House, 2005.

———. *Loaded*. 1995. Reprint, London: Random House-Vintage, 1997.

———. *The Slap*. Crows Nest, Australia: Allen and Unwin, 2008.

Tsiolkas, Christos, Gideon Haigh, and Alexis Wright. *Tolerance, Prejudice and Fear: The Sydney Three Writers Project*. Crows Nest, Australia: Allen and Unwin, 2008.

Tuan, Yi-Fu. *Cosmos and Hearth: A Cosmopolite's Viewpoint*. Minneapolis: University of Minnesota Press, 1996.

Turnbull, Neil. "The Ontological Consequences of Copernicus: Global Being in the Planetary World." *Theory, Culture & Society* 23, no. 1 (2006): 125–39.

Turner, Jonathan H. *On the Origins of Human Emotions: A Sociological Inquiry into the Evolution of Human Affect*. Stanford, Calif.: Stanford University Press, 2000.

Uricchio, William. *We Europeans? Media, Representations, Identities*. Bristol, Eng.: Intellect, 2009.

Vidal, Gore. "The Bookchat of Henry James." In *Armageddon? Essays 1983–1987*, 157–67. London: André Deutsch, 1987.

Virilio, Paul. *The Aesthetics of Disappearance*. Translated by Philip Beitchman. New York: Semiotext(e), 1991.

———. *The Information Bomb*. Translated by Chris Turner. New York: Verso, 2000.

Wallerstein, Immanuel Maurice. *The Essential Wallerstein*. New York: New, 2000.

———. *Geopolitics and Geoculture: Essays on the Changing World-System*. Cambridge, Eng.: Cambridge University Press; Paris: Maison des Sciences l'Homme, 1991.

———. *The Modern World-System*. 4 vols. Berkeley: University of California Press, 2011.

———. "New Revolts Against the System." *New Left Review* 18 (November-December 2002): 29–39.

———. *Utopistics, or Historical Choices of the Twenty-First Century*. New York: New, 1998.

Walljasper, Jay. *All That We Share: How to Save the Economy, the Environment, the Internet, Democracy, Our Communities, and Everything Else That Belongs to All of Us*. New York: New, 2010.

Wark, McKenzie. *Telesthesia: Communication, Culture, and Class*. Cambridge, Eng.: Polity, 2012.

———. *Virtual Geography: Living with Global Media Events*. Bloomington: Indiana University Press, 1994.

Warnier, Jean-Pierre. *La mondialisation de la culture*. 3rd ed. Paris: La Découverte, 2004.

Weber, Steven. *The Success of Open Source*. Cambridge, Mass.: Harvard University Press, 2004.

Wegner, Phillip E. *Life between Two Deaths, 1989–2001: U.S. Culture in the Long Nineties*. Durham, N.C.: Duke University Press, 2009.

Wehrs, Donald R. "Sartre's Legacy in Postcolonial Theory, or, Who's Afraid of Non-Western Historiography and Cultural Studies?" *New Literary History* 34, no. 4 (2003): 761–89.

Weibel, Peter, and Andrea Buddenseig, eds. *Contemporary Art and the Museum: A Global Perspective*. Ostfildern, Ger.: Hatje Cantz, 2007.

Westphal, Bertrand. *La géocritique. Réel, fiction, espace*. Paris: Minuit, 2007. Translated by Robert T. Tally Jr., as *Geocriticism: Real and Fictional Spaces*. New York: Palgrave Macmillan, 2011.

———. "Une lecture géocritique des structures anthropologiques de l'imaginaire." *Iris* 33 (2012): 23–35.

———. *Le monde plausible: Espace, lieu, carte*. Paris: Minuit, 2011.

Wigan, Kären. Introduction to "AHR Forum: Oceans of History." *American Historical Review* 111, no. 3 (June 2006): 717–21.

Williams, Jeffrey J. "The Plutocratic Imagination." *Dissent* (Winter 2013). http://www.-dissentmagazine.org/article/the-plutocratic-imagination.

Williams, Sam. *Free as in Freedom: Richard Stallman's Crusade for Free Software*. Sebastopol, Calif.: O'Reilly, 2002.

Wilson, Rob. "Afterword: Worlding as Future Tactic." In *The Worlding Project: Doing Cultural Studies in the Era of Globalization*, edited by Rob Wilson and Christopher Leigh Connery, 209–24. Santa Cruz, Calif.: New Pacific; Berkeley, Calif.: North Atlantic Books, 2007.

———. *Be Always Converting, Be Always Converted: An American Poetics*. Cambridge, Mass.: Harvard University Press, 2009.

Wilson, W. Daniel. *Unterirdische Gänge: Goethe, Freimaurerei und Politik*. Göttingen, Ger.: Wallstein Verlag, 1999.

Winton, Tim. *Dirt Music*. Sydney: Pan Macmillan, 2001.

———. *The Riders*. Sydney: Pan Macmillan, 1994.

———. *Shallows*. 1984. Reprint, Sydney: Allen and Unwin, 1985.

Wittgenstein, Ludwig. *Philosophical Investigations*. Translated by G. E. M. Anscombe. Oxford: Blackwell, 1958.

Wright, Alexis. *Carpentaria*. 2006. Reprint, Artarmon, Australia: Giramondo, 2007.

Zalasiewicz, Jan, et al. "Are We Now Living in the Anthropocene?" *GSA Today* (February 2008): 4–8.

Zegher, Catherine de, and Gerald McMaster, eds. *All Our Relations: 18th Biennale of Sydney*. Sydney: Biennale of Sydney, 2012.

Zijlmans, Kitty, and Wilfred van Damme, eds. *World Art Studies: Exploring Concepts and Approaches*. Amsterdam: Valiz, 2008.

Žižek, Slavoj. *First as Tragedy, Then as Farce*. New York: Verso, 2009.

———. *The Fragile Absolute; or, Why Is the Christian Legacy Worth Fighting For?* New York: Verso, 2009.

———. Speech presented at Occupy Wall Street after a march near Washington Square Park in New York City, Oct. 9, 2011. http://www.youtube.com/watch?v=Xjcm2djpimQ&feature=player_embedded.

———. *Welcome to the Desert of the Real: Five Essays on September 11 and Related Dates*. New York: Verso, 2002.

Zournazi, Mary. "On Believing—with Christos Tsiolkas." In *Hope: New Philosophies for Change*, 98–121. Annandale, Australia: Pluto Press Australia, 2002.

CONTRIBUTORS

Hester Blum is an associate professor of English at the Pennsylvania State University. Her work on nineteenth-century American literature, oceanic studies, and print culture has been published in *PMLA*, *American Literature*, *J19*, and *Early American Studies*, as well as in multiple collections. She is a founder of C19: The Society of Nineteenth-Century Americanists. Her book *The View from the Masthead: Maritime Imagination and Antebellum American Sea Narratives* (2008) received the John Gardner Maritime Research Award; her critical edition of *Horrors of Slavery*, William Ray's 1808 Barbary captivity narrative, appeared in 2008. Blum is completing a book entitled *The News at the Ends of the Earth: Oceanic Studies and the Print Culture of Polar Exploration*.

Wai Chee Dimock is William Lampson Professor of English and American Studies at Yale University. Her recent publications include *Through Other Continents: American Literature across Deep Time* (2006) and a collaborative volume, *Shades of the Planet: American Literature as World Literature* (2007). She has coedited special issues of journals such as *PMLA* ("Remapping Genre," coedited with Bruce Robbins in 1997); *American Literary History* ("Transnational Citizenship and the Humanities," coedited with Gordon Hutner in 2006); *ESQ* ("American Literary Globalism," coedited with Lawrence Buell in 2006); and *American Literature* ("Literature and Science," coedited with Priscilla Wald in 2002). She now writes movie reviews for the *Los Angeles Review of Books* and works on two books, *Weak Theory and Low Epic* and a web-and-print anthology, part of an online teaching initiative, *American Literature in the World*, at http://amlitintheworld.commons.yale.edu/.

Laurie Edson is a professor of comparative literature and French at San Diego State University. Her research interests include nineteenth- and twentieth-century French and comparative literature and theory, postcolonial and African literatures, relations between literature and visual art, and gender, transnational, and postcolonial theory. Her most recent book on inter-arts relations is *Reading Relationally: Postmodern Perspectives on Literature and Art* (2000). In addition to her monograph on the poet and painter Henri Michaux (*Henri Michaux and the Poetics of Movement*, 1985), she is the editor of *Conjunctions: Verbal-Visual Relations* (1996); *Contemporary Feminist Writing in French: A Multicultural Perspective*, a special issue of *Studies in*

Twentieth-Century Literature (1993); and *Henri Michaux,* a special issue of *L'Esprit Créateur* (1986). She is also the translator of *Mother Death* (1988; Jeanne Hyvrard's *Mère la mort*).

Amy J. Elias is a professor of English at the University of Tennessee, Knoxville. She has published numerous articles and book chapters concerning contemporary literature and cultural theory, narrative theory, and history and time studies, and she is the founding president of ASAP: The Association for the Study of the Arts of the Present, hosted its launch conference, and is founding coeditor of its scholarly publication, *ASAP/Journal.* Her books include the award-winning *Sublime Desire: History and Post-1960s Fiction* (2002). She is completing a monograph titled *Dialogue at the End of the World: Art and the Commons.*

Raoul Eshelman is a lecturer in Slavic languages at the Ludwig-Maximilians-Universität in Munich. His main research interest during the last ten years has been to define the transition from postmodernism to post-postmodernism in terms of cultural and literary history. He is the author of numerous books and articles on Russian and Czech modernism and postmodernism and has written extensively on the epoch of post-postmodernism, or on what he calls "performatism." His most recent monograph is *Performatism, or the End of Postmodernism* (2008).

Paul Giles is Challis Professor of English at the University of Sydney, Australia. His books include *Antipodean America: Australasia and the Constitution of U.S. Literature* (2013); *The Global Remapping of American Literature* (2011); *Transnationalism in Practice: Essays on American Studies, Literature and Religion* (2010); *Atlantic Republic: The American Tradition in English Literature* (2006); *Virtual Americas: Transnational Fictions and the Transatlantic Imaginary* (2002); *Transatlantic Insurrections: British Culture and the Formation of American Literature, 1730–1860* (2001); *American Catholic Arts and Fictions: Culture, Ideology, Aesthetics* (1992); and *Hart Crane: The Contexts of "The Bridge"* (1986).

Alan Kirby is an independent scholar who holds degrees from Oxford University and the Sorbonne and has completed a Ph.D. on British fiction at Exeter University. Of late, his research has focused on contemporary cultural reconfigurations under the impact of the digitization of the text in the aftermath of postmodernism. His work includes a monograph, *Digimodernism* (2009), the polemical essay "The Death of Postmodernism and Beyond" (2006), articles including "Endgames: Some Versions of the Passing of Postmodernism," as well as essays on writers such as John Fowles, Stephen Poliakoff, and Ian McEwan. He is currently at work on a monograph reconsidering the narrative contexts of textual reflexivity from the altered cultural perspective of the present.

Christian Moraru is a professor of English at the University of North Carolina, Greensboro. He specializes in contemporary American literature, narrative, literary-cultural theory, and comparative studies with emphasis on the modern history of ideas, as well as on postmodernism and the evolving relations among culture, ethics, and the imagination in the globalizing world. He is the author of numerous volumes and articles in English and other languages. His latest books include monographs such as *Rewriting: Postmodern Narrative and Cultural Critique in the Age of Cloning* (2001); *Memorious Discourse: Reprise and Representation in Postmodernism* (2005); and *Cosmodernism: American Narrative, Late Globalization, and the New Cultural Imaginary* (2011), as well as the edited collection *Postcommunism, Postmodernism, and the Global Imagination* (2009). His forthcoming monograph is titled *Reading for the Planet: Toward a Geomethodology.*

John D. Pizer is a professor of German and comparative literature, and chair of the Department of Foreign Languages and Literatures, at Louisiana State University. His research interests include eighteenth- to twenty-first-century German literature and thought, comparative literature, and the theory and practice of world literature. He has been the recipient of a Fulbright Scholars Award. His books include *Imagining the Age of Goethe in German Literature, 1970–2010* (2011); *The Idea of World Literature: History and Pedagogical Practice* (2006); *Ego-Alter Ego: Double and/as Other in the Age of German Poetic Realism* (1998); and *Toward a Theory of Radical Origin: Essays on Modern German Thought* (1995).

Terry Smith is Andrew W. Mellon Professor of Contemporary Art History and Theory in the Department of the History of Art and Architecture at the University of Pittsburgh and Distinguished Visiting Professor, National Institute for Experimental Arts, College of Fine Arts, University of New South Wales, Sydney. In 2010 he received the Mather Award for Art Criticism (College Art Association, U.S.) and the Australia Council Visual Arts Laureate Award (Australia). He was a member of the Art & Language group (New York) and a founder of Union Media Services (Sydney). He is the author of *Making the Modern: Industry, Art, and Design in America* (1993); *Transformations in Australian Art* (2002); *The Architecture of Aftermath* (2006); *What Is Contemporary Art?* (2009); *Contemporary Art: World Currents* (2011); and *Thinking Contemporary Curating* (2012).

Robert T. Tally Jr. is an associate professor of English at Texas State University, where he teaches American and world literature, literary theory, and the history of criticism. He is the author of *Fredric Jameson: The Project of Dialectical Criticism* (2014); *Poe and the Subversion of American Literature: Satire, Fantasy, Critique* (2014); *Spatiality* (2013); *Utopia in the Age of Globalization: Space, Representation, and the World System* (2013); *Kurt Vonnegut and the American Novel: A Postmodern Iconography* (2011); and *Melville, Mapping, and Globalization: Literary Cartography in the American Baroque Writer* (2009). The translator of Bertrand Westphal's *Geocriticism: Real and Fictional Spaces* (2011), Tally is also the editor of *Geocritical Explorations: Space, Place, and Mapping in Literary and Cultural Studies* (2011) and *Kurt Vonnegut: Critical Insights* (2013).

Bertrand Westphal is a professor of comparative literature at the University of Limoges, where he leads the research team "Espaces Humains et Interactions Culturelles" ("Human Spaces and Cultural Interactions"). His work is interdisciplinary, and he regularly collaborates with designers, architects, and geographers. A leading geocritic, he is the author of numerous works on geocriticism, Austrian literature, the Mediterranean, and the theory of the novel, such as *L'oeil de la Méditerranée: Une odyssée littéraire* (2005); *Geocriticism: Real and Fictional Spaces* (translated into English by Robert T. Tally in 2011); and *The Plausible World: A Geocritical Approach to Spaces, Places, and Maps* (translated into English by Amy D. Wells).